THE TYRANNY OF NOSTALGIA

THE TYRANNY OF NOSTALGIA

Half a Century of British Economic Decline

Russell Jones

LONDON PUBLISHING PARTNERSHIP

Published by London Publishing Partnership
www.londonpublishingpartnership.co.uk

All Rights Reserved

ISBN: 978-1-913019-79-2 (hbk)
ISBN: 978-1-913019-80-8 (iPDF)
ISBN: 978-1-913019-81-5 (epub)

A catalogue record for this book is
available from the British Library

This book has been composed in
Adobe Garamond Pro

Copy-edited and typeset by
T&T Productions Ltd, London
www.tandtproductions.com

Printed and bound by TJ Books Limited,
Padstow

For Ronald Fitzgerald Jones, 1926–2021

Contents

Foreword

Born in 1967, I am certainly one of Thatcher's children. I grew up in Dundee, Scotland, which is by some accounts one of the first western cities to deindustrialize when nylon displaced jute in packaging in the 1940s. Born in a city on the skids, my childhood was filled first with blackouts, strikes and three-day weeks and then, later, by ever-rising unemployment, poverty and a pervading sense of hopelessness. When I left school in 1983 the only jobs I saw in the job centre for young people were on oil tankers in the gulf.

These feelings were attenuated by a move to Glasgow in 1986 and then extinguished by a move to New York in 1992. Despite my transfer across the pond, I follow events in the UK closely. I still read the *Financial Times* and check the BBC for UK news and football. I travel to London every couple of months. I teach political economy in the US, and I am as well versed in the genre of 'UK decline' as the next man. But I can honestly say that nothing in my past or in my studies prepared me for the shock of Liz Truss. I mention her because – despite not featuring much in Russell's book, mainly because he wrote the book before she became prime minister – in many ways she 'bookends' Russell's narrative rather well.

I had heard her name on Radio 4 in parody and comedy, and when she became prime minister I watched the infamous 'cheese speech' on YouTube to catch up. My first thought was: 'So this is how far you can fall as a country.' The next week she met the Queen, who promptly died, which made me reflect further on the British predicament. Imagine starting with Churchill and ending with Truss? What a metaphor for decline.

The problem with metaphors, though, is that while they illuminate they do not explain. How did the UK end up with Liz Truss as prime minister? Indeed, if you travel backwards in time, the past decade or so has been a veritable rogues gallery of less than successful politicians. But was it really any better in the 1990s and 1980s? Was I simply jaundiced by the mendacity of the current crew in comparison to the more subtle foibles of prior decades? Indeed, what does focusing on leadership really tell us about the fundamental policy choices made by states and the drivers of demand, supply, skills and investment in their economies?

As a political economist I prefer bigger fish. I like to think about countries as having particular 'growth models': that is, an ensemble of economic and regulatory institutions and markets that determine how a state produces gross value added (GVA) and turns it into gross domestic product (GDP). When one thinks of Germany in this way, one sees a permanently undervalued currency, demand constriction and export promotion. When one thinks of Ireland, one sees tax arbitrage for foreign multinationals and a nice sideline in film production. When I think of Britain, I think of credit-fueled domestic consumption, financial services exports, an overvalued exchange rate and boom–bust cycles. But when you think about the world this way, it makes you question where the people are who chose that growth model, defended it, argued about it, transformed it and, in some cases, crashed it.

This is where Russell's brilliant book does us all a favour. He reminds us that beneath such macro-structures there are the people that run the model. In particular, the politicians, civil servants and key technocrats that are, for better or worse, 'in charge'. Russell does more than give us an excellent economic history of Britain since the gloss peeled off the Keynesian welfare state in the 1970s: he shows us how each administration was effectively handed a set of problems to solve, how they each tried to solve them in the shadow of the prior administration's failures, and how that process always produced the next set of problems.

For example, notwithstanding the 1973–74 oil shocks, Heath's gamble with the 'Barber boom' set up the industrial relations and inflation mess that Wilson and Callaghan had to deal with. The limits of their solutions in turn discredited organized labour and incomes policies, setting the stage for Thatcher's experimentation with monetarism. The failure of that strand of numerology eventually morphed into the grab bag of policies that was the 'medium-term financial strategy' plus financial deregulation – a combination that effectively deindustrialized the UK while powering a series of asset price bubbles, especially in housing, that have both propelled it forward and crippled it ever since.

As the policies of Thatcher and Lawson evaporated in a housing bust and the poll tax debacle in the very early 1990s, the search for inflationary anchors – the focus of the decade – moved offshore to the European Monetary System and anchoring to the Deutschmark, in classic 1925 style, at too high a rate and for no good purpose. Eventually, under Major, self-imposed economic distress and organized speculation ended that particular monetary fetish – and perhaps (un)surprisingly, once it was abandoned the economy rebalanced quite nicely and handed the incoming New Labour government a very benign environment with which to get started.

However, rather than accepting this benign environment as the product of luck, New Labour wanted 'credibility', so they needed to turn that luck

into a claim of skill to garner that holy grail of credibility. New Labour therefore switched from anchors to its 'five tests', its 'golden rule(s)' and a host of
other indicators that they tried to hit – and when they did hit them, luck was
declared to be skill. Of particular importance here was Gordon Brown's move
to make the Bank of England 'operationally independent', hoping to thereby
ensure low inflation (which was already low), monetary stability ('no more
boom and bust') and (again) policymaking credibility. These policy choices
happened to coincide with the 'NICE Decade'/the 'Great Moderation'. But
again, was this luck or skill? After all, lots of other countries with very different growth models, policy mixes and central banks all had a very nice decade
too between 1997 and 2007.

But in a competitive world, ascribing good outcomes to skill rather than
luck is what gets you elected. No one seeking the highest office is going to
say out loud: 'Wow, we really got lucky there with Chinese deflation, a global
collapse in rates, a ton of new tech that came on line at the right time, the
consolidation of global supply chains, and the end of labour militancy – vote
for me!' Even if it was those things that were, at least partly, driving the result.
And even the most skilled operators – and Blair and Brown were, by Russell's
account, the best the UK have produced over the last fifty years – have their
limits. Sometimes it is simply down to poor choices, such as with Blair and
Iraq. Sometimes it is hubris, as seen with Brown's tinkering towards utopia
with rules and targets while being blind to the downside of massive asset
bubbles and financial fragility.

And so, following hubris, the UK pitched once again back to its nemesis:
back to a hardline anti-Keynesian stance that sought to grow the economy
by shrinking it as fast as possible. The austerity gamble of the Cameron and
Osborne years failed miserably, and in its wake British politics fractured. The
Bank of England heroically kept the ship afloat during this period through
large-scale interventions and endless rounds of quantitative easing, but the
state was continually trying to bore a hole in the ship at the same time. Public
and private investment fell, wages stagnated, productivity effectively stopped,
regional inequalities and wealth inequalities multiplied, and bullshitter politicians weaponized the sense of grievance that all this produced outside of
London and channelled it into a new fetish: Brexit. If only we could get away
from the source of all our self-inflicted woes (the EU), they opined, all would
be restored.

Quite how it ever made sense to leave the world's largest free trade zone so
that one could better sign free trade agreements remains a mystery to many,
but as political theatre it worked. Now, rather than politicians and technocrats running the model, an imaginary and impossible model – an economic
unicorn of vague design called 'global Britain' (yours for only 3% of global

GDP) – drives the actions of the governing classes. Despite no one really being able to say quite was Brexit was, is or should be, 'getting Brexit done' became the only game in town. And the only folks who could deliver that unicorn were not the serious – but flawed – politicians and technocrats, who the public had apparently had enough of. Brexit could only be delivered by the pure showmen: Nigel Farage, Boris Johnson and their billionaire backers.

Once Brexit had been delivered in its 'oven-ready' but indigestible form, and after the country was subsequently battered by a pandemic that eventually brought down the showman-in-chief, the last woman standing was up next to bat. That is how, and why, the UK ended up with Liz Truss. But aside from the comedy, and the handy proof that Truss provided that bond markets really can screw you up if you try hard enough, there lies another deeper lesson with Truss. That is that when all else fails, the UK does 'the politics of nostalgia' better than anyone else.

As Russell once again shows us, if the period from Heath to Callaghan represented the end of an era, it was an era when most people, most of the time, got better off and their life chances improved. Thatcher through Major was a flawed attempt to get to the same place through very different means – means that really did not work and that exacerbated inequality. Blair and Brown managed to do what they said they would do, and things got better again – for a while. But they got there through luck as much as skill. Importantly, however, and despite all their differences, all of these projects had one thing in common: they looked forward.

But then the UK stopped looking forward. Cameron and Osborne were more like the national government of the 1930s when it came to policy beliefs than they were like a government of the 2010s, and they governed like it too. Austerity met benefits brutality. Class warfare through fiscal retraction. Strivers against skivers. Benefits Street. All aided and abetted by the UK's uniquely rabid press. It got ugly. But more importantly, it simply did not work.

If we could not go back to the 1930s, maybe we could go back to the 1950s, when Britain was still 'Great', and we did not have the EU to push us around? And thus the UK settled for a fantasy version of the 1950s called Brexit, and government by nostalgia became normalized. Little wonder, then, that Truss's post-Brexit playbook was to live in the 1980s all over again. I guess that the 1980s are the only place to go when you exit from the 1950s in the Brexit imaginary. The problem with all this is, of course, that you cannot live in the past. You can only live it forward, into a permanently uncertain future, which brings me to the last thing I want to say about Russell's tremendous book.

Russell correctly notes that the real environment of economic policymaking is deep Knightian uncertainty, not tractable and quasi-normally distributed risk. As such, reliance on fragile economic ideas that assume the world is, for example, populated by a single sexless, ageless, raceless agent, drifting through an atemporal time, being slapped with shocks that revert to the mean over time – as most central bank models still do – is probably not a good guide to policy. Again, I would agree. But I think that there is a deeper insight here.

Right at the start of the book Russell quotes his mentor Sir Alec Cairncross, who warned him, above all, to 'avoid dogma'. That is always good advice for an itinerant professional economist. But can *states* really avoid dogmas? Or, to put my question more strongly, do they in fact need them? After all, if the world is truly random, if the shocks are asymmetric and if there is no mean to revert to, what should one do? We would be adrift. Perhaps, then, to reduce uncertainty to at least a sense of risk, we invent fetishes – dogmas – that focus our attention on one particular set of variables as the light under the proverbial drunk's lamppost just as the prior lamppost fails.

Heath was the last devotee of the Phillips curve. Callaghan of incomes policies. For Thatcher it was the quantity theory plus tax cuts wedded to a Ricardian conception of society. Major sought refuge in offshore anchors; Brown in rules that he got to write. Osborne found guidance in the 'Treasury view' redux. Cameron gave everyone else Brexit. To her credit, Truss at least knew that growth and productivity were what really mattered. Unfortunately, the only map that Truss and Kwarteng could find to get there seems to have come from a comedy version of Thatcherism – on steroids.

So where does that leave us? As Russell concludes, the current plight of the UK is bleak, and signs of improvement are fleeting at best. The incumbent Conservative government staggers from scandal to scandal, teetering about on its last corrupt legs, while the opposition Labour Party still seems to crave 'credibility' – whatever that actually means – above having an actual plan to increase investment, raise productivity and make people's lives better again.

Russell does not quite tell us how to get out of this mess, but he does identify the key elements required for any 'reboot' of the UK economy. And he is very good at telling us how we got where we are, which was usually down to real people making the wrong choice in a critical moment. There is good news in that, because it means that, in principle at least, we can perhaps begin to make some better choices by being honest about the errors – and the successes, however fleeting – of the past.

Mark Blyth
Providence, Rhode Island

Preface

This book chronicles the enduring relative decline of the British economy over the past fifty-odd years. In the process, it details the often-humiliating crises and the desperate – and ultimately unsuccessful – attempts on the part of numerous governments, of both the left and the right, to arrest and reverse this process and return the country to the supposed glories of the past.

It is, for the most part, a sad and frustrating tale. The capacity of policymakers to countervail the powerful and inexorable forces impinging on the economy was always more limited than they and the commentariat supposed, and, if anything, that capacity has diminished over time. Nevertheless, there is throughout the narrative a recurrent theme of those in charge – and those who set the wider political agenda – fixing upon a panacea that they hoped would rapidly transform the nation's prospects and encourage some sort of economic rebirth.

In reality, however, there was never a simple solution for what was an increasingly complex and obdurate problem. The despairing search for a magic bullet repeatedly failed, and merely descended into inconsistency or outright (ideologically driven) experimentation. The extraordinary events of the autumn of 2022 – when Liz Truss, the short-lived prime minister, and Kwasi Kwarteng, her even more ephemeral chancellor of the exchequer, briefly sought to impose an absurdly inflationary, unsustainable and unfair set of macro policies on the nation – is just the latest example, albeit a particularly egregious one.

In writing the book I have drawn on the knowledge I have accumulated and the lessons I have learned as a globe-trotting professional economist over the past forty-odd years. Hopefully, this has helped to put Britain's numerous trials and tribulations since the 1970s into a broader perspective. In particular, how does Britain's economic performance stack up in historical and international terms? What were the successes, and what were the failures? Why and how were certain decisions taken? What alternative strategies could have been pursued and did they stand much chance of success? Could more lessons have been learned from abroad? Where might our recent experience leave us placed for the future?

My personal introduction to economics came first as an A level student and then as an undergraduate during the latter half of the 1970s. It was early in the following decade that it became clear to me that I had found my metier. I was consumed by a subject that seemed to affect everything around me – not least the contemporary political debates both in the UK and elsewhere. And, of course, this was a time of extraordinary turbulence. Many long-standing assumptions about how economies should be run were being called into question, if not entirely turned upside down.

By late 1981, my first degree behind me, I was immersed in postgraduate research into the inflationary dynamics of the UK's post-war full employment policy.[1] This evolved into a brief academic career during which I worked as an assistant to two eminent former senior government advisors, Sir Alec Cairn-cross and Lord Plowden, as they set down for posterity their reminiscences of the past, their judgements on the present, and their advice for the future.[2] Both were extraordinary men, and extraordinary public servants.

Sir Alec's breadth of knowledge was incredible, and I found his ability to rapidly absorb information, summarize a complex argument or arrive at the nub of an issue astonishing. He also provided me with one piece of advice in particular that I was to cherish: 'Whatever you do, Russell,' he said, 'avoid dogma. It's toxic.'

Edwin Plowden was a rather different character. More businessman than academic, he was outwardly self-effacing but equally astute. He had been more of a fixer, working between the lines of government, patiently and calmly finding practical compromises that could satisfy those with opposing views, and opposing characters. His career was one of getting things done. He had a remarkable nose for what was politically possible, and what was not.

In assisting these two brilliant – and, I should add, kind and generous – individuals I came into contact with other members of the great and the good of the post-World War II British policymaking community. Some were still active in that field, while others had returned to academia. A few were Nobel laureates. Almost all were only too happy to share their experiences and pass on their wisdom.

This was a privileged education and introduction to the discipline, and one that laid a very solid foundation for my long professional career. I received an expert grounding in how theory and policy interact, and in the messy prac-ticalities of running a large, advanced economy. I learned to appreciate how imperfect our knowledge of contemporary economic conditions was – the amount of available data may have increased dramatically over time, but much of it has remained unreliable and subject to revision. The myriad uncertainties about how the economy functions and evolves also became clear to me over time, as did the difficulties inherent in spotting turning points in advance. My eyes were opened to the chaos or salvation resulting from unforeseen external events, the unavoidable and painful trade-offs encountered at every turn, the strategic inconsistencies wrought by swings of the political pendulum, the narrow-mindedness and wishful thinking of some important actors, the malign influence of personal and institutional animosities – and much more. When all this was considered, it is no surprise that optimal policy responses, or anything that even approximates to them, are rare. Policymakers muddle through, hoping to get things 'generally right' and that the inevitable costs associated with a particular strategy do not overwhelm them.

An early lesson I absorbed from this period of my life was the importance of history to the progression of economic development and the process of macroeconomic management. To downplay or, worse, disregard history's influence is to risk serious misunderstanding and analytical error. Historical experience – and associated perceptions of achievements and failures – fashions the present and colours the future. History echoes through generations. Its influence on policy choices is pervasive and relentless, and along the way it can encourage both constructive feedback loops and destructive ones. As the title of this book suggests, too much conceptual inertia and hankering after the glories of the past can cast a long and ruinous shadow.

Equally, however, it was soon clear to me that the critical influences on the paths of economic advancement and policymaking do not stop at history. Contrary to the perceptions of many laypeople, who are wont to view economics as a bounded subject, an appreciation of other disciplines is required to grasp the dynamics of the business cycle (to the extent that such a phenomenon exists[*]), to contextualize the relative performance of individual sectors and economies, to appreciate the intricacies of the different strands of government strategy or the progress of international economic relations, and to get to grips with the often seemingly random gyrations of financial markets.

Armed with numerous insights from my mentors, this framework of thought and the arrogance of youth, in 1985 I abandoned academia for the City of London, hoping to tap into the burgeoning opportunities that were available – and, it should be said, the pecuniary rewards on offer there – as it geared up for the programme of market liberalization known collectively at the time as the 'Big Bang'. The Conservative government of the day felt that

---

[*] There is evidence that output does not cycle around a long-term upward trend. Rather, shocks also result in a shift in the trend line itself. Hence, the 'business cycle' is not really a cycle. This traditional paradigm should be replaced with a new paradigm of output dynamics that incorporates hysteresis: the dependence of the state of a system on its history.

the UK financial services industry had been held back by excessive regulation. It was determined to give it free rein to flourish.

Economists were in high demand, and freed from many long-standing restrictive practices, this was an industry on a tear as it made up lost ground, particularly on its US counterpart. In this sense I was present at the creation of one of the foremost drivers of late-1980s British free-market capitalism: finance-led growth. I had a ringside seat as the Thatcherite revolution first seemed to sweep all before it before succumbing to an all-too-familiar and predictable demise.

I was initially employed by one of the two global banks that offered fee-based foreign exchange advisory services to major corporations. Currency derivatives, such as options, had recently been created. Currency trading for the purposes of hedging risk and speculation was burgeoning. Yet currency economics was barely in the profession's lexicon. Today, virtually every major international bank and financial institution employs at least one currency economist, but when I began my career, there were hardly any. I was therefore one of the few in my profession that was able to observe at first hand, and participate in, the explosive development of a major financial market.

My purview was a wide one, extending to most of the world's major currencies. But given the pound's volatile and painful history, and the violent swings in monetary and fiscal policy both at home and abroad at the time, I often found myself focused intently on the entrails of the UK economy and consumed by the national economic debate. There was rarely a dull moment as I tried to get to grips with the vicissitudes of financial market sentiment and predict sterling's uncertain future trajectory.

By the time of Thatcher's exit from 10 Downing Street in November 1990, however, I had been posted to Tokyo to cover Japan's economy as the collapse of its 1980s 'bubble' ushered in a remarkable reversal of fortune for a nation that had been held up as an example for all to follow. It was there that I spent much of the next decade. My responsibilities were subsequently extended to Asia as a whole, and in due course I learned a huge amount about the importance of asset prices, credit markets and the functioning of financial intermediation to macro performance, while also getting early insights into the mechanics and complexities of operating monetary and fiscal policy close to the zero-interest-rate bound. Along with the knowledge I had accumulated of the interwar international economy during my academic career, this experience stood me in excellent stead later in my professional life. The misadventures of Japan and the rest of Asia in the 1990s provided something of a template for the development of the other advanced economies.

My years in Japan marked the onset of a peripatetic career. Between intermittent sojourns back in the UK, I spent extended periods based in the Middle

East and Australia, while also travelling the world to service the global client bases of a number of major international financial institutions.

Much of the time, therefore, I monitored the UK's progress from the external vantage point of its competitors. This gave me insights into how alternative policy institutions and different strategic options succeeded or failed. Moreover, as I progressed up the corporate ladder I began to manage larger and more varied teams of economists, and I was therefore able to benefit from their expertise, and to further broaden my understanding of other economies and the different paths their respective policymaking communities chose. Indeed, as my role evolved to becoming a figurehead for the articulation of a comprehensive view of the entire global economy and its asset markets, I had little choice but to lean heavily on the knowledge of others. This included some of the best UK economists in the marketplace.

Over the years I was also lucky enough to tap into the thoughts and judgements of those employed by the largest asset management firms on the planet, as well as the opinions of the international policymaking community, including those employed by the International Monetary Fund (IMF), the Organisation for Economic Co-operation and Development (OECD), the World Bank, and the Bank for International Settlements (BIS). Their perspectives helped to bring Britain's relative performance, and its successes and failures, into yet sharper relief, and never was this more the case than during the global financial crisis (GFC).

The last stop on my forty-year career journey was at a consultancy based in the City of London, where, from 2013, I was reunited with Dr John Llewellyn, whom I had worked closely with for ten years previously. An economics polymath, John had seen and done it all: first in academia, at both Oxford and Cambridge; then during an extended spell at the OECD, where, among other senior roles, he ran economic forecasting for a period; then as chief economist for a major investment bank; and finally, as a UK Treasury official in the aftermath of the GFC.

Together we could offer a deep well of macroeconomic experience and insight, but we were also keen to extend our analytic reach into more specialized and burgeoning areas of importance such as climate change and technology. With these various arrows in our quiver, we were employed as trusted advisors to key players in the investment community, and to various international corporations and industry bodies, while also acting as expert witnesses in a series of pathbreaking UK legal cases.

In this guise we were witness to a further series of remarkable and traumatic events that stand to have enduring consequences. This was the era of Trump, populism and post-truth politics; the age of Brexit; and the period in which the fabric of UK society was stretched almost to breaking point. It also coincided with a global pandemic that, in the UK, brought along the deepest economic downturn in more than 300 years in its wake. It was an epoch in which central bank balance sheets and public sector deficits and debt swelled to unprecedented peacetime levels, and yet interest rates had never been lower – in some important instances plumbing depths lower even than those I had witnessed in Japan.

This final sojourn brought additional opportunities to learn from, and collaborate with, a number of top economists from around the globe, former senior civil servants, and proven champions in different fields of industry. This was especially the case when, in 2019, John and I, along with John's son Preston, initiated the Policy Reform Group (PRG). The PRG is a politically non-aligned body that seeks to develop and advance policy proposals that stand to enhance countries' political and economic health; to present them as a basis for rational, informed, evolving debate; and to contribute where possible to the vigour of that debate. Indeed, in many ways it was this latter venture that paved the way for the writing of this book.

This was hardly the gentle glide into retirement I had pictured, and I will not deny that – for all the fascinating moments during the later years of my career – I found many events, to varying degrees, both unexpected and disturbing. As ever, the ability of economic and political developments to surprise knows few bounds.

But what the recent period also demands is an answer to the question of how we got here. This book is my studied response, at least as far as the UK is concerned.

The structure of the book is straightforward. It is in essence a historical narrative, although it begins with an effort to consider the nature of economics and how it can and should be applied. I then attempt to set the scene for the trials and tribulations of the 1970s – the period when I first became economically literate – before looking in detail at that most vexed decade. Thereafter, I go on to examine the progress of the British economy under various political leaders and policy regimes over the next four decades or so while occasionally taking a detour to review how macroeconomic theory was evolving and affecting policy. There is also a special chapter on the GFC, which takes a broader perspective and looks in detail at the faultlines in the international financial system at that time. In the concluding chapter I try to draw together all the themes I have identified, in the hope that they can help to improve the way in which the economy is run in the future.

On starting to write the book I determined, arbitrarily, that my analytic cutoff point should be the end of 2019. However, given the speed, gravity and interconnectedness of recent events, this proved to be easier said than done. The chronological conclusion of the narrative is therefore somewhat uneven.

Acknowledgements

The book draws overwhelmingly on secondary sources, the most important of which are listed in the section on 'Main Sources and Further Reading' at the conclusion of the main text. The reality is that there is little that is entirely original here. The book is largely a mosiac of others' research and ideas. I have merely provided a framework for them, and intermittently applied additional context and drawn out certain conclusions.

There are a number of individuals without whose support and encouragement the book's publication would have been impossible. First and foremost, I would like to express my gratitude to my wife and family for their endless patience and understanding. I also thank my former colleagues at Llewellyn Consulting – John and Preston Llewellyn, Silja Sepping and Soyon Park – working with whom was a constant source of intellectual stimulus and discovery. Certain other additional people were kind enough either to engage with me on the subject matter of the book or to provide detailed comments on the manuscript, including Mark Blyth, Alastair Campbell, Paul Chertkow, William Keegan, John Nugée, Jim O'Neill, Terry Scuoler, Phillip Turner, Nick Vanston, David Vines and Dimitri Zenghelis.

Finally, I must also thank my publishers, London Publishing Partnership, and in particular Sam Clark and Richard Baggaley. They were a pleasure to work with and did a marvellous job of converting my initial efforts into something more fit for purpose.

Needless to say, the responsibility for any errors in the text lies with the author.

CHAPTER 1

A Very Social Science

The master economist must possess a rare combination of gifts. He must be mathematician, historian, statesman, philosopher – in some degree. He must understand symbols and speak in words. He must contemplate the particular, in terms of the general, and touch abstract and concrete in the same flight of thought. He must study the present in the light of the past for the purposes of the future. No part of man's nature or his institutions must lie entirely outside his regard. He must be purposeful and disinterested in a simultaneous mood, as aloof and incorruptible as an artist, yet sometimes as near to earth as a politician.

— John Maynard Keynes, 1933[1]

NO LIMITS

Before embarking on the history of the British economy over the past fifty years, it is worth taking a moment to consider what economics is. What does it have to offer? What are its strengths? Its limitations? Is it all about facts and figures? Is it really a science? Does it embody certain fundamental laws and truths?

As Keynes suggested in the 1930s, economics is a vast, sprawling discipline, with endless quirks, subtleties and hidden mysteries. Its focus on people and how they behave, both as individuals and in groups, marks it out from the natural sciences. The subject matter is humanity, with all its talents, foibles and imperfections. It touches all our lives. To get to grips with economics is to appreciate both what shapes people's hopes, fears, aspirations, reasoning and actions and how all these things relate to one another. This requires the acquisition of knowledge relating to geography, politics, culture, philosophy, anthropology, psychology, even language. And the economic environment is constantly evolving, responding to sudden unexpected events; slow but inexorable natural forces; ever-changing tastes and preferences; the shifting balance of wealth and power; our accumulated stock of knowledge; and the inspiration of new ideas, not least in the guise of technological advancement. In every sense it is a social and moral science.

In such a broad context, economic debates tend to be prolonged – some at the core of the subject have ebbed and flowed over centuries. This reflects two overriding considerations: first, that economists frequently disagree about how the economy works; and second, that individuals have different perceptions about what constitutes a 'free', a 'virtuous', a 'fair' or a 'well-ordered' society, and that they desire to establish an economic system that conforms with their particular vision of how humanity should be organized and how it should conduct itself and fit into nature more broadly.

Unfortunately, given these diverse perceptions and value judgements, in the process of debate, like all human beings, economists can downplay or ignore new information or proven facts that are at variance with their established standpoint. They may claim objectivity, but predispositions and self-deception can pollute judgements. The activities of research groups can take on the form of ideologies, even cults, where non-believers are deemed heretics.

Economists' investigations therefore rarely approach the unanimity achieved by, say, physicists or mathematicians. All too frustratingly for others, and especially for the political classes, economists sponsor a wide gamut of often-fluid opinions and populate numerous conflicting schools of thought, the influence of which is rarely constant.

Research agendas and the structure of power within the profession reflect the development and structure of power in broader society. There have been what might be described as 'epochs of economic theory'. Systems of economic thought have evolved in response to economic circumstances and the great questions of the day. Big disturbances upset the ideological status quo and encourage people to look at things in different ways and focus on different priorities. Economics is endogenous to the world it seeks to explain.

As the subject of economics relates to the activities of people, ethics dictate that controlled experiments, and certainly those of any scale, are inappropriate or impossible. Economists are not usually in a position to construct uncontaminated environments from which potential sources of external interference can be excluded, or from which generalized conclusions can be drawn and subsequently broadly applied.

For example, changes in policy are just one of many influences on an economy, yet it is impossible to simply disable all the other 'acting forces' in order to isolate the policy effect. Often, the best that can be done is to use large data samples, coupled with various statistical filters and techniques, to even the other influences out. Moreover, even if all the other relevant influences could be deactivated, it would never be morally acceptable to, say, arbitrarily raise interest rates or taxes to see what happens to people's income, jobs or wealth. The macroeconomy cannot be a research laboratory.

What tends to happen is that policy reacts to events at least as much as it triggers them. It is the impact of the economy on policy, rather than the reverse, that dominates data. Interest rates tend to rise when an economy is strong, and inflation is rising, and fall when an economy is weak, and inflation is in retreat. But it should not be concluded that low interest rates are a catalyst for weak growth and that high interest rates are the source of price instability. Rather, the effects run the other way: when an economy is weak, it requires the support of looser monetary policy; when inflation is high, the necessity is for tighter monetary policy.

Economic analysis is therefore, by its nature, less pure and more opaque, and its conclusions more tentative and open to dispute, than is the case with the natural sciences. That said, it is encouraging to note that the 2021 Nobel Memorial Prize in Economics was won by three US-based economists for their work on real-world (or natural) experiments – situations in which chance events or policy decisions created conditions akin to a clinical trial.[2]

Furthermore, in the world of economics, the present depends not only on the past but also on the future, or at least on how people expect the future to pan out. This feature of the discipline adds to its complexity and can render it particularly hard to come to terms with. Natural scientists can comfortably assume that the direction of causality of a relationship extends from the past through the present and into the future. In economics, for all the importance of history in shaping thinking and action, this is not necessarily the case. The dynamics of causality can be more convoluted, and counterintuitive. In particular, expectations of how the future will evolve can change things in the present, which in due course will impinge upon the future.

Nowhere are these feedback loops, or unexpected secondary consequences, more important than where investment activity is concerned. As has been seen since the UK's Brexit referendum, a sudden wave of pessimism about future economic conditions will depress willingness to invest and slow contemporary economic activity down. But less investment today also means less productive capacity – and, consequently, slower economic growth – tomorrow. That some relationships within economic systems can take on this reflexive quality means that they can lack stationarity – or parameter time invariance – from period to period.

NUMBERS, SYMBOLS, GRAPHS AND MODELS

Nevertheless, despite its complexities, its largely non-experimental nature and its peculiar processes of cause and effect, economics is a quantitative discipline.

Indeed, most of the relationships that economists delve into can be quantified. This means that the subject can be less descriptive and more abstract and disposed to arithmetic and algebra than other social sciences, such as politics, sociology and the majority of history. Unfortunately, however, this can lead practitioners down blind alleys. Human relationships are messy and opaque; they are rarely sharply defined. The human subjects of economics have their own minds and free will. These allow them to observe, to organize, to plan and thereby to avoid the unpleasant consequences of particular circumstances and actions. They are prone to do what they want, when they want.

Modern economies, even the smaller and less developed ones, are intricate systems, hard-wired into the even more complex universe that is the global economy. For practical purposes, some level of simplification is inescapable if we are to get to grips with them, or even elements of them, and to generate forecasts of important economic variables. This simplification typically takes the form of a small number of proven behavioural relationships – cause and effect linkages between certain economic quantities – plus a few equilibrium conditions that must be satisfied for economies to exhibit stability.

These behavioural relationships and equilibrium conditions can be captured in algebraic equations and geometric diagrams, which can in turn be applied more broadly in so-called models.

Models are rudimentary maps or frameworks established in the hope that the process of simplification has not garbled them to the extent that they become an inappropriate guide to the real world. They embody exogenous variables (those from outside the model) that provide the model's inputs and endogenous variables (those from inside the model) that provide the model's output. That is to say, the exogenous variables are fixed at the moment they enter the model, while the endogenous variables are determined within the model. The purpose of the model is to demonstrate how the exogenous variables impact the endogenous variables.

The fact is, however, that economic models tend to focus on the variables and relationships that fit most easily into an algebraic format. They can neglect other considerations – ones that are more complex, that take longer to play out, and that are less straightforward to incorporate – many of which reflect the breadth and richness of the subject. Model builders can also be slow to update their assumptions and their ways of working to reflect the evolving structure of modern-day economies. For example, the role of greatly expanded financial sectors from the 1980s onwards was long downplayed, or even ignored altogether. Equally, digital technology is today seemingly all-pervasive in society and yet absent from many economic statistics and inadequately mirrored in econometric models.

In describing their models, economists tend to employ particular linguistic tics – analogies, metaphors and descriptive techniques – as short cuts to help laypeople understand how the economy functions. Hence, the word 'market' is used to describe vast, complex and decentralized processes of movement and exchange, as in 'labour market' or 'commodity market'. As suggested above, 'equilibrium' is used to describe the situation when the economy, or some part of it, is in balance, and the concept of equilibrium is central to economic analysis. Once such points of balance are identified, it is easier to understand how fast various forces will return an economy, or some part of it, to these loci. Indeed, the search for equilibria, together with the examination of the speed of adjustment to those equilibria, are two of the most common procedures in economic analysis.

Economists put to use the fact that graphs and equations are two different portrayals of the same reality. Indeed, the pictorial representations of analytic geometry are often more intuitive and easier to grasp than the mathematical symbols, Greek letters and obstruse conventions of algebra. Quantified behavioural relationships become curves on a graph. Equilibria are points where the curves describing these behavioural relationships cross (and thus both behavioural relationships are satisfied). Changes in economic conditions or economic policy are represented by shifts in the position of particular curves. Many complex economic theories and arguments can be summarized in this way, and it is crucial to the teaching of the subject.

It should be stressed again, however, that models are simplifications to facilitate the omission of detail and complexity judged to be superfluous to the core underlying relationships. Economists must not therefore become fixated on the elegance of their mathematics, and the apparent richness of their model's output, and in the process lose track of the ever-changing complexity of the actual experience from which it was drawn, and which it is meant to proxy. Such fixations risk subjecting oneself to disappointment and failure, or even ridicule.

Unfortunately, there are no rules for how much simplification a model should embody. The predictions of some basic models can be as accurate as those of more complex alternatives. Model building therefore inevitably involves considerable trial and error, or 'learning by doing'. It is a work in progress, and economists would benefit from being more outward looking, and seeking to work with engineers, climate scientists, computer scientists and ecologists to better understand the challenges facing society. How, for example, will the development of artificial intelligence or quantum computing improve the process of econometric model building?

There are, however, certain fundamental characteristics that the most effective models embody. These include the use of representative agents, or the notion that all participants in an economy are, for practical purposes, the same; opportunity cost, or the notion that there is at the heart of every behavioural relationship always a choice, but that in making that choice the alternatives are excluded; and some assumption about the nature of expectations about the future. In particular, are expectations static; backward looking and adaptive to past experience; or what economists call 'rational', and the result of a comprehensive effort to understand not just the past and the present but also the future – and, if taken to the limit, to know as much about the structure and the behaviour of the economy as the model builders themselves?

Finally, there are the equilibrium conditions: the conditions that must be true if the economy is in balance. And if an equilibrium condition does not hold, then the economy must be moving towards a situation where it does. In macroeconomics, it is the demand-must-equal-supply condition that is most important – as this implies that the economy is operating at its effective limit and prices are stable – although there are countless others.

Modelling can only take economists so far. Models cannot know what particular forces are driving the economy at a particular point in time, or why. Therefore, when describing economic conditions or forecasting the future trajectory of an economy, a clear and thoughtful narrative, transparency around the assumptions made, and the employment of appropriate adjectives can be more powerful and revealing than the precise numerical output of a model. It is worth repeating again that economies are complex, adaptive systems. They are not stable entities, occasionally disturbed only by exogenous shocks. They are capable of endogenously driven volatility, and multiple equilibria, both of which are huge challenges for macroeconomists.

The experience of the past seventy-odd years provides ample evidence of all this. By and large, post-World War II macroeconomic history can be characterized as runs of many years of comparatively small perturbations and fluctuations punctuated by a few large shocks and commensurately big consequent fluctuations. Unfortunately, the small fluctuations contain little information that is useful in discerning what will happen in response to a larger shock. The nature of large shocks usually differs qualitatively from the impulses that determine minor fluctuations, and they can be complicated by nonlinearities.

This might lead to a supposition that the most useful evidence for analysing the likely consequences of a large shock is therefore to be found mainly in previous large shocks. But, unhelpfully, that is not generally the case. Most of history's large shocks have differed from one another in important respects. And, furthermore, the underlying conditions in which those various large shocks struck and worked their way through economies typically varied importantly from one episode to another.

Most post-war recessions before 1990 were caused by policy instability or the need to reduce inflation or the external deficit (things that tended to occur after prolonged periods of full employment) and were relatively minor, frequently amounting to slowdowns rather than outright contractions. However, the shocks related to the oil price in 1973–74 and 1979–80 were different, simultaneously impacting both demand and supply, making them harder to address.

After 1990 successive downturns were caused, or exacerbated, by instability in asset prices and related balance sheet adjustment – in particular, a requirement to reduce excess indebtedness. This pattern extended from the collapse of the Japanese 'bubble economy' to the East Asian crisis, the 'dot-com bust' and, of course, the global financial crisis.

Latterly, the Covid-19 pandemic has delivered another unfamiliar and very damaging kind of shock, again embodying both demand-side and supply-side effects. The only previous example to draw on over the modern era was the Spanish flu pandemic of 1918–21, but unfortunately this episode preceded the collection of national accounts and other important economic statistics. Moreover, the effects of Spanish flu were obscured by the impact of demobilization and the return of economies to a peacetime footing at the end of World War I. It can therefore provide few insights, beyond the most general. And the impact of the Covid-19 pandemic was itself complicated both by the sharp rise in energy prices that went hand in hand with war in Ukraine and, in the UK's case, by Brexit, both of which also represent significant negative supply shocks. Over recent years economists and policymakers have therefore essentially been flying blind.

A major implication of this history of the post-war period is that macro forecasting errors divide into a large number of comparatively small errors, made in the years when fluctuations were modest, and a few large errors, made following shocks that were both sizeable and novel.

In this context, the only viable approach to understanding, and thence forecasting, the effects of a large shock such as the coronavirus pandemic is to take from past shocks anything that may be relevant – discarding all that which is not – and put together a composite analysis. And where there is no relevant evidence, one must fall back on a priori reasoning.

Therefore, even if some quantitative assessment of the outlook is worthwhile, it should be the account of the forecast that matters most, rather than the numbers. It is the narrative that gives policymakers and economic agents a framework for thinking through what they see happening and for adjusting course when necessary. The numbers are merely illustrative.

Moreover, this does not just hold for forecasting: the same is true when looking backwards. The numbers can only tell you so much. The whys and wherefores are inevitably much richer and more revealing. And the story of the British economy over the past fifty years or so is a remarkable one.

CHAPTER 2

Losing the Plot

Truth is provisional, to be deserted if it conflicts with experience.

— Sir Alec Cairncross, 1988[1]

THE CLASSICS AND MR KEYNES

The birth of modern economics is usually associated with the publication of Adam Smith's *An Enquiry into the Nature and Causes of the Wealth of Nations* in 1776.[2] Economic theory burgeoned over the next 160 years, but the core message remained that, if left to its own devices, capitalism was a near-perfect system. Shocks of one sort or another might come and go, but rational self-interest, coupled with the unfettered operation of the price mechanism, would encourage economies to smoothly gravitate back to a position of optimal equilibrium. It was therefore important to trust free markets to work their allocative magic.

Market failures – where the freely functioning forces of supply and demand failed to distribute scarce resources in a way that optimized social welfare – were believed to be few and far between. The role of government should be confined, therefore, to the establishment of a stable currency, to private property rights (despite the fact that most of the population owned little or no property), to the creation of courts to enforce contracts, to basic education, to infrastructure to facilitate commerce, and to the security of the nation state. From the middle of the nineteenth century onwards there was also recognition that to prevent a breakdown of the financial system, a central bank should intervene and lend when others were too fearful to do so. Apart from these limited interventions, though, governments should adopt a 'laissez-faire' approach, and disengage from the economy, in so doing, entrenching much of the distributional status quo.

In the eighteenth and nineteenth centuries this ideology was frequently reinforced by experience. Much of what the state did beyond these minimum functions was damaging or unsuccessful, so few believed that governments should seek to influence the course of business cycles.

Notwithstanding some limited dilution of this doctrine in the face of unavoidable political pressures and enduring hangovers from the interventions necessitated by wars, laissez-faire held sway until the Wall Street Crash of 1929 ushered in the Great Depression of the early 1930s. Those who hankered after a more active role for government remained largely on the fringes of debate until the catastrophic events of 1929–33 changed everything. The global slump shattered faith in laissez-faire.

With the establishment convinced that whatever the market system yielded must be appropriate, and that the private sector should be left to its own devices, many prominent economists of the time – such as Joseph Schumpeter, Friedrich von Hayek, Ludwig von Mises and Lionel Robbins[3] – averred that government interventions would only encourage a false revival that would ultimately make the situation worse. Depressions were seen as cleansing processes – necessary to eradicate previous excesses, reimpose discipline on workers and businessmen, facilitate structural change and breed future dynamism. In the meantime, government budgets should be balanced, households and firms should be permitted to default on mortgages and loans, and social security should largely be eschewed so that people are encouraged to price themselves back into work by accepting lower wages. What is more, the pegging of currencies to gold should be maintained as an overarching guarantee of long-term price stability, financial rectitude and political discipline. Indeed, the fixed link to gold should be prioritized, even to the extent that, in the short term, it stands in the way of interest rates declining to levels more appropriate to domestic economic conditions, drives prices and wages sharply lower, undermines collateral values and pushes the real value of debt obligations upwards.

The most famous – even infamous – example of such thinking is attributed to Andrew Mellon, the US Treasury Secretary of the time and one of the world's richest men. He is reputed to have said: 'Liquidate labor, liquidate stocks, liquidate the farmers, liquidate real estate.' The result, he claimed, would be that 'rottenness [will be purged] out of the system … people will … live a more moral life … and enterprising people will pick up the wrecks from less competent people'.[4] Similar views were to be found in the UK, too, not least in the Treasury, where considerable time and effort were given over to defending the laissez-faire status quo and attempting to refute heterodox theories of how the economy operated and should be managed.[5]

I would strongly argue that the record shows, however, that to the extent that the policies that flowed from laissez-faire thinking were employed, they manifestly made things worse. It was the lingering attachment to the precepts of nineteenth-century economic thought that ensured that the Great Depression was great. Output proved reluctant to stabilize. International trade and capital flows slumped. Rapid deflation became entrenched. Governments chased their tails in futile efforts to slash their spending to match their slumping revenues. The Gold Standard collapsed in the face of a series of financial crises. Banking systems imploded. Credit premia surged. Financial intermediation froze. Investment spending dried up. Unemployment and poverty skyrocketed. Political and social instability mounted. One government after another fell. Democracy withered as totalitarian regimes multiplied.[6] The supposedly perfect system of capitalism seemed to be on the verge of collapse. For many, Soviet-style communism appeared to be the only viable solution.

It was at this juncture that John Maynard Keynes entered the story in the UK. Keynes had long been a thorn in the side of the government. He was brilliant, intuitive, self-confident, practically minded, outspoken and persuasive, yet never one to close himself off from new ideas or allow his thinking to stagnate. Indeed, his imagination was extraordinarily fertile. And when he changed his mind, it was usually for the better. He was not just an innovative and wide-ranging economic thinker, but was also possessed of one of the finest and most agile intellects of the twentieth century.

He had famously condemned the post-World War I Versailles financial settlement as a disaster for Europe and the world, and he dismissed the 1920s Gold Standard as a 'barbarous relic': an outmoded and unsustainable financial architecture that transmitted shocks rather than dampened them, and threatened to consign Britain and others to deflation and depression.[7] But by the onset of the slump, his criticisms of orthodox – or what he was to call 'classical' – economic opinion had gone much further. Keynes was disparaging of laissez-faire economics, characterizing it as being divorced from the practical realities of the day, and likely to be a source of misery to much of the population. He hated the reality of poverty in the midst of plenty.

As an alternative, Keynes put the case for active monetary management to stabilize the domestic price level. He even explored how central banks might use purchases of long-term government securities – what we know today as quantitative easing, or QE – to go about this when short-term interest rates approached the zero bound.[8] He also became an outspoken supporter of using fiscal policy to support monetary interventions, especially when the latter lost their potency and the private sector remained reluctant to spend more. His particular focus was on the use of a programme of public investment spending to support aggregate demand, and in conjunction with his Cambridge University colleague Richard Kahn he developed a theory about how government investment outlays would cascade through an economy such that their aggregate effects could greatly exceed the initial sum spent.[9]

In his 1936 magnum opus *The General Theory of Employment, Interest, and Money*, Keynes sought to demolish the 'classical' approach to economics once and for all.[10] He challenged the notion that markets were close to perfect. Rather, he claimed that they were beset by frictions and distortions – not least those related to monopolistic powers on both the supply side and the demand side. Spending was constrained by both income and liquidity, and high unemployment could last for years and limit supply – a decidedly 'bad' macroeconomic equilibrium. In short, there was outright – and often systematic – failure. Contrary to the ever-full-employment theories of most of his forerunners, the reality was that economies tended to spend much of their time divorced from high levels of resource utilization.

Markets failed because actors within them did not have enough knowledge of how others would react and could not possibly act simultaneously to maximize their shared interests in the way that had been suggested by the 'classical' school. They failed because they could not by themselves ensure that social costs were borne by those who incur them. And they failed because they could not ensure the delivery of necessary public goods. Keynes had a special level of contempt for financial markets, where participants could rarely see very far into the future, which encouraged them to indulge in short-term speculation. This made their investment choices prone to becoming disassociated from underlying economic fundamentals.

At the core of Keynes's economic philosophy was the logic of choice in circumstances of uncertainty. He believed uncertainty – as opposed to measurable risk, presented in the form of probabilities – to be a fact of life. Not only did people often have little or no idea what was going to happen, they also had a limited ability to describe, or even imagine, what might happen. To cope with such uncertainty, human beings fall back on conventions, or rules of thumb. But these could vary greatly in nature from person to person and were likely to be very unstable. Uncertainty could become radical in nature. The shortcomings in our knowledge and understanding, and the caution and hesitations they encouraged, could come to dominate decision-making – and they could do so at every level, from the individual upwards. By damping 'animal spirits', or confidence in the future, uncertainty could encourage saving, constrain spending (particularly investment spending, which once initiated can be difficult to reverse) and fundamentally undermine aggregate demand. Bound up with this was the so-called paradox of thrift, whereby if there is a generalized desire to save more, aggregate income is bound to fall and so, therefore, will overall savings. Rather than a virtue, saving could become a vice from the point of view of economic stability.

Keynes's bottom line was that quantities – of output and employment in particular – adjust more than prices in response to economic shocks, and economies do not therefore necessarily rapidly self-regulate and self-heal, smoothly returning to some harmonious equilibrium. The gravitational pull towards full employment could be weak. Economies could become detached, for a protracted period, from any notion of full resource utilization. And the social and political consequences of these things could be dire in the meantime, leading nations down very unfortunate and damaging paths.

Because markets and economies are able to behave in this way, they should not be left to their own devices. The state should become involved in them, although what he meant by this was state intervention in the market not state suppression of the market – an economy where the supply of goods and services is determined largely by market processes but in which the state has an important oversight and management role. Never an overt supporter of nationalization, Keynes saw his mission as saving and improving capitalism rather than replacing it. In practical terms, this meant government activism via monetary, fiscal and (to a lesser extent) regulatory policy, and especially when economic activity was prone to drop some way below potential. In such circumstances, it was important that government pulled all the levers available to it in an effort to re-establish growth and prosperity.

Despite Keynes being an external government advisor during the depression and the subsequent recovery, his ideas continued to be greeted with official scepticism. His insistence that low short-term interest rates might be insufficient to secure full employment and that the Bank of England should be ready to buy bonds on a large scale was ignored, and real long-term interest rates therefore remained high. Notwithstanding Treasury proposals to prepare a reserve fund of public works projects in advance of the next downturn, the evidence that government rearmament programmes exerted a profoundly positive impact on UK economic activity in the late 1930s was never accepted as proof of the case for fiscal activism in 'normal' circumstances. The fear across government remained that significant resort to Keynesianism would prove a recipe for state excess, that private sector confidence would be further undermined rather than enhanced, that unsustainable trade deficits would be accrued, that the exchange rate would collapse, and that runaway inflation would result.

Indeed, it is fair to say that Keynesian policies, or Keynesian-like policies, achieved greater acceptance in the 1930s beyond the UK's borders than within them. In the US, Roosevelt's New Deal encompassed certain Keynesian elements, including major public works programmes, even if it was a hotchpotch of often-incoherent and conflicting interventions.[11] A number of European authoritarian states, including Germany and Italy, also applied heavily interventionist strategies that extended to significant government investment outlays beyond those earmarked for rearmament.[12] And in Japan, under the guidance of its finance minister Korekiyo Takahashi, the Bank of Japan was mandated to underwrite certain debt-financed government spending programmes that again went beyond those earmarked for the military. Japan exited the Great Depression faster than any other large economy.[13]

It was only during the course of World War II that, supported by the development of national income accounting, and the identification and estimation of what we would now describe as the 'output gap', Keynesian thinking and macroeconomic management made more conspicuous headway in the UK.[14] Significant elements of the Keynesian approach were then incorporated into the 1944 White Paper on Employment Policy. Even though this was a cautious and often-contradictory document, it committed future British governments to strive for a high and stable level of employment through the use of monetary and fiscal policy to influence the total level of spending.[15] In other words, it stated that macroeconomic policy should endeavour to be countercyclical and could and should prevent sharp downturns.

There is a broader point to be made here. The adoption of Keynesian economic policy in the UK and beyond, even if its precise form varied from country to country, was a consensus-building strategy to protect the capitalist status quo against revolutionary assaults. Keynes's desire to preserve capitalism rather than bury it was implicitly recognized.

AN INGLORIOUS END

Keynes effectively invented the science of macroeconomics, and forty years on, when I began to study the subject seriously, it was the exegesis of this Keynesian approach to macroeconomics and policy that was still in the ascendency in the UK. For several decades, fearful of repeating the painful experiences of the 1930s, successive governments had presided over a 'mixed economy', encompassing a significant – indeed burgeoning – public sector share in overall activity while prioritizing the management of aggregate demand, focused in particular on securing full employment. Dissenters in either of the two main political parties had either been frozen out or forced to disavow their old opinions. The same was largely true of nonconformists in academia.

But the picture was changing. My 'economic awakening' coincided with an epoch of tempestuous economic, social and political upheaval in this country and beyond – upheaval that had a profound effect on economic thinking. The 1970s saw the demise of the post-war Keynesian era. Just as had been the case with the previous orthodoxy during the interwar years, Keynesianism – at least as it had been applied – had stopped delivering.

The basic macro statistics of that decade tell a grim story. After an unsustainable boom that peaked in the middle of 1973, the years 1974 and 1975 were noteworthy because annual average real gross domestic product (GDP) declined in outright terms for the first time since the war. Previous post-war recessions had merely represented slowdowns in the rate of growth. The mid 1970s also saw labour productivity growth per hour and per head go negative for the first time since the war. Furthermore, the share of profits in national income hit an all-time low of around 32% in 1975,[16] which in turn depressed business investment. It contributed nothing to growth in the middle years of the decade. Thereafter, recovery gradually took hold, but it was not until the final quarter of 1976 that output returned to its previous peak, and it was only in late 1977 and 1978 that the economy again grew consistently. It has been estimated that, if proceeds from North Sea oil were omitted, output was some 9% lower in 1979 than its extrapolated pre-1973 trend. The equivalent shortfall for labour productivity was 7%.

The headline unemployment rate had run persistently under 3% of the workforce in the 1950s and early 1960s, was frequently around 2%, and at one stage fell as low as 1.6%. This meant that in some particularly vibrant areas, the unemployment rate was often as low as 1%, and throughout this period much of the joblessness that was in evidence was confined to specific regions such as the North East, Clydeside and South Wales. However, the jobless rate began to edge higher in the late 1960s, reaching 4.3% in 1972. It then jumped again during the recession of 1974 and 1975, not to return to the levels seen early in the decade until 2019.

Consumer price inflation also took off during this period. Between the end of the Korean War in the early 1950s and 1967, inflation was never much more than 5%, and it averaged considerably less. Indeed, in 1959 and 1960 it ran under 1%. It was, however, typically higher in the UK than it was in other major advanced economies.

Just as with the unemployment rate, the late 1960s saw the inflation trend break higher. By the early 1970s, the average was in high single digits, and the annual figures for 1974 and 1975 were 15.75% and 22.75%, respectively, with a peak of 25.25%. In previous epochs, prices had fallen more or less as often as they had gone up. Moreover, there had been only three years since 1700 (1800, 1917 and 1918) in which inflation was comparable to 1975. Thereafter, it was not until January 1978 that annual inflation fell back into single digits, and it did not remain there for long.

The UK also suffered from persistently large twin deficits in the 1970s. The overall public sector shortfall, which included the operations of the nationalized industries, never dropped below 3.5% of GDP between 1973 and 1979, and it is estimated to have peaked at 6.25% of GDP in 1975. Meanwhile, driven by rapidly rising welfare payments, unemployment benefits and public sector pay, the share of government spending in GDP lurched upwards to crest at more than 46% of GDP. There was a keen sense through this period, therefore, that government activities were 'crowding out' those of the private sector and necessitating an ever-higher tax take.

For its part, despite a consistently depreciating exchange rate,[17] the current account balance experienced a sharp deterioration: from a surplus of around 1.5% of GDP in 1971 to a deficit of 3.75% of GDP in 1974 – and apart from a small surplus in 1978, it remained in the red for the rest of the decade. Britain's share in total global manufacturing trade, meanwhile, fell as low as 6.3% in 1976, down from more than 20% in 1950. The external situation was only rendered manageable through considerable official financial support from the international community, including the IMF.

Interest rates swung wildly, but they were frequently negative in real terms, often substantially so, which in turn fuelled the inflation described above. The policy rate – which was set by the chancellor of the exchequer at that time, with the Bank of England merely providing an advisory, and often peripheral, role – began the decade at 8%. It was reduced to 5% in 1971 but had hit 13% by the end of 1973 – a level it revisited and then exceeded towards the end of 1976. Thereafter, within less than a year it had tumbled as low as 5%, before once again reversing course to end the decade at 17%.

The stock market also suffered exaggerated swings. A vigorous bull market in the early 1970s was followed by a catastrophic bear market in 1973 and 1974 and then another dip in 1976. Recovery took hold after 1976, but the upswing in equity prices levelled off in 1979.

The 1970s saw an average of 13 million working days lost per year because of strikes, with a peak of 29.5 million in 1979, during the so-called Winter of Discontent. To give some context, a little over 4 million days were lost per year in the 1960s, just over 3 million per year in the 1950s, and some 7.25 million in the 1980s, although this latter number was skewed upwards by the 27 million or more days lost in 1984 during the miners' strike. Thereafter, as trade union power waned, the figures dropped to a mere fraction of the first four post-war decades.

The decade's dreadful reputation can be overplayed, however. After all, notwithstanding its ups and downs, the 1970s saw real GDP growth average 2.25% per year. While this was well below the pace recorded in the 1950s (just over 3%) and the 60s (almost 3.5%), it was not far short of the rate seen in the 1980s (2.75%), which was supposedly an era of renaissance for the British economy, and it was some way above the figures seen in the 1990s (just over 2%) and in the past two decades (1.75%). Furthermore, although unemployment was on a rising trend after 1973, and was generally higher than it had been in the 1950s and 1960s, it was to become a much greater source of blight for society in the 1980s, when the rate averaged just shy of 10% of the workforce, peaking at 11.75% in 1984 and not dropping into single digits for six years in the middle of the decade.

The 1970s also saw a number of other, often-forgotten, landmarks and achievements, many of which were bound up with the welfare state being at its zenith during this decade. For example, women were given the right to equal pay, and more than 50% of all women were employed for the first time. Pathbreaking legislation was passed on racial equality, maternity leave and universal child benefit, and overall income inequality, as measured by the Gini coefficient, declined to its lowest level on record. Finally, the growth in real wages, at some 3% per annum, was higher than it was in the 1990s and the 2000s.

These considerations aside, however, there was a sense towards the end of the decade that macroeconomic instability had reached extreme proportions, and that the overall political and social situation in the UK was increasingly unsustainable. Indeed, there was a fear that the very fabric of society was being torn apart.

So how did Britain get into such an unenviable situation? And how culpable were those policymakers who claimed to be the standard bearers of Keynesian doctrine? To answer these questions, it is necessary to divide the post-war era into two parts. Outwardly, the first twenty-five or so years after World War II was a period of considerable achievement. Indeed, it has been characterized by many commentators as a 'golden age'. Beneath the surface, however, a deepening malaise can be detected, especially towards its end. Then, in the ten years that followed, that malaise deepened alarmingly.

TOO MUCH OF A GOOD THING

The fear among most economists and government officials when preparations were being made for the post-war world, as well as during the initial period of demobilization, was that conditions akin to the 1930s would soon reassert themselves. Mass unemployment and the poverty associated with it would be the overarching problems that faced governments.

This proved to be grossly pessimistic. The dominant issue for governments in the UK and beyond was instead the control of a secular private sector boom. In Keynes's 1930s terminology, uncertainty was low and 'animal spirits' ebullient. Growth was, therefore, historically robust, underlying fluctuations in activity were mild (ripples rather than waves), deflation was absent,[18] and, in overall macro policy terms, there was a requirement for restraint rather than largesse. The record shows that there were five mini-cycles – six periods of faster growth interspersed with five periods of slower, at times minimal, growth – between 1949 and 1973, yet there was no major contraction in output.

This surprisingly upbeat outcome reflected a number of overlapping and reinforcing considerations, including

- rapid global population growth and an associated strong demand for capital;
- the requirement for industrial reconstruction in Europe and Japan;
- a period of catch-up with the technological best practice of the United States, which also provided generous financial assistance to its wartime allies and others;
- weak energy and commodity prices, such that the UK's terms of trade (the price of UK exports relative to the sterling price of UK imports) improved consistently from the Korean War until the early 1970s, and by more than 35% in total; and
- the progressive liberalization and rapid expansion of global trade.

Britain, meanwhile, became as strongly committed to full employment as any western nation. By February 1951 the second Attlee government had already instructed the United Nations that the maximum level of unemployment it would tolerate was 3% of the workforce, and that action to keep joblessness below that level would be initiated well before the threshold was reached.[19] Indeed, full employment became a sacred cow, and the idea of what should constitute full employment became more and more extreme – certainly more radical than anything Keynes himself had imagined to be practicable for any length of time. In late 1944, for example, Keynes wrote a letter to Sir William Beveridge about the latter's book, *Full Employment in a Free Society*, in which it was mooted that governments should aim to reduce unemployment to 3% of the workforce. He commented: 'No harm in aiming at 3 per cent unemployment, but I shall be surprised if we succeed.'[20]

As the expectation of very full employment became increasingly embedded in the nation's political superstructure, it became harder for governments to row back on previous commitments and those who argued that it might be wise for the economy to be run with a greater degree of spare capacity were dismissed as reactionaries. Hence, any remotely significant deviation from full employment tended to be met with howls of dismay from the commentariat, fears of a haemorrhaging of political support for the government, and, in due course, a bout of panicky reflation.

This was also the era of what might be described as 'Meccano economics', where pulling policy lever x was confidently expected to produce result y. Based on the so-called Phillips curve, it was widely believed that there was a stable inverse relationship between the level of unemployment and the rate of change of worker remuneration, and therefore that governments had a menu of choices between degrees of joblessness and inflation.[21] However, this article of faith was dependent on people acquiescing to a certain amount of inflation. It gave no heed to the dynamic nature of market economies, and it entirely ignored the role of expectations in private sector behaviour. And, unfortunately, price expectations became increasingly sensitive to actual experience. 'Money illusion' – the tendency to see money wage increases as real – lasted for shorter and shorter periods of time, before evaporating altogether. Workers increasingly put in wage demands to match expected rises in prices. The decline in real wages required to make unemployment-reducing policies effective became increasingly ephemeral, yet the higher prices endured.

By the late 1960s the Phillips curve relationship was breaking down. It was revealed to be only an interim phenomenon. Higher and higher inflation seemed to result following each successive attempt to achieve full employment, and the employment levels achieved struggled to match what had previously been experienced.

Governments responded to these inconvenient truths with greater interventions. In particular, policies that had a direct effect on wages and prices were introduced, in the hope that the earlier inflation–unemployment trade-off might be rekindled. In essence, the hope was to shift the Phillips curve back to the left.

Temporary wage freezes in the context of major crises tended to be the most successful variant of prices and incomes policy. However, these were not sustainable for long in a predominantly free market economy, and some thawing of the freeze inevitably became necessary after a few months. But often working against the grain of the balance of demand and supply in the labour market, and what many trade unions and employers saw as their underlying interests, these less draconian variants of such policies were doomed to failure and collapsed. To the extent that wage and price inflation were temporarily slowed down by these policies, they tended to subsequently bounce back, while in the meantime price sensitivity was enhanced and industrial relations were poisoned.

Keynes wrote little about wages policy during his life (he died in 1946), and there was certainly nothing that could be described as a formal incomes policy in his voluminous output. He recognized the potential for wage inflation to become a problem in a full-employment economy, but beyond viewing it as a political issue that was unlikely to respond to a formulaic approach, he offered no specific solution. Ever the optimist, however, his expectation seems to have been that the possibility of achieving consistently high employment, and the benefits to society that went with doing so, would over time be sufficient to encourage both sides of industry to behave moderately in the way that they went about fixing wages. This proved to be an empty hope – and one that was shared by numerous post-war governments.[22]

POLITICAL FINE-TUNING

The tendency to seek to run the economy as hot as possible for as long as possible led to the so-called stop–go era in the 1950s and 1960s, and to the emergence of a politically driven business cycle. Moreover, the influence of political considerations in the timing and magnitude of policy changes was increasingly reflected in risk premia on long-term interest rates and in the currency markets.

Ahead of a general election, the economy would typically be stimulated through what might be summarized as 'fiscal Keynesianism'. This was a combination of tax cuts and increases in current public spending, supplemented by looser direct controls on bank balance sheets and credit availability (in particular 'hire-purchase' schemes), in order to reap the vote-winning benefits these measures would bestow.

There were also efforts to accelerate the pace of public investment sometimes, but in practice it tended to take a long time to get new work started: there was likely to be a rise in public investment two years after it was approved. Such policy initiatives were much better suited to deep and extended downturns than to offsetting minor fluctuations in activity.

With the Bank of England having been nationalized in 1946, and now under direct Treasury control – and, at least, beyond the influence of the residential construction sector – interest rates were seen as a relatively blunt instrument with which to manage domestic demand, so monetary policy played a subordinate role to fiscal policy until the 1970s. There was a general desire to keep interest rates relatively low to sustain investment if possible, but the money supply was ignored altogether. It was not until the mid 1960s that any effort was made to compile extended series for the monetary aggregates, and, as we shall see, it was only from the mid 1970s that any effort was made to detail an objective for monetary growth.[23]

After a general election, the economy would regularly have to be slowed down to address the resultant overheating of demand. It should be stressed, however, that in the 1950s and 1960s, overall policy changes were limited. The current budget of the government – that which was most impacted by tax and short-term expenditure changes – remained in surplus throughout. Moreover, the overall annual changes in the broad cyclically adjusted budget balance – the aggregate impulse of fiscal policy – were generally in the region of just half a percent of GDP.

Nevertheless, it could prove difficult to fully reverse the pre-election expansionary budget measures taken. Once taxes were lowered, they were hard to raise. Public investment projects were difficult to abandon once they were underway. During a fiscal expansion, the chancellor of the exchequer was popular, and their cabinet colleagues were only too pleased to lend their support. But during a fiscal contraction, the chancellor cut a more isolated figure. It could take several rounds of reluctant deflation to bring a rapidly expanding economy fully to heel.

To the extent that it proved necessary to prop up the exchange rate, official interest rate changes also tended to come into play more during 'stop' phases – as, on occasion, did direct controls on imports. However, interest rates were never employed as the primary weapon with which to restrain inflation during this period.

The underlying commitment of successive governments to full employment and to avoiding any return to the pre-war conditions of mass unemployment helped, in a broad sense, to underpin confidence and the long post-war boom.[24] However, the persistent fine-tuning of demand around the electoral cycle was not without cost. Besides helping to ratchet inflation higher, it was, at the margin, a source of instability and uncertainty that somewhat moderated the inducement to invest. What we can see with hindsight is that macro policy during this epoch appeared both to cause small deviations from trend and, later, to reverse them, such that growth would have been closer to trend had policy been less active or been held constant.[25]

The failings of fine-tuning no doubt in part reflected the fact that, despite the apparent confidence of economists in Meccano economics, macroeconomic forecasting at the time was relatively crude and the data on which it relied often grossly inadequate. The editions of the national accounts and other data series at the time often differ substantially from contemporary estimates, with the more recent figures tending, if anything, to look more benign. Both reflation and deflation were attempted when they were less necessary than they appeared to be – or, at least, the degree of policy adjustment undertaken was excessive relative to what was actually required. The events of mid 1966 offer a prime example: deflation was undertaken to address a slide into external deficit following the March general election that was won by Labour. We now know that the current account had actually been on an improving trend and was in rough balance at this time.

MISSION CREEP

The emphasis placed on expansion in macro policy was deepened by a growing recognition from the late 1950s that Britain was falling behind its neighbours and competitors. Growth might have been historically high, but it was less impressive than that being achieved by most other advanced economies, including those across the channel in Europe. Between 1954 and 1960, West Germany grew by 7.75% per year, Italy by 5.75% per year, France by

4.5% per year, and the UK by 2.75% per year. It was, in significant part, envy of the apparent accomplishments of the continental European economies that led Britain to look to belatedly join the EEC, the forerunner of the European Union.

In the immediate post-war years, it was no exaggeration to say that the typical British attitude was to look down on the rest of Europe, where democracy had proved incapable of resisting fascism in the 1930s, and with much of the continent having suffered military defeat, or surrender. Britain found itself in a quite different situation. It was not a failed state that had been occupied, and although it had paid a heavy physical and financial price for its role in defeating Nazi Germany, there was no lack of faith in its political institutions. Supranational solutions that reduced national sovereignty therefore had less resonance than they did elsewhere in Europe, and the British population had little confidence that they could rely on the rest of Europe for protection against the Soviet Union. Britain had been on the winning side in the war, and that victory had been facilitated by the closeness of its relationship with the US. Its natural tack, therefore, was towards Washington.

Perceptions had changed after a decade and a half of economic underperformance and the military and political disaster that was the Suez Crisis. The so-called Common Market seemed to be going from strength to strength, and by 1960 Prime Minister Harold Macmillan had grown sufficiently concerned about the economic and political threat posed to the UK by Europe that he saw fit to hedge his geopolitical bets and apply for membership of the club – even if he was reluctant to fully come clean with the public about the potential implications for national sovereignty.[26]

But Macmillan's application to join, as well as a subsequent effort by Harold Wilson's Labour government in 1967, foundered on French opposition, and in particular on the veto of President Charles De Gaulle. De Gaulle no doubt had gripes with Britain and its governing classes stretching back to the war, but he also believed that Britain's past meant that it could not be trusted to be a 'good European'.

It was only in the early 1970s, with De Gaulle gone, that British efforts to join the EEC proved successful under the stewardship of Edward Heath, and the UK became a member on 1 January 1973. The community was presented to the electorate as largely an economic, rather than a political, entity – one that would foster Britain's modernization. The ambition of 'ever closer union', enshrined in the founding Treaty of Rome, was downplayed, if not ignored, throughout. The underlying issues of governance and the potential erosion of British national sovereignty were never fully acknowledged. This was the 'original sin' of the Europhiles, and it stored up huge problems for the future.

PLANNING AHEAD

At the same time as Britain was looking to Europe for inspiration, concern developed that British governments were having to apply the policy brakes to the economy too often. There were, in short, too many 'stops'. Consequently, successive governments of the right and the left in the 1960s and early 1970s supplemented their full-employment objective with specified targets for economic growth. Efforts were made to develop a longer-term policy framework, worked out in consultation with both sides of industry. The experiences of countries like France and Japan with forms of so-called indicative planning – the coordination of private and public investment through common forecasts and output targets, and the identification of the major obstacles to their achievement – had a significant influence on these initiatives. This was despite the fact that it was unclear whether the apparent accomplishments of such *dirigiste* strategies reflected the broader record of success of these economies or vice versa.

'Growthmanship' was never in the original Keynesian playbook. Furthermore, the targets that were announced were invariably unreasonably high, underpinned by little more than aspiration and the hope that a further enhanced, but in reality fanciful, commitment to expand demand would deliver the desired outcome.[27] Rhetoric tended to greatly exceed detailed policy substance.

This is not to deny that demand management had an effect on supply. High pressure on demand coupled with a low unemployment rate can help to sustain skill levels and encourage the diffusion of innovations, both of which can augment potential output. However, productive capacity cannot necessarily be routinely created merely by a diet of fiscal and monetary expansion. One can only conclude, therefore, that there was only a limited understanding at the time of the processes of productivity enhancement and economic growth, and of the structural policies that were necessary to sustainably raise output growth. Indeed, it was only in the 1980s and 1990s that a remotely adequate literature on such initiatives was to become available.

Few took on board the fact that many countries had an automatic productivity advantage over the UK, in that they retained considerable scope to shift resources out of agriculture and into manufacturing, which had considerably higher productivity. Britain had already largely exhausted this dividend. Britain's productivity problems were also most evident in the services sector, where regulation was high and competition muted. This was certainly the case in financial services, where the City of London was a shadow of its pre-war self, and persistently losing market share.[28]

Equally, the analytic shortcomings of the time are also evident in the debate about the role of private investment in plant and equipment in Britain's apparent decline. The low propensity of businesses to invest was regularly touted as a major – if not *the* major – source of slow productivity growth. But was low productivity growth caused by low business investment or was low business investment down to low productivity growth? After all, for the private investment that was undertaken during this period, the subsequent returns in the form of additional output consistently proved to be disappointing.

This suggests that the reasons for Britain's sub-par productivity and growth performance went well beyond weak private investment per se. Rather, they were complex and they were reflective of a broad range of underlying considerations: considerations that differed from sector to sector, that evolved in prominence over time, and that were prone to feed off one another. They included aged and inadequate infrastructure networks; slow-growing external markets; shortcomings on the part of management and labour, both of which were too defensive, often resistant to change, and wedded to adversarial industrial relations; a lack of spending on research and development; an embedded faith in existing institutions, rooted in being on the winning side in the two World Wars; educational shortcomings, which extended from poor basic attainment levels across much of the population to inferior skills training and retraining; the low esteem attached to occupations such as engineering relative to the more traditional professions; and limited access to finance for entrepreneurs, not least in the small to medium-sized enterprise (SME) sector. Two issues in particular, however, are deserving of further attention.

BINDING CONSTRAINT I:
THE EXTERNAL BALANCE

'Stop–go' – or, more specifically, the regular emphasis put on 'go' to reduce unemployment and stoke the engines of growth – meant that UK governments were repeatedly confronted by the threat of a more significant loss of price stability than our competitors, a deteriorating external balance and, as a result, a loss of confidence in the pound and a forced devaluation of sterling's fixed exchange rate under the Bretton Woods system. Even relatively small variations in the growth rate of world trade, or the UK's terms of trade, could make the difference between relative calm on the foreign exchanges and a sense of overwhelming crisis. Yet there was a persistent failure to develop a balance of payments strategy that was consistent with more ambitious growth targets – indeed, there was a persistent failure to develop much of a balance of payments strategy at all.

A more competitive pound could have been a valuable stimulus to faster growth, and indeed without it, faster growth could not really be sustainable for any length of time. Yet voluntary, preplanned devaluation was something of a political taboo to governments of both the left and right.

Prior to sterling being floated in June 1972, it was explicitly devalued twice: in 1949 and 1967. But there were numerous other close calls, which sent hitherto-expansionist governments into headlong retreat. Indeed, there were thirteen greater or lesser runs on the pound over this period, all of which triggered domestic policy adjustments and often required external financial assistance to address.

The reality was that, *in extremis*, the balance of payments overrode full employment or growth as a policy goal. In this sense, the UK behaved like a client state of the US. As the world's second reserve currency, sterling was the first line of defence for the dollar as the US economy's dominance of the post-war international monetary system waned and it began to run up twin deficits in the context of the Vietnam War. Anxious to keep the US government onside, UK policymakers were reluctant to let the pound go, unless the rate was completely untenable; simultaneously, recognition of the UK's role in stabilizing the overall system meant that international support for sterling was more readily available than might have been expected. The devaluation of 1967, when it was finally forced on the Labour government of the time, signalled the beginning of the end for the Bretton Woods dollar standard.

Britain's balance of payments problem was not just down to a tendency towards excess demand. The fragility of sterling's position was exacerbated by a number of important underlying structural weaknesses in the economy's external position.

First, Britain's post-war trade performance was enfeebled by the lingering geographical skew of UK exporters towards sluggish traditional Commonwealth markets, and by the British consumer's particular predilection for imported manufactures – a phenomenon that was itself symbolic of the modest quality and choice of much UK output. The merchandise trade deficit was actually typically much smaller than it had been before 1939, but had the geographical composition of trade been different, and had there been a lower propensity to import, it would have been closer to – or actually in – surplus.

More important is the fact that World War II had been exorbitantly expensive. Indeed, it almost bankrupted the nation. Over the course of the hostilities, some 28% of the nation's wealth had been wiped out by disinvestment in foreign assets and increased foreign indebtedness. Once comfortably the world's largest net creditor, Britain's net overseas asset position was by 1945 in the red.[29] The nation's earnings from interest, profits and dividends were therefore greatly reduced. In the late 1930s the UK typically ran an 'invisible' trade surplus of around 5% of GDP. In the 1950s and 1960s, however, it averaged closer to 1% of GDP, leaving the overall current account balance prone to deficit in cyclical upswings.

A third consideration behind the external balance's perpetually precarious condition was a consistent and substantial deficit (typically amounting to around 1.5% of GDP) in the government's international transactions. This reflected its significant overseas military presence, much of it east of Suez, and an unwillingness on the part of successive administrations to rapidly adjust Britain's geopolitical aspirations to match its diminished post-war economic and political status.

A fourth weakness was a persistent and significant net long-term private capital outflow, despite a range of capital controls, largely reflecting foreign direct investment. Although the outflow was much smaller than it had been before the war – unsurprisingly, given the current account's fragility and the relative decline of the City of London's international role and reputation – it was sufficient to frequently leave the 'basic balance'[30] in deficit. This implied a reliance on short-term capital inflows, often highly speculative and mercurial in nature; a running down of official reserves; or substantial official borrowing from sympathetic central banks or the IMF to compensate. Between 1947 and 1971 – that is to say, well before the huge IMF loan of 1976 – the UK had benefitted from some $7.25 billion of direct IMF support, together with standby arrangements, both drawn on and unused, totalling more than $8 billion.[31]

The fifth and final vulnerability was sterling's role as a reserve currency. While the pound's importance to international transactions diminished after the war, around a third of international trade was still settled in the currency in the early 1960s, the sterling–dollar exchange rate remained the world's pivotal currency relationship, and sterling was a vital component of the official reserves of many countries. A substantial proportion of the total stock of sterling was therefore owned offshore.

One element of this was the so-called sterling balances. The official sterling balances, owned by other governments and central banks, had increased dramatically during World War II, when payments for war supplies were made in sterling retained in London. The sterling balances can be thought of as current account bank deposits, withdrawable at any time, and where 'withdrawn' meant converted into gold or other currencies, threatening a sterling crisis. They were a Sword of Damocles hanging over UK policymakers.[32]

This problem was all the more acute because the UK's gold and foreign exchange reserves were inadequate to shoulder the role of a reserve currency. They were lower than those of all the other major western European nations, for example, and the persistent weakness of the current account balance left few opportunities for their replenishment. Up until 1970 they never exceeded $4 billion, while the sterling balances held in London had for many years run at $20 billion or more. The position improved a little in the early 1970s, when reserves rose to $7 billion, but from then on they remained between $5 billion and $7 billion: a level that was not only inadequate in relation to the liquid liabilities in the form of the sterling balances but that would have paid for only two months of imports.

Overall, taking all these considerations into account, it could be argued that the UK was the most conspicuous casualty of the failure of the UK delegation to prevail during the negotiations with the US at Bretton Woods in 1944 to establish the rules for the post-war trading and payments system. Drawing on Keynes's original idea of an International Clearing Union, the UK strove for the establishment of symmetry in the obligations of debtors and creditors. In short, in the event of fundamental disequilibria in external balances, it should be just as incumbent on creditor nations to reflate and revalue as it was on debtor nations to deflate and devalue. The US, however, as by far the world's dominant creditor nation, rejected this notion outright. Hence, in the post-war era the overwhelming burden of policy adjustment fell on the shoulders of those countries that ran persistent current account deficits.[33] And, indeed, this remains the case to this day, as the events of the euro area sovereign risk crisis of 2012 amply demonstrate. It was the debtors Greece, Ireland, Portugal, Spain, Italy and Cyprus that had to adjust, rather than the creditors, such as Germany.

BINDING CONSTRAINT 2: THE LABOUR MARKET

The inflation of the post-war period did not just reflect a tendency for over-stimulation of the economy and for aggregate demand to exceed aggregate supply: it also had its roots in more institutional, social and cultural considerations. As such, it involved both 'demand-pull' and 'cost-push' factors, and the latter became increasingly strong from the mid 1960s onwards.

These broader societal influences were numerous and tended to interact malignly. They began with historical considerations. British employers had always been weak, by international standards, in a collective sense. They had never developed strong industry-wide coalitions, and they had always highly valued their independence. They rarely provided a strong and consistent stance on wages.

This lack of a united front on the part of employers had repercussions on the trade union movement. The British economy was highly unionized, and the unions' legal strength was increased by legislative changes in the 1950s and 1960s. However, the Trades Union Congress (TUC) lacked coherence and authority. It was made up of a large number of individual unions organized on an occupational basis, while the shopfloor, where piece-rates and local supplementary payments were set, was increasingly militant and powerful, and the venue for numerous unofficial strikes. In the absence of a tough and unified bargaining posture on the part of employers, the unions were given little incentive to restructure, reorganize or increase coordination. Decentralization in wage bargaining was allowed to progress more or less unchecked.

And there were other important structural pro-inflationary influences too. For example, there was a general intensification of the struggle for a high relative wage, as individual groups came to appreciate the power they possessed. Consistently increasing affluence tended to raise both aspirations for the future and the desire for income growth continuity. With income tax thresholds not automatically adjusted for inflation until 1977, there was a reaction against rising and more widespread taxation. The aggressive pursuit of full employment in tandem with the extension of the welfare state and the maintenance of a strong defence commitment meant that public sector activities and taxation came to account for higher and higher proportions of GDP. And finally – and, as noted above, most importantly – there was growing inflation-consciousness among workers in what was historically a rare period of protracted rising prices. It is noteworthy, for example, that prior to 1939 the notion of an annual wage round was unheard of, whereas by the early 1970s the question was being raised by trade unionists as to whether a single wage round each year was sufficient.

SWANSONG

The 'last hurrah' of the post-war Keynesian era, in which the vulnerabilities and failings of the previous two decades metastasized, came in the early 1970s, but it coloured the rest of the decade and sorting out the resultant mess took a lot longer. Such was the extent of the debacle that followed that it warrants a chapter of its own.

CHAPTER 3

The Barber Boom and Bust – and Beyond

It is not often that a government finds itself confronted with a possibility of simultaneous failure to achieve all four main policy objectives – of adequate economic growth, full employment, a satisfactory balance of payments, and reasonably stable prices.

— *National Institute Economic Review*, February 1974[1]

THROWING CAUTION TO THE WIND

When the Conservative Party came to power in the middle of 1970, it was ostensibly committed to a more laissez-faire strategy of 'industrial disengagement', and macro restraint, than previous post-war governments had been. This approach did not last long. Although the economy was expanding consistently, with unemployment heading towards the politically sensitive figure of a million, or about 3% of the workforce, Prime Minister Edward Heath and his only-too-willing chancellor, Anthony Barber, were panicked into a dramatic reflationary U-turn over the course of 1971 and 1972. One eminent historian has characterized their policy as 'Keynesianism gone mad'.[2]

With a low and falling public debt burden, a budget close to balance, and a rare current account surplus all inherited from the previous Labour government, macro policy was relaxed aggressively in an attempt to achieve another arbitrary target for the growth rate: this time of 5% per year. The change of tack was presented – as it had been on previous occasions when prudence was cast aside – as a strategy to reverse the economy's relative decline.

This particular bout of reflation went some way beyond the usual fiscal fine-tuning. In addition to a range of tax cuts and increases in public spending, it included the lifting of quantitative controls on bank lending, which had been in place since World War II, as part of a liberalization of the financial system that the government called Competition and Credit Control.[3] This ill-prepared initiative proved to be a disaster. Years of heavy-handed

regulation had left banks eager to diversify and expand, but bank regulators and supervisors failed to adapt to the new risks that banks were
taking. With policy interest rates under political control, and held below
appropriate levels, this sparked what can only be described as a bout of
monetary debauchery. Just as a global boom was getting underway, private
credit and monetary growth exploded: the broad monetary aggregate M3,
for example, expanded by some 60% over two years. In this environment, a
property bubble was inflated, and a wave of unsavoury financial speculation
was encouraged.

Furthermore, in June 1972, as the Bretton Woods system of fixed exchange
rates unravelled, sterling was unpegged from the dollar and allowed to float.
This was viewed by many domestic commentators as a measure that would
lift the economy's long-standing external constraint, allow the expansion to
be sustained for longer, and establish growth on a higher trajectory in the
context of impending EEC membership. The reality, though, was rather different. With monetary policy super loose, the pound rapidly sank – not just
against the dollar but also in trade-weighted terms. This fall also embodied
sterling's precipitous ejection from the 'snake in the tunnel' system of European exchange rate management that was heralded as a first tentative step
towards European monetary union. Britain had abandoned perhaps the most
important anti-inflationary discipline on employers and trade unions.

There was a significant degree of monetary and aggregate demand
excess throughout the advanced economies in the early 1970s, but Britain's
experience was exceptional. The Heath government's reflationary strategy
– nowadays widely derided as the 'Barber boom' – amounted to a poorly
timed, incoherent and astonishingly destabilizing cocktail. Inflation had
already been elevated at its outset; the government was ridiculously optimistic about the economy's ability to grow without running into capacity
constraints (the UK's potential growth rate had oscillated around 2.75–3%
per year since the war); and the lack of consideration given to monetary
trends and the implications of a persistently depreciating exchange rate were
inexcusable oversights.

Statutory controls on wages and prices were adopted from November 1972,
including an initial freeze on both, but the former were greeted with hostility
by workers and the latter accepted only grudgingly by industry. Besides, the
incomes policy had no chance of holding back the inflationary tide of a super-
charged cyclical upswing. At one stage, output increased not at the targeted
rate of 5% per year but at a post-war record clip of 7.25% per year; at the same
time, the unemployment claimant count bottomed out at just 200,000, or
around 1.5% of the workforce. In such circumstances, prices and wages were
bound to chase each other higher, and as imports were sucked in to meet

the overabundance of domestic demand, the current account balance swung rapidly from surplus towards what was then a record peacetime shortfall.

After an extended period of denial, recognition that things were running out of control gradually took hold through 1973. The Bank of England was belatedly allowed to move interest rates sharply higher and reimpose controls on bank lending, and the expansive public spending plans were pared back. With stock levels in industry clearly excessive, industrial confidence ebbing away and the property bubble bursting, a significant downturn already seemed to be in prospect.[4]

DOUBLE WHAMMY

Two other considerations then intervened to deepen the sense of burgeoning calamity.

The end of that year saw a mining industry overtime ban in support of a 16% pay claim that forced the government to declare a formal state of emergency and, in due course, to impose a three-day working week to preserve coal supplies.[5]

What is more, this period also saw the Yom Kippur Arab–Israeli War. Enraged by US support for Israel, OPEC announced an embargo on oil exports and sharply cut production. After decades during which cheap oil had been taken for granted, the price of crude quadrupled over the course of two months. In this environment, fatally misconceived indexation clauses built into the incomes policy – so-called threshold payments – kicked in, providing a built-in inflation accelerator.

The increase in oil prices was at the heart of a 27% peak-to-trough deterioration in the UK's terms of trade. Not only did it push up the overall price level and headline inflation rate, but it also delivered a huge negative shock to the supply side of the economy and to productivity. Oil was the source of about half of energy consumption in the advanced economies, so the sharp increase in crude costs significantly changed the pattern of demand. Meanwhile, much energy-rich capital was rendered obsolete, and considerable organizational disruption was triggered. The difficulties of adjustment were further compounded in the UK by the long-standing inefficiencies of industry and the by-now-entrenched reluctance of workers to accept cuts in real incomes.

Spectacular boom had turned into equally spectacular bust. By the beginning of 1974, ration books had been distributed; the press was comparing the UK to the Weimar Republic and to Salvador Allende's Chile; and some middle-of-the-road commentators were warning of a military takeover, while Marxist academics speculated whether Britain was witnessing the final crisis of capitalism.

Then, with inflation running at around 14% and heading higher, and the economy falling into a deep and extended contraction, the miners' dispute escalated into an all-out strike. At this juncture, and with the IRA also mounting a major bombing campaign on the British mainland, William Armstrong – the head of the civil service, an outspoken supporter of the reflationary gamble of 1971–73, and Heath's closest advisor – suffered a nervous breakdown and had to be committed. The beleaguered prime minister felt he had no alternative but to call a snap general election on 28 February, supposedly to determine 'who governs Britain'.

HOSPITAL PASS

Unfortunately, from the point of view of a robust economic policy response to the situation, the electorate's answer to the question of who should be in charge was that it wasn't sure, although it didn't think it should be Mr Heath and his Conservative Party. To his barely disguised surprise, if not chagrin, Labour's Harold Wilson – as leader of the largest, and the most ideologically divided, party in the House of Commons – became prime minister for a second time.[6]

Wilson was no longer the man that had initially become prime minister in 1964, having been ground down by his time in office and by the challenges of keeping his party together while in opposition. There is also evidence that he had already begun to exhibit the first symptoms of early-onset Alzheimer's disease, which was to cause his formerly excellent memory and his powers of concentration to deteriorate.

Furthermore, the economic legacy he inherited from his predecessor was catastrophic. As the new chancellor, Denis Healey, put it in his introductory statement to the first cabinet of the new administration: 'The country is confronted by an economic situation which might be the worst which had ever been faced in peacetime, and which is deteriorating.'[7]

Labour's victory in the February 1974 election – such as it was a victory – reflected in part a belief that the party was better equipped to work with powerful trade unions than were the Tories. As well as being a result of the industrial relations chaos of the final months of Tory rule, this belief was encouraged by the 'Social Contract', a deal struck in 1972 between the TUC and the Labour Party covering food subsidies, nationalization plans, government-controlled prices, taxes and pensions. In essence, it was hoped that by consulting the unions on policy, mitigating the effects of inflation, and maintaining the 'social wage' through welfare benefits, the conditions could be created for pay restraint and industrial harmony.

This was wishful thinking, but from a narrow political perspective, Labour's return to power was not the time for a change of tack. The left of the party was very strong and vehemently opposed to anything that smacked of serious austerity or the dilution of workers' rights. Wilson was always a leader who was more focussed on compromise and the tactical here and now than on any longer-term strategic vision, so his approach was to settle the miners' strike as soon as possible (by giving them much of what they had demanded); end the three-day week and state of emergency; abandon the unpopular statutory incomes policy; accept a number of comparability-based claims for significantly increased public sector pay; abandon Heath's controversial industrial relations laws; and provide enough budgetary largesse to allow the party to win a stronger mandate at a second election later that year. He also determined to keep the disastrous threshold payments in place, so that real wages were maintained. More fundamental issues of policy could be addressed once Labour had a majority – or not.

Healey – an experienced minister and pugnacious intellectual heavyweight, but a politician with no experience in economic management – was acutely aware that his primary initial task was to keep Labour in power.[8] In this he was helped by a Treasury that, while bamboozled by the stagflationary impact of the oil price shock, was still largely wedded to core Keynesian principles – not least the commitment to full employment. His key advisors – the three Cambridge economists Nicholas Kaldor, Sir Robert Nield and Wynne Godley, plus Maurice Peston of Queen Mary College, London – certainly fell into this category.

Despite policy lacking a credible anchor, underlying inflation pressures being severe, and the external deficit becoming cavernous, Healey's advisors were reluctant to deflate aggressively while real activity was so weak and there appeared to be a significant degree of excess capacity. Moreover – and this was forgotten two years later – this was the response officially recommended by the IMF at the time, even if the UK was one of the few nations to actually put the advice into practice.[9] Others preferred to instead focus more intently on addressing the inflationary implications of the oil price shock.

Healey's first budget was broadly neutral. However, he sought to massage the headline inflation rate lower through a combination of price and rent controls; food subsidies; increased financial support to the increasingly inefficient, if not loss-making, nationalized industries; and a reduction in value-added tax (VAT). He also raised the top income tax rate to an eye-watering 83% and imposed a 15% surcharge on 'unearned income'. Together these measures amounted to a marginal tax rate of 98% for a small proportion of the population. The policy rate was also cut, and monetary policy remained relaxed for the next two years, with real borrowing costs significantly negative. Just as had been the case under the Conservatives, the Bank of England's influence was limited.

FROM BAD TO WORSE

In narrow political terms, Wilson's strategy worked. Despite the first real recession of the post-war era, a second general election in October 1974 gave Labour an overall majority of three. However, the significant number of MPs elected from small parties meant that negotiations over support for the government were always a possibility, as indeed proved to be the case.

As the effects of Healey's various policy palliatives faded, the awful underlying situation reasserted itself. The economy was in a state of profound disequilibrium. Inflation was headed to 20% and beyond, and after eleven successive automatic threshold-related monthly pay increases, hourly wages were growing even faster, not least across the public sector. Unemployment was also rising sharply. Corporate liquidity was in short supply, as companies were being taxed on the basis of the value of inventories inflated by sharp price increases. In real terms, profits were falling rapidly.

Insofar as the Social Contract was meant to be a disinflationary device – or, for that matter, a means to improve industrial relations – it failed dismally. Meanwhile, the budget and current account deficits remained excessive, and continued to outstrip official forecasts, while the share of public spending in GDP seemed to be rising inexorably towards 50% – a proportion far above that of most of the UK's major competitors.

EUROPEAN DISTRACTION

The prime minister was for much of this time absorbed by the renegotiation of the terms of the UK's membership of the EEC – something that had been promised in both of Labour's 1974 election manifestos and that was to be followed by a referendum on whether or not the country should remain in the bloc. Wilson's personal position on Europe was less than enthusiastic, and his leadership of the 'Yes' campaign was as much a matter of political necessity as of personal conviction. Nevertheless, he recognized that staying in the EEC in 1975 was better for the country's future prosperity than the alternative of exiting after less than three years of membership.

During the discussions with Brussels, little energy was expended on the major issues of principle involved in Britain's membership. These were largely dealt with by broad assurances that Britain's leeway on issues like regional and industrial policy, public ownership, the management of sterling, and VAT would not be overtly circumscribed. Furthermore, the specific dispensations ultimately granted to the UK by the EEC were limited, being chiefly confined to greater access to New Zealand dairy produce and a cap on budgetary rebates.

During the subsequent referendum campaign, in which his cabinet was split between the two camps, Wilson played a low-key role, shunning the limelight and content to sidestep the smouldering underlying issues of sovereignty and the longer-term trajectory of the UK's budget contributions: topics that would haunt future administrations. The choice he opted to put to voters was framed as one between 'moderates' who wanted to remain and 'extremists', on the left and the right, who wanted to leave, and it resonated in a way that was conspicuous by its absence in the referendum of 2016. A majority of both Tory voters and Liberal voters were happy to follow Wilson's lead.

In the end, an electorate consumed by more pressing issues and burdened by a sense of national frailty overwhelmingly endorsed the limited renegotiation in a referendum held in June 1975.[10] In the process, Wilson – ever the astute political fixer – managed to reinforce the foundations that Heath had laid, reconcile his party to membership, encourage Britain to play a constructive role in a maturing European community, and largely keep the subject out of the headlines for the next five years. The significance of these achievements was only to increase with hindsight.

All that said, the underlying commitment to Europe of both the Labour Party and the public remained lukewarm. For the UK, this was an instrumental and transactional arrangement, when for others in the EEC it was more fundamental: a means to end a long cycle of war, an escape from fascism, or a guarantor of freedom. Britain, by contrast, had been on the winning side in two major global conflicts, had remained a democracy throughout, and had not been conquered for a millennium. The next forty years were to see Britain's – and particularly the Conservative Party's – relationship with Europe characterized by an ever-changing cocktail of hubris, anxiety and injustice. Hubris arising from Empire and from Britain's historically global purview. Anxiety about being left behind economically. And a sense of injustice rooted in a suspicion that the rest of Europe was conspiring against the UK. Wilson's European settlement was not an enduring one.

TOO LITTLE, TOO LATE

Wilson's focus on Europe inevitably distracted him from other matters, and from the economy in particular. Furthermore, he was frequently exhausted, and on doctor's orders his officials were reducing his workload.

During this period of economic policy drift, two considerations served to maintain market confidence in the UK. First, oil producers needed to invest their newfound wealth somewhere, and out of habit they continued to place a significant proportion in London. Second, oil had been discovered in the North Sea, output was picking up rapidly, and the UK was expected to become self-sufficient in what was an increasingly expensive and scarce energy resource.[11]

By early 1975, however, Bank of England and Treasury officials, including Healey's influential advisor Nicholas Kaldor, were increasingly convinced that the market would not suspend its judgement on the shortcomings of UK economic policy forever. Time was running out, especially if the economy's malaise were to deepen further. Fiscal policy had to become more restrictive, and public spending needed to be cut back in real terms.

Political decisions aside, it was proving very hard to control government outlays, not least at the local authority level, and spending on social security and wages was soaring. Public spending totals were initially set in volume terms and automatically adjusted for prices, but the outturns were consistently overshooting official forecasts by wide margins. The projections therefore lost all credibility.

Healey was cautious about spending restraint, however, for fear of alienating the unions and the left of his party. He raised the basic rate of income tax to 35% in his spring budget, but most of the adjustments to the spending plans he announced at that stage were deferred until the 'out years' of the official projections. Healey also continued to pour money into industrial policy, which, for all its social and regional policy merits, was increasingly a vehicle to support 'lame ducks' rather than dynamic companies. He did, however, pay lip service to the monetarism that was growing in popularity within academia, as well as taking root in the City of London, and he announced a long-overdue intention to rein in monetary growth.

Equally importantly, this period also saw the beginning of efforts to develop a new incomes policy and to move on from the Social Contract as originally defined. The advice of the Treasury and the Bank of England was, despite the disasters of the Heath years, to go down the statutory route of wage control. But the Number 10 Policy Unit – led by Bernard Donoghue and including future City economics grandee Gavyn Davies – put up a convincing case for a less confrontational, voluntary approach, backed by sanctions on firms. There was considerable wavering on the part of both Healey and Wilson before the Policy Unit's proposals were finally embraced. In adopting their proposed strategy, the government was encouraged by the fact that some trade union leaders, including certain leftwingers such as Jack Jones, the head of the Transport and General Workers' Union, had grasped that runaway inflation was devastating UK competitiveness, hurting those on fixed incomes and with little bargaining power the most, and that if it was allowed to continue it would guarantee Labour's removal from office.[12]

An announcement limiting wage increases to £6 a week for those earning less than £8,000 a year, supported by penalties on employers that breached the norm, was announced in July 1975. Inflation soon began to retreat, but things came to a head again in early 1976. Healey's far-from-radical plans to roll back the size of the state were defeated in the House of Commons because of a rebellion by the Labour left, and the government was saved only by a knife-edge confidence vote. Five days later, a spent Harold Wilson resigned in a move that took the country by surprise.

James Callaghan, the familiar and experienced foreign secretary, took his place. Healey retained his position as chancellor. The delicate balance of power within the cabinet changed little. Nevertheless, this was a time of great uncertainty across the nation and in the markets.

It was not clear at the time why Wilson had resigned at that precise moment. He subsequently claimed that he had always intended to do so when he was 60, but that was still very young for a prime minister (Callaghan was older than Wilson). That Alzheimer's disease had made his continuing in the role impossible only came to light later.

Callaghan had been the chancellor disgraced by the devaluation crisis of 1967. It was debatable if he could sustain the close relationship with the trade unions and match Wilson in holding the fissiparous Labour movement together. Would he grasp the nettle of fiscal retrenchment? Would he cut and run for an election? The questions were many; the answers far from obvious.

A CRISIS OF CONFIDENCE

Around this time, the Treasury discussed using a lower exchange rate to stimulate exports and rein in the current account deficit, and although no ministerial authority was secured for a devaluation, the Bank of England was instructed to sell sterling on 4 March and the next day a small cut in interest rates was announced. Unfortunately, these initiatives coincided with heavy official sales of sterling, particularly by Nigeria (a large oil producer) as its government, like many others, sought to diversify its reserve holdings. The pound slumped, necessitating heavy intervention in the opposite direction. Market sentiment had soured and it became increasingly fixated on the UK's significant twin deficits; the government's apparent lack of authority and political will; and, despite the incomes policy, the relatively high inflation rate. Over the course of March and April 1976, almost a third of the UK's limited foreign exchange reserves were expended.

As it transpired, agreement with the TUC on a second round of voluntary wage restraint was reached in May, but only after Healey announced income tax concessions in his April budget. Union influence on macro policy remained profound, and despite further heavy intervention in support of the pound, pressure on sterling continued, much of it reflecting the unrelenting withdrawal of official central bank holdings. The sterling balances remained a heavy burden.

With the help of the BIS and a number of sympathetic central banks, the UK negotiated $5.3 billion in standby credit from the G-10 in early June. However, $2 billion of this was provided by the US Federal Reserve, and the US authorities required repayment within six months. If the government could not repay any resort to the credit by that date, it would have to seek a longer-term loan from the IMF, which would only come with strict macro policy quid pro quos.

There is an irony here, in that elements of the UK's economic situation were starting to turn around at this time. It would certainly be difficult to claim that the country's overall position in mid 1976 was any worse than it had been in 1974 or 1975. The economy was now expanding, inflation had fallen sharply (although it remained in double digits), competitiveness had been improved by the depreciation of the pound, and the external deficit had peaked. The problems were that the impression in the markets and elsewhere was that public spending and the budget deficit remained excessive, that the government could not be sure of a majority in the House of Commons, and that important aspects of policy were effectively subject to a trade union veto. The paramount issue was one of confidence.

With the UK having effectively been handed an ultimatum by the US, Healey and Callaghan accepted that further exhausting efforts to cut the country's spending plans were unavoidable. Unsurprisingly, however, the cabinet was split over the issue. The prescribed target was cuts of £2 billion – equivalent to a little more than 1.5% of GDP. But after seven cabinet meetings, only £1 billion of cuts had been agreed, and the deflationary package had to be topped up by what amounted to yet another tax hike: a two percentage point increase in employers' national insurance contributions. This was widely branded as another political cop-out, and one that would add significantly to business costs and reduce the incentive to employ people. On the other hand, Healey did strengthen his commitment to rein in the money supply by announcing an 'expectation' (not a target) that broad monetary growth would be kept to 12% during that financial year.

THINGS COME TO A HEAD

Sterling held steady in August, but thereafter confidence again began to ebb away. In particular, it was becoming increasingly difficult to sell enough government bonds to finance a budgetary shortfall that immediately ran in excess of the official July estimates, while forward exchange rates against the dollar were becoming increasingly discounted, sparking a 1.5 percentage point increase in official interest rates, bringing them up to 13%.

Late September saw two key events: the annual Labour Party Conference, in Blackpool; and the annual IMF Conference, held in Manila. Although

Healey was by now convinced that there was no alternative to calling in financial assistance from the IMF, he did not want to make an announcement to that effect before he returned from the Philippines. But as left-wing delegates were quick to flex their muscles in Blackpool, proposing a number of radical motions (including one against any more public expenditure cuts and another in favour of restoring all previous cuts), sterling went into a tailspin.

Taken aback by developments on the currency markets, Healey and the governor of the Bank of England, Gordon Richardson, were forced to turn back from London's Heathrow Airport on their way to Manila. On the same day, Callaghan gave a speech in Blackpool aimed as much at the international political and financial community as his own party. In it, he effectively sounded the death knell of the post-war Keynesian consensus. In a now-famous passage, he asserted:

> We used to think that we could just spend our way out of a recession ... I tell you in all candour that that option no longer exists, and insofar as it did exist, it only worked by injecting a bigger dose of inflation into the economy, followed by a higher level of unemployment.[13]

Callaghan appeared to have adopted the clothes of Milton Friedman (Nobel laureate in that year) and other outspoken critics of Keynesianism, if not going so far as the laissez-faire school of the 1920s.[14] While the Ford administration in the US might have been impressed by his apparent Damascene conversion to conservative economic doctrine – indeed, this seems to have been Callaghan's intention, at least in part – it went down very badly with the majority of his party colleagues and the trade unions.

Healey immediately announced that an application was being made to the IMF for $3.9 billion of support, which was the largest sum that had ever been requested of it. Indeed, the proposed loan was so substantial that the IMF would have to seek supplementary resources from, *inter alia,* the US and Germany.

The next day, the beleaguered but irrepressible chancellor himself gave a speech from the conference floor* in which, despite incessant heckling, he sought to educate the party faithful about the extent of the crisis. Healey also expressed his intention to negotiate with the IMF on the basis of existing policies, although this was manifestly wishful thinking: the IMF would insist upon its pound of flesh in return for such substantial financial assistance.

---

* Left-wingers had voted Healey off the party's executive committee as punishment for his previous efforts to rein in their excesses, so he could not sit on the podium with Callaghan.

Sterling continued to slide, only stabilizing after further interest rate hikes and curbs on bank lending.

TOUCH-AND-GO

The IMF delegation that arrived in London on 1 November was, ironically, headed by a former Bank of England official, Alan Whittome. The drama of the five weeks of negotiations with the IMF has gone into folklore. To this day, the Conservative Party presents them as a moment of national ignomity, while rumours and conspiracy theories about the episode abound. There are stories of clandestine meetings with US officials in a Savile Row tailor's shop; of a flood of leaks and misinformation; of massaged economic forecasts; of Britain playing its allies off against each other; of threats to pull British forces out of Germany; of Treasury officials siding with the IMF against their own government; and even of IMF officials' hotel rooms being bugged. And many of those stories are true. This was a government and a nation in the last-chance saloon. The discussions were bound to be feverish and labyrinthine, and they frequently came close to collapse.[15]

In a precursor to many future structural adjustment programmes, the IMF's initial demand was for new public spending curbs of £3 billion in 1976–77 (equivalent to some 2.25% of GDP) and a further £4 billion in 1977–78, stricter control of the money supply, and further depreciation of sterling. The first part of this policy cocktail was politically impossible for this Labour government (and perhaps, indeed, for any Labour government), and Callaghan told the IMF so. The question was whether a compromise could be reached.

The cabinet essentially split into three factions: the anti-deflationists led by Tony Crosland, the foreign secretary and a former Oxford economics don, who thought the economy was already on the mend and wanted to call the IMF's – and the markets' – bluff by refusing to deflate in a meaningful way at all; the protectionists on the left, led by Tony Benn, the energy secretary, who, rather than being dependent on the IMF, favoured a retreat into a reflated siege economy, shielded by import and capital controls; and the moderates, or 'Healey's men', who recognized the need to counter the widespread perception of UK profligacy and policy ill-discipline. They saw the IMF's seal of approval for a degree of deflation as essential to ensure that the UK rekindled its international credibility, that the government had a chance of survival, and indeed that the country remained governable.[16]

Callaghan was certainly no fan of Tony Benn, or of the siege economy option. Rather, he was by nature practical and moderate in approach. However, he was also haunted by history, and not just the events he had presided over in late 1967. He feared that if the conditions for a loan were unduly stringent, the consequence might be a rupture in the party akin to that of 1931, when a Labour government was replaced by a national coalition and its parliamentary representation was subsequently reduced to a rump of a mere fifty-two MPs.[17]

In the end, after endless cabinet meetings in which he let the various factions talk themselves to a standstill, Callaghan finally made it clear that he intended to back his chancellor's judgement. Agreement was subsequently reached on £2.5 billion of planned cuts in the budget deficit over the next two years, with £2 billion resulting from expenditure restraint and the remaining £500 million coming from the sale of 17% of the government's holdings of BP shares. Remarkably, no cabinet minister resigned. Even the Bennites toed the line.

On 15 December Healey laid out the details of the deal in parliament. The public sector borrowing requirement (PSBR) had hitherto been forecast to be £10.5 billion in 1977–78 and £11.5 billion in 1978–79. As a result of the new measures, it was projected to fall to £8.75 billion in 1977–78 and remain at a similar level in 1978–79. It would therefore fall from an estimated 9% of GDP in the current year to some 6% of GDP in 1977–78 and 5% of GDP in 1978–79. In addition, reflecting not just the opinion of the IMF but the wider perception of extended UK monetary excess, the chancellor committed to limiting domestic credit expansion (DCE) to contain inflation expectations and wage inflation. Monetary rules – rather than unalloyed, politically motivated discretion – had become a fact of life.[18]

Britain was able to repay the $1.6 billion drawn from the June standby credit, the beleaguered government lived to fight another day, and the battle-weary Healey remained as chancellor. What is more, with the help of the BIS, the UK secured agreement for a funding scheme that allowed official holders of sterling balances to convert their pounds into foreign-currency-denominated securities of 5–10 years' maturity. The weight of the sterling balances was finally lifted. Sterling's role as a reserve currency was over. Another pillar of the chimera of Britain's post-war power posturing had collapsed.

The budget cuts, while being larger than originally desired, were more modest than initially feared and considerably less onerous than those being proposed by the Conservative opposition. Nevertheless, the record shows that they hit hard. Local authority housing completions fell by a quarter between 1976 and 1978. Education spending in 1978–79 was reduced to its 1973–74 level in real terms, at a time when there were 10% more secondary school pupils and 18% more university students (including the author) than there had been in the earlier period. The welfare state was in decline before Margaret Thatcher took office.

SNATCHING DEFEAT FROM THE
JAWS OF VICTORY

With global growth robust, neither the spending cuts nor an overall tightening of the fiscal stance of more than two-and-a-half percentage points of GDP between 1975–76 and 1977–78 stood in the way of the economy's expansion. Furthermore, once market confidence in the public finances was restored, sterling quickly recovered and the foreign exchange reserves were rapidly replenished. From a low of $1.55, sterling had risen to $2.02 by early 1979. Monetary policy could also be loosened and, remarkably, official interest rates were a mere 5% – ten percentage points down from their peak – by October 1977. All this was despite the fact that, because of left-wing abstentions, the chancellor had initially failed to secure the approval of the House of Commons for his expenditure plans. In the end, with Labour having lost its overall majority in parliament by this stage in a series of by-election defeats, the plans were only passed into law because the centrist Liberal Party entered into an informal coalition with the government (the Lib–Lab Pact) and lent its support in a no-confidence vote.

Courtesy of the IMF's imprimatur, the tide had turned. Healey was soon able to announce more tax concessions conditional on another year of wage restraint; North Sea oil was starting to flow in significant amounts; and annual consumer price inflation dropped below 10% for the first time since 1973. In a further 'letter of intent' delivered to the IMF in December 1977, Healey could confirm that despite the easing of monetary and fiscal policy through the year, the targets for both the PSBR and DCE had been comfortably met. Indeed, the progressive adoption of formal cash limits on expenditure programmes during this period led to government underspending to the extent that it would comfortably have met the IMF's initial – seemingly draconian and politically intolerable – demands.[19] Subsequent estimates suggest that the budget deficit dramatically undershot Healey's December 1976 PSBR estimates over the next three years. Over the course of 1977, only half of the IMF loan was utilized.

Nineteen seventy-eight was the best year for the UK economy for some time. Output grew steadily, unemployment started to fall, inflation remained below 10%, and both the budget and the current account imbalance were improving; indeed, the latter returned to approximate balance for the first time since 1972. Repayments of a billion dollars were made to the IMF in both January and October.

That year also saw the UK eschew the opportunity to join the fixed but adjustable exchange rate mechanism (ERM) of the European Monetary System (EMS), which was to come into operation in March 1979. The ERM

represented the resurrection of the idea of a zone of European monetary stability as a precursor to a single currency.[20] Although the Foreign Office was
keen on membership and the Bank of England was, on balance, supportive,
the generally Euro-sceptic Treasury was unconvinced. Even with the arrival of
North Sea oil, there was little confidence that sterling could remain a member
without experiencing successive destabilizing devaluations and further bouts
of deflation.

Healey was agnostic about the whole initiative, while Callaghan was concerned it might open the old wounds on Europe, which Wilson had managed
to salve, and split the Labour Party.[21] As it turned out, reflecting divergent
inflation rates and policy mixes, the initial four years of the system were characterized by frequent currency realignments against the Deutschmark, which
acted as its anchor. It was only after 1983, and in particular after 1987, that
the system began to exhibit the sort of monetary stability originally mooted.

In the summer of 1978 the Liberal Party announced that it would withdraw from the Lib–Lab Pact in November. Callaghan, like his predecessor
four years earlier, therefore became the head of a minority government. He
was forced to operate on a day-to-day basis, depending on backing from Scottish and Welsh nationalist and Ulster Unionist MPs (support that had its roots
in Labour's proposals for greater devolution).

In these circumstances, the prime minister thought long and hard about
calling an early general election, and such an event was widely expected in the
press. Support for Labour had rebounded with the improvement in the economy's performance, and the party enjoyed a small overall lead in the polls. The
avuncular Callaghan's personal popularity also exceeded that of the dry, and
still largely untested, opposition leader Margaret Thatcher, and he had secured
the endorsement of the major trade unions for such a move. But in a decision
he was later to rue (and which he made against his chancellor's advice), he got
cold feet at the last minute.

Callaghan saw the next election as being of particular consequence, given
the potentially transformative arrival of North Sea oil, and he wanted to be
certain that he would secure an overall majority. Voter intentions in a number
of marginal constituencies argued against him achieving one, and his judgement was therefore that circumstances were likely to become more propitious
for Labour in 1979. Sadly for him, the economic and political environment
was about to sour – and sour badly – once again. He missed his chance, and
the rest, as they say, is history.

The problems were an overambitious incomes policy and a trade union
movement that felt betrayed on the issue of general election timing. Like
its various predecessors, the policy to restrain wages, adopted in 1975, had
gradually been loosened over the succeeding couple of years – but also in

common with previous efforts at wage control, support for it was ebbing away on the shop floor and beyond after an initial period of acceptance and reasonable success. The government and the TUC failed to agree on a new pay norm in mid 1978, but Callaghan and Healey decided to adopt a target for wage increases of 5% per annum regardless, backed by yet more sanctions on employers that paid over the odds. They did so in spite of union warnings that their plan was unrealistic (inflation was running at around 8% at the time), especially for public sector workers looking to make up for the sacrifices of the previous period.

The result was the so-called Winter of Discontent, during which any residual belief that Labour could manage the unions was swept away by an ugly catalogue of disruptive pay-related strikes, many of them in the social services sector, and episodes of violent picketing. Rubbish piled high in the streets, and schools were closed because caretakers, cleaners and cooks stayed away. It was sometimes hard to buy bread, and in Liverpool the dead went unburied.

The government had no option but to back away from the 5% pay norm, but the damage had been done. It never recovered from the sense of ungovernability and social chaos that descended on the nation in the winter of 1978–79. Callaghan, who as home secretary had been instrumental in vetoing the first Wilson government's trade union reforms in the late 1960s, saw his administration undermined by trade union power a decade later.

Labour's unhappy time in office – during which, for the most part, it just about survived rather than governed – drew to a close in May. The Conservative Party, led by Margaret Thatcher, was elected with an overall majority of forty-four. She proved to be a leader with rather different priorities, and rather different methods when it came to how to achieve them.

FROM HUBRIS TO NEMESIS

And so it was that the post-war Keynesian era drew to an ignominious close. Over the course of three decades it had curdled into a sour quagmire of chronic macro instability, overbearing government interference, industrial strife and political dyspepsia, where the abnormal came to seem all too normal.

Full employment had become harder and harder to secure. Inflation had surged to unprecedented peacetime levels and become hard-wired into the superstructure of the economy. The budget and the current account were both prone to significant deficit. The price mechanism had, in important respects, been bent out of shape. Major downturns, involving substantial output falls, seemed to once again be a fact of life. The underlying trend of economic growth appeared to have slowed. In the eyes of many, the trade unions had become a law unto themselves, or even a threat to the entire democratic process. The events of 1973–79 were a chastening experience for both policymakers and the electorate, and they left a lasting bruise on Britain's polity.

Notwithstanding the damaging effect of the large – and at that time unique – supply-side shock represented by the first oil crisis, the Keynesian era came to an end because of a litany of wrong turns and policy errors, which seemed to multiply over time. These were grounded in overoptimism about what could be achieved through demand management, and in particular through fiscal fine-tuning; in mission-creep into corporatism and excessive intervention in its pursuit; and in the often-crass political manipulation of the business cycle, to which Keynesianism was unfortunately always wide open. Keynes's followers perverted much of what he had said, succumbed to 'group-think', failed to question the basic premises of their approach sufficiently, and ultimately proved both hubristic and naive.

All too quickly it was largely forgotten that Keynes's central thesis was less about offsetting minor fluctuations in aggregate demand than it was about dealing with large and persistent shortfalls in macro resource utilization. He was against self-defeating attempts to balance the budget during a recession through austerity that would prolong the downturn rather than achieve the professed objective, but he was equally distrustful of elaborate economic forecasts and he was no supporter of either persistent budget deficits or unbridled 'tax and spend'.[22] It is likely that he would have had strong reservations about the fine-tuning of demand, or the employment of a formal incomes policy, while 'growthmanship' would have been anathema to him.

What he argued for most strongly was the stabilization of volatile investment, the main source of domestic instability. He believed this should be encouraged by persistently low interest rates, although *in extremis* this strategy could lose potency, and the speeding up or slowing down of a separate government capital budget (while the ordinary current budget remained in balance) would be warranted. He was also open to the idea of varying national insurance contributions to sustain the spending of the income or liquidity constrained, but – in a precursor of Friedmanite theory, and the latter's notion of the relative stability of the consumption function – Keynes was critical of too-regular small variations in taxation to manage demand, 'as people have established standards of life'.[23]

Neither was Keynes an inflationist. He believed in the merits of relative price stability, and for much of his life he suggested that the authorities should seek to achieve this through preventing excessive monetary growth. Furthermore, he essentially agreed that the quantity theory of money, which related changes in the price level to prior changes in the supply of money, was operative at full employment.[24] An increase in effective demand when resource utilization was high would translate into higher prices rather than higher output.

Furthermore, during World War II Keynes became persuaded that British workers had become increasingly '[price] index-conscious'. That is to say that inflation expectations had become more important to them.[25]

Depression was not the primary problem in the post-war years. Rather, as much of Europe and Japan reconstructed, businesses sought to catch up with technological best practice, and global trade flows were progressively liberalized, the priority was boom control. Yet the Keynesians, just as they embellished and distorted much of Keynes's original framework of thought, remained trapped in a mindset of depression economics. They failed to adapt Keynesianism appropriately to this new world. In particular, there were too few policy rules, too much misapplied policy discretion in pursuit of too many unrealistic goals, and too little use of interest rates.

Finally, far too much emphasis was placed on the management of aggregate demand in pursuit of a real variable – full employment – that was from the outset ill-defined; and far too little emphasis was placed on structural, or supply-side, policies that would encourage flexibility in the face of shocks, help to maintain competitiveness, and generally facilitate the flow of resources from low-productivity to high-productivity sectors and firms.[26] Indeed, many seemed to think that if the authorities got aggregate demand right, supply would largely look after itself. To the extent that structural policies were employed, they were either piecemeal, largely aspirational or bound up with increased government influence over, if not control of, production. Many of the most egregious, and long-standing, underlying problems were for the most part left unaddressed.

Overall, therefore, the Keynesian era fell foul of arrogance and overreach, and a failure to intellectually renew itself. How the blame for this should be apportioned between economists, officials and politicians is difficult to judge. The standing of economists in the eyes of the public has varied, just as the influence of economists on policy has fluctuated from period to period, often depending on the forcefulness of individuals and their ability to synthesize the thinking going on around them and translate it into practical initiatives. That said, there can be little doubt that the intellectual corruption that convinced economists they had the knowledge and tools to accurately control the economy and society from the top down infected officials, and politicians were only too happy to go along for the ride, taking the easy, immediate, vote-winning option, and too often eschewing the potential costs – or at least being content to worry about them later. The important message that you cannot have your cake and eat it was not delivered strongly enough.

Wherever the culpability lay, Keynesianism's failings left the door open to the New Right, whose ideas were in many ways restatements of old – pre-Keynesian – ideas, but which embodied an appealing uncomplicatedness.

All this said, there was much in the Keynesian era to admire. Keynesian-ism was employed with the best of intentions. Furthermore, it embodied – or, at least, the ideas of Keynes embodied – many important fundamental truths about the economy, how it behaved and how it should be run that would in due course reassert themselves. The contrast between the richness of Keynes's intellectual inheritance and the poverty of the UK's economic performance in the 1970s was stark.

Britain clearly could not go on as it was in the late 1970s. There was a broad consensus that enough was enough. Macro-stability had to be re-established. The role of the state had to be scaled back to something more modest. The power of the trade unions and their role in policymaking had to be reduced. And the broader institutional architecture and incentive structure of the econ-omy needed to be reformed. The danger, though, was that the baby would be thrown out with the bathwater. After all, much of what the New Right espoused had already been shown in previous epochs to be an overly simplistic and dangerous path to go down.

CHAPTER 4

Counter-Revolution

By taxation, by inflation, by the remorseless flood of regulations and legislation, by controls and by the constant and arbitrary interventions of authority,
successive governments since the war have cumulatively taken away both the
pleasure and the rewards that once made risk-taking worthwhile. By this attitude we have driven out some wealth creators; discouraged others; shrivelled
the impulse to expand and throttled enterprise.

— Sir Keith Joseph, October 1976[1]

THE TORIES MOVE ON

The Barber boom and bust, together with its political fallout, was a chastening
episode for the Conservative Party, while the subsequent trials and tribulations of the Wilson and Callaghan governments did nothing to encourage the
Tories to abide by Keynesian principles of economic management.

When Margaret Thatcher somewhat surprisingly replaced Edward Heath
as party leader in February 1975 and became the first female leader of a major
UK political party, she was a symbol of right-wing protest against both the
style and the substance of the latter years of the Heath regime. Hers was a
more radical and old-style version of Toryism, and there soon developed a
powerful sense that a different approach to economic policymaking would be
practised as and when the party returned to office.

The change of course was strongly influenced by Keith Joseph, a tor-
tured eccentric, a politically maladroit right-wing intellectual and a minister
under Heath. Joseph's ideas drew heavily on the monetarist theory popularized by Nobel laureate Milton Friedman, which had garnered considerable
support in the US in the 1960s but which, in the thirty years leading up
to the mid 1970s, had largely been viewed as anathema in the birthplace
of Keynes.

THE FRIEDMANITE AGENDA

Friedman, like Keynes, was an excellent communicator, debater and popularizer of his own ideas. These ideas, however, were in many significant respects very different to those of Keynes. Indeed, they were a throwback to the 'classical' economics of the pre-Keynesian era.

At the core of Friedman's theoretical framework was his research on the dynamics of the largest component of domestic spending: personal consumption. His analysis suggested that personal outlays were dependent not only on current income but also on future expected income. Consumption behaviour therefore tended to be smoothed out over time, and both the demand for money and overall private sector activity were therefore more inherently stable than Keynes had believed.[2] The suggestion was that it was government interference and mismanagement that must be the primary sources of macroeconomic instability.

He presented powerful evidence for this in a sweeping monetary history of the US, which *inter alia* blamed the Great Depression on policy error and, in particular, on an excessively tight monetary stance. According to Friedman, the extent of the downturn in the US between 1929 and 1933 was the Federal Reserve's fault.[3] This assertion was no doubt narrow and oversimplistic, but he nevertheless had a point. The Fed had tightened monetary policy in the teeth of the downswing to protect the dollar's fixed link with gold, and it had subsequently soft-pedalled in its open-market operations, fearing generous liquidity provision would fuel renewed stock market speculation rather than support output. It presided over a one-third contraction in the broad money supply, which was bound to be associated with sharp falls in nominal expenditure, real activity and the price level.

In much of his work, Friedman placed special importance on the old quantity theory of money (QTM). He believed first and foremost that 'inflation was always and everywhere a monetary phenomenon'.[4]

Friedman further contended that budget deficits financed by borrowing from the commercial banks were typically to blame for much of the excessive increases in the money supply during the 1960s and 1970s. This practice should therefore be avoided if monetary stability was to be encouraged. The less the government had to borrow, the less it would be likely to turn to the commercial banks to take up its debt. Budget deficits should therefore be avoided.

At the same time, he asserted that fiscal policy per se was relatively powerless to affect aggregate demand and activity unless it was accommodated by monetary expansion. Fiscal largesse without any change in trend in the money supply would merely 'crowd out' an equal amount of private demand through the tendency of an increased demand for money to drive up interest rates.

Friedman accepted that changes in the rate of growth of the money stock could affect the rate of growth of output as well as prices in the short term, but over the long run – beyond a period of around two years, he asserted – they merely influenced prices. Moreover, as discretionary monetary policy adjustments tended to be subject to long and variable time lags in their effects on output, they had an inherent tendency to be destabilizing. It was therefore prudent to obey a strict monetary policy rule that kept the money supply growing at a steady rate, preferably commensurate with the long-term trend in the growth rate of nominal national income. This would help both to maintain the economy at close to full employment and to ensure long-run price stability.

Friedman's focus was on monetary policy consistency and predictability, in contrast to forever adjusting policy to match changing conditions. Moreover, he strongly believed that exchange rates should be left to market forces. Indeed, if the emphasis was to be on domestic monetary stability, it was impossible to manage the exchange rate simultaneously. The two were mutually exclusive.

Friedman also made a critical contribution to macroeconomic theory in identifying the role of evolving inflationary expectations in the widespread tendency for post-war inflation to accelerate, not least in the UK.[5]

As already noted, Keynes had accepted that the QTM was essentially valid at full employment – an increase in aggregate demand in such circumstances would merely tend to raise prices, not output. Friedman concurred with this, but his concept of full employment was different to that of Keynes. Friedman referred not to a widespread absence of spare capacity but to an equilibrium level of unemployment defined as the 'natural rate' – or the rate that was manifest under conditions of stable inflation and that reflected the structural characteristics of the labour and commodity markets. These extended to market imperfections, such as employers' monopsony, the influence of trade unions on workers' wages and conditions of employment, geographical and occupational immobility, and shortfalls in information about job vacancies.

The Friedmanite concept of the natural rate of unemployment – the natural rate hypothesis (NRH) – was alien to Keynesian post-war UK policymakers. They believed that in the absence of an absolute limit on labour supply, the expansion of aggregate demand would always generate output gains, even if these were a declining proportion of price increases. This was, after all, an important foundation of their belief in the Meccano economics of the Phillips curve: the enduring menu of choice between different levels of unemployment and inflation supposedly available to policymakers.

To Friedman's mind, this tariff of options was a red herring, as it was merely transitory. It existed solely because workers were temporarily fooled into accepting lower real wages than they desired by neglecting to factor in

rising prices sufficiently. But if, in pursuit of a commitment to 'full employment', the authorities repeatedly resorted to monetary expansion to reduce
unemployment below its 'natural rate', workers would adapt, or learn from
their mistakes, and frame their wage demands to match the expected rise in
prices, so rendering the reflationary action ineffective. To his mind, there was
no autonomous – or 'cost-push' – source of wage pressure. Wage dynamics
were merely a logical reaction to previous monetary excess.

Friedman's framework also provided a theoretical explanation for the
simultaneous increases in inflation and unemployment – 'stagflation' – that
Keynesians found so hard to understand when they began to arise in the late
1960s and that UK policymakers had struggled to come to terms with in the
1970s. He believed that, just as monetary excess would push up inflation,
increased structural rigidities in the labour market would raise the natural
rate of unemployment. And in the UK's case, such rigidities were on the rise
in the post-war era. In addition to the increased strength of the trade unions
in terms of membership numbers and legal position, there were, for example,
important changes in the level, breadth and duration of unemployment pay;
declines in the size of the private rented housing sector; and greater provision
of council housing.[6]

Friedman's writings went beyond monetary primacy and long-term policy consistency and restraint. They also went beyond the formalization of
the limitations and inevitable inflationary consequences of repeated efforts
to secure full employment, such as the policies employed in the UK in the
1950s, 1960s and early 1970s. In highlighting government mismanagement
and interference in the economy as the primary source of macro instability,
he resurrected two pre-Keynesian principles: that macroeconomic outcomes
should be inferred from optimizing microeconomic behaviour, and that private enterprise should, as far as possible, be left to its own devices. He was a
standard bearer for the free market and for small government.

Keynes's ideas had come to dominate political thinking when overcoming
mass unemployment was perceived to be the principal economic problem.
Friedman's simple, and seemingly practical, ideas came to the fore when the
control of inflation, excessive government intervention and unduly powerful
trade unions were the overriding issues confronting society.

MORE RADICAL THOUGHTS

As Friedman's framework for macroeconomic policymaking began to make
headway in the Conservative Party and beyond – including, importantly, in
the City of London – a new generation of supposedly mathematically minded
so-called new classical economists, led by Robert Lucas, one of Friedman's

former students at the University of Chicago, began to challenge some of his ideas. They did this not from a Keynesian perspective, but because Friedman's approach retained a number of important logical inconsistencies and because his emphasis on the micro precepts of economics did not in their eyes go far enough.

Lucas and his disciples asserted that to be entirely credible, macroeconomics had to be fully grounded in the same foundations as microeconomics, and particularly in the idealized, ultra-efficient, perfect-market world of Walrasian general equilibrium theory.[7] Analysis of the behaviour of 'aggregates' – such as consumption, investment and financial markets – should be based on the behaviour of individuals, such as the householders, firms and investors that made up those aggregates. And their behaviour was likely to be self-interested and based on the maximum pursuit of those interests in the context of markets that always cleared. They were all 'optimizers'.

At the heart of the criticism of Friedman by Lucas and the new classical school was Friedman's assertion that that economic agents would, over time, learn from their mistakes and adapt their behaviour to changing market signals. Lucas argued that Friedman's 'adaptive expectations' were themselves irrational, in that they would lead to systematic errors.

Building on the work of the mathematical economist John Muth in the early 1960s, Lucas believed that individuals could do better if they made efficient use of all the information available to them.[8] This was the rational expectations hypothesis (REH). In this context, rationality did not just mean 'behaving in a reasonable manner under the circumstances'. Rather, it meant that economic agents would be best served by rapidly accumulating extensive and precise knowledge of the future based on past and present developments. Armed with such information, while they might make random forecasting errors, they would not fall into the trap of making systematic mistakes in predicting prospective events. On average, their decisions would match those of a correct model of the economy, and that meant a model based on economically rational behaviour and the principles espoused by Lucas and his followers.[9]

This was heady stuff. If expectations were indeed rational in this sense, the implications were truly radical. Keynes's distinction between uncertainty and risk disintegrated: all uncertainty could be reduced to a probability calculus. The world had an inherently stable, unchanging structure, conducive to learning speedily by experience and to the extrapolation of past behaviour into the future. Keynes's supposed insights into the psychology of markets, the variability of investment and the role of money as a store of value become worthless and irrelevant. Equally, there could be no interim period during which agents could be wrong-footed or fooled by governments or central banks. If policy were systematically deployed according to Keynesian principles, agents would instantaneously anticipate it and adjust to it, and it would have no effect on output, even in the short term. The only impact would be on prices, which would rise *pari passu* with any related increase in the money supply.

In such a world, macro-stabilization policy was redundant. There was no such thing as involuntary unemployment. The only unemployment that could exist must be voluntary, as shocks to output are immediately offset by rationally dictated changes in wages and prices. The notion that government could not improve on market forces – that they could only distort them, and that they should, as far as possible, disengage – was thereby greatly strengthened.

Another group of counter-revolutionaries went a step further still. Confronting the inconvenient fact that the business cycles that seemed to be impossible if the REH was taken to its logical conclusion were an undeniable reality, economists led by Edward Prescott, then of the University of Minnesota, developed real business cycle (RBC) theory. This posited that these cycles must be the result of variations in potential output, such as those that result from random fluctuations in the rate of technological progress, which then reverberate through the economy as the result of a tendency of workers to work more in favourable times and less in unfavourable times. It was not that the economy cycled around the natural rate of unemployment. Rather, it was the natural rate that oscillated.[10]

RBC theory confirmed that economies are always effectively at full employment since fluctuations in output are fluctuations in the natural rate of unemployment. Of course, unemployment may be observable, but it must in essence be 'voluntary' – a matter of personal choice – no matter how much there is of it or how long it endures. Unemployment is merely the result of an individual's desire to seek leisure rather than work. Even the Great Depression amounted to a mass decision to take an extended vacation. Policy should therefore be aimed at increasing the incentives for individuals to minimize their leisure time, by cutting income taxes and reducing unemployment and other social security benefits.

In the same vein as the REH and RBC theory was the efficient markets hypothesis (EMH), which was popularized by another Chicago economist, Eugene Fama. Fama's central assertion was that financial markets work perfectly. An individual stock price will accurately embody the knowledge and understanding of financial analysts, investors and the firm's management about its earnings potential. In the case of commodities, spot prices will reflect everything known about resource stocks. In the case of bonds, the price will incorporate the likely default risk. Financial market prices therefore fully reflect underlying fundamental considerations. They cannot mirror undue optimism or pessimism. Any tendency for prices to deviate from these fundamental levels is offset by the actions of well-informed speculators.[11]

Taking things still further, this suggested that shadow banks – the plethora of opaque financial intermediaries that largely escape the regulatory net – served the real banks by providing additional liquidity and facilitating transfer of risk. Derivatives, meanwhile, added to the safety of the financial system by increasing the ability of individuals to sell risk to those who wanted to buy it – those who were, because of this, presumed to be best suited to holding it. And the banks themselves would be best equipped to assess the risks they were taking using the models that they designed themselves.

Another implication of Fama's theory was that investing is essentially 'a random walk'. Its outcome is determined by luck rather than judgement. Hence, fundamental analysis by the average investor is a pointless exercise.

The conclusion that it was impossible to 'beat the market' consistently was in due course to encourage the popularity of stock index funds. It also drove quantitative finance, and the development of new techniques such as the mean–variance approach to portfolio diversification, the capital asset pricing model, and so-called Black–Scholes option pricing, all of which depended on market behaviour conforming to a standard normal distribution.

None of this makes it easier to predict specific random events, but it does facilitate the ability to make forecasts about the overall probability of those events occurring. Once the mean of a sample of price movements in a financial asset over a particular period has been calculated, the standard deviation can then be deduced. From that, the chances of that asset price rising or falling by more than the standard deviation can be worked out. And from that, the likelihood of extreme outcomes – and thereby the nature of the risk of investing in an asset over a specified period – can be gleaned.

Perhaps most importantly of all, however, if financial market prices are always appropriate, finance could be excluded from analysis of economic equilibrium.

THROUGH THE LOOKING GLASS

The new classical school's theories possess logical consistency and mathematical elegance, but they are also arcane – even faintly absurd – when viewed through the lens of the enduring vicissitudes of the business cycle, the historical struggles of the trade union movement, the poverty and human suffering of major recessions, and the intermittent episodes of mania and panic in financial markets. Indeed, where some aspects of new classical theory are concerned, one is drawn to Keynes's withering critique of Friedrich von Hayek that 'how, starting with a mistake, a remorseless logician can end in Bedlam'.[12]

The EMH, for example, is itself built on a logical inconsistency. If stocks always reflected all the relevant information available about them, then investors would have no incentive to seek out that information and process it. But if no one undertakes this task, the stocks will not reflect that information, and the market will not be efficient. There must therefore be some inefficiency for the market to work.

There is overwhelming evidence, moreover, that at least beyond the short-term, there is a predictable component to movements in share and other asset prices. In particular, periods of high returns are likely to be followed by periods of low returns. There is low-frequency negative serial correlation.

More broadly, markets are not universally efficient, and they do fail. In this, Keynes was correct. They fail because of imperfect information and the inevitability of unquantifiable uncertainty about the future. Monopolistic or oligopolistic power is a fact of life. Price signals get distorted. Externalities arise – both positive and negative. Discontinuities, herding, tipping points and price cascades are observable. Positive and negative feedback loops develop.

Equally, the reality is that people are not always rational in the sense defined by Muth and Lucas. They are social animals driven by context. They might not be stupid, but they take time to learn from some of their mistakes. They do not instantaneously know what they want and where their best interests lie. They can struggle even to grasp the range of things they might be confronted with in the future.

GETTING REAL

The fact is that the performance of economic models based purely on assumptions of rational expectations has been and continues to be poor, in both an absolute sense and a relative one. Furthermore, although they might be beguiled by its theoretical logic and purity, not even its most ardent adherents would suggest that the various tenets of new classical economics should be a viewed as a literal description of how people behave. Rather, overlapping with the notions of 'the wisdom of crowds' and 'the law of large numbers', its supporters instead present it as the most appropriate and workable *approximation* of reality within which to frame policy. It is a better analytical framework than any of the alternatives

They contend that market prices do tend to efficiently incorporate a huge amount of relevant information, and that people do utilize it to plan ahead and make decisions. They believe that government intervention does tend to reduce welfare, and that government failures are more common than market failures. They assert that the QTM is generally valid and that reflation yields inflation and little or nothing else. They think that the focus of macro policy should be price stability, and that expectations – and the tendency for politicians to always promise more than they can deliver – should be managed by a set of consistent and transparent policy rules. They argue that supply matters more than demand, and that private sector activity should be encouraged by appropriate incentives delivered by a small state, and through the tax system and a programme of deregulation, not least where labour is concerned.

What is perhaps more fascinating is that many Keynesian economists, dis-illusioned by the failures of discretionary macro policy in the post-war period, had by the late 1970s begun to take on board and embed elements of the thinking of Friedman and the new classical school in their own ideas and models. They accepted much of the QTM, the NRH, the REH, the EMH and even RBC theory, although their sense was that the new classicists had gone beyond their skis, especially in how they denied a demand-driven expla-nation for recessions and regarded all unemployment as voluntary.

This so-called new Keynesian school baulked at the notion of instantane-ous market clearing because it takes time for contracts to change, because not all prices embody new information, and because information can be costly to acquire. Prices could therefore be 'sticky' for extended periods, and markets can fail to clear, so both supply and demand shocks can lead to involuntary unemployment. In such circumstances there remained a role for government – or more specifically for monetary policy intervention – to address the risk that an economy might fail to rapidly self-equilibrate and that unemployment might remain above its natural rate for some time.

This was a far cry from the original Keynes, however, and in particular two of its basic tenets: the notion of radical uncertainty rendering econo-mies inherently unstable, and his scepticism that monetary initiatives – espe-cially changes in short-term interest rates – would be sufficient for macro-stabilization policy, especially during a slump.[13] And like the new classicists, the new Keynesians had no room in their models for financial market bubbles or banking system collapses.

FROM HIGH THEORY TO PRACTICALITIES

The policy implications of these developments in economic theory during the 1960s and 1970s significantly influenced the manifesto of the Conservative Party ahead of the 1979 general election. Party leader Margaret Thatcher was no trained economist but, tutored by Keith Joseph, the economic philosophy she instinctively cleaved to was drawn from the monetarism of Friedman and the new classical school's restatements of pre-Keynesian principles, together with Friedrich von Hayek's exaggerated claims that attempting to deliver social justice in a market economy was a chimera, and that economic planning was a slippery slope that would inevitably lead to dictatorship.[14]

Thatcher came to power in May 1979, determined to control inflation, create a more stable macroeconomic environment, roll back the borders of the state and promote self-reliance, thereby transforming the country's economic performance for the better and reversing its relative decline. She also saw herself as something of a teacher, or even a preacher: someone who could enlighten the masses and bring them round to her way of thinking through persuasion – or failing that, through determination and ruthless singlemindedness.

A succession of progressively lower published targets for monetary growth, backed by sympathetic restrictive objectives for government borrowing and public spending, were expected to bring inflation expectations and wage claims to heel. Fiscal fine-tuning and incomes policy were eschewed. To the extent that workers ignored these targets and insisted on pricing themselves out of a job, it was not the government's role to create new jobs at the cost of inflation and broader instability. In this sense, any tendency to higher unemployment was perceived as voluntary.

Meanwhile, a shift in the balance of taxation from direct to indirect levies would encourage enterprise. Market forces would be strengthened by the reduction of subsidies, lower regulation, the scaling back of regional policy and a series of labour market reforms.

The new government was deeply suspicious of the civil service. Officials, not least those within the Treasury, were ill-prepared for the changes in both ideology and the policy framework with which they were to be confronted. Terry Burns and Alan Budd, two monetarist academics, were hired as senior Treasury advisors, while much of the Keynesian establishment that had dominated policymaking for so long was subsequently either exiled from Whitehall or had little choice but to keep their qualms about the new government's strategy to themselves.[15] There was, however, one conspicuous exception: the battle-hardened Sir Douglas Wass was retained as Permanent Secretary to the Treasury because of his all-round wisdom and experience.

Thatcher presented her initial economic programme as one of self-evident common sense, and of applying the rules of good housekeeping to the nation's finances. There was a strong moral – indeed Victorian – element to the counter-revolution, albeit a selective one. Her philosophical outlook notably omitted Dickens, Disraeli, Arnold and Ruskin, among others.

The underlying belief was that people had been sheltered from the consequences of their own actions for too long. The dependency culture of previous decades had left the country ethically compromised. Markets, on the other hand, were a realm of freedom. Thrift, enterprise and self-reliance were the fundamental pillars of prosperity. Inequality was a necessary dynamic force for change and renewal. A return to these fundamental values could restore Britain to its nineteenth-century position of economic pre-eminence.

In the process of developing the new government's philosophy, important shortcomings in monetarist and new classical thought – as well as many practical considerations in their transformation into policy – were glossed over or ignored. For example, could the supposed stability of the demand for money identified by Friedman be depended on, especially in the short term? Could the authorities actually control the money supply, especially in the context of institutional and technological change and high interest rates that might, by encouraging people to hold more money, produce perverse effects? Is the stock of money endogenous to the progress of the economy, and therefore co-determined with the price level and output? What is the most important measure of the money supply to use? Is it a narrow or a broadly defined measure, and how would that measure respond to being subject to control? How quickly and comprehensively would workers and employers adjust their inflationary expectations to a monetarist regime, and at what interim cost in terms of output and employment? How easy would it be to restrain government spending? And finally, would taking a long-term view and avoiding fine-tuning make the process of returning an economy struck by a large shock much harder, leading to, as Keynes suggested, potentially dangerous implications for social stability, democracy and freedom?

The implications of brushing aside these important considerations would be revealed in spades over the following decade.

CHAPTER 5

Blemished Renaissance

Ubi solitudinem faciunt, pacem appellant.
[Translated here as 'They create a desert and call it stability.']

— Tacitus, 98 CE[1]

A GAME OF TWO HALVES

The 1980s were very much a period of contrasts. It was a decade of haves and have nots; of those in work and those who were unemployed; a time of bounty for the asset rich and for many professionals and homeowners, especially those in the South East, but one of despair and deprivation for many blue-collar workers and their families in the old industrial regions – despair that has echoed through the decades.

The clearest successes of the 1980s flowed from microeconomic policy. The interventionist and corporatist thrust of post-war industrial strategy was rejected, and many of the Thatcher government's initiatives were retained by subsequent administrations of both the right and the left. That said, even in this area the picture was patchy.

After an initial deep recession and a further period of elevated inflation, the 1980s were noteworthy for a long episode of continuous economic expansion – sluggish at first, then rapid. However, high unemployment was a consistent blight across the decade, especially in the economy's traditional manufacturing heartlands, and inflation made a disturbing comeback towards the end of the period, as indeed did a large external deficit.

The 1980s can therefore be divided into two halves. The average growth rate in the first half of the decade was marginally above 1% per annum, which was far below the OECD average despite the fact that all the advanced economies were growing more slowly than hitherto. In the second half of the decade average growth amounted to an impressive 4.25% per annum, although 1987 and 1988 saw the development of an unsustainable boom and by 1990 a serious recession beckoned.

The primary driver of the 1980s expansion was personal consumption, underpinned by robust real income growth for those in work, a rapid accumulation of household debt, and an associated sharp dip in the personal savings rate. This was especially so after 1986, when imports also surged. The strength of private consumption was in stark contrast to public spending on goods and services, which was heavily curtailed, albeit not by as much as public investment, which especially in net terms fell sharply, most notably towards the end of the period. Private fixed investment initially dipped dramatically but then rebounded strongly, in significant part because of a boom in residential construction. Exports performed well in the middle of the decade but suffered badly once domestic demand became excessive.

North Sea oil output grew strongly in the first half of the decade, before peaking in 1985 and 1986. Against this backdrop, and given the initial precipitous downswing, the current account moved into significant surplus. It remained close to balance as the recovery began, but the boom of the second half of the decade plunged the external balance back into the red. In 1989 the current account shortfall amounted to almost 5% of GDP, exceeding that which followed both the Maudling boom of the early 1960s and the Barber boom and first oil shock of the 1970s.

Unemployment rose to levels that surprised the government, and which would have been unconscionable in the three previous decades. This was despite the basis of calculation being repeatedly adjusted to flatter the published figures. The jobless total would have risen close to 4 million if it had been calculated in the same way as it had been in previous decades: around 750,000 higher than the official number.

The peak in the unemployment rate saw nearly 12% of the workforce out of work during the course of 1984, compared with a rate of 5.5% when the Conservatives took office. The rise was particularly dramatic during the initial downturn, when youth unemployment in the inner cities exceeded 50%. The overall jobless rate remained in double digits until 1987, before falling away in the late-cycle boom. Unemployment ran persistently far above the OECD average throughout the 1980s, and long-term joblessness peaked just below 6% of the workforce in 1984 and 1985. However it was measured, the jobless rate was higher in its best year in the 1980s than it was during its worst year of the 1970s.

The rise in joblessness was overwhelmingly driven by a contraction in manufacturing employment, with a particularly precipitous decline evident between 1980 and 1982. Most of the jobs that were lost were full-time ones, held by men in unionized factories, and they were concentrated in the Midlands, the North of England, Scotland and Wales. Greater London, by contrast, was spared the worst of the recession.

The primary explanation for the initial surge in unemployment appears to have been the tightness of monetary policy, and especially the high level of interest rates and, thereby, the exchange rate. Official interest rates were at 14% or higher for twenty-one consecutive months from June 1979, and respite did not appear quickly thereafter.

It is hard to attach much blame to the second oil shock, as there was no dramatic deterioration in the UK's terms of trade akin to that seen in 1973 and 1974. Sharply higher oil prices did, however, push up headline inflation at the beginning of the decade, as indeed did public sector wage settlements that the government felt compelled to honour, and a decision to sharply raise indirect taxes.

The annual CPI inflation rate averaged 8.25% in the first five months of 1979, but it had leapt to 18.5% by April 1980 and still averaged almost 12% in 1981. It fell rapidly to an average of 4.25% in 1984 and then to around 3.25% in 1986 and 1987, as oil prices collapsed back down from their early-decade highs. However, the boom of the decade's later years saw inflation climb once again, and it peaked at more than 8% in October 1990, the month before Margaret Thatcher resigned as prime minister. Inflation had returned to the level seen when the Conservatives came to power.

THE FIRST HALF: GETTING OFF
ON THE WRONG FOOT

Thatcher appointed Sir Geoffrey Howe as her first chancellor. A successful, albeit dour, lawyer, he was a hawk on economic policy. He seems to have been attracted to monetarism as it offered the opportunity to apply the logic of what its devotees presented as fundamental laws to the procedures of economic management. Howe was no intellectual lightweight, but like another lawyer, Anthony Barber, before him, he was to find that the prime minister was invariably at his shoulder when it came to steering the economy: as a confirmed control freak, Thatcher lived up to her formal title of First Lord of the Treasury. Her willingness to apply the basic monetarist tenet of keeping discretion to a minimum was bounded from the outset.

The centrepiece of Howe's first budget, delivered in the summer of 1979, was a sharp shift of emphasis from direct to indirect taxation. There were cuts in personal allowances and in the basic and top rates of income tax, while VAT, previously set at 8% and 12%, was conflated into a single 15% rate, petrol duty increased sharply, and the nationalized industries were given greater latitude to set prices. Public spending plans were cut by £1.5 billion (the equivalent of around 0.75% of GDP) and official interest rates were increased from 12% to 14%. The chancellor also announced sales of state-owned assets of around £1 billion.

The budget was designed to be deflationary, and it embodied lower targets for the budget deficit and for monetary growth, but its immediate impact was to push the price level – and hypersensitive inflation expectations – sharply higher. This was then exacerbated by generous awards made to public sector employees by the Clegg Commission on pay comparability, which had been established by the previous Labour government as its final incomes policy collapsed, and which the Conservatives had honoured for electoral purposes.

The government went ahead with this incoherent strategy because of its almost evangelical faith in the ability of monetary restraint to curb inflation. Implicit in this was a belief that it could adequately control whatever definition of the money supply was prioritized, and an assumption that the mere announcement of a desire to bring down monetary growth would be reflected in lower pay claims. Both proved hopelessly unrealistic.

Commencing around the time of the first budget, in part to encourage more outward foreign investment when sterling was very strong, the government first loosened exchange controls and then abandoned them altogether. But capital inflows initially swamped any additional outflows, and the pound appreciated further, rising an additional 10% in nominal effective terms over the following eighteen months, to the end of 1980. This process was only encouraged by a three-percentage-point rise in official interest rates to 17% in November 1979, in an unsuccessful effort to bring wayward broad monetary growth to heel.

In the two years from the first quarter of 1979 to the first quarter of 1981, sterling appreciated by some 25%, while domestic UK labour costs – which were going up by more than 20% a year – were rising at twice the average of the other major economies. It was hardly surprising, therefore, that real GDP experienced a peak-to-trough fall of some 5% or that the downturn both came earlier and was deeper than those experienced elsewhere.

The influence of the second oil shock on sterling's rise and the depth of the UK's downturn was limited. Higher oil prices would certainly make an oil producer more attractive to international investors, especially as North Sea oil production was rising rapidly at the time, improving the UK's current account position. However, if oil prices were the predominant driver of sterling, why did the exchange rate slump in 1981 as dramatically as it appreciated in 1980? Oil prices really began to fall only in 1982, and the process was initially hesitant. A shift towards looser monetary policy better explains sterling's decline.

THE MEDIUM-TERM FINANCIAL STRATEGY

The UK's overly tight monetary policy can be traced back to the unduly low annual monetary growth target set in the 1980 budget. The 7–11% range for the M3 aggregate announced for 1979–80, which was dramatically overshot, was not only retained but incorporated into the so-called 1981 Medium Term Financial Strategy (MTFS).

The MTFS was prepared under the supervision of Nigel Lawson, then Financial Secretary to the Treasury. Although he was nominally the third-ranked minister at the Treasury, this abrasive, supremely confident, former financial journalist was the cabinet's most powerful proselytizer of the monetarist counter-revolution. While they did not necessarily share Lawson's passion for monetarist theory, senior officials appreciated the MTFS's clarity and simplicity and, after the painful policy vicissitudes of the 1970s, they saw merit in its underlying message of enduring macro restraint.

The MTFS was unapologetically presented as the antithesis of the efforts of previous post-war administrations to fine-tune aggregate demand in an effort to target real variables. It was aimed primarily at reducing inflation through a combination of progressive declines in broad monetary growth – engineered through official interest rate adjustments and reductions in the budget deficit – that would mean the government impinged less and less on the financing requirements of the private sector.[2] The government's aim was to reduce annual M3 growth to 4–8% by 1983–84, while cutting the budget deficit to a mere 1.5% of GDP.

In contrast to the previous thirty-odd years, but consistent with new classical theory, fiscal policy was principally viewed as a facilitator of monetary control, while the money supply and the budget deficit were judged to be predominantly exogenous considerations, largely independent of the progress of economic activity or financial assets. The exchange rate was disregarded, with the thinking being that, so long as the money supply was brought under control, sterling would in due course find an appropriate level. Also consistent with new classical doctrine, the MTFS was built on the notion that inflation expectations, and thereby wage growth, would rapidly respond to the new focus on monetary and fiscal restraint by moderating.

The MTFS therefore embodied five propositions: there was a predictable and causal relationship between M3 growth and inflation; public borrowing was a key determinant of M3;[3] public borrowing levels had a dominant effect on the level of long-term interest rates; the exchange rate could be left to its own devices; and inflation expectations could be encouraged to fall rapidly. All of these proved overly simplistic, if not entirely wide of the mark. The MTFS ran into trouble from the outset.

Actual and projected rates of M3 growth consistently failed to remotely coincide. Monetary targets were missed as financial deregulation and the increasing globalization of capital markets rendered their achievement practically impossible. M3 growth increased by more than 19% in 1980–81, after 'the corset' – a system of quantitative restrictions on bank deposits that was used by both Barber and Healey to try to control monetary growth but which was erroneously thought to have lost its potency – was removed in June 1980.

Monetary growth was further swollen both by the fact that with the elimination of capital controls British banks could now both borrow from abroad and repatriate cash held overseas and by what became known as 'distress borrowing': the tendency for firms to borrow more in an attempt to stay in business.

Monetary targeting fell foul of Goodhart's law: the notion that when a measure becomes a target, it tends to lose its usefulness.[4] Hence, in subsequent versions of the MTFS, M3 was supplemented by various other monetary targets (both narrow and broad), and in the end set aside entirely in favour of M0, or notes and coins in circulation. This happened despite it seeming absurd that, in a complex and mature economy, inflation could be determined by what amounted to individuals' small change.

Meanwhile, the real economy and the public finances were performing worse than expected. The slump in output meant that, both in real terms and as a percentage of GDP, government spending increased rather than declined, revenues disappointed and the budget deficit significantly exceeded official forecasts.

The neglect of any reference to the exchange rate in the original MTFS was an oversight that had initially concerned many senior officials at the Treasury and the Bank of England. It was unsurprising, therefore, that before long, as with previous governments, sterling's performance became a key consideration in monetary policy. Indeed, by the second half of the decade it – along with the eradication of the budget deficit – had superseded monetary targeting in terms of importance.

At the same time, there was insufficient understanding that one-off positive shocks to the price level could elevate inflation expectations or that policy credibility was a key consideration in how those that set wages and prices would respond to the MTFS. Credibility had to be earned, and after fifteen years of rapid inflation, and with a new government experimenting with new ideas, it was in short supply.

Yet despite the various mis-steps, overshoots and changes of tack, it should be stressed that monetary and fiscal conditions in the early 1980s were manifestly very restrictive. Industry was under acute duress and the jobless rate was surging. The collapse in output and employment, and the fear that that collapse engendered among workers – rather than the supposed message of the MTFS – furthermore eventually began to moderate wage claims, and inflation fell.

BUDGET CONTROVERSY

The budget of 1981 was controversial at the time and remains so now. The government and the monetarist and new classical economists who supported it, presented it – and the MTFS – as symbolic of the new approach to policy, and in due course they claimed that this approach had worked: the green shoots of an extended recovery can be traced more or less exactly to its delivery. To Keynesians, it was anathema, encouraging 364 of them – including five of the six then-surviving former chief economic advisors to the government – to write a letter of protest to *The Times*, claiming that the budget was a recipe for a deeper depression, higher unemployment and political and social unrest.[5]

The reality is that, while the 364 signatories might have been being overly pessimistic in their judgements, they were not far off the mark, and the monetarist rhetoric about the budget went a lot further than the substance – and continues to do so to this day. In important ways, the 1981 budget was an admission of failure. What followed it was a more flexible and practically minded – even Keynesian – strategy than is generally appreciated.

What is not open to debate is the political and economic backdrop to the budget of 1981. It was grim. Thatcher's approval ratings were very low. The exchange rate was crushingly high, at $2.40 to the pound, and it had risen some 30% in trade-weighted terms since the May 1979 election. Factory closures and bankruptcies were soaring. The unemployment count was rising by around 100,000 a month. There were few job vacancies. Manufacturing profitability had collapsed, and the sector had shed around a tenth of its workforce in a year, while those regions of the economy dependent on it were experiencing mounting deprivation and social unrest. The collapse in industrial capacity would come back to haunt the government later, playing a considerable role in the subsequent deterioration of the external balance.

Dr Otmar Emminger, a former president of the Bundesbank, summed up the pound's strength most succinctly when he opined to a House of Commons Select Committee that the rise in sterling's real value at this time was 'by far the most excessive overvaluation which any major currency has experienced in recent monetary history'.[6] In the meantime, criticism of the government was mounting, and the cabinet, many of whom were far from true believers in the Thatcherite strain of Conservatism, was growing restless.

The prime minister publicly eschewed any formal policy U-turn akin to those of the stop–go era.[7] But beyond her public bravado, and the continuing support of Nigel Lawson for a tough line on the money supply and interest rates, it was clear that a strategy of benign neglect towards the currency was no longer viable. Sterling needed to fall, and this meant cutting official interest rates. Moreover, this was something that, throughout her term of office, always appealed to a prime minister who saw homeowners as her core constituency.

What was more contentious was that a lower budget deficit was central to this goal. Nevertheless, encouraged by Alan Walters, Thatcher's recently appointed personal economic advisor, and by the prime minister herself, the chancellor chose to tighten fiscal policy in the midst of a deep recession to expedite a significant easing of monetary policy. There were no explicit tax increases as such, but the indexation of tax allowances to inflation was suspended, which amounted to the same thing, especially at a time when the inflation rate was still running well into double digits.

The target for the budget deficit in 1981–82 was set at 3% of GDP, as against an outturn in 1980–81 of 5.75% of GDP. This translated into a decline in the UK's structural, or cyclically adjusted, budget balance – that is to say a fiscal tightening – of some three percentage points of GDP between 1980–81 and 1981–82. By any standard this represents an onerous degree of fiscal restraint over a short period of time when real activity was so depressed, but the chancellor actually wanted to go further in cutting spending. He was only prevented from doing so by a cabinet revolt.

The stance of fiscal policy in 1981 was the antithesis of the strategy adopted by Denis Healey in 1974 and 1975. And unlike Healey, Howe faced no external constraint on domestic borrowing. Almost the only saving grace of the UK economy at the start of the 1980s was that the country's current account balance was in healthy surplus. Howe's leeway to borrow more was therefore considerable, but he eschewed it because he believed a larger budget deficit would have swollen the money supply and inflated prices, despite there clearly being copious excess capacity in the economy.

Official interest rates were immediately cut by two percentage points, to 12%, and the effective exchange rate began a long, if by no means uninterrupted, downtrend that continued until 1987, aided by very high interest rates in the US. However, when monetary growth once again significantly overshot the target level of 6–10%, official rates were pushed back up to 15% (the same level they had been in July 1980).

This was perhaps the last occasion on which the government obsessed about monetary growth. Judgement and discretion gradually returned to monetary policy. In 1982, with the exchange rate relatively stable, interest rates were reduced to around 10%. By the end of that year there was a growing focus within the Treasury and beyond on the UK's relative loss of competitiveness, and on the fact that despite the significant contribution of North Sea oil, the external surplus was expected to disappear in 1983. This triggered a renewed desire on the part of the government to see sterling lower, and the markets were only too happy to oblige.

Despite the tight fiscal squeeze that followed the 1981 budget, recovery was prompted by a turn in the inventory cycle. It was initially a sluggish process, though, with capital spending being particularly slow to pick up, and while consumer spending was a source of stability throughout, unemployment continued to rise inexorably for more than three more years.

What is less commonly understood is that the fiscal years 1982–83, 1983–84 and 1984–85 saw almost all of the restraint of the 1981 budget unwound. The Falklands War, which in total cost some £2 billion (around 0.65% of GDP) when allowance is made for the replacement of equipment,[8] had some stimulative effect, while efforts to cut public spending ran into continued political opposition within the cabinet and the Conservative Party (despite the sacking or demotion of ministerial critics of the economic strategy), never mind from the population in the areas devastated by the recession. Meanwhile, the tax burden on both individuals and businesses continued to be lightened.

Just as pertinently, official interest rates finally fell back into single digits, and the broader effects on borrowing of the progressive abandonment of credit controls – a tried-and-trusted technique of demand management during the four previous decades – became manifest.

With the fiscal and monetary squeeze on the private sector significantly reversed, and the exchange rate coming down, the cyclical upswing gathered momentum. Real GDP growth exceeded 3.5% in 1983, and a cavernous output gap finally began to close. And 1983 was, of course, an election year. Whatever the initial claims around the longer-term focus of the MTFS, the political manipulation of the business cycle that characterized the 1950s, 1960s and 1970s lived on.

Despite the high level of unemployment, a combination of fiscal largesse, lower interest rates, economic recovery, military success in the Falklands War and a Labour Party opposition beset by internecine warfare and espousing policies that were too left-wing resulted in a landslide victory for the Conservatives in the June 1983 election. This had seemed almost unthinkable eighteen months earlier.[9]

LAWSON TAKES OVER

Nigel Lawson took over from Geoffrey Howe as chancellor in the new parliament, and his inheritance was considerably more satisfactory than that of his two immediate predecessors. After four years of often-chaotic struggle and numerous self-inflicted wounds, the economy appeared to be back under control. He also had good reason to believe that his relationship with a similarly minded prime minister would be a constructive one, and that he would be able to rely on her for support. Sadly for him, and for the coherence of policy, this became less and less the case. Indeed, their relationship completely collapsed over time, and if there is one cabinet relationship that needs to function well for effective government, it is that of a prime minister and their chancellor.

One of Lawson's first initiatives was to instigate a renewed attack on the level of public spending, so that taxes could in due course be reduced, but he too found the going tough. His initial attempts to cut overall spending outright morphed first into an effort to stabilize it in real terms and then into the pursuit of a gradual fall relative to nominal GDP. A key stumbling block was a burgeoning social security bill. Bloated by rising unemployment and its related consequences, by the middle of the decade it was absorbing some 12% of GDP, as against 8% of GDP a decade earlier.

The new chancellor also instigated a review of monetary policy, which extended to an examination of the case for ERM membership. The Treasury, however, whose new Permanent Secretary, Peter Middleton, was ideologically aligned with Lawson, continued to favour domestically focused monetary control, not least because the supposed – but in reality questionable – tight relationship between public borrowing and interest rates gave it continued leeway to restrain public spending.

MONETARY TARGETING: FROM THE UNMANAGEABLE TO THE IRRELEVANT

In the end, the review proved inconclusive, encouraging pragmatic shifts in emphasis more than fundamental changes in direction. M3 growth remained a formal target variable, but it was given little weight in policy decisions, with the chancellor blaming structural changes in the demand for money related to the removal of exchange controls and the direct controls on bank lending outlined above for its unreliability. Instead, taking his lead from Alan Walters and other hardcore monetarists, who favoured the use of narrower definitions of money as intermediate objectives because they were less subject to distortions, he switched the focus of monetary policy towards M0, thereby letting a target that was apparently easier to hit overshadow one that, although it was badly behaved, at least had some meaningful relationship with the overall price level.

The MTFS was overhauled in the budget of 1984. It was given a five-year time horizon, rather than one of three or four years as previously, and M3 and M0 were presented as parallel monetary targets. The monetary targets were then supplemented in 1985 by medium-term projections for nominal GDP growth, in effect reinstating the demand management in cash terms that had been at the heart of the 1944 White Paper on Employment Policy. In reality, however, even if it was not yet subject to a formal target, it was the exchange rate that was increasingly afforded the greatest weight in policy.

It is ironic that the years 1983, 1984 and 1985 finally saw both monetary growth and the budget deficit and the inflation rate largely coming to heel, but the weakness of the exchange rate – fed in part by erratic communications on currency policy, falling oil prices and production, and a growing deficit in manufacturing trade – kept interest rates in double digits for the most part. It was also around this time that Lawson, initially the most outspoken defender of the finer print of the MTFS and of monetary targeting, began to seriously consider a more formal exchange rate objective, and in particular hitching sterling to the Deutschmark, which anchored the ERM.

As noted above, the UK's CPI inflation rate was well below its 1980 peak by the middle of the decade, typically running between 4% and 5%. It then fell to around 3% in 1986, 1987 and early 1988, before rebounding over the rest of the decade.

Wages dominate industrial costs, and slower wage growth was therefore a key consideration in the overall disinflationary trend. Wage inflation had begun to subside during the summer of 1980. In July of that year wages were some 26% higher than a year previously. By December the rate of increase was under 20%, and by the following December it was falling towards 10%. The low was 5.25% in mid 1984. Thereafter, the trend was upwards once again.

The moderation of wage inflation in the first half of the decade can be ascribed to three considerations: labour market legislation, government policy towards its own employees, and high and rising unemployment. Labour market legislation was initially more concerned with secondary picketing and the trade union closed shop than the more explicit attacks on trade union power of later years, and its impact on wage inflation was therefore probably limited. On the other hand, the government's attitude to wage claims in the public sector seems to have exerted greater influence. In 1982, after inflation had begun to fall, the government set an annual pay target of a 3.5% increase for the public sector. By providing departmental funding on this basis, it confronted public sector unions with a stark choice between sustaining employment and higher earnings. Overall, however, the most powerful factor in restraining wage inflation in the first half of the decade was probably the increase in corporate bankruptcies and the dramatic rise in private sector joblessness, especially in those sectors that had traditionally set the pace in wage bargaining. Workers were quite simply cowed into submission.

THE SECOND HALF: FROM RECOVERY
TO UNSUSTAINABLE BOOM

Nineteen eighty-three marked the onset of a more conspicuous recovery. Personal consumption was encouraged by a sharp fall in the savings ratio, which more than halved between 1980 and 1988. A key element in this was a housing boom. House prices rose to unprecedented levels relative to current incomes, with the rise particularly marked in London and the South East. The boom was underpinned by easy access to finance. Building societies began to offer 100% mortgages, while the major banks provided them with stiff competition for housing loans for the first time. The accumulation of mortgage debt for house purchases did not itself reduce personal savings, but the additional funds made available were channelled into higher spending.

The housing boom soured and turned to bust after 1988, as higher rates of interest squeezed incomes and house prices began to turn downwards, especially where the boom had been most intense. Borrowing declined and the savings ratio rebounded higher, not peaking until the early 1990s, by which time it had reached more than 15% of disposable income. This was a key driver of the downturn at the end of the 1980s. Moreover, the rapid accumulation of household debt meant that changes in short-term interest rates came to exert increased influence over consumer spending.

The progress of the savings ratio was not driven entirely by developments in the housing market. Hire purchase controls were withdrawn in July 1982, while the financial sector in general was subsequently subjected to a comprehensive programme of deregulation. Other asset values also enjoyed steep price rises. The FTSE share index rose from 440 at the beginning of 1980 to 1,855 in July 1987, equating to average gains of more than 20% per annum. Then, after a sharp correction to under 1,300 in October 1987, the index rebounded to register new highs as central bank policy around the world was relaxed to assuage fears of a repeat of the 1929 Crash.

In retrospect, this monetary response was inappropriate, and only served to exaggerate a well-established boom. But the fears that the sudden market adjustment presaged a global recession were at the time very real, and to have failed to react would have risked a more damaging and sustained downward adjustment in asset prices.

UK monetary policy in general was a strong contributory factor to the economy's strength and to the asset price boom of the later 1980s. Where interest rates had been focused exclusively against domestic inflation at the start of the decade, by 1985 and 1986 exchange rate stability had increasingly become the primary goal.

Sterling had weakened materially in the second half of 1984, as the miners' strike of that year dragged on, slowing the pace of recovery, and the US dollar surged higher against all currencies. By January 1985 the sterling–dollar rate was threatening to reach parity: a prospect viewed with horror in Number 10 Downing Street. In trade-weighted terms, the currency was some 28% lower than its 1981 peak. In response, the Bank of England was instructed to raise official interest rates by four percentage points in a single month, bringing them back to 14%. Sterling fell to a low of $1.04 in February 1985, and it remained weak throughout the year both against the dollar and in trade-weighted terms. Parity with the dollar was, however, avoided.

The mid 1980s saw coordinated international efforts to restrict exchange rate movements among the major economies, with the so-called Plaza and

Louvre Accords designed to curtail large swings in the US dollar.[10] Lawson identified this as an opportune moment to lock in a low inflation rate by bringing sterling into the ERM, and towards the end of 1985 he presided over two internal seminars on the subject.[11] His essential argument was that ERM membership would allow the UK to 'import' enduring low-inflation credibility via a fixed, or quasi-fixed, link to the Deutschmark, long one of the world's strongest currencies.

In his quest to join the ERM, Lawson could count on the support of a number of senior Treasury and Bank of England officials, while the Foreign Office, now led by Geoffrey Howe, was also keen on such a move. The problem the chancellor faced was the prime minister.

Thatcher generally took a narrow view of the EEC's raison d'être. Moreover, her relationship with the bloc had been fraught from the outset of her premiership, when she was treated with what can only be described as disdain by the then leaders of Germany and France, Helmut Schmidt and Valéry Giscard d'Estaing. She went on to achieve a significant political victory in sharply reducing the UK's EEC budget contribution in 1984, but in the process her confrontational approach and refusal to work constructively on other issues alienated many of her interlocutors.[12] Her distrust of Germany burgeoned thereafter, and she encouraged an 'us against them' mentality within her own party, in the UK press and across the country at large. She was also sceptical of the ERM's merits more generally: it went against her instincts.

Buttressed by the arguments of monetarist purist Alan Walters – who remained influential with the prime minister despite having left Number 10 for academia – she had a number of specific concerns. Thatcher was reluctant to buck market forces and present currency speculators with a clear target; she feared membership would encourage greater interest rate volatility; she hesitated at reducing the leeway for policy flexibility ahead of a general election; and why, she asked, should she feed the perception that her monetarist experiment had failed, and that Britain had to fall back on the Bundesbank for policy credibility?

Although it soured her relationship with her chancellor, and stored up many political problems for later, Thatcher was probably right to veto ERM entry at this time. UK membership in 1985 or 1986 could have ended in disaster. Sterling was still, to a degree, a petrocurrency. The downward pressure on the pound that followed the collapse in oil prices during that period (to as low as $10 a barrel) might have triggered a repeat of Britain's humiliating six-week experience with the European 'snake' in 1972. And, of course, Thatcher had been a minister in Edward Heath's cabinet at the time. At a minimum, UK interest rates would have had to have been increased sharply, potentially crushing output and employment, and terminating the nascent recovery.

Undaunted, and without the prime minister's imprimatur, Lawson subsequently instead adopted an unofficial strategy of shadowing the Deutschmark under a cap of 3.00 to the pound, particularly once the Louvre Accord of February 1987 had put a floor under the dollar against the other major currencies. He later claimed that by resisting upward pressure on sterling he sought to encourage the belief that downward pressure would also be resisted, although quite how is unclear.

Whether or not Lawson's logic was sound, the underlying implication of shadowing the Deutschmark was that joining the ERM was a matter of when, not if. But events continued to conspire against him. The tide of international currency market cooperation turned in 1988. Money was flooding into London in anticipation of a further term – or terms – for Thatcher. And as Britain's recovery matured into an out-and-out boom there was a growing need for greater domestic monetary restraint.

Yet Lawson's fixation on sterling's stability against the Deutschmark led him to pursue a very different, and very destabilizing, path – and not just around the time of the October 1987 stock market crash. By the end of that year, Lawson had effectively abandoned any predetermined domestically orientated framework for interest rate decisions. Monetary policy was down to his own subjective judgement, and at the core of this was his pursuit of currency stability. The rules once deemed so important to the monetarist counter-revolution had been abandoned in favour of the discretion of a headstrong and blinkered chancellor. The markets would just have to trust him as the self-styled architect of Britain's economic renaissance. This was dangerous territory, especially once the economy began to hit choppier waters, and it only added to his difficulties with the prime minister.

In the end, despite aggressive sterling sales by the Bank of England and a succession of interest rate cuts, Lawson's policy of shadowing the Deutschmark proved unsustainable both economically and politically. With the prime minister at the height of her authority and ultimately no longer willing to allow the chancellor to plough his own furrow – it is remarkable she let him tread this path for so long – the cap on sterling was lifted in March 1988. Lawson contemplated resignation, but drew back, not wanting to miss out on delivering the tax-reforming budget that he had long been aiming for.

Soon after the lifting of the cap, however, and as the chancellor desperately fought to rekindle his own authority, policy rates were cut to a low of 7.5% in an effort to moderate sterling's subsequent rapid rise. This happened despite broad money and credit growth once again being rapid, despite income tax being reduced, and despite the economy expanding strongly – indeed, much more strongly than was appreciated at the time.

The bigger political picture was that the relationship between the prime minister and the chancellor had soured beyond repair, and economic policy was in disarray. The expansion was running out of control, inflation was picking up, the external deficit was widening, and excessive monetary laxity in the context of undue policy discretion was an important reason why.

Disconcertingly, the cut in rates to 7.5% had to be reversed within two weeks, and over the next twelve months or so policy rates were progressively doubled to 15%, where they remained for an entire year. By then, reference to the interaction of interest rates with the money supply had been largely disregarded. Instead, the most commonly touted mechanism of policy transmission was seen as being through the impact of higher mortgage payments on purchasing power.

Neither was fiscal policy used to slow the impetus of the late 1980s boom until it was too late. Trend or potential growth was overstated in official forecasts, building a consistently positive bias into spending plans and revenue projections. The average annual growth rate assumed in the documentation published alongside successive budgets was raised progressively, from 2.25% per year in 1984 to 3% per year in 1988. Lawson, meanwhile, had long been reluctant to admit that fiscal policy had much impact at all on aggregate demand: that was just the discredited view of old-school Keynesians. In his eyes, fiscal policy's biggest effects were on supply-side incentives and distribution. This proved to be a painful misjudgement. Lawson's tax cuts went further than simply putting money into people's pockets: the boost they also provided to already-elevated business and consumer confidence and asset prices encouraged them to spend it.

Corporation tax had already been reformed in 1984. The tax relief for stock appreciation introduced at the end of 1974 to save many companies from bankruptcy was now abolished. With the retreat of inflation, it was no longer deemed necessary. Investment allowances were also swept away, but the standard rate of corporation tax was reduced sharply over two years to compensate, from 50% to 35%.

The standard rate of income tax was lowered in 1986, again in the election year of 1987, and yet again in 1988, bringing it down to 25% – or eight percentage points lower than when the Conservatives took office. The top rate of tax was also cut, from 60% to 40%, in 1988.

The lower rates of tax were more than compensated for by the buoyancy of tax revenues as incomes increased, while privatization – one-off sales of publicly owned assets in nationalized industries – brought in progressively larger amounts to the Treasury's coffers. The government therefore ran an overall budget surplus equivalent to around 1% of GDP in 1988 and 1989. However, this provides an unduly restrictive picture of the impetus of fiscal policy. In cyclically adjusted terms, the budget remained in significant deficit, and in both 1986 and 1987 the structural shortfall increased by around half a percentage point of GDP a year. Fiscal policy was being loosened. It was only in 1988 – when public spending was curbed to a greater extent than in any other year of the Thatcher governments – that overall fiscal policy exerted any degree of restraint on the economy, and in the eyes of Lawson's advisors, it did not do so enough.

THE END OF THE AFFAIR

The downturn that commenced in 1989 began when the unemployment rate was still running at more than 7% of the workforce, the CPI inflation rate was above 5% (and rising rapidly), and the external deficit was consistently exceeding expectations.

Lawson argued that the record current account shortfall was of little import, claiming in his annual address to the IMF Conference in September 1988 that, unlike previous deficits the UK had run up, it was a private sector phenomenon rather than reflecting public sector excess, and it would prove self-correcting.[13] This was, once again, wishful thinking. As noted above, the fiscal position was flattered by the strength of the cyclical upswing. The picture was in fact worse than it looked, and history strongly suggested that a persistently large external deficit is indicative of a fundamental imbalance in the economy and that a major policy readjustment was required to put things right.

The UK seemed to still be afflicted by a number of structural weaknesses and rigidities. Foremost among these was a shortage of capacity, as indicated by the early emergence of numerous bottlenecks and shortages and by a tendency for manufacturing imports to grow at about twice the rate of manufacturing exports.

A further problem was continuing inflexibility when it came to wage settlements. While much of the earnings inflation after 1986 was at the top end of the income scale, rather than the bottom, the main source of inflationary pressure, since productivity rose consistently, still remained wages. The long-standing habit of workers asking for more than their output warranted was not readily abandoned. Earnings growth ran at consistently high-single-digit annual rates in the late 1980s, and it breached 10% in 1990.

As the economy gradually came off the boil in 1989, the dominant policy issue behind the scenes remained the vexed matter of ERM membership. The prime minister – still profoundly influenced by the arguments of Alan Walters and unapologetically antagonistic towards Europe, and in particular the close Franco-German alliance of François Mitterrand and Helmut Kohl – hardened in her opposition. But against the background of the all-too-familiar ignominy of an unsustainable inflationary consumer boom turning to bust, her authority began to wane, and there was a perception in the markets and beyond that the UK required a new policy anchor. Although Lawson had by now clearly lost the prime minister's favour, he continued to push hard for ERM entry and he retained the support of other cabinet Europhiles, such as Geoffrey Howe at the Foreign Office, as well as the governor of the Bank of England, Robin Leigh-Pemberton.

In the meantime, with a customs union in place and the EEC budget settled, the rest of Europe became increasingly determined to extend the reach of the bloc and make further progress towards the 'ever closer union' referred to in the Treaty of Rome. Under the influence of Jacques Delors, a former French finance minister who became president of the European Commission in 1985, it was agreed that the next major initiative should be the creation of a 'single market'. This implied the removal of all outstanding obstacles to trade, ranging from customs and passport controls to fiscal barriers (such as varying levels of indirect taxes) and technical barriers (such as conflicting standards, laws and qualifications).

Notwithstanding her narrow view of the EEC's raison d'être, Thatcher believed that being part of this single market was in the UK's interests. The necessary legislation to incorporate the Single European Act into UK law was passed in a mere six days, even though it also embodied increased powers for both the European Parliament and the European Commission, together with the extension of qualified majority voting in the Council of Ministers on single market issues. Thatcher seems to have believed that if countries surrendered their vetoes, the single market that ultimately emerged would be more open to competition and cleansed of government interference. By signing up so readily, she probably gave away more British sovereignty than did Heath in 1973.

Others, however, wanted the establishment of the single market to dovetail with a broader suite of initiatives extending to social policy and monetary union. In April 1989 the European Commission published a three-stage route map towards a single European currency, with the ERM at its core.[14] The first stage required the completion of the single market, plus a currency's membership of the ERM within the system's narrow bands. The second stage involved the creation of the necessary institutions for a monetary union, including a European Central Bank. And the third consisted of the launch of the single currency. It was subsequently decided that these initiatives, together with the necessary amendments to the original Treaty of Rome, would be discussed at a special intergovernmental conference in Maastricht in the Netherlands in December 1991.

It was not widely known or advertised that Britain had committed in principle to monetary union in both its initial EEC accession treaty and when it signed up to the Single Market Act. However, neither Thatcher nor Lawson saw these as binding near-term obligations. Rather, they each viewed monetary union as a dangerous and unwarranted step towards political union, and a threat to the British nation state. Nevertheless, the long-buried issue of British sovereignty in the context of a maturing and evolving European community was beginning to rear its ugly head, and it would subsequently blight Conservative Party politics for more than thirty years.

Lawson's antipathy towards monetary union did not deflect him from his view that ERM membership was at that time the best low-inflation anchor for the UK, or from his trying to bring it about. Together with Geoffrey Howe, in the summer of 1989 he sought to obtain something more definitive than Thatcher's oft-repeated filibuster that the UK would join the ERM when 'the time was ripe'. Eventually, increasingly isolated in cabinet and facing the potential resignation of her two most senior colleagues, the prime minister made a clearer pledge, albeit one with conditions worked out with the help of Alan Walters. The UK government would consider membership when there had been more progress in bringing inflation down to the average of its competitors; when exchange controls had been abandoned across Europe; and when the single market was complete, including a free market in financial services and the strengthening of community competition policy around state aid.

Even then, Thatcher's hostility towards the ERM, compounded by her broader antipathy towards Europe, continued to fester, and her commitment to her own conditions wavered. It was only when there appeared to be little alternative to joining that she accepted membership as a fait accompli. She would later also claim that she always saw the ERM as a flexible system of exchange rates for the UK, and that on her watch there would have been neither heavy intervention nor an interest rate structure that was at odds with the demands of the domestic economy. In other words, she never really bought into the ERM – and certainly not in the way that others did.

Neither did Thatcher accept what was a significant political defeat graciously. She was determined to never again be held hostage by her foreign secretary and chancellor. In an increasingly poisonous political atmosphere, Howe was demoted to Leader of the House of Commons in July 1989, and then, in October, Lawson resigned following the prime minister's repeated public characterizations of his Deutschmark-shadowing policy as the primary source of the UK's inflationary problems, and her re-employment of the virulently anti-ERM Alan Walters as her personal economic advisor. It also emerged that Walters was opposed to Lawson's final interest rate hike to an eyewatering 15%.

Lawson told Thatcher that she had to choose between him and Walters. There could not be two chancellors. She effectively chose Walters. Lawson walked out, although Walters's position was also untenable and he too resigned.

Lawson's replacement as chancellor was John Major, a lesser-known and more modest and down-to-earth politician than his predecessor. Major was driven more by practicality than by ideology, but four things were clear: he could master a brief; he was clear-thinking; he was politically savvy; and he was serious about bringing down inflation, which he viewed as not just economically harmful but socially pernicious.

The pound had once again come under heavy selling pressure at the end of 1989, and this dashed hopes that headline inflation would rapidly come to heel. Indeed, it would continue to rise well into 1990. Major considered pushing official rates beyond the already excruciating 15% level, but short rates were at their highest level in real terms since the 1930s, and with Thatcher against such a move he backed off.

Major, however, recognized that UK macro policy had lost credibility following the Lawson boom, and he rapidly needed to re-establish it. He had no time for a return to doctrinaire monetarism, while an aggressive fiscal squeeze was by this stage both economically inappropriate and politically unacceptable. Bank of England independence – which the frustrated Lawson had presented to the prime minister as an alternative to ERM membership in late 1988 and which might have made more sense – was viewed by Thatcher as another humiliation, while any formal inflation target would also initially have to be set at an embarrassingly high level. He therefore saw ERM membership as the only viable strategy available. With the Treasury, the Foreign Office and much of the Bank of England in agreement, with industry eager for greater macroeconomic stability, and with many in the City and the opposition Labour Party also onside, all Major had to do was what his predecessor had failed to do and persuade the prime minister to take the plunge.

Despite Major's placatory skills, the fact that Thatcher could hardly afford to lose a second chancellor in short order, and support from the equally emollient new Europhile foreign secretary, Douglas Hurd, this was not a smooth process. Thatcher was increasingly isolated, paranoid and mercurial in this (final) interlude of her premiership, and she vented many of her frustrations on Europe. Moreover, Walters retained her ear, and continued to advise strongly against entry.

In the end, the die was cast by a combination of factors, foremost of which were fear that Britain would lose influence to the Franco-German axis in the EU, not least around monetary union; a warning from the Bush administration that British influence in Washington depended on its occupying a central role in Europe; desperation to find a policy apparatus that would end Britain's experience of boom and bust; and the hope that membership would facilitate a declining trend in official interest rates into the next election.

The conditions marked out for entry the previous year were progressively softened and redefined, while other considerations pertinent to the timing of sterling's entry to the system were given short shrift. For example, the risk that the UK economy was headed for recession and would therefore require both policy largesse and a competitive currency was given too little weight. The threat that German reunification, which was already a fact of life, would push German interest rates (and thereby other ERM interest rates) sharply higher and disrupt the whole system was similarly played down, despite the fact that German currency strength had tended to cause severe strains elsewhere ever since the ERM's inception. Finally, there was the simple fact that eleven years of Conservative rule had failed to transform the pound from a currency consistently prone to devaluation and crisis to something more robust. It was simply not a strong currency, or even a very credible one.

Sterling joined the ERM on 5 October 1990 at the prevailing central rate of DM2.95, which, given the UK economy's cyclical vulnerability, seemed somewhat elevated. There is some suggestion that Thatcher wanted to enter at an even higher rate, while on the other hand she insisted that the fluctuation margins around this central parity were, at 6%, wider (and thereby less demanding) than those accepted by most other members. Furthermore, official interest rates were cut by a percentage point to 14%: a policy departure that the Bank of England had argued against but which, true to form, the prime minister had demanded as the ultimate condition for her acquiescence.

Hindsight indicates that each of these three decisions was a mistake. The central rate against the Deutschmark translated into a challengingly high rate for sterling against the dollar. The decision to choose a high exchange rate was no doubt influenced by the need to bear down on inflation, but it was a hostage to fortune that would do little to help an already weakening economy or moderate an already large external deficit. The wide parity bands were from the outset viewed in financial markets as indicative of the UK authorities' relatively loose commitment to exchange rate stability, and of a desire to maximize the room within the system for policy flexibility. Finally, with inflation yet to peak, the rate cut could only be seen as a cynical political move: it was hardly symbolic of steadfast intent.

The reckoning for these errors would not fall into the lap of Margaret Thatcher, however. After eleven years in power, a burgeoning recession, high inflation, high interest rates, collapsing house prices and a disastrous decision to introduce a poll tax destroyed her reputation as a winner with much of the electorate. Moreover, her remote, overbearing and imperious style, her growing inflexibility and her anti-Europeanism had alienated her from many of her cabinet colleagues. She had become a political liability. She was replaced by John Major, who became the youngest prime minister for a century.

THE SUPPLY SIDE

Even before the Conservatives came to power in 1979, they went out of their way, as we have seen, to reject the post-war Keynesian consensus. However, it was in a lecture given by Nigel Lawson early in his tenure as chancellor that perhaps the clearest exposition yet of how the Tories believed economic policy should be framed is to be found.[15]

Lawson stressed that the macroeconomic instruments of interest rates, taxation and public spending would be focused on containing inflation rather than on real variables such as employment or output. Meanwhile, microeconomic, or supply-side, measures would be directed at reducing the influence of the government on the economy, promoting greater flexibility in the face of shocks, and encouraging faster and more sustainable underlying growth, rather than, as had often been the case in the past, being used to suppress prices and wages or to act as a rather clumsy means to ameliorate social or regional disparities.

The progress, shortcomings and failures of the first of these two policy pillars have been outlined in detail above. The programme of structural reforms was more coherent and, with the fatal exception of the poll tax, more successful.

The Thatcher governments' micro, or supply-side, policy evolved considerably over the course of their time in power, and it had many elements. The most important can be summarized as a reduced dependence on government expenditure; the privatization of state-owned assets; deregulation to encourage increased competition in product markets and to breathe new life into the financial industry; the reduction of trade union power; the encouragement of home ownership; and reform of the tax system to reduce the burden of direct tax, especially on high incomes via a switch to more regressive levies such as VAT and a poll tax.

ROLLING BACK THE STATE

From the outset, the Conservatives were keen to reduce the share of public spending in national income. This proved much harder to do in practice, however, than was initially foreseen. Major economies in some areas, such as pensions, defence, and law and order, were not possible because these outlays were considered central to the preservation of Tory values, while large cuts in health and education were both impracticable, and also electorally fraught. It was possible to massage some current expenditure down, but the only large immediate economies that could be effected were in capital outlays, such as infrastructure spending, which hardly amounted to 'waste' and where cuts came with a long-term cost to productive potential. In the end, significant savings were also made in housing, subsidies and so-called miscellaneous items. In addition, charges were introduced or increased, and some welfare payments were linked to prices rather than wages. But even with subsidies, progress was slow. Many financial grants, both to private industries and to nationalized ones, continued to be paid into the middle of the decade.

Rather than declining, public spending increased by about 14% in real terms between fiscal years 1978–79 and 1990–91. The sense at the time that public services and physical infrastructure were being starved of cash reflected a surge in outlays on unemployment and other welfare benefits, which squeezed the funding available for other programmes. This was despite the fact that eligibility criteria for welfare payments were significantly tightened.

Towards the end of the Thatcher governments period, rapid nominal GDP growth exceeded growth in public spending, so that the latter fell as a proportion of GDP despite the absolute total continuing to trend upwards. Public spending accounted for some 44% of GDP in 1978–79. By 1982–83 the figure had increased to around 47.5%. By 1988–89 it had fallen back to just over 39%, but the decline was short-lived, with recession pushing it back above 44% by 1992–93. In relative terms, the size of the UK government remained much as it had been at the beginning of the Thatcher years: significantly larger than the G-7 and OECD averages, and than the US and Japan in particular, albeit smaller than the vast majority of its European competitors.

Public sector net investment's share in output fell sharply in the early 1980s, accelerating the downward trend seen under the previous Labour governments. By 1981–82 it accounted for less than 1% of GDP, down from some 5.5% of GDP in the first year of the Wilson government. There was some limited recovery in the middle of the decade, but it subsequently hit new lows, declining to less than 0.5% of GDP in 1988–89. The dearth of net public investment did not reflect only government austerity, however: from 1983 onwards it also reflected large declines in capital outlays by the nationalized industries as the privatization programme picked up steam.

The restraint of public spending was meant to facilitate tax reform and a lower tax burden, thereby unleashing greater entrepreneurial spirit. As we have seen, following an initial near-doubling of VAT from 8% to 15%, the standard rate of income tax was progressively lowered to 25% and the top rate was cut to 40%. Then, in the middle of the decade, the government also resorted to corporate tax reform in pursuit of supply-side improvement.

Towards the end of Thatcher's time in office, a flat-rate per-capita poll tax (officially known as the Community Charge) was substituted for domestic rates in an effort to reform the funding of local government. Thatcher had been in favour of getting rid of rates since serving as shadow environment secretary in 1974, and, encouraged by Alan Walters, she saw their removal as a flagship policy of her third term. Rates, which had effectively been in place since the seventeenth century, were widely disliked by property-owning Tory voters, who thought it unfair that an important tax was levied on the rental value of their homes rather than being spread across all individuals. The government's aim was also to restrain free-spending Labour councils. The financial burden of any local government spending largesse would in future fall on the shoulders of everyone.

As predicted by Lawson, the Community Charge was a political disaster, however.[16] It was introduced at too high a level (in part because Lawson was reluctant to subsidize its initial launch) just as the economy soured, and many unemployed people, students and poor large families occupying small homes suddenly found their tax liabilities greatly increased, sparking vehement opposition. Widespread riots ensued in March 1990, while extensive refusals to pay resulted in large-scale shortfalls in revenue for many local authorities. The poll tax was subsequently abandoned, being replaced in 1993 by a levy that was similar to the old system of rates.

Despite the government's plans to reduce the tax burden, the proportion of government receipts as a share of GDP initially rose sharply from 40.25% of GDP in 1978–79 to peak at some 46% of GDP in 1981–82. It really only began to fall persistently in 1985–86, and it did not drop back below 40% of GDP until 1989–90. Just as had been the case at the outset of the Thatcher years, this still left the UK's tax take significantly higher than the G-7 or OECD averages, even if it was well below that seen across Europe.

The second element of reducing the role of the state was deregulation. As already noted, exchange controls and hire-purchase controls were abandoned, and banks were given greater freedom of action during Thatcher's first term. In the process, the government eschewed a number of weapons of stabilization policy that had been used in the past, and important destabilizing effects of these initiatives became manifest, especially during the consumer boom that took hold in the second half of the 1980s. These could only be brought under control through an extended period of sharply higher interest rates.

The removal of exchange controls also encouraged greater diversification of financial and direct investment portfolios. Outward financial flows were greatly stimulated, particularly in the second half of the decade, when the current account balance swung sharply into deficit.

Financial deregulation did not stop there, however.

In the late 1970s the City of London had become increasingly uncompetitive. It was inward-looking and it operated in an old-fashioned, anachronistic way, while financial repression – the creation of captive markets through mechanisms such as artificial price ceilings, trade limitations, barriers to entry and other market controls – was pervasive. In global terms, it was becoming a backwater, especially when compared with New York. Since the collapse of the Bretton Woods monetary system in the early 1970s, the US's major financial hub had enjoyed a period of increasingly innovative growth, as securitization burgeoned, as a welter of mechanisms to raise capital more cheaply than bank loans emerged, and as new risk management products (such as interest rate and currency swaps) flourished.

A comprehensive set of reforms introduced in the autumn of 1986 was designed to encourage the City to reinvent itself and catch up. The 'Big Bang', as it was known, sparked a revolution in UK financial sector modi operandi. At a stroke, the stock exchange outlawed fixed commissions for trades and abolished the 'single capacity rule', with its traditional distinctions between 'jobbers', who traded on the floor of the exchange, and 'brokers', who acted on behalf of investors. At the same time, the London markets were opened up to foreign companies.

The result was a typhoon of 'creative destruction'. Old constraints on doing business were swept away and a new era of more intense competition, economies of scale, rapid innovation, and investment in new technology began. With the release of these dynamic forces, the City was not merely saved from irrelevance but rapidly transformed back into the world's foremost financial centre for the first time since 1914. Trading volumes surged, the fees related to privatization further boosted profits, and the sector became a substantial direct contributor to the UK's economic growth and to the Treasury's coffers. The financial sector's share of GDP rose from 3.5% to more than 5%: an increase that brought with it greatly increased political clout.

Over time, however, numerous malign side effects of light-touch financial regulation were to become manifest, and significant pockets of vulnerability in areas such as capital adequacy, liquidity and risk concentration were stored up for the future. Furthermore, as it subsequently transpired, the Big Bang proved to be a recipe for the triumph of large, multifaceted, mainly US international conglomerates or 'securities houses' that could more readily benefit from the broader eradication of the world's financial boundaries. Few of the City's old indigenous firms survived as independent entities.

Financial deregulation also went hand in hand with a loosening of moral restraints. Traditional banking emphasized long-term relationships with customers, while in the new environment the focus was all too often on short-term opportunism and risk-seeking.

Deregulation went well beyond finance, too. Numerous government quangos were wound up, competitive tendering for the private provision of local government services was introduced, and efforts were made in areas such as telecommunications to sharpen competition, allowing producers more freedom of action and consumers more freedom of choice. The hope was that all of this would encourage greater efficiency, lower unit labour costs and therefore prices, and improve the quality, breadth and innovativeness of output.

It should also be noted that the effects of these regulatory initiatives dovetailed with the delayed effects of the UK's entry into the EEC in 1973. Membership had led to sharp reductions in tariff barriers – the average tariff on imports fell from 9% in the late 1960s to less than 5% in 1979, and then to just over 1% in the mid 1980s – and easier access to a much-expanded developed marketplace.

In addition, Britain was at the forefront of efforts in the middle of the 1980s to rejuvenate the supply side of the EEC economy. Lord Cockfield, a former junior UK cabinet minister and subsequently vice commissioner of the European Community, authored a White Paper in 1985 that identified 300 barriers to trade that would need to be dismantled in order to complete a comprehensive pan-European single market.[17] The White Paper was well received across the continent, where there was a growing sense that excessive regulation was stifling growth potential, and it proved to be an important catalyst for the adoption of the Single European Act: a treaty that set a deadline of 31 December 1992 for the completion of the single market. It was duly launched on 1 January 1993.[18]

The third element of state contraction was privatization. Little was made of the concept in 1979. Indeed, it barely appeared in the Conservative Party's election manifesto. However, the idea subsequently proved popular and developed remarkable momentum, interacting with the broader efforts at deregulation. Indeed, it became a defining policy of the Thatcher era and was subsequently adopted in many other countries.

By 1979 the original post-war arguments for the nationalization of the major utilities and a number of heavy industries – to enable clearer long-term planning and to unleash greater opportunities to harness economies of scale in what were natural monopolies – had been found wanting. The structures that were used to monitor and control the nationalized industries had proved ineffective; ministerial interference in their running, often dictated by the state of the business cycle and by technological nationalism, had distorted their operation and undermined their ability to make appropriate strategic decisions; and disruptive trade union power had been amplified by the fact that many union members worked for a single employer. Low productivity and a lack of profitability, which were problems from the outset, had only worsened, and the nationalized industries had increasingly morphed into wasteful mechanisms of social and regional policy as well as becoming a drain on the taxpayer.

Privatization was attractive to the Thatcher governments on three levels: it promised to bring greater market discipline and efficiency gains to a number of sectors of the economy; the shares sold in nationalized industries would diversify wealth and help to encourage entrepreneurship and a share-owning democracy, just as the sale of council houses helped to diversify the population of property owners; and the proceeds generated by the sales of hitherto-public assets could contribute to the reduction of the budget deficit and government debt, thereby facilitating lower taxes.

In truth, just as with the initial process of nationalization, the evolution of privatization was driven more by politics and ideology than by any careful sector-by-sector examination of the case for different industrial structures. Furthermore, it was by no means clear that large private monopolies would be any more efficient than large public monopolies.

Privatization began slowly. It started with the sale of BP shares and of licenses to prospect for oil, and with the running down of oil stockpiles. And then in 1981 Nigel Lawson, who was then the secretary of state for energy, gave the process important momentum by contending that 'no industry should remain under state ownership unless there is a positive and overwhelming case for it doing so'. Thereafter, the attitude that state ownership should be the exception rather than the norm was increasingly hard-wired into government strategy. True public ownership was presented as putting shares into the hands of the electorate.

The rapid expansion began in 1983–84 and followed two routes: private sales of companies, including Ferranti, the National Bus Company and the Royal Ordnance Factories; and public offerings, which extended to the major public utilities, such as British Gas and British Telecom, and to a wide range of other large undertakings, including British Airways, British Steel, Britoil and Rolls Royce. In some cases the government initially retained a substantial holding, and in many it retained a 'golden share', giving it the power to preserve significant powers of control.

In the end, the number of public corporations in the economy was cut by half, employment in them was reduced from 8 million to 3 million, and their contribution to GDP was cut from above 10% to under 5%. Some of these privatizations created markets where previously there had been none, with the telecoms sector perhaps representing the most obvious example – competition flourished and prices fell as a consequence. Others merely saw private monopolies replace public ones, with disappointing results for those who were expecting long-term transformative change.

The ending of ministerial accountability for and control of an industry that was brought about by an instance of privatization did, however, mean that there was now a need for regulatory regimes and bodies to enforce acceptable market behaviour and the protection of consumers, not least from excessive pricing. Oftel was set up to regulate the new telecommunications industry when British Telecom was privatized, for example, and Ofgas was created when British Gas went the same way.

Privatization initially brought about a large increase in the number of shareholders in the UK, with the sale of British Telecom proving particularly attractive to those who had previously never owned shares. Many merely sought to make a quick profit and sell, but it is nevertheless estimated that the number of British shareholders increased from 3 million in 1979 to 10 million by 1991. The proportion of all shares in the hands of individuals (rather than institutional investors) fell by a third in the same period, however, to around 20%. The new shareholdings were of little import in economic terms, but they seem to have had a bigger, psychological, impact on the attitudes of individuals towards business.

By the end of 1987 the government had raised around £25 billion in total through privatization, and the sum of some £9 billion collected that year exceeded the budget deficit. By 1991 the cumulative proceeds had nearly doubled again.

Privatization also extended to the housing market. The Housing Act of 1980 allowed tenants to purchase council houses at a significantly discounted price under the 'Right to Buy' programme. Again, the intention was to encourage aspiration and entrepreneurship, while also fostering labour mobility in an effort to reduce the 'natural rate' of unemployment described by Friedman.

This was further underpinned by 'mortgage interest relief at source', or MIRAS. In the 1983 budget Geoffrey Howe raised this tax allowance from £25,000 to £30,000, while unmarried couples with joint mortgages could pool their allowances to £60,000. This provision, known as Multiple Mortgage Tax Relief, remained in place until the 1988 budget, when Nigel Lawson ended the option to pool allowances, from August 1988. Lawson later expressed regret at not having implemented the change with effect from the time of the budget because a rush to beat the deadline poured fuel on to the fire of an already rambunctious housing boom.

Millions of homes were sold off under the extremely popular Right to Buy scheme, and by the end of the Thatcher period owner-occupied housing had risen by a fifth, from 55% in 1979 to some 66% of the total. The problem was that little or no thought was given to replacing the social housing sold. In the thirty years from 1948 council house building never fell below 100,000 a year, and in some years it exceeded 250,000. By the end of the 1980s less than 20,000 council houses were being built each year.

For all the hype and the hopes of the government, whether or not privatization led to higher productivity is hard to discern. According to the official history of privatization, the measured productivity of privatized utilities was higher in the 1990s than the 1980s, but this seems to have been down to the adoption of new technologies as much as anything else.[19]

TACKLING TRADE UNION POWER.

Following the 1978–79 Winter of Discontent, public sympathy for the trade union movement was in short supply, and there was widespread agreement across most of the political spectrum that trade union power had become excessive, that is was damaging the economy, and that is had to be reined in. The Thatcher governments took advantage of this consensus to confront organized labour with a progressively more forceful succession of laws and actions designed to moderate unions' influence significantly, to inject greater flexibility into the labour market and to raise productivity.

The first step that was taken was to restrict, and then abolish, closed-shop agreements. Thereafter, secondary strikes and picketing were outlawed to ensure that industrial disputes remained firmly between employees and their immediate employers only; membership ballots were required for the election of union officials, for sanctioning the existence of political funds, and for industrial action; and unions were made liable for damages arising from industrial action. Many of these measures had been proposed by the Wilson government of the late 1960s and enacted by the Heath government of the early 1970s, but trade union opposition at the time meant that those initiatives were rapidly abandoned.[20] The Thatcher governments made greater headway in part because they avoided the error of trying to do everything at once.

The miners' strike of 1984 proved to be a further crucial episode in the assault on the unions. The Conservative Party had been seared by the Heath government's defeats at the hands of the National Union of Mineworkers (NUM) in the early 1970s, and Thatcher was determined to avoid a similar debacle. She also understood the broader political importance of vanquishing what was, in the early 1980s, one of the last bastions of union militancy, if not the movement's vanguard. She saw the miners, or at least their leaders, as 'the enemy within', and she prepared assiduously for a confrontation that she knew would come, even backing away from a conflict in 1981 because she was not yet convinced that she could prevail.

When conflict with the miners occurred over the issue of pit closures, the government was well primed, not least in the sense that coal stockpiles were high. It was also lucky that the NUM's leader Arthur Scargill was an unreconstructed Marxist: a rabble-rouser lacking in political subtlety, who alienated the political middle ground. Nevertheless, it was a ghastly, often violent, year-long strike that disrupted the economy and resulted in huge financial and social distress for the miners, their families and their communities, which subsequently received only limited government support. Ultimately, however, the government's victory did more than just facilitate much-needed reform of the mining industry: together with the following year's assault on the print unions in London, it marked an important turning point in UK industrial relations.

By the end of the 1980s the balance of power in the labour market had shifted conclusively. Trade union membership fell from some 52% of those employed in 1979 to around 37% in 1990, while the number of days lost to strikes averaged just over 6 million a year in the 1980s (including 27 million days in 1984 alone) as against an average of around 13 million a year during the 1970s.

However, the reduction in both union membership and militancy was not entirely down to the government's legislative programme and a few stage-managed confrontations. It also reflected the collapse in manufacturing sector output and employment. Indeed, this was arguably the most important consideration.

FLAWED REVOLUTION

The Thatcher years evoke sharply divergent opinions and emotions, which is appropriate for a prime minister whose style was uncompromising and who people were either with or against. For the same reasons, the period and its legacies are more than usually subject to myths, half-truths and misrepresentations, with judgements indelibly coloured by politics and philosophy, not to forget class, profession and geography.

What is not open to doubt is that the UK was at a crossroads in 1979. The widespread perception, both internally and around the world, was that the country's relative decline had accelerated – had maybe even become terminal – and that the UK was mired in a swamp of inflation, toxic industrial relations, onerous government intervention and suffocating levels of taxation. There was therefore a strong desire for, or at least an acceptance of, a change of tack, and a release from what many viewed as a shabby purgatory. Indeed, it is difficult but to conclude that whoever came to power in that year would have had to operate in a different fashion and pursue a different agenda from those of preceding governments.

Against this backdrop, Margaret Thatcher clearly struck a particular chord with the electorate. However simplistic it might have looked to her critics, her powerfully articulated commitment to sound money, laissez-faire, nationalism and supposed common-sense values was appealing to many at the time, representing as it did a clean break with recent failures and disappointments. She offered an alternative vision, and one that held out the prospect of a return to past glories for a country that had seemingly lost its way.

Engineering significant and enduring change in both economic performance and national self-esteem proved a tough challenge, however. Individual economies are complex and reflexive systems inextricably linked into other complex and reflexive systems. Disruptive events have a habit of interceding with great regularity and considerable force. Some of the electorate were sympathetic to the government's agenda. Many rather less so.

Although it can be argued that Britain changed dramatically under Thatcher's leadership, that she fundamentally shifted the locus of political debate, and that the 1970s appeared a far off place by the time she left office in 1990, significant societal evolution was to be expected over a ten-year period. Moreover, the 1980s had rather more in common with other post-war epochs than is sometimes realized.

Unpleasant trade-offs, unintended consequences, and painful setbacks proved to be as unavoidable as ever. Strongly held principles inevitably gave way to practicalities and seat of the pants ad hocery. The promised land of a clear and simple macro policy panacea remained out of reach. The political manipulation of the business cycle continued, often in crass fashion. For all the often fiery rhetoric, there was little consistency of strategy. Policy roles and responsibilities were neither clear nor stable. Transparency and accountability in policy were patchy at best, completely absent at worst. Personal enmities intervened to make successful economic governance harder. Successes gave way to hubris and myopia, rendering mistakes and countervailing failures inevitable – and those mistakes and failures had damaging political consequences, ultimately not least for Thatcher herself.

The record shows that despite all the hyperbole and the hopes and fears, many aspects of the UK's economic performance in the 1980s proved all too familiar. And even what might be seen as victories were frequently short lived and were achieved only at great cost.

It was a time of errant economic forecasts, ungrounded optimism, dangerous oversights and policy error, most egregiously at the beginning of the decade and towards its end. The 1980s witnessed stop and go and stop again. It was an epoch when cyclical excess was confused with structural renaissance. It was a period in which the pound's value fluctuated wildly; where inflation was temporarily pacified, but subsequently rebounded alarmingly; and of persistently high and volatile interest rates. It was an era where, despite the sizeable boon of North Sea oil revenues, the external account once again plunged into unsustainable deficit. It was a phase when both the public sector and the tax burden proved hard to rein in.

The particular shortcomings of policy are numerous.

Initially, there was the almost-religious commitment to an MTFS noteworthy for its reliance on naive monetarist principles; to misguided judgements about the importance of the budget balance to the trajectory of monetary growth; to a misunderstanding of the dynamics of inflation expectations; and to an underappreciation of the importance of sterling to financial conditions. Rather than encouraging a smooth and relatively painless process of disinflation, the monetary restraint of 1979–81 amounted to catastrophic shock therapy that imposed huge costs on output and employment. It did not simply cut out the dead wood from the economy: it ended up destroying swathes of potentially viable manufacturing industry and putting millions on the unemployment register, the legacy of which was a lack of productive capacity and enormous social problems that reverberated for decades to come.

Later, changes in the formulation of the MTFS – and particularly the modification both of monetary target ranges and of the monetary targets themselves – created confusion and uncertainty and made it harder for policy credibility to be established.

Fiscal policy was misunderstood and misapplied, and its potency was underestimated. Furthermore, these shortcomings left too much onus on monetary policy stabilizing the economy. The fiscal stance lacked balance and was initially too tight, particularly in 1981, and it necessarily had to be loosened thereafter, even if furtively. However, fiscal policy was subsequently too expansive in the middle of the decade and during its latter stages, with the positive impact of lower direct taxation on consumer and business confidence proving particularly destabilizing. There was also an excessive reliance on one-off privatization receipts, a short-sighted failure to apply resources to public investment, and a disastrous and divisive effort to reframe local government finance. In the meantime, Britain became the most centralized country in western Europe.

North Sea oil revenues rose from 0.3% of GDP when Thatcher came to power to peak at almost 3% of GDP in 1984–85, before falling to trivial levels in the early 1990s. But for ideological reasons and political expediency, Britain's energy bonanza was frittered away on tax cuts skewed towards the upper income brackets rather than, for example, being invested for the future through infrastructure upgrades or the mechanism of a sovereign wealth fund.

The government failed to grasp the full consequences of financial deregulation. In particular, it underappreciated its distortionary effects on the monetary aggregates; the onus it left on official interest rates for macro-stabilization; its role in stoking an unsustainable housing boom; the perverse incentives it encouraged in banks and investment banks; and its damaging longer-term implications for financial stability.

Financial deregulation interacted with tax reform to encourage consumerism and materialism, and together with persistently high unemployment fostered an extraordinary rise in inequality that has never been remotely unwound. The UK's Gini coefficient* rose from around 24 to 34 during the Thatcher years, while income at the ninetieth percentile relative to that at the tenth percentile jumped from 3.1 to 4.4 and the share of income going to the richest 1% of the population more than doubled, from 3% to above 6%. Poverty rates also increased significantly, for working-age adults, for children and for pensioners, and by considerably more than they did in other advanced economies around this time.

Competition in product markets was no doubt enhanced by a series of overlapping and, on occasion, mutually reinforcing measures. However, some credit must also go to the delayed impact on trade barriers of joining the EEC, something that also encouraged economies of scale.

Work incentives were no doubt improved by tax reform, even if such initiatives were highly regressive and added significantly to the issue of inequality.

Trade union legislation, coupled with some elements of privatization and the frontal assault on the miners and print workers, helped to temper worker militancy and inject a greater element of flexibility into the jobs market, but it did so at considerable social cost, and wage inflation remained an issue throughout the period. Moreover, it was the catastrophic industrial recession of 1979–81 and the structural demise of manufacturing, rather than changes in labour laws, that were perhaps the most powerful factors in changing the balance of power in the labour market.

In broad terms, the record of privatization was mixed. Yes, some new markets were created, people had their eyes opened to new investment opportunities, and the sale of council houses bred aspiration, even if it again deepened the divide between the haves and the have nots. Elsewhere, public monopolies or quasi-monopolies just became private monopolies or quasi-monopolies, and their subsequent regulation has left a great deal to be desired.

There were also significant gaps in supply-side policy. In particular, public infrastructure investment was neglected, active labour market policies and research and development were persistently underfunded, and the government's record on education was poor. The share of national income allocated to public education declined throughout the 1980s and actually fell in real terms between 1979–80 and 1986–87.

Overall, however, for all the caveats and painful side effects, the new micro framework seems to have changed for the better the environment in which

---

* The Gini coefficient is the measure of statistical dispersion most commonly used to represent income or wealth inequality. A Gini coeffcient of 0 represents perfect equality, where all income or wealth values are the same. A Gini coefficient of 100 represents maximum inequality.

investment decisions and bargains between management and labour were made, and it also had direct positive effects on the use of capital and labour.

In coming to a comprehensive judgement about the Thatcher years, it is important to examine the UK's productivity performance. As Nobel laureate Paul Krugman put it: 'Productivity isn't everything, but in the long-run it is almost everything.'[21]

The strength of the UK's recovery in the 1980s was undoubtedly also accompanied by a significant rise in profit share and productivity growth, especially in manufacturing, relative to much of the previous decade and to the country's major competitors. GDP per capita expanded on average by just over 2% per annum, compared with a figure of 1.5% per annum between 1973 and 1979 and an average elsewhere of just under 2%. Britain did, therefore, close its long-standing 'productivity gap' somewhat.

As discussed above, detailed analysis suggests that much of this can be traced to higher total factor productivity, or efficiency in factor usage, rather than to increased capital accumulation or technological proficiency, where Britain remained something of a laggard.

All this said, there is always a strong cyclical element to productivity, as employment tends to lag output. This flattered the improvement in productivity between 1981 and 1989 just as it had exaggerated the initial decline in productivity in 1979–80.

For manufacturing, the average annual improvement in productivity over the course of 1979–89 was more than 4%, which again compares well both with the UK's European competitors and against the historical record. But in truth, it is not so dramatically different to what might have been expected to arise from an extended cyclical upswing where the absolute level of productivity was considerably lower than in its neighbours. Moreover, the productivity record in other sectors – financial services aside – is much less impressive.[22]

Perhaps the best conclusion to draw about productivity is that the 1980s saw the UK regain much of the ground that was lost during the 1970s. Britain was no longer generally considered to be the sickest man in Europe, but nor had the country exactly reinvented itself.

CHAPTER 6

Humiliation Gives Way to the 'NICE Decade'

The government has concluded that Britain's best interests can be served by suspending our membership of the exchange rate mechanism.

— Norman Lamont, September 1992[1]

AN UNLIKELY LEADER

John Major, born in 1943, came from humble, working class origins. He left school before he was 16, and after many years as a local councillor in south London he became an MP in 1979. He entered the cabinet only in 1987, and he held no prominent post until he became foreign secretary in July 1989. He held this post for just three months before taking over from Nigel Lawson as chancellor. Then, following the act of regicide against Margaret Thatcher by Conservative MPs, including much of her cabinet, just over a year later, in November 1990, he became prime minister. The dominant reason for his remarkable rise seems to have been that he was not Michael Heseltine, or, for that matter, any of the other senior party figures complicit in his predecessor's demise.

The seventeen months of Major's first administration, which prefaced his shock general election victory in April 1992, was a tough period for the British economy, and this makes his electoral success all the more extraordinary. The Conservatives' overall majority of twenty-one, their fourth successive victory, was a personal triumph for Major. For a while, his calm and reassuring demeanour put a human face on Thatcherism and encouraged the electorate to believe that there had already been a change of government. He was also wise enough to abandon the Community Charge, saving his party from losing hundreds of thousands more votes.

Major's success was also, however, a stunning indictment of an opposition Labour Party that had failed to convince the electorate it was ready to govern.

This is particularly the case where taxation was concerned. The fear remained that public spending would be allowed to run out of control under Labour, and that taxes would have to rise sharply to fund it.

Although the overall economic record of Major's second administration looks reasonably impressive from a distance and was to provide a rare benign inheritance for a Labour successor to a Conservative prime minister,[2] it will forever be defined by the Sterling Crisis of September 1992, after which both the political landscape and the opinion polls were transformed. Despite the achievements of the years between 1993 and 1997, the Tories' reputation for economic competence had been eviscerated.

The ejection of the pound from the ERM represented a political and economic upheaval from which neither Major nor his government could recover. The event also served to hothouse the vexed issue of Europe within the Conservative Party. Differences over Britain's prospective role in the European Community had been an important factor in the internal coup that led to the removal of Margaret Thatcher from Downing Street in November 1990. But for Major, Europe became an irresolvable conundrum with which he had to grapple for the next four and a half years.

BUST FOLLOWS BOOM AGAIN

The UK economy initially seemed relatively immune to the high level of interest rates that was the legacy of the Lawson boom, but it tumbled into a deep recession in the second half of 1990, with house prices collapsing and with onerous levels of private sector debt sparking severe balance sheet adjustments for both consumers and businesses. The private sector financial balance swung from a deficit of around 6% of GDP in 1989 to a surplus of similar proportions in 1991 and 1992, as households and firms cut back on investment and saved cash to pay down debt. In the process, the personal saving ratio jumped from around 4% of post-tax income to some 12%.

Real GDP declined for six quarters out of eight, and it barely increased at all in the other two. The peak-to-trough decline in output is now estimated at more than 2%, with gross fixed capital formation falling by more than 13% and the ratio of business investment to GDP establishing a post-war low relative to its long-term mean. The large positive output gap that had characterized the latter stages of the 1980s was dramatically reversed. The headline unemployment rate, which had bottomed out at around 7% of the workforce in the first half of 1990, was back above 10% by the end of 1992 and stayed there until early 1994. Long-term unemployment rose beyond 4% before subsiding in the middle of the decade. In contrast to the early 1980s, however, the fallout from this downturn was focused more on white-collar workers than on those employed in manufacturing. The people who had benefitted most during the previous boom were frequently the biggest casualties of the bust.

As recession made it harder for individuals and companies to repay their debts, housing repossessions reached a record high. There was also what was termed 'a small banks crisis'. At one stage, the Bank of England had forty small banks under surveillance, and it was forced to help some of them secure long-term funding and others to wind down their activities. In the end, twenty-five banks failed in the early 1990s.

Burgeoning excess capacity at the onset of the new decade encouraged inflation to fall steeply. Having peaked in high single figures in mid 1991 on a CPI basis, it dropped below 4% in mid 1992 and was not to return above that threshold until 2008. Inflation expectations followed suit. The long-standing tendency for wages and prices to feed off one another in a vicious upward spiral was finally ended.

Within the constraints of the ERM, sterling interest rates were cut seven times in 1991, falling from 14% in January to 10.5% in September. However, with inflation also in rapid decline, real borrowing costs and monetary conditions in general remained punishing for such a depressed economy.

Major appointed Norman Lamont as his chancellor. Lamont was a late developer in political terms, having been passed over numerous times where senior cabinet positions were concerned. A Cambridge-trained economist, he had been a junior Treasury minister since 1986, serving under both Nigel Lawson and, briefly, Major himself. He also ran Major's successful campaign for the Tory leadership in late 1990. A sceptic about both Europe and fixed exchange rates, and very much against EMU, he supported the UK's ERM membership merely as a short-term disinflationary device.

The recession and the policy response to it resulted in a dramatic deterioration in the headline fiscal position. The broadly defined headline budget balance swung from a small surplus in 1988–89 and 1989–90, as the Lawson boom peaked, to a deficit of almost 8% of GDP in 1993–94. This represented what was then the largest shortfall of the post-war era. In his first budget, in March 1991, Lamont considered raising direct taxes, as it was clear that Lawson's mid-1980s cuts had dangerously denuded the income tax base. But with a general election on the horizon, this strategy was rejected. Instead, mortgage interest tax relief was moderated, and VAT was raised from 15% to 17.5% to pay for an across-the-board reduction in the widely despised Community Charge and a two percentage point cut in corporation tax.

In his second budget, brought down just before the 1992 election, caution was less in evidence. The direct tax burden was reduced through the introduction of a new 20% income tax band, and public spending plans, not least capital outlays, were boosted.

With monetary policy constrained by sterling's ERM membership over the course of the first two years of Major's premiership, fiscal policy was employed to take up at least some of the slack. The rise in the share of total government spending in GDP seen towards the end of the Thatcher era accelerated, peaking at around 46%; net public investment spending was increased sharply to make up for some of the restraint of the previous decade; and the cyclically adjusted budget deficit expanded by some three percentage points of GDP between 1989–90 and 1992–93, including a two percentage point deterioration in 1992 alone. This represented a significant pre-election fiscal expansion.

Fiscal policy could only do so much to ameliorate the recession, however, and ERM membership was increasingly blamed for the depth and obstinacy of the UK's downturn. Calls for a more competitive exchange rate became more commonplace, especially as sterling also remained strong against the US dollar. Some commentators even began to compare Britain's ERM membership with the decision to return to the Gold Standard in 1925.[3]

EXTERNAL EVENTS INTERVENE

Major indicated that the UK would look to move to the narrower ERM bands employed by the system's stronger currencies as soon as possible (this was also a 1992 Conservative Party manifesto pledge), but this never materialized. Rather, the pros and cons of a devaluation within the existing system were already being explored within Whitehall as early as the autumn of 1991 – just a year after sterling had joined. The principal problem confronting the UK was German reunification. As the Bank of England acknowledged in early 1991, in a world of floating exchange rates, economic theory implied that reunification should result in a once-and-for-all increase in the Deutschmark's real value.[4]

A realignment of the ERM based on a German revaluation lacked widespread support, however. Since the last general recalibration of central parities in January 1987, the ERM had increasingly been viewed by its members as a 'fixed', rather than a 'fixed but adjustable', exchange rate system. After France suffered a series of damaging devaluations in the early 1980s, and with EMU increasingly in its sights, the French had become particularly wedded to a hard currency policy known as 'Le Franc Fort'. In the absence of any formal change in central parities, the warranted adjustment in the real Deutschmark exchange rate could come about only via lower inflation in the other ERM member states than in Germany.

Reunification was causing the home of the ERM's anchor currency to overheat. Chancellor Helmut Kohl had decided to overrule the monetary conservatives at the Bundesbank for political reasons, and to base German monetary union on the notion of parity between the international safe haven that was the West German Deutschmark and the near-worthless, previously unconvertible East German Ostmark. At the same time, the process of rapidly modernizing the backward East German economy extended the boom of the late 1980s and led to a sharp expansion of the budget deficit. Germany's cyclically adjusted budget balance went from approximate balance in 1989 to a deficit of around 4.5% of GDP in 1991 and 1992. In this environment, CPI inflation picked up to very un-German rates of more than 3.5% in 1991 and 4% in 1992.[5] Moreover, the nation began to run a current account deficit for the first time in a decade. This deterioration in Germany's fundamentals was insufficient to arrest the upward pressure on the Deutschmark however.

Confronted by this difficult set of circumstances, the Bundesbank, as guardian of the nation's steadfast commitment to price stability, believed that it had no option but to tighten monetary policy aggressively. By late 1991 the discount rate and the Lombard rate – the German central bank's two key policy interest rates, between which money market rates oscillated – were set at 8% and 9.75%, respectively. With Lamont and Major reluctant to push UK rates up because of the weakness of the domestic economy, this meant that UK–German interest rate differentials were wafer thin. The spread between UK and German short-term market rates had averaged above six percentage points since 1985, yet by late 1991 the disparity was less than one percentage point. With such a slim interest rate premium to reflect the long-standing risks associated with holding sterling, the UK's currency was acutely vulnerable.

Unlike his worldly wise predecessor Karl Otto Poehl, the Bundesbank's new president, Helmut Schlesinger, was a very traditional German central banker. He had spent his entire career at the 'Buba' and viewed the ERM as a political apparatus that threatened to distract him and his colleagues from their central task of keeping domestic prices stable. Schlesinger was therefore not greatly disposed to offer Britain a sympathetic ear. By late 1991 the UK government was on a collision course with the German central bank.

DECEPTIVE CALM

Nevertheless, in the aftermath of his unexpected election victory, Major, at the height of his authority, was in an optimistic frame of mind where the ERM was concerned. Sterling seemed to have overcome a wobble around the turn of the year, during which it fell below DM2.84, to the extent that Lamont felt able to cut UK official rates further in early May 1992, by half a percentage point to 10%. As a consequence, the gap with German short rates vanished almost completely. But rather than viewing this as a potential risk, there was talk in Whitehall that the UK might be able to decouple its interest rates from

Germany, and even that the pound could displace the Deutschmark as the ERM's anchor.

This was to prove tragically hubristic. Broader European issues were about to intervene greatly to complicate the prime minister's task in economic policymaking and elsewhere.

Keen to differentiate his approach to the EEC from the abrasive tone of his predecessor and to keep Britain close to the centre of the European debate, Major had achieved some notable diplomatic successes towards the end of 1991 during the negotiations for what was to become the Maastricht Treaty. His task was to square the circle of his party's meagre enthusiasm for 'more Europe' with the desire of the rest of the community to finalize both a timetable and the economic criteria for EMU, to establish a new social policy framework and to sketch out a roadmap for the greater political integration that would transform the European Community into the European Union.[6]

This was a treacherous path to tread, especially with a bitter Margaret Thatcher making mischief on the backbenches by providing regular encouragement to dyed-in-the-wool Eurosceptics and reversing her previous antipathy to referenda on important constitutional issues. Nevertheless, ably supported by his foreign secretary, Douglas Hurd, Major managed, after extensive negotiations, to have the word 'federal' dropped from the treaty, to secure an opt-out for the UK from the treaty's Social Chapter on issues such as employment rights and health and safety at work, and to ensure that parliament would make the final decision on any UK commitment to EMU. He could also reasonably argue that the Maastricht Treaty's principle of 'subsidiarity' meant that more decisions would be devolved to the national level.

Despite some mutterings of discontent, the initial response to these efforts to protect British interests while not preventing others from pursuing theirs was sufficiently positive in the press, and acquiescent across the Conservative Party, that European issues were largely absent from his successful April 1992 election campaign.

THE HONEYMOON ENDS

The party truce did not last long, however. The election saw fifty-odd Tory Europhile MPs retire, many of whom were replaced by more Eurosceptic members. Thatcher, still rancorous about her defenestration, continued to provide a rallying point for Eurosceptic opinion. And Major had yet to deliver the parliamentary ratification of the Maastricht Treaty. There had seemed no urgency to do so in the run-up to the election. He had his party's support, the opposition Labour Party was onside, and other countries would undoubtedly take their time. There were also other important bills to see through a busy parliamentary timetable.

Then, in early June 1992, just a month before Britain assumed the six-month rotating presidency of the European Community, Denmark rejected Maastricht in a referendum. The rule was that if even one country failed to ratify the treaty, it was null and void. Thatcher hailed the result as a victory for democracy and called for a halt to the British ratification process. Others on the right of the Conservative Party followed suit. Demands grew for the complete abandonment of the treaty.

Major had no choice but to delay the Maastricht-related legislation, especially when opposition leader John Smith sought to maximize the divisions in the Tory party by insisting Labour would only vote for the treaty if the Social Chapter was re-inserted. A small number of Tory rebels could now sink the whole process. In the end it was decided to postpone the completion of the ratification process until after a second Danish referendum and after a similar plebiscite, scheduled for 20 September, had been held in France.

The political vacuum over the early summer was filled by concern about the economy's continued weakness, and about the ERM's, and Germany's, chokehold on UK monetary policy. In the markets, meanwhile, the Danish referendum result raised questions over the very sustainability of the ERM. After all, if it was not intended as a means for beating a path towards EMU, what was it for? Speculators began to set their sights on the weaker currencies in the system, and increasingly this group included sterling.

Still worried about the strength of post-reunification monetary growth, the Bundesbank was reluctant to sanction any easing of interest rate policy. Meanwhile, US interest rates were at thirty-year lows, sparking further international capital flows into the German currency and adding to the strains in the ERM. France and Italy, however, remained opposed to any devaluation of their currencies, thus ruling out a wide-ranging realignment of the system.

Against this backdrop, UK officials were again asked to review the exchange rate policy options, although in an echo of the devaluation debate of the mid 1960s, the cabinet was not involved. The view that emerged from Chief Economic Advisor Alan Budd and backed up by Terry Burns, who was now Permanent Secretary to the Treasury, was that devaluation should be eschewed unless it was part of a formal Deutschmark revaluation.

The principal concern was that any other form of devaluation within the ERM would lead to higher UK interest rates, not lower ones, as it would result in a sharp rise in sterling's risk premium. Policy credibility would be badly damaged and further downward adjustments in the currency likely. Furthermore, based on the experience of the mid-to-late 1980s, any benefits to the UK's competitiveness of a lower currency would be fleeting, as higher import prices would rapidly push up both domestic costs and inflation. This was a highly pessimistic view. Between 1986 and 1988 excess capacity in the economy was rapidly disappearing and the demand for labour was strong, yet the UK's negative output gap in 1992 was approaching some 4% of GDP: a much less sanguine environment for wage and price setters.

The only caveat to Budd's judgement about the downside of a unilateral parity adjustment was that a very large devaluation of, say, 20% might convince investors that the next move in sterling was likely to be up. The dynamics of such a departure were highly uncertain, however, and it would in any case be unacceptable to the other ERM members.

There were a few dissenting voices in Whitehall, but the Budd–Burns thesis that there was little or no practical alternative to the exchange rate status quo in the absence of a comprehensive recalibration of parities rapidly came to dominate the government playbook. What is more, these conclusions were also expressed with increasing fervour by Major and Lamont.[7] Of course, no prime minister or chancellor should publicly acknowledge that he or she is considering a devaluation. To do so is to guarantee that it happens. But the willingness of Major and Lamont to go beyond the customary ritual denials of any policy adjustment, and to double down repeatedly on the UK's commitment to the existing ERM parity, verged on foolishness. They painted themselves into a corner. As long as France, in particular, vetoed a general realignment of the system, the UK had only two choices: stick with the existing parity and endure the associated costs; or abandon the system altogether, and once again have to seek out and establish confidence in an entirely new macro policy anchor.

The hope was that the situation might improve following a positive vote in France's Maastricht referendum. After all, unlike Denmark, France was at the core of the entire project. Opinion polls suggested that the French vote was likely to be close run, however, and the risk was therefore of even greater turmoil on the foreign exchanges. A rate hike was considered to build confidence in sterling, but the idea garnered little official or political support. It would have only added fuel to the fire of the Eurosceptics, while there were growing concerns about not just the frailty of the real economy but about outright deflation, and the potential for associated financial sector distress. A particular worry was that negative equity in the housing market already stood at some £6 billion, or the equivalent of 1% of GDP.[8]

THE GATHERING STORM

It was against this backdrop that the UK authorities made a series of unforced errors.

First, at the beginning of July 1992, National Savings issued a high-interest-rate bond with a guaranteed return of more than 10%.[9] This went down badly with the building societies, which were struggling to attract deposits. The

Treasury therefore cut the return on offer to 9.7%, and policymakers thereby indicated to the markets that they could not afford to allow interest rates to rise.

Then, in the middle of the month, the Bundesbank raised its discount rate, the lower boundary for German short-term money market rates, by three quarters of a percentage point to 8.75%. In a sign that the German central bank was not entirely immune to the tensions in the ERM, the Lombard rate, the upper boundary for market rates, was left at 9.75%. Nevertheless, other European central banks followed the Bundesbank's example and hiked rates to underpin their currencies. But the Bank of England did not, meaning that sterling unsurprisingly lost further ground within the system, and in early August it fell below the so-called divergence level that obligated a country to begin to actively defend its currency.[10]

Finally, another intrusion was made by the Treasury to prevent mortgage rates rising: it cut the returns on offer to investors in National Savings again.

Major and Lamont were becoming increasingly troubled, to the extent that the latter seems to have tried, unsuccessfully, to convince the prime minister to suspend sterling's membership of the system. In the meantime, an ERM crisis contingency plan was assembled at the Bank of England by Eddie George (who would go to become its governor in 1993). The plan had three stages: large covert purchases of the pound followed by massive public intervention in its support and, as a last resort, a rise in interest rates.

At the same time, diplomatic efforts to persuade France of the merits of a general ERM realignment, and to encourage the Bundesbank to change tack and cut official interest rates, were increased. For the French to voluntarily abandon Le Franc Fort after nine years of painful sacrifice would have amounted to a catastrophic political defeat for President Mitterrand, however, and it would also have guaranteed that the French Maastricht referendum vote would be lost. As for the Bundesbank, the German central bank considered its independence to be sacrosanct, and it was particularly reluctant to make public policy concessions in response to external pressure. Behind the scenes, meanwhile, Helmut Schlesinger and his colleagues were increasingly convinced that the UK's worsening fundamentals were such that a sterling devaluation was unavoidable.

This was the background to one of the more acrimonious international gatherings of policymakers of recent economic history. Lamont chaired the regular EEC finance ministers' meeting in early September in Bath. In an extraordinarily maladroit example of diplomacy, rather than striving for consensus on how to approach what was likely to be a challenging period ahead for all ERM members, he launched a full-frontal attack on German macro policy and sought to browbeat the Bundesbank president into at least guaranteeing that the German central bank would not tighten monetary policy any further. This was not what was done at these events. It was certainly not what was done to the Bundesbank. It was at the very least tone deaf, and at most a spectacular own goal – one that smacked of arrogance and desperation. An incandescent Schlesinger nearly walked out.

In the end, it was only the intervention of the emollient Terry Burns that avoided a rift in Anglo-German relations that would have guaranteed an immediate ERM meltdown when markets opened the following Monday. A communiqué was cobbled together that included the phrase: 'The Bundesbank in present circumstances has no intention to increase rates.' Lamont tried to spin this as a victory. Schlesinger agreed to it only because he thought it was completely vacuous. In the meantime, the chancellor's antics had exhausted much of the remaining sympathy the other ERM members might have had for the UK's predicament.

There is also evidence that if there had been agreement on a general realignment of parities around this time, the Bundesbank would have been open to a rate cut. By ploughing his own wayward furrow, Lamont scuppered the last chance for the UK government to avoid the debacle that befell it a few days later.

THINGS COME TO A HEAD

Although Major was presumably livid about his chancellor's diplomatic deficit, his response to what went on in Bath was to raise the 'no sterling devaluation' rhetoric another notch. However, by this stage the die was cast. Speculation about a realignment built, with the Italian lira the first target. Despite heavy intervention in its support by the Banca d'Italia and the Bundesbank, on 12 September the Italian government agreed to a 7% parity adjustment. However, in response to what amounted to only a minor tightening in German financial conditions, the Bundesbank offered a quarter-point cut in its Lombard rate. This again suggested that a broader realignment would have resulted in a larger German interest rate quid pro quo.

At a secret meeting on Monday 14 September, senior Treasury and Bank of England officials, including Alan Budd and the bank's newly appointed chief economist Mervyn King, belatedly sought to persuade German officials, including the Bundesbank's chief economist Otmar Issing, that DM2.95 was a sustainable rate for the pound. They left their hosts unconvinced. The UK was, after all, still running an external deficit equivalent to around 1.5% of GDP, even though the economy was cyclically acutely depressed.

The markets increasingly echoed the judgement of the German authorities. Sterling was widely viewed as the next domino to fall. Back in Whitehall, the atmosphere darkened. With the French Maastricht referendum offering the only possible hope of salvation for the pound, Major and Lamont again discussed sterling withdrawal from the system, flirting with the argument that membership had, after all, done its disinflationary job. But in the end they baulked at such a move.

The pound came under mounting selling pressure on the Tuesday, and despite heavy intervention in its support it traded barely above its ERM floor of DM2.7780. Then, that night, the news broke that Schlesinger had suggested in an interview with the *Handelsblatt* newspaper that it would have been better for all concerned if the lira devaluation had instead been a general realignment. He had naively assumed that he had been speaking off the record. Lamont was furious. He demanded a retraction and got one. The German central bank duly stated that its president's injudicious remarks were not authorized, and that what was reported was not what he intended to say. Lamont also issued yet another uncompromising statement that sterling would not be devalued. By this stage, however, it is difficult to imagine that the chancellor believed it, and in any case the markets were no longer listening. They were primed to call the British government's bluff.

DISASTER

What transpired on 16 September 1992, now widely referred to as 'Black Wednesday', was a national humiliation. It cast a pall of gloom over the Treasury and the Bank of England for years, and it also stripped Major of his authority and much of his already-fragile self-confidence. For the next four and a half years he was, in prime ministerial terms, a 'dead man walking'. From that point until the general election of 1997, the Conservatives were never ahead in the opinion polls, although sterling's expulsion from the ERM did, ironically, provide the economy with something akin to blessed relief in due course.

The day began with a tsunami of sterling sales on the European foreign exchanges that, according to the ERM's rules of engagement, had to be met by unconstrained Bank of England intervention. The problem was that the pound was under siege from speculators convinced that devaluation was inevitable. Many officials have subsequently said that, in watching the market price action that morning, they knew immediately that the game was up. Nevertheless, after urgent discussions with the Treasury and the Bank of England, Lamont convinced the prime minister that interest rates should go up, and by a significant amount, to preserve sterling's existing parity. At 11.00 a.m., a two percentage point rate hike, to 12%, was announced – the first tightening of monetary policy since the UK joined the system. The pound, however,

failed to budge. It remained stuck at its ERM floor, while the central bank
continued desperately to support it.

The morning also saw a number of senior cabinet ministers with no formal
responsibility for monetary policy corralled together by the prime minister to
experience events as they unfolded and to debate strategy. This was unusual,
to say the least, and was seen as entirely inappropriate by some Treasury and
Bank of England officials. As Kenneth Clarke, the home secretary, later appo-
sitely put it: 'We were there to dip our hands in the blood.'[11]

There have also been suggestions that the prime minister broke down
at one stage, the collapse of the centrepiece of his economic strategy – and,
potentially, of his administration – too much for him. True or not – and it
should be said that the rumours have subsequently been vociferously denied
by many of the day's key actors, including Major himself – they hint at the
chaotic progress of events that day.

At 2.15 p.m. a further rate hike to 15%, effective the next day, was
announced, but again to no avail. The frantic intervention in support of the
pound continued, with the Bank of England in effect the only purchaser of
sterling in the market. Ultimately, approaching $28 billion was spent, which
was to leave the Bank's net reserve position negative to the tune of some
$15 billion.[12] The UK has not engaged in foreign exchange intervention since.

Extraordinarily, however, this all proved to be merely window dressing.
After the failure of the initial rate hike, the chancellor, the prime minister and
the other senior cabinet members brought in to share in the decision-making
process recognized that sterling's withdrawal from the ERM was unavoidable. Thereafter, the UK authorities were merely going through the motions,
putting up a show of resistance to demonstrate to the rest of Europe and the
markets that they cared. It was clear not only that the rate hikes had failed to
stem the tide of sterling sales, but also that the elevated structure of interest
rates was completely unsustainable. It was just a matter of getting through to
the close of the trading day, and as far as possible meeting the legal requirements of European treaties.

One has to question, however, where any legal challenge to the UK government would have come from had Major and Lamont accepted the inevitable
when trading began, or indeed in the middle of the day. Whether any other
ERM member would have trod a similar path, and in the process frittered
away a significant portion of the nation's foreign currency reserves, is doubtful. In hindsight, and especially given the way latter-day British governments
have behaved towards the rule of international law, the probity of the Major
administration in this regard is remarkable.

When the European exchanges officially closed for the day and the legal
niceties had been observed, sterling was suspended from the system. The

government made a last-ditch effort to persuade other members to suspend the entire ERM but, unsurprisingly, their entreaties fell on deaf ears. Later that evening the decision to raise rates to 15% was reversed, and the next day so was the first two-percentage-point hike to 12%.

Subsequently, the British government sought to blame everyone but itself, reserving particular ire for the German government and the Bundesbank. This was especially the case when, after the French government only narrowly won its Maastricht referendum and the franc came under pressure, Chancellor Kohl went out of his way to encourage the German central bank to help the beleaguered French currency. In truth, though, most of the culpability for Black Wednesday clearly lay at home.

First of all, the time chosen for sterling's entry into the system was anything but 'ripe'. In October 1990 the collapse of the inflationary Lawson boom and the effects of German reunification had left the UK and Germany travelling along very different trajectories and requiring very different macroeconomic policy mixes. The tensions this encouraged within the system were insurmountable.

Sterling's central parity of DM2.95, meanwhile, was too high. Greater effort should have gone into securing a more competitive exchange rate; one that embodied some leeway in the event of the economy underperforming expectations, as indeed it subsequently did. Together with the eye-watering level of real interest rates that prevailed in 1990–92, DM2.95 imposed far too tight a squeeze on the economy. As some officials recognized in the run-up to sterling's ejection from the system, without significant changes in policy, the country was headed for outright deflation and serious financial turmoil. Fiscal laxity in 1991 and 1992 – understandable in the context of a deep recession, but also partly in pursuit of electoral gain – only added to the perception of an unsustainable exchange rate configuration.

As for the Treasury's conclusion that devaluation within the ERM would inevitably raise inflation, and result in higher interest rates rather than greater domestic policy freedom, it was far too strongly held. It reflected the experience of the late 1980s, when cyclical conditions were manifestly more robust, excess capacity was exhausted and inflationary pressures were much more intense. Things had moved on.

Turning to the tactics that the UK authorities employed during this period, it is hard but to conclude that important mistakes were made at almost every turn.

First, the government did not have to treat the ERM as quite so much of a fixed-rate exchange rate system. In this sense, Thatcher had perhaps been right – if, indeed, this was her true opinion prior to entry. In the early to mid 1980s other nations had taken time to acclimatize to the strictures of the ERM, going through a series of initial parity realignments. Moreover, following the Maastricht Treaty, the UK, in contrast to other members, was not committed to using the ERM as a glide path to EMU.

Second, the UK should have raised rates – even to a limited extent – when sterling encountered a rough patch at the end of 1991. A significant gap was left in the authorities' credibility by the fact that the UK had never tightened monetary policy as a member of the system by the time the pound came under more acute pressure the following year, and the gap was exacerbated by the decisions taken around the returns on National Savings.

Third, intervention in support of the pound should have begun earlier, while the defence of sterling would also have been helped by a more sophis-ticated interest rate structure. Other members had developed mechanisms to push short-term interest rates up to three figures or more in financial markets without significantly impacting domestic borrowing costs.

Fourth, the UK was too isolated, and it was often too arrogant in its deal-ings with other members of the system. Britain was never an ERM insider, and relations with the rest of the EEC had never fully recovered from the Thatcher era. Many Treasury and Bank of England officials seemed to see themselves as superior to their European counterparts, and they therefore failed to cultivate the connections and external support they might one day need. Britain, mean-while, was seen by many Europeans as an opportunistic latecomer: a country that was only too happy to play fast and loose with the rules and conventions of the ERM, and one whose underlying commitment to the system fell short of that of others. The behaviour of Norman Lamont towards the president of the Bundesbank at the disastrous Bath finance ministers' meeting seemed to provide a convenient case in point.

Finally, there was the progressive elevation of the exchange rate by Major and Lamont into something akin to a Roman legion's standard. The political stakes around devaluation were repeatedly raised as the crisis unfolded. The maintenance of the DM2.95 central rate was presented as a panacea for the UK's economic ills, when the reality was that addressing Britain's range of deep-seated structural problems, which went back decades, required a range of interlocking strategies. The government gave the markets a target – again as Thatcher had feared – and left itself no escape route.

AFTERMATH

Sterling's ejection from the ERM saw it fall rapidly towards DM2.50. In trade-weighted terms, the pound dropped some 20% by the end of 1992. It steadied thereafter but remained 15–20% lower than its September 1992 level for the remainder of the parliament.

Both Major and Lamont considered resignation in the immediate aftermath of Black Wednesday, but in the end they both took the decision to stay on. Indeed, Lamont was soon dropping less-than-subtle hints that he was far from unhappy to be released from the straitjacket of the ERM.

Meanwhile, there was a need to rapidly establish a credible new framework for monetary policy while reining in the large budget deficit and providing much-needed support to a still acutely depressed economy. With anti-EEC feeling running high within the Conservative Party, there was no rush to seek to ratify the Maastricht Treaty.

The Treasury and the Bank of England remained wary of the potential for higher borrowing costs that had been at the core of the government's case against unilateral devaluation within the ERM, and they were cautious about proceeding with cuts in official interest rates. Although many commentators urged a dramatic volte-face, the initial adjustment in domestic monetary policy was confined to a single-percentage-point cut on 22 September. Three further tentative one-percentage-point adjustments were then made over the next four months.

The new monetary regime, for which the Bank of England's chief economist and future governor Mervyn King provided considerable input, was launched in October, with details set out in a letter from Lamont to the House of Commons Treasury Select Committee. Following the example of New Zealand and Canada, and ironically taking on aspects of the Bundesbank's approach, the UK adopted a formal 1–4% target for underlying annual inflation for the rest of the parliament, with the stated desire being to see the rate in the lower half of the range by the time of the next general election.[13] The thinking was that if this target was hit, it would keep inflation low enough that the public would not be constantly considering how to keep up with it from day to day but also sufficiently high to aid economic adjustment and give the Bank of England enough room to set real interest rates low enough to deal with any downturn.

It is also worth bearing in mind that the direct targeting of inflation was just about the only remaining regime open to UK policymakers. Everything else had been tried over previous decades and had been found wanting or had been abandoned because of policy errors.

At the time of the new strategy's announcement, the annual rate of change in the targeted retail price index less mortgage interest costs (known as RPIX) was running just below the 4% level. The strategy to meet the target was to be based on regular assessment of asset prices, the exchange rate and the trends in both narrow and broad money, together with a much greater degree of transparency and accountability for policymakers.[14] This was to extend to the publication of a note on the regular monthly meetings between the chancellor and the governor of the Bank of England and to the release of a detailed quarterly 'Inflation Report' by the Bank of England, together with full explanations of the rationale behind policy changes. Furthermore, a group of seven independent advisors, or 'wise men', was appointed to provide supplementary analysis and forecasts to the government.[15]

After more than fifty years of playing second fiddle to the Treasury where monetary policy was concerned, the Bank of England's influence was significantly increased by the changes ushered in after Black Wednesday. Indeed, influenced by Nigel Lawson's brief flirtation with central bank independence in 1988, Lamont had wanted to go further still, but he was unable to convince Major, who thought that interest rate decisions ought to remain directly accountable to parliament. In addition, he was reluctant to see the Bank of England, rather than the government, receive the plaudits for defeating inflation.

As it transpired, because of the softness of the labour market and the broader overhang of excess capacity, together with the weakness of private sector balance sheets, the Bank was rather more sanguine about the post-devaluation prospects for inflation than the Treasury had been. And despite the persistently weak exchange rate, inflation continued to fall, running between 2% and 3% during 1993. Indeed, although sterling remained acutely depressed in trade-weighted terms for the next four years, inflation was benign throughout the remainder of the Conservatives' time in office.

Turning to fiscal policy, it too needed a significant reorientation in the wake of sterling's ejection from the ERM. The budget deficit was running at an unsustainable level, and the burden of public sector debt had been rising rapidly since the end of the previous decade. To bring government borrowing to heal, the March 1993 budget embodied a rising wedge of direct and indirect tax increases – £0.5 billion in the first year, £6.5 billion in the second and £10.25 billion in the third – together with greater public spending restraint.

Although the budget provoked a fiercely critical reaction – it was, after all, replete with broken election promises and was followed by major losses for the Tories in the May 1993 local elections – its reputation has been transformed over time. It is now widely regarded as being both politically courageous and essential to the stabilization of the public finances in the 1990s. In total, the cyclically adjusted budget balance was to improve from a deficit of around 5.5% of GDP in 1992–93 and 1993–94 to less than 1% of GDP in 1997–98. In the first year of Tony Blair's subsequent Labour government the headline deficit also accounted for less than 1% of GDP, and the net debt ratio was established on a consistently declining path.

While UK macro policy was being reorientated, both the prime minister and the chancellor were the targets of unrelenting criticism by the parliamentary opposition as well as often-vitriolic condemnation in the press. The latter was particularly the case for Lamont, who fell foul of a scurrilous tabloid scandal about his private life. Meanwhile, the once-close relationship between Major and Lamont fell apart.

Having for months largely withdrawn from public view, often leaving other ministers to articulate the government's new economic strategy, Lamont resigned towards the end of May 1993 rather than accept a cabinet demotion. Beyond his identification by the public as the principal personality behind the ERM debacle, he had lost the confidence of the cabinet and of a political party that was by now completely on the defensive.

By this stage Lamont was a bitter man. He felt betrayed and he subsequently pulled few punches in his criticisms of Major. He accused the prime minister of being unduly influenced by opinion polls, of being too short term in focus, and of generally failing to offer adequate leadership. He added that Major had vetoed his desire to give the Bank of England independence and had interfered excessively in the timing of interest rate cuts. He also suggested that Major had only kept him in his job to act as a lightning rod in the politically toxic post-ERM environment. Over subsequent years he continued to snipe at his former colleague from what became an increasingly Eurosceptic standpoint. Indeed, in 1994 Lamont became the first senior Conservative politician to raise the idea that the UK should contemplate leaving the EU. This did nothing to salve the party's post-ERM wounds.

A NEW BROOM AT THE TREASURY

Lamont's successor was Kenneth Clarke, an experienced politician and an ardent Europhile. While he was no trained economist, he had occupied a number of secondary economic roles in the cabinet over the years. He exuded good sense, was willing to listen to advice and had something of a common touch. In many ways he cut a similar avuncular figure to Jim Callaghan.

Despite his pro-European credentials, Clarke was savvy enough to realize that there was no prospect of an early return to the ERM. However, when the system came close to collapse in July and August of 1993, he was not one of those European finance ministers who called for it to be scrapped, and nor did he abandon his long-held view that the UK should retain the option of eventual participation in EMU. To his mind, a single currency would be essential to make the most of the single market.[16]

Major, on the other hand, unsurprisingly proved more prone to schadenfreude. He saw the system's near-death experience as evidence of its underlying frailties and proof that the UK was not itself to blame for the previous year's sterling crisis. Rather, the Germans and the French had much to answer for.

He was also happy to declare that the idea of a single European currency was to all intents and purposes an irrelevance.

Clarke's second key judgement was to realize that Lamont had put UK economic policy back on track, and to appreciate that there was little need for additional root-and-branch reform. The priority was more to maintain the newly established direction of travel. That said, Clarke imposed additional fiscal austerity in November 1993 in an effort to bring the budget into balance over the course of the business cycle, instituting a £10 billion cut in public spending plans (equivalent to 1.5% of 1993–94 GDP) over the next three years and imposing a further £5 billion of tax increases (0.75% of GDP). Nigel Lawson's late-1980s tax cuts were completely unwound.

Clarke instituted two further guidelines for fiscal policy. First, he declared his support for the so-called Maastricht Criteria of an annual budget deficit equivalent to less than 3% of GDP and a national debt burden equivalent to no more than 60% of GDP. Second, he expressed his desire to bring the proportion of GDP accounted for by public spending below 40% from its 1993 level of 46%. This was to be achieved in 1998, the year after the Conservatives left office.

Where monetary policy was concerned, Clarke was, like Lamont, a supporter of greater central bank independence, so he took further steps to strengthen the authority of the Bank of England. It was agreed that once a decision had been taken to adjust official interest rates, the precise timing would be left to the Bank. He also ended the Treasury's advance vetting of the Bank's Inflation Reports, and from the spring of 1994 the minutes of the chancellor's regular monthly meeting with the Bank's governor were published after a six-week delay. This was a particularly important change as it meant that if the chancellor had rejected the governor's advice, the markets would know why. The scope for the political manipulation of monetary policy was thereby restricted.

Major was reluctant to agree to some of these changes, as they represented a dilution of prime ministerial power, but this was, after all, a central element of the whole exercise. Moreover, he could hardly afford to lose a second chancellor in short order.

Eddie George, who had been at the Bank of England since the 1960s, took over as governor from the patrician, and rather ineffective, Robin Leigh-Pemberton in July 1993. George was street smart, and quick to exploit the changes in modus operandi, even though he was initially sceptical about the monocular focus on the inflation target, preferring instead that the Bank should retain greater freedom of action. In the meantime, he and Clarke forged a constructive relationship. They were both Cambridge graduates, of a similar age, and were renowned for their plain speaking. They had also reached their elevated positions through ability rather than privilege.

The problem was that two such forthright personalities were not always able to agree. The autumn of 1994 saw Clarke take two days to accept George's advice to hike rates, while a bigger difference of opinion emerged in the spring of 1995 when Clarke, following the Conservatives' heavy losses in local elections, rejected George's (and, it should be said, his own Treasury officials') recommendation for a half-a-percentage-point rate hike to support sterling.

These new institutional arrangements represented a substantial improvement on the old opaque and frequently brazenly politically distorted system of monetary policy determination. However, there was a danger that the 'Ken and Eddie show', as it became known, would develop into a form of soap opera for the financial markets and come to damage policy credibility. It was therefore only a halfway house. If a line was to be drawn under the political exploitation of interest rates, it would require the granting of full operational independence to the central bank.

A REMARKABLE TRANSFORMATION

Judging by standard metrics, the net result of the post-September 1992 reorientation of UK macro policy was admirable. The economy became much better balanced. Real GDP growth resumed in the very quarter in which sterling left the ERM, and it averaged a little over 3% a year over the period to 1997, such that the output gap progressively closed. Real exports of goods and services expanded at close to double-digit annual rates between 1994 and 1997, and the contribution of net exports to growth was positive from 1993 to 1995. Personal consumption and housing were much less to the fore in the cyclical upswing than had been the case in the late 1980s, and the household saving rate remained around 10% of disposable income throughout. After a sluggish start, business investment spending grew rapidly, especially in 1996 and 1997. By 1997 unemployment was back under 7% of the workforce, but wage inflation and various measures of inflation expectations remained benign by the standards of previous decades, even if the latter proved reluctant to converge fully with the inflation target. Labour productivity growth initially rebounded strongly as the recovery gathered momentum, although it disappointingly more than halved, to around just 1%, in the last three years of the parliament. The external balance improved throughout Clarke's time as chancellor, with the current account deficit disappearing in 1997. Britain's share of world exports was more or less stable. Inequality, which had risen so sharply in the 1980s, levelled off, while most measures of poverty, which had moved higher at the beginning of the decade, retreated as the cyclical recovery developed.

Against this backdrop, the Bank of England comfortably met its mandated 1–4% annual inflation target without having to resort to any aggressive tightening of the monetary stance. The selected RPIX measure of inflation spent much of the middle years of the 1990s around or below 3%, and it was at exactly 2.5% in May 1997 when the Conservatives left office. CPI inflation dropped below 2%.

Official rates oscillated within a tight 5–7% range, far lower than in the previous two decades. Following the global bond market sell-off in 1994, longer-term gilt yields trended downwards until Major left office. UK stocks experienced a tough year in 1994, but the FTSE 100 rallied consistently thereafter in line with other developed markets, and the real return on UK equities between 1991 and 1997 amounted to some 70%, compared with just over 85% in the Thatcher era of 1980–90 and a mere 2.5% in the years 1970–79. UK house prices remained subdued into the middle of the decade relative to their 1990 highs, rising in real terms only in 1996 and 1997.

STRUCTURAL REFORM INTERACTS WITH EXTERNAL INFLUENCES

This impressive statistical summary suggests that we ask how supply-side policy contributed to the performance of the economy under the Major governments.

The years 1991–97 are best described as a period of supply-side policy consolidation rather than intense reform. Importantly, there were no major backward steps, even if gaps remained around infrastructure, active labour market policies and education. This allowed the longer-term consequences of the various reforms of the 1979–90 period to bear fruit while at the same time encouraging the constructive forces unleashed by the establishment of the European single market, and various other beneficial external influences, to percolate gradually through the economy.

As we have already seen in chapter 5, the deregulation and privatization of the Thatcher era increased competition, raised contestability and helped to bolster productivity. Extending to labour markets, and with an associated reduction in trade union bargaining power, these initiatives stimulated a reduction of labour share in national income, especially in industries facing higher import penetration, and they also helped to change the responsiveness of some sectors, so that a given demand shock no longer caused as large a price response as it would have done in earlier epochs. Procyclical movements in profit margins were constrained. Furthermore, by severing some of the linkages that tied prices (including relative wages) together, these reforms moderated the propagation of shocks. And finally, they supported, even encouraged, three other disinflationary forces that increasingly came on stream in the 1990s: globalization, the integration of new technologies, and price transparency.

Globalization can be defined as a worldwide intensification of cross-border flows of goods, services, factors of production (labour and capital) and financial instruments. The spread of globalization is difficult to measure with precision, but trade and foreign direct investment statistics help to capture the broad trends. The share of trade relative to GDP increased sharply following World War II, and this process picked up again in the 1990s and through the early years of the twenty-first century. For the world as a whole, the combined share of imports and exports in GDP rose from 20% in 1950 to nearly 42% in 1992, increasing further, to some 60%, by the time of the 2008 global financial crisis. This reflected the success of the General Agreement on Tariffs and Trade (GATT) negotiations in reducing trade barriers (which resulted in cheaper and improved transport and communications infrastructure) and gains from specialization as developing countries became more important producers and exporters of manufactures.

The economic liberalization that followed the dissolution of the Soviet Union in 1991 brought much of eastern Europe into the world economy, but the most crucial new entrant at this time was China. In purchasing power parity terms, China's shares of global exports and GDP doubled from 1.0% and 2.0%, respectively, in 1980 to 2% and 4% in 1990, and then doubled again to 4% and 8% by 2000. Moreover, this increase in economic heft coincided with the rising importance of global value chains (GVCs), whereby a country imports intermediate goods to produce goods for export. This vertical specialization accelerated greatly in the 1990s, with low-cost China often at its epicentre.

The foreign direct investment (FDI) channel of globalization was especially important for service sectors, which typically account for more than two-thirds of the output of developed economies. World FDI flows more than tripled in the 1990s, easily outpacing the rise in global GDP and trade. Total FDI inflows peaked at $1.5 trillion in 2000, following the cyclical downturn at the turn of the decade, although they picked up again in the noughties, rising above $2 trillion in 2007, just before the GFC struck.

Globalization had two important effects on the inflation process.

First, greater integration between economies widened the supply base. It helped businesses to source from lowest-cost suppliers, it encouraged them to develop a global investment strategy, and, by increasing competition, it constrained domestic pricing power. For consumers, it brought cheaper imports and greater choice, whether they shopped locally or, as they increasingly did from the 1990s, via the internet. For workers, it constrained bargaining power on pay and conditions and reduced job security, particularly in those sectors previously sheltered from external competition.

All this demonstrates the importance, in the analysis of inflation determinants, of the global output gap or excess capacity rather than the domestic output gap or excess capacity. Supply shortages are less frequent and, generally, less extreme at the global level.

Second, global competition encouraged a more rapid spread of state-of-the-art management and methods of cost control, raising efficiency within firms and productivity across economies.

The wave of innovation in information and communications technology (ICT) that began in the 1990s improved the speed, quality and accessibility of information, and at very low marginal cost. This provided opportunities to increase the efficiency with which capital and labour are combined in the production process. The result was shorter design times, better quality control and – because firms can respond more rapidly to changes in customer preferences – a diminished requirement for precautionary stockpiling in the production chain. It also encouraged more outsourcing to the cheapest global supplier.

The internet enhanced this process, allowing consumers and businesses to compare prices, specifications and conditions of sale more easily, and to bypass middlemen and extract discounts from local suppliers.

Increased price transparency is closely related to the rise of ICT, but other aspects have contributed to the disinflationary process too. For example, by removing the background noise of higher and variable general inflation, greater price stability can itself make it easier for consumers to identify changes in relative prices.

In summary, these global developments represented a quantitatively important set of finite, disinflationary forces that reinforced the potency of the UK government's efforts to squeeze inflation out of the system and keep it at bay. Moreover, they interacted constructively. By reducing the impact of unanticipated inflation on output and employment, they also reduced the incentive for monetary authorities such as the Bank of England to try to raise output through an unduly expansionary policy. As a result, central bank credibility was enhanced and inflation expectations were held in check.

Where there were new domestic supply-side initiatives on the part of the Major governments, they had rather mixed results. The extended fiscal restraint of the years 1993–97 succeeded in reining back what was perceived to be a bloated public sector, while Ken Clarke improved labour market incentives by increasing Family Credit, the main in-work benefit, and by generally increasing the conditionality of the benefit system. The UK labour market remained more flexible than that of most of its competitors.

Of more questionable value was the Citizen's Charter of 1991. Ostensibly, this prime ministerial initiative represented a laudable effort to apply some of the standards and competitive forces that acted on the private sector to the public sector. It sought, for example, to enhance choice, to subject government activities to performance targets and complaints procedures, to create internal markets, and to strengthen the oversight of independent agencies to monitor performance. This was a big change from the Thatcher era, when the government view was that no public sector activity could possibly match the efficiency of the private sector, meaning that the only logical solution was privatization and as small a state as possible.

Unfortunately, however, the Citizen's Charter was widely derided at the time as amounting to a series of bureaucratic trivialities of negligible importance. More pertinently, it is hard to detect it having much of an impact either in public perceptions or in the public sector productivity figures, although in fairness these are frequently little more than educated guesswork. There were undoubtedly some achievements – NHS waiting lists declined somewhat, and better performance criteria were introduced in schools – but public service standards in many areas remained lamentable.

Another dubious initiative was the privatization of the railways, instigated after the 1992 election. This was something that even Thatcher had backed away from, and it did not go well. It proved both messy in form and deeply unpopular. It was not long before opinion polls suggested that the public favoured renationalization.

This period also saw the commencement of the private finance initiative (PFI), whereby private sector investment was used to deliver public sector infrastructure and/or services according to a specification defined by the public sector. An idea first sketched out by Keynes in his *General Theory*, as he explored ways to bring greater stability to investment, the PFI was formally justified on the basis that the private sector is usually better at delivering services than the public sector. However, it was also established in an effort to keep liabilities off the public sector balance sheet at a time when government deficit and debt levels were high and rising. The reality was that the PFI made very slow progress until it was employed more aggressively by the Blair and Brown governments.

POLITICS TRUMPED ECONOMICS

From an economic perspective, the Major years can be divided into four sub-periods. The first saw a deep and sharply disinflationary recession that was in significant part the result of the hubris and excesses of the previous boom. The second was characterized by a surprising election victory and an ephemeral honeymoon period that bred another bout of excessive optimism. The third yielded a traumatic sterling crisis. And the fourth saw a subsequent period of macro policy reorientation and micro policy consistency, the positive effects of which were reinforced by sympathetic global trends. This was the beginning of what has been termed the 'Great Moderation' or the 'NICE Decade' (with NICE standing for non-inflationary, consistent expansion).[17]

In defending his cautious, if not austere, approach as chancellor, Ken Clarke would often recite the mantra that 'good economics is good politics'. Unfortunately, this was not the case for the Conservatives after 1992. Despite the commendable economic record of the mid 1990s, the government was doomed from the moment sterling was chased out of the ERM. The public confidence lost at that juncture was never regained, while sterling's humiliating exit was red meat to the Eurosceptics on the right of the party in the meantime. Major was never forgiven by them for replacing Margaret Thatcher, for championing the ERM and Maastricht, or for wanting to keep the UK close to the heart of Europe.

The government became trapped in a web of rancorous infighting, backbench rebellions, resignations, sackings and intermittent withdrawals of the whip, from which it never emerged. Nor did a spate of sleaze allegations against Conservative MPs, some of them cabinet members, help its popularity. By the end of 1996, through a series of by-election defeats and with one member crossing the floor of the House, Major headed a minority government, effectively dependent on the cantankerous Ulster Unionists to survive.

The Maastricht Treaty was ultimately ratified in July 1993, but only after more than a year of acrimonious parliamentary debate, a regular requirement for the support of the minor parties, and a knife-edge vote of confidence in the government, which would have resulted in a general election had it been lost. To keep his government afloat while also seeking to maintain influence in Brussels, Major was constantly tacking between Europhilia and Euroscepticism, while having to resort to every parliamentary trick in the book.

To fend off the repeated challenges to his authority from both within and outwith his cabinet, he even resorted to resigning in mid 1995, going on to fight a party leadership election against one of his own cabinet members: the arch Eurosceptic John Redwood. He was victorious, but it proved a hollow victory. Nothing much changed. The Conservative Party had become unmanageable where Europe was concerned, and whenever Major tried to shift the debate to focus on domestic issues, he found it impossible. This was the beginning of the road that led to Brexit in 2016.

The second Major government was finally put out of its misery in May 1997, by which time the country was no longer listening to the Conservatives. Just as in 1979, the electorate expressed their desire for a change, and on this occasion it was mesmerized by the youthful, modernizing figure that was Tony Blair, and by the dour earnestness of Gordon Brown.

CHAPTER 7

New Labour, New Keynesianism

The central problem of depression-prevention has been solved for all practical purposes.

— Robert Lucas, 2003[1]

THESIS, ANTITHESIS AND SYNTHESIS

By the time the Blair government came to power in May 1997, economic theory had moved on from the 1970s anti-Keynesian counter-revolution described in chapter 4. A consensus had developed about the appropriate macroeconomic framework of thought, and about how macroeconomic policy should be conducted. The arcane Panglossian certainties of new classical theory, which embodied elements of monetarism, the rational expectations hypothesis (REH), real business cycle (RBC) theory and the efficient markets hypothesis (EMH) had been synthesised with new Keynesianism, or the attempt to incorporate certain Keynesian features into micro-founded models, by emphasizing how market 'frictions' could cause deviations from the optimal level of output.

The stickiness of wages and prices within an REH framework was explained by considerations such as imperfect information and imperfect competition. This meant that markets did not clear instantaneously: they took time to do so. There could therefore be temporary demand shortages that pushed the actual unemployment rate above its 'natural rate', and on which macro policy, largely in the form of central bank action on official interest rates, could have an impact. New Keynesians acknowledged that there was no long-run trade-off between price stability and employment but claimed that government could affect employment over the short term.

BACK TO EARTH

Behavioural economists had by this time also succeeded in modifying elements of the REH. It had originally been grounded in the notion of a near-unlimited

ability to obtain and process information. Behaviourists suggested that this
was both unrealistic and, more to the point, unnecessary. When faced with
a mass of data, people fell back on short cuts, or heuristics, which included
'anchoring' (relying heavily on the initial information received), availability
(focusing on prominent examples) and familiarity (extrapolation from previous experience), all of which, it was asserted, were reasonable methods of
forming expectations and, more importantly, could be influenced by efforts
on the part of the authorities.

Hence, a central bank with a specific inflation target could, by establishing a reputation for hitting that target, secure expectations around it.
This would both reduce the impact of shocks on an economy and afford the
central bank policy room to manipulate real interest rates via changes in
its own nominal policy rate, thereby returning an economy to equilibrium
more rapidly.

Whether it is entirely sensible to view heuristics as valid approximations of
a comprehensive assessment of all available information is an open question.
As we saw in chapter 2, Keynes also believed that people fell back on heuristics
when confronted by uncertainty, but he did not see these as computational
shortcuts, as he doubted that calculation was even possible in most situations.
Furthermore, he feared that if a pretence of knowledge was exposed as that –
as being a sham – an economy could suddenly collapse and struggle to recover,
because confidence was hard to restore.

KEYNES ABANDONED

In taking on board much of the new classical framework for macroeconomics,
however, the new Keynesians abandoned one of the basic tenets of Keynes's
General Theory: the often-radical, or unbounded, nature of intertemporal
uncertainty; its potential role in encouraging large and extended downturns;
and thereby the establishment of an undeniably strong and enduring rationale
for policy activism. In the new classical world there was no uncertainty, just
imperfect information within known probability distributions, and there was
thereby little or no scope for major recessions.

The theoretical compromise between the new classicists and the new
Keynesians was increasingly built into most mainstream macroeconomic
policy models from the 1980s onwards. These assumed rational expectations,
or at the least some hybrid of rational expectations and Friedman's adaptive
expectations, but they assumed a degree of wage and price stickiness, such that
policymakers were confronted by at least some short-term trade-off between
output and employment, and inflation.

STRUCTURAL INTEGRITY

In the meantime, reflecting in part RBC theory, but also the observed tendencies for economic growth to generally slow, and for certain economies to be more inflexible than others, there was a growing focus on 'real', or 'supply-side', shocks to economic activity. This led to exploration of how microeconomic policies should be designed to reduce the impact of these shocks, and to generally improve the working of markets and, thereby, the ability of economies to expand in a sustained fashion.

These structural reforms were increasingly elevated to the forefront of policy, not just in the UK but around the world. Nowhere is this more obvious than in the quid pro quos attached to the assistance provided to financially compromised countries by the IMF and the World Bank. Loans were conditional on commitments to pursue financial deregulation, privatization, labour and product market liberalization, and the curbing of the influence of the state through tighter public spending control and tax reform.

A further influence impinging on policy at this time was public choice theory. This essentially posited that democratic governments were not, as suggested by Keynes, generally benevolent guardians of the public interest: they were in fact more malign, and in particular more interested in maximizing votes than stabilizing economies. Hence, they were prone to short-termism, policy incoherence and, ultimately, failure.[2] Again, therefore, the most sensible course of action was to eschew sophisticated government interventions, limit the size of the state, and curtail policy discretion as much as possible. In practical terms, this meant explicit fiscal rules, budget watchdogs, independent central banks, formal inflation targets and free markets.

A final theoretical inspiration for policy at this juncture emanated from the analysis of economic growth by economic historians such as Douglass North, another Nobel laureate. This work emphasized the importance of political, economic and social institutions and incentive structures, including constitutions, legal systems, private property rights and moral codes.[3] It suggested that in looking to encourage development, seeking just to raise aggregate savings and investment totals – as was fashionable during the Keynesian heyday of 'growthmanship' – could get you only so far. It was also vital that the 'rules of the economic game' were appropriately set.

POLICY MANIFESTO

If all these various theoretical influences were distilled down into practical policy steps, they might be summarized as follows.

- Rules should dominate discretion. Every effort should be made to provide a transparent, and accountable, modus operandi and to minimize the risk of short-term political manipulation of policy levers.
- The fine-tuning of demand should be avoided. It tends to destabilize rather than stabilize. Macro policy should be constrained to assisting the economy's own underlying self-correcting properties.
- Monetary instruments, and in particular official interest rates, should be the primary tools of stabilization policy, and they should focus on the pursuit of long-term relative price stability as an essential precondition for high and stable levels of growth and employment.
- The anchoring of inflation expectations around the price stability target should be prioritized. This will ensure that deviations from that target are minimized, and it will enhance the leeway for monetary policy interventions, if required.
- Fiscal policy should be of secondary importance and should be largely confined to the unencumbered operation of the 'automatic stabilizers' and to the sustainable management of public debt.
- The roles of public sector institutions in applying policy rules and reaching specified objectives should be clear and consistent and must avoid potential conflicts of interest.
- Markets should be encouraged to function as freely as possible. Government interference should be constrained. Positive incentive structures, not least through the tax and welfare systems, should be encouraged.

There is a good deal of sense in these policy guidelines. They seek to address the flaws in Keynes's 1930s approach; to deal with the even bigger flaws in the way that that approach was often applied by his disciples; and to apply many of the broader lessons learned from several decades of policy activism, both in the UK and abroad, and including during the monetarist heyday of the early 1980s.

PRIDE COMES BEFORE A FALL

The enthusiasts for this modus operandi got rather carried away with themselves, however. The godfather of the new classical school, Robert Lucas, remarked as early as 1980 that: 'At research seminars, people don't take Keynesian theorizing seriously anymore – the audience starts to whisper and giggle to one another.'[4] By 2003, as suggested by the quote at the beginning of this chapter, he was proclaiming that he and his disciples had effectively conquered the business cycle.

There was more than a hint of 'the end of history' in all this. But the reality was that the new consensus itself retained numerous shortcomings.

Besides the manifest difficulties of achieving the requisite degree of monetary control, the REH was not always the most workable approximation of reality that it was claimed to be. Market failures and the encouragement of perverse incentives, not least in finance, were less rare than was presupposed. But most pertinently of all, the new classical dictum that all uncertainty could be collapsed into measurable risk seemed intuitively questionable. It was at the very least a hostage to fortune, and at most a recipe for disaster. After all, collapses of confidence and large downturns remained an intermittent fact of life. Even in the late 1990s and early 2000s, the catastrophic East Asian crisis and the collapse of the dot-com bubble seemed to suggest that the new consensus did not have all the bases covered, although it was not until 2007 that its inadequacies were fully exposed.

NEW LABOUR JOINS THE CONSENSUS

Nevertheless, Tony Blair and his putative chancellor, Gordon Brown, were to take much of the menu of policies outlined above to heart. This meant that they worked within a similar overarching framework to that applied by Thatcher and Major, even if much of the detail was different.

This dyarchy rose to prominence in the Labour Party in the 1980s, as it embarked on a long and painful process of modernization. At the time of then-leader John Smith's untimely death in May 1994, the party had lost four successive elections, and for all its previous efforts to reinvent itself, and move away from the corporatism and heavy-handed intervention of the past, it still had a significant trust deficit with the electorate. This judgement applied in particular to economic policy.

By this stage, it had become obvious that of the two friends, Blair – a non-traditional, non-partisan politician, and natural public performer – was the better communicator. His charm appealed more to the middle ground that the party had to cultivate if it was to return to power than did Brown's seriousness. Notwithstanding his intellect, sense of duty and appreciation of the Labour Party's heritage, Brown was much less the sort of modern political figurehead that Labour needed if it was finally to win an election.

For all his competitiveness and burning ambition, Brown had enough political nous in the mid 1990s to recognize the way the wind was blowing in the party and the country. He stood aside on the condition that if, or rather when, he became chancellor, he would enjoy a wide-ranging remit that went beyond macroeconomic strategy, to include welfare and social policy, and that he would be Blair's designated successor. Indeed, Blair was to cede an unprecedented amount of control over economic policy to his chancellor. His own engagement with economic policy was to be limited to how it would serve his broader political strategy. In time, however, it became clear that Brown never fully reconciled himself to the fact that he had had to give way to Blair on the leadership.

One of Blair's most important early acts as leader was to drop Clause IV of the party's constitution. This was a highly symbolic, but increasingly anachronistic, commitment to the public ownership of the means of production, distribution and exchange – a commitment that left many centrist voters fearing that the Labour Party could at any time lurch violently to the left. There were, however, many other signals to the effect that New Labour, as the party was rebranded in 1994, would be a very different, less doctrinaire, less socialist entity to previous incarnations of the movement. Blair even went so far as to admit that the Thatcher years had irreversibly shifted the terms of the political debate.

Brown, meanwhile, spent the next three years planning meticulously for his expected entry into Number 11 Downing Street. In so doing, he worked closely with his chief advisor Ed Balls (who was a former *Financial Times* leader writer) and with a number of distinguished academics and City figures, and he even sought the advice of Alan Greenspan, the revered Federal Reserve chairman.

Balls, for his part, had spent time at Harvard University, where he came under the influence of future US Treasury Secretary Larry Summers and other new Keynesian cheerleaders. He also passed on to his boss a cautious approach to Europe and to a European single currency – certainly a more cautious attitude than that of Blair – together with a greater understanding of the importance to the economy and to economic policymaking of the financial sector and financial markets. Balls recognised that the City would have to be placated.

Brown was desperate to change perceptions of Labour's economic competence for the better, and he wanted to avoid at all costs the sort of financial catastrophe that had plagued previous Labour administrations. Taking Balls's advice onboard, he recognized that it was vital that, on coming to power, Labour looked to build trust in the markets and with the public. If it did this in its initial years in office, then it would be possible to pursue a more expansive policy agenda in the run-up to the next general election and beyond. This implied a good deal of short-term consistency with Ken Clarke's approach and also that, as Blair had suggested, New Labour accepted much of what might be termed the 'Thatcherite settlement'.

The policies that were developed and that found their way into Labour's 1997 election manifesto were circumspect – even pusillanimous – in tone.[5] Stability and consistency were the watchwords. There was an emphasis on the need for a transparent and predicable macro policy framework: 'constrained discretion', with accountable divisions of responsibility aimed in large part at price stability. This constrained discretion was to be combined with microeconomic policies that would promote sustainable growth and high employment. These should not look to respond to market failures by replacing markets, as they had in the past, and neither should they seek to 'pick winners' in industry. Rather, they should endeavour to make markets work more efficiently. In the labour market, for example, while protecting people from the worst ravages of poverty and social exclusion the tax and benefit systems should be focused on rewarding work.

Brown embraced fiscal rules that sought to balance current public spending over the cycle, and he aimed to borrow only to finance public investment. At the same time, there was a commitment to low and stable net government debt. To underline this emphasis on fiscal restraint, Brown promised to eschew any hikes in the basic and higher rates of income tax and to retain the Conservatives' existing departmental public spending plans for two years. Tax and spend was to be a thing of the past – at least initially.

Where monetary policy was concerned, Brown pledged to retain the existing 2.5% inflation target and, further, to ensure that interest rate decisions were more open, accountable and free from short-term political influence, although quite what this was to mean in practice was not yet clear.

THE PENDULUM SWINGS

Labour won a remarkable 179-seat majority in May 1997: far bigger than either of Thatcher's two landslides in 1983 and 1987. It could be argued that the Conservatives were in disarray and were never going to win this election, and that, just as in 1979, change was inevitable. But tellingly, New Labour received more votes from the middle classes and from homeowners than did the Tories. Blair and Brown's transformation of the party had worked. The nation was beguiled by its youthful and, in Blair's case, charismatic leadership, which eschewed the discredited classist dogma of the Old Left and the divisive social Darwinism of the New Right in favour of a technocratic approach it characterized as the 'Radical Centre' or the 'Third Way'. In truth, it was fixated more than anything else on 'what worked' – New Labour was remarkably hollow in ideological terms. Nevertheless, May 1997 was a time of optimism and hope.

CHAPTER 8

Blair, Brown and the Great Moderation

The government will pursue the long-term strategy that is necessary to achieve stability. We will not return to the stop–go, boom–bust years which we saw under the Conservatives.

— Gordon Brown, April 1998[1]

BENIGN INHERITANCE

Sustained by a benign international environment, the UK economy had performed surprisingly well once it was released from the strictures of the ERM, and this was to continue under New Labour. The period between the third quarter of 1992 and the onset of the GFC in the third quarter of 2007 saw fifteen years of continuous expansion. Despite various international disturbances such as the Asian Crisis of 1997, the collapse of Long-Term Capital Management in 1998 and a global downturn in the early years of the new millennium, there was no British recession. Indeed, growth continued with barely a pause for breath.

Real GDP growth averaged some 3% per year, far in excess of the euro area and OECD averages. The unemployment rate fell more or less continuously. Productivity growth remained firm. Inflation was consistently low and relatively stable. There was no whiff of crisis relating to the public finances, to the external balance or to sterling akin to those that undermined previous Labour administrations in 1931, 1949, 1967 and 1976. This was a remarkable and unprecedented record, standing in stark contrast to the rollercoaster ride of the previous twenty years, and for once it left the UK as one of the more successful performers among the major industrial economies.

Many of the seeds of this improvement in performance were sown in the supply-side initiatives of the 1980s, including the development of the European single market, and in the restructuring of the macroeconomic policy framework initiated by Norman Lamont, and further advanced by Ken Clarke, during the Major era. The powerful forces of globalization that were detailed in the previous chapter and that were so conducive to macro-stability in the mid 1990s also continued to exert their influence. It was no wonder that this era was to be characterized as the 'NICE Decade' or the 'Great Moderation', even if the more malign effects of the expansion of international trade and capital flows on the income distribution were at the time underappreciated.[2]

The bulk of this extraordinary period of macroeconomic tranquillity was presided over by Tony Blair and, more specifically, by Gordon Brown, Blair's all-powerful chancellor, who was to remain in post for more than a decade.

Brown, the son of a Church of Scotland minister, was ferociously intelligent, single-minded and possessed of a formidable work ethic – together with a volcanic temper. Furthermore, he was driven by a passionate desire to improve the lot of the poorest and most disadvantaged. Like Blair, Brown had no previous ministerial experience, but unlike many of his predecessors he arrived in Number 11 Downing Street with something of a plan of action, and with a commitment to run the Treasury his way. Indeed, there was a ruthlessness about his approach to policymaking that curdled into toxicity in his personal relations with both officials and cabinet colleagues.

That said, reflecting the growing consensus in macro theory, the gap between Brown's thinking and that of the Treasury's was narrow – certainly narrower than had been the case when the Conservative Party came to power in 1979. Brown was also lucky not to have his plans for the economy immediately scuppered by a requirement to address an emergency inherited from the previous government. Growth was running a little above trend when Brown became chancellor, and the labour market was tight. Inflation was close to the outgoing administration's target, and while it was expected to rise, it was not anticipated to to do dramatically. The external account was, moreover, in rough balance. There was no need, therefore, for a dramatic reorientation of the impetus of policy. A gentle touch on the tiller would suffice. This left him free to pursue grander designs.

INDEPENDENCE DAY

Brown's extended period as economic overlord* began with one of the most important changes in the way the economy was managed of the modern era. On 6 May 1997, just days after Labour's landslide election victory and following the regular meeting between the chancellor and the governor of the

---

* I use this term deliberately because, in contrast to the situation under the Labour governments of the mid 1970s, when economic policy was argued over endlessly in cabinet, Brown brooked little, if any, debate.

Bank of England, Brown announced not only that official interest rates were to rise by a quarter point to 6.25% but also that the Bank of England was to become operationally independent. Brown's rate rise would be the last made by a chancellor of the exchequer. This was a bombshell, not least because of the often-vexed relationship between Labour and the Bank, stretching back all the way to Labour's first (brief) minority government in the 1920s. And it was after all a Labour chancellor, Hugh Dalton, who had nationalized the central bank in the first place (in 1946).[3]

Encouraged by Ed Balls – his main advisor, and in due course his de facto deputy – and by various members of the great and good of the international policymaking community, Brown had been considering such a move for some time.[4] However, the ultimate decision to make this leap was finalized only the weekend after the election, when Treasury officials, not least high flyer Tom Scholar, were forced to hurriedly make the necessary preparations, in the process resurrecting work done during Nigel Lawson's flirtation with central bank independence in 1988.[5]

The move also marked the beginning of the end of the Treasury careers of its Permanent Secretary, Terry Burns, and its chief economic advisor, Alan Budd. While they had become increasingly pragmatic over the years, they were tarred with the brush of monetarism and with having been appointed at the onset of the Thatcher era.[6] Indeed, Brown proved rather particular about the civil servants he was willing to trust. Burns was replaced by Andrew Turnbull, but it was only when Turnbull was elevated to the position of cabinet secretary in 2002 that Brown acquired the Permanent Secretaries he was comfortable with: Gus O'Donnell initially (O'Donnell was a former academic economist and press secretary to John Major) and then, in 2005, the long-term Treasury official Nicholas MacPherson.

As for the detail of Brown's 'bolt from the blue', the responsibility for meeting the government's monetary policy objectives was to be transferred to a newly created Monetary Policy Committee (MPC) located at the Bank. The new arrangements were set out in a letter from Brown to the governor and in a subsequent statement to parliament. A month or so later, the government published its remit for the MPC, in which it specified an inflation target, and it outlined the mechanisms by which it would be held to account for meeting this target.[7] After acting on a de facto basis for twelve months, the new framework for monetary policy was formalized in the June 1998 Bank of England Act.

The Bank's primary responsibility was to be relative price stability, although subject to this it was required to support the government's other economic policy objectives, including those for growth and employment. Price stability was viewed not as an end in itself but as being necessary to achieve those other goals. The level of the exchange rate was downplayed in all of this.

The price stability goal was initially set by the government at 2.5% per year in terms of the RPIX – the same index prioritized by the previous government. However, the focus was to be placed on a single point rather than on the range favoured under Lamont and Clarke. This was in order to provide a clearer and more effective anchor for inflation expectations and to make it easier for the public to assess policy success. For similar reasons, the MPC was required to aim to hit the target all the time rather than on average over some arbitrary period.

The target was symmetrical. Deviations below it were to be responded to in the same way as deviations above it, hence ensuring that growth and employment were appropriately supported. The framework also recognized that when inflation failed to meet the target, as it was bound to do at times, it might not be desirable to seek to restore it to target too abruptly for fear of generating undue instability in output and employment. That said, when inflation deviated from target by more than a percentage point in either direction, the governor was obligated to write an open letter to the chancellor. The letter needed to detail why the deviation had happened, what measures were being taken to address it, how long those measures were likely to take to bring inflation back on track, and how the government's objectives for growth and employment were likely to be affected in the interim.

Decisions would be made by majority vote by an MPC of nine: four external members, who would bring a range of alternative views and expertise; the governor; his or her deputies; and two further senior Bank officials.[8] The votes would be made public after a brief delay, along with the minutes of the meetings. Further transparency relating to the Bank's deliberations would come in the form of the publication of regular detailed Inflation Reports, speeches made by MPC members,[9] and through the scrutiny of the MPC's operations by the House of Commons Treasury Select Committee. The government could override the central bank only in exceptional circumstances.

The decision to grant the Bank operational independence went down very well with its governor, Eddie George, who had already had a number of meetings with Brown, Balls and, occasionally, Tony Blair over the previous two years. However, he was much less enamoured with Brown's subsequent choices to hive off the Bank's responsibility for the management of government debt to a Treasury agency (the Debt Management Office) and, in particular, to strip the Bank of its long-held responsibility for banking supervision and transfer it to a new regulator (the Financial Services Authority (FSA)). Indeed, the governor considered resignation over the latter judgement and the precipitous nature of its announcement.

This rendered relations between the Bank and the Treasury fraught for a period, not least because it created a reputational problem for the Bank among the international central banking fraternity. George also felt a strong responsibility towards his staff, some of whom were bound to be moved on. In due course, however, Brown and George were to forge a strong and mutually respectful relationship, helped by the fact that, to the surprise of many, Brown was scrupulous about not seeking to second-guess the governor on interest rate decisions.[10] In due course, George's reappointment as governor in 1998, for a further five years, was a shoo in, particularly as the government recognized his paramount reputation across a financial community it was anxious to appease.

The decision to divest the Bank of much of its supervisory role reflected a judgement that the largely self-regulatory system of financial sector oversight established by the Conservatives in 1987 was no longer appropriate. It also reflected the Bank's perceived culpability for a number of policy failures in the 1980s and 1990s (the collapse of Barings Bank, for example), plus a desire to prevent it being captured by City interests, to the detriment of the economy as a whole.

However, the amputation of the Bank's micro supervisory role was to leave the responsibility for financial stability in the event of a crisis split between three entities: the Bank, which retained a remit to oversee the overall health of the financial system and remained the lender of last resort; the FSA, which undertook individual bank assessments; and the Treasury. The Treasury retained control over the government's purse strings and was the paramount ministry of state.

A memorandum of understanding between the three entities was cobbled together, but the tripartite arrangement lacked hierarchical clarity and was ill-equipped to deal with uncertainties about whether a struggling entity's problem was a liquidity issue or one of solvency. Moreover, especially under the governorship of Eddie George's successor, Mervyn King, the arrangement encouraged the Bank to focus on monetary analysis and policy, and on the achievement of the inflation target. The budget of the Bank's financial stability division was cut sharply, interactions with the other two departments on the stability issue were limited, and King himself showed little interest in the technical issues of the matter.[11]

The regime's inadequacies, and particularly its opacity and the lack of a clear pecking order, were to come into stark relief during the lead up to the GFC of 2007–9.

HITTING THE TARGET

The record shows that the MPC was fairly active over the first four years of its existence. Policy rates were raised in 1997 to head off modest inflationary pressures but were then cut in 1998 and early 1999 to address the risks posed by the Asian Crisis and the collapse of Long-Term Capital Management. They were briefly edged up again in late 1999 and early 2000 but then reduced in response to the collapse of the US technology stock bubble and to fears that a US recession would spread to the UK. At 5.25% in May 2001, official rates were a percentage point lower at the end of New Labour's first term than they were at its beginning.

Annual RPIX inflation averaged 2.4% between 1997 and 2001, so the Bank can be said to have met its inflation target, but there was a tendency for it to undershoot the mark from the spring of 1999. Eddie George never had to write an explanatory letter about a significant inflation 'miss' to the chancellor. Indeed, it took ten years of Bank independence until such a missive proved necessary. Most pertinently, continually benign inflation encouraged lower nominal interest rates across the yield curve, as both inflation expectations and the inflation risk premium declined. At the same time, sterling moved sharply higher in trade-weighted terms and remained elevated for the next decade, and the spread of UK long-term bond yields over their German equivalents narrowed sharply. There was a clear credibility windfall from UK central bank independence.

However, while the UK's inflation performance under the new regime was historically impressive, it was less remarkable in relative terms. While inflation roughly matched the US experience, it ran significantly higher than in what was to become the euro area and, in particular, in Japan. The average inflation rate across the OECD economies during this period was just 1.6% per year.

A NEW FRAMEWORK FOR FISCAL POLICY

Turning to the other major lever of macro-stabilization, Labour inherited a healthy overall fiscal position, by international standards, thanks to the efforts of Lamont and Clarke. In 1997 the UK's broadly defined budget deficit was equivalent to just over 2% of GDP. This was similar to the OECD average and below the EU average. A net debt burden of around 41.5% of GDP was some way below both the OECD and EU standards, while the UK government's net interest payments, equivalent to just 3% of GDP, were similarly modest.

This is not to deny that there were concerns about the health of the public sector balance sheet, however. There had, for example, been decades of underinvestment in the country's infrastructure. Net public investment in 1996–97 and 1997–98 accounted for well under 1% of GDP. Perceptions of the public services were generally very poor. For all the burgeoning private affluence observable in late-90s Britain, there was – as J. K. Galbraith had so eloquently observed about the US in the 1950s – considerable 'public squalor'.[12]

Labour adopted four main principles for the future management of the public finances: the eschewal of an unsustainable and damaging accumulation of public debt; the avoidance of future generations paying for spending that gave them no benefit; refraining from the sort of bias against investment spending that was evident in previous periods of fiscal restraint; and a commitment to support monetary policy in the achievement of price and broader macroeconomic stability.

To meet these principles, Brown established a new framework for fiscal policy. Its key elements were in a 'Code for Fiscal Stability' that was approved by the House of Commons in December 1998. This document set out the broad guidelines of the approach, as well as requiring the Treasury to embrace full transparency in its operation, forecasting and reporting procedures, and to publish clear fiscal rules.[13] The latter were designed to translate the notion of sound fiscal policy into operational targets, to govern annual budget assessments, and to provide metrics against which judgement on the success or failure of policy could be reached.

The government settled on two such criteria.

First, it would abide by what economists termed the 'golden rule': over the course of the business cycle, the public sector would borrow only to finance capital investment or spending on lasting assets. The 'current' budget, reflecting outlays on non-durable items such as wages, would be kept in balance or run with a small surplus. This would promote fairness across generations, in that the bill for today's current outlays, which mainly benefit today's taxpayers, would be paid by today's taxpayers. Moreover, the rule would be consistent with stable public sector net worth, or the government's net asset position.

Second, the government adopted a so-called sustainable investment rule: public sector debt would be kept at a stable and sustainable level in net terms (that is to say, adjusted for the government's liquid financial assets, which also affect its solvency). For practical purposes, this was defined as less than the equivalent of 40% of GDP at the end of each financial year across the economic cycle. This was a relatively low debt burden in both historical and relative terms.

In contrast to the Keynesian era, the two rules envisaged only a limited role for fiscal policy in demand management. Support for monetary policy as the primary tool of macro-stabilization should be confined, except *in extremis*, largely to the operation of the 'automatic stabilizers' – the natural tendency for current public spending and tax revenues to ebb and flow with economic activity – over the course of the business cycle. The rules were also consistent with the objectives of the EU's 'Stability and Growth Pact', which was designed to prepare members for monetary union.

There is no single definitive set of fiscal rules and, for all Labour's good intentions, those fixed upon by Brown, and the concepts that underlay them, had their shortcomings. In particular, they were always likely to be easier to describe in the abstract than to successfully manage in reality. Indeed, it can at least be said that all fiscal rules have a shelf life, and perhaps even that they are made to be broken.

It is hard to say, for example, which types of public spending yield benefits for future generations and which do not. The distinction between current and capital spending is opaque. How, for example, are education and investment in human capital to be treated?

At the same time, it is only possible to pass definitive judgement on whether the golden rule has been met in retrospect – and perhaps only considerably after the fact. Assessing whether the golden rule will be met in future is complicated by the need to establish precisely where the economy is in any particular cycle – something that Treasury and other forecasters had always struggled with. Cycles vary greatly in duration, in amplitude and in terms of their driving forces. They can also be asymmetric. Forecasting the rate at which productive potential is likely to grow and the associated output gap is by its very nature difficult, and estimates invariably evolve over time.

It is also hard to argue on theoretical, or historical, grounds that a ceiling of 40% of GDP for the net public sector debt burden is more prudent than 30%, say, or 50%, or some other number. There is evidence that sustained high levels of public debt can impose significant costs on economic performance, raise risk market premia and require a damaging reorientation of fiscal policy, but it is impossible to definitively establish an optimal level of public indebtedness. Much depends on the size and frequency of economic shocks, and on how borrowing costs evolve relative to nominal growth. Additionally, concentrating on contemporary debt to the exclusion of potential future liabilities resulting from, for example, demographic changes may fail to provide an accurate picture of the long-term sustainability of the public finances.

In judging and policing the stance and sustainability of fiscal policy, there would remain considerable margin for error and plenty of scope for the government to massage its conclusions, and its policy initiatives, to meet its political priorities.

PRUDENCE WITH A PURPOSE

Brown's first budget in July 1997 was a cautious affair. As suggested in the previous chapter, the hope was that building policy credibility would afford him greater leeway to take a more expansive stance to address key issues and his own favoured projects later. This approach was to become known as 'prudence with a purpose'.[14]

The most obvious demonstration of this restrained approach was Brown's determination to persist with the Major government's parsimonious public expenditure plans for the next two years – plans that the previous chancellor himself was subsequently to characterize as 'eye-wateringly tight' and to which he claimed to have no strong attachment.[15] At the same time, Brown raised the overall tax burden. He and Blair might have agreed to eschew any changes to the basic or top income tax rates for the whole parliament, but he imposed a £5.2 billion windfall tax on the profits of the quasi-monopoly privatized utilities and he instituted a £5 billion raid on pensions through abolition of the dividend tax credit. These were to prove the first of numerous unorthodox revenue-raising schemes that punctuated Brown's time as chancellor – schemes that were, over time, to erode his reputation. He was by far the most tax-active of recent chancellors.

Brown used some of the additional funds raised from these sources to cut the corporate tax rate from 33% to 31%, and he also instituted a 'New Deal' to help the young unemployed. The latter initiative drew on the 'Welfare to Work' policies common in the US and Scandinavia. Those aged between 18 and 24 who had been jobless for more than six months could no longer stay on benefits, but were instead offered a range of options including a subsidized job, full-time education or training, or a placement in the voluntary sector. This was to mark the first of a series of such schemes designed to provide financial help and raise work incentives for specific groups towards the bottom end of the income scale.

Future years would see a growing focus on tax credits targeted at families with children, single parents, pensioners and the disabled that were to cumulate to the equivalent of some 4–5 percentage points on the standard rate of income tax.[16] Furthermore, a minimum wage was introduced in the UK for the first time in April 1999. Although initially set at the relatively low level of £3.60 an hour (£3.00 for the under 20s), the intention was both to stop employers with monopsonist market power holding down pay and to reduce welfare spending. It was subsequently increased in each year New Labour was in power, reaching just under £6.00 an hour in 2010, seemingly without pricing many workers out of jobs or raising unemployment.

Overall, the 1997 budget and its immediate successors delivered a remarkable degree of fiscal restraint, particularly given the public investment deficit and the lamentable condition of the public services. The budgetary stance was tightened by some three percentage points of GDP between 1997 and 2000, by which time the consolidated budget was in significant surplus and the net burden of debt was falling.

From 1998 Brown also introduced a new system of public expenditure planning and control in the form of biennial 'Comprehensive Spending Reviews' (CSRs) that would look ahead three years and that separated capital spending from current spending.[17] These reviews embodied 'Public Service Agreements' (PSAs), which set out the aims and objectives of departmental and cross-departmental programmes, together with quantified performance targets against which progress could be gauged. The goal was, on one level, to encourage longer-term strategic thinking and greater spending efficiency in the context of the fiscal rules outlined above. But what PSAs also did was enhance the Treasury's leverage across the entire gamut of domestic policy, and thereby Brown's powerbase.

EASING OFF

The tide of fiscal policy began to turn ahead of the new millennium and as the next general election came into view. In 1999 the government introduced a new 10% income tax rate on the first £1,500 of income, and then in 2000 it cut the basic rate of income tax to 22%. Spending plans were also upgraded, especially for health and education, while Brown began to throw his weight behind the PFI as a means of mobilizing private funds and expertise for public investment purposes. Again, the intention was to distance New Labour from the supposed excesses and errors of past Labour administrations, and to moderate the increase in public sector liabilities.

The PFI replaced spending financed by public debt with spending undertaken by private firms, for which the firms were compensated by leasing agreements over periods of up to thirty years. This helped New Labour to meet its fiscal rules in the short term, but it did so at considerable future expense. For a creditworthy government, the cost of borrowing to finance private-built infrastructure will almost always be lower than it would be for a private company. Furthermore, projects that are privately financed and run clearly need to generate profits, which in turn leads to higher costs.

Up to the point when the GFC intervened in the autumn of 2007, at which point many sources of private capital dried up, the total value of PFI contracts signed was some £68 billion, committing the British taxpayer to future spending of £215 billion over the life of the contracts. Under New Labour, the PFI was focused to a significant degree on the delivery of social infrastructure, and especially schools and hospitals. The PFI undoubtedly helped to sustain economic growth and high levels of employment, and the projects funded in this way performed better than did traditional infrastructure projects in terms of delivery dates and cost overruns, which by definition were borne by the private contractor. But PFI schemes became notorious for poor design, for optimism bias, for questionable oversight, for a lack of transparency in regard to the financial and operational performance of projects, and for generally offering poor value for money for taxpayers. A scheme to modernize the London Underground proved a particularly expensive example of the initiative going awry.

The PFI also carried high levels of underlying political risk, as many of the deals had a lifespan in excess of the UK's five-year electoral cycle. This meant that a significant number of contracts signed by New Labour locked subsequent governments into making fixed payments for investments with which they had little sympathy.

Away from the impetus given to the PFI, and in a remarkable contrast to the 1970s and 1980s, actual government outlays were slow to pick up once the shackles were loosened. It was as if government departments had forgotten how to spend. Furthermore, revenues were boosted by some 2.3% of GDP through the auction of third-generation mobile phone licences and through the termination of mortgage tax relief and the married couples allowance, both of which had been in existence since the end of World War I.

The budget surplus continued to mount, therefore, reaching the equivalent of more than 1.5% of GDP at the end of Labour's first term. Over this four-year period, total public spending fell by some three percentage points of GDP. Most of the decline was in current outlays, but contrary to the government's avowed principles of fiscal management, net public investment fell from 0.75% of GDP to just 0.5% of GDP, and it was lower on average than in any other four-year period since the war. Over the same quadrennial, total government revenues increased by more than two percentage points of GDP, while total public sector debt dropped by more than ten percentage points of GDP, to around 31%. By these metrics, Gordon Brown was very much the 'Iron Chancellor'.

INTO A SECOND TERM

New Labour enjoyed a second landslide general election victory in June 2001, losing a mere six seats and retaining a huge overall majority of 194. Helped by a buoyant economy, New Labour had built up considerable trust with the electorate over its first four years in office, and especially among the middle classes and floating voters. Blair seemed to have realized Harold Wilson's dream that Labour should become 'the natural party of government'. It now had a mandate for a more expansive programme.

New Labour's 2001 manifesto recommitted it to the maintenance of low inflation and broader macroeconomic stability, while also emphasizing the need to increase investment and to pursue public service reform, especially in health and education. The party again explicitly eschewed any rise in the basic or top rates of income tax, and yet the fiscal shackles were about to be loosened. There was also a sense that the issue of euro membership would have to be addressed. Indeed, by the time of the election the Treasury had already begun a detailed assessment of the case for the UK joining. In due course the matter would widen an already-deepening rift between the party's two major personalities and would generate broader political turbulence for the government.

Rather than macroeconomic considerations, however, it was external events – in the form of the 9/11 attack on the US and the subsequent invasions of Afghanistan and Iraq – that more than anything else were to dominate the politics of this parliament. In hindsight, the decisions made in that context were to mark the beginning of the end for New Labour, and those mistakes still resonate in the minds of the electorate today.

MORE PRICE STABILITY, BUT ...

Ostensibly, the Bank of England continued to do an admirable job in delivering on its price stability mandate during New Labour's second term. Monetary policy remained free from political influence and more systematic and predictable. Inflation expectations were subdued. That said, it should be acknowledged that the Bank was assisted in its quest for stable prices by the global environment. The accession of China to the World Trade Organization in 2001 augmented the competitive forces that had been exerting downward pressure on wages and prices in all the advanced economies, and which were being amplified by the rapid spread of information technology and, with it, price transparency and market contestability.

While the economy avoided the shallow recession that afflicted the US in 2001, continuing to expand at a pace a little above its underlying potential growth rate of 2–2.5% a year, inflation remained reasonably close to target. Indeed, if anything, the Bank continued to undershoot its objective slightly, as it had done for much of the period from 1999 to 2001. This was particularly the case after the Treasury adjusted the Bank's goal from 2.5% a year on the basis of the RPIX index to 2% a year on the basis of the consumer price index (CPI), a measure used across the rest of the EU, in the autumn of 2003.[18] UK inflation remained slightly above the OECD average, however, although that was largely because of Japan's slide into outright deflation.

Keeping inflation subdued also required much lower policy rates than had prevailed in previous decades. Official rates fell in quarter-point stages during 2001, from 5.75% in February to 4.0% in November, where they remained until a cut to 3.75% in February 2003. They were then reduced to 3.5% in July 2003, the month in which Mervyn King took over from Eddie George as governor. This marked their lowest level since January 1955, and the bottom of the cycle. They subsequently rose progressively, getting back to 4.75% in August 2004, where they remained until the May 2005 election. But this was still a level that had not been witnessed since the early 1960s.

Monetary policy cannot be judged purely on the basis of the achievement of a price stability target, however. Inflation targeting is not the answer to every macroeconomic question – or even, for that matter, every monetary question. Away from consumer price developments, a number of disturbing trends were emerging. For example, UK growth in the early noughties was driven overwhelmingly by domestic demand and service activity. With sterling persistently elevated, the manufacturing sector struggled, the external balance was in stubborn and widening deficit, import penetration increased further, and the UK's share in world trade declined. The current account shortfall and difficulties in the tradable-goods sector did not trigger a currency crisis, but they were nevertheless indicative of burgeoning underlying disequilibria and unsustainable processes within the economy.

Following an extended phase of falling long-term government bond yields, this period saw a deepening 'stretch for yield' and an accumulation of risk on the part of investors. It also saw considerable financial innovation and asset price appreciation, not least in the real estate market. From the low in December 1995 until the onset of the GFC in 2007, the average price of a house increased by some 260%, rising from the equivalent of just over four times average earnings to more than eight times. This was the longest and most ebullient bull market in housing on record, and it had a significant impact on the distribution of wealth.

Hand in hand with rapid asset price appreciation went a sharp increase in the burden of debt. Total credit extended to the household sector, much of it in the form of mortgages, rose from 57.75% of GDP in 1997 to 68.75% of GDP in 2001, continuing up to 93.75% of GDP in 2007. For the non-financial corporate sector, the equivalent figures were 54.5% of GDP in 1997, 75.5% of GDP in 2001 and 81.75% of GDP in 2007. Taken together, these figures represented by some distance the fastest growth in private indebtedness the UK had ever experienced.

The accumulation of debt left individual and company balance sheets – and, thereby, the banks and other financial institutions – increasingly vulnerable to economic shocks. And excessive indebtedness had been a theme common to so many financial crises of the past. This led some commentators to suggest that the Bank should broaden its focus in an effort to reduce the degree of debt in the system and bear down more explicitly on asset prices. The problem was that this was easier said than done. As made clear by Dennis Robertson (a Cambridge economist, and a contemporary of Keynes) as long ago as the late 1920s, it is difficult to apply monetary policy directly to asset markets without greatly adding to broader macro instability, including the risk of deflation.[19]

For example, while stock prices and house prices rose sharply after 2001, suggesting a requirement for greater monetary restraint, the exchange rate was persistently strong, indicating that monetary policy should be more accommodative. The Bank of England could not simultaneously respond to both pressures with adjustments in interest rate policy. The Bank's avowed approach of assessing asset prices through the lens of their impact on the balance of overall supply and demand therefore made considerable sense. But this is not entirely to deny that the Bank's critics had a point, especially given King's increasingly narrow fixation on the inflation target.

Equally, the FSA and the Treasury could have sought to make more use of fiscal and regulatory measures that were arguably better suited to addressing excessive asset market exuberance head on. But it is always difficult for a government to be seen to be deliberately deflating an asset bubble. Acting directly to reduce peoples' wealth, either via their stock portfolios or the value of their houses, is never popular, and New Labour was of course keen to retain the support of the asset-rich middle-income groups that had swept it to power in 1997 and then kept it there in 2001. Furthermore, there was the financial sector itself to consider. The government did not want to alienate it, as various previous Labour administrations had tended to do. Financial entities' profits were often directly linked to asset market performance, and these profits were an important source of tax revenues. By 2007, housing and financial sector receipts had risen to the equivalent of 4.25% of GDP.

FISCAL EXPANSION

There was a very different bias to fiscal policy during New Labour's second term. Tony Blair set the tone, suggesting ahead of the 2001 election that he wanted to raise public spending on health to the European average of some 8.5% of GDP from its existing level of around 5%. Gordon Brown resented the prime minister straying on to his policy patch in such an overt way, allegedly going so far as to accuse Blair of 'stealing my fucking budget'.[20] However, he had little choice but to acquiesce in this, especially given his own strong desire to address the shortcomings of the public services. He therefore appointed Derek Wanless, former head of NatWest Bank, to examine the future funding of the NHS. When Wanless submitted his report around the time of the 2002 budget, he recommended an increase of £40 billion in spending, or annual increases of more than 7% in real terms over the period to 2007. After the famine was to come the feast.

The problem Brown faced at this time was that despite debt interest payments having fallen because of the decline in the UK's risk premium following the Bank of England being granted independence, tax revenues had weakened unexpectedly in 2000 and 2001 because of the correction in the UK stock market that followed the US 'tech wreck'. Because he was keen to also apply greater spending largesse to other areas of the public sector, while boosting infrastructure investment and continuing to attack poverty through his strategy of targeted tax credits, Brown was therefore compelled to raise the tax burden if he was not to see the public finances run off track. He settled on a one percentage point increase in national insurance contributions for both employees and employers, which he successfully presented to the population as a hypothecated levy to fund NHS renewal.

The extent of the recalibration of budgetary policy in the early years of the twenty-first century is revealed by the fact that the fiscal impulse was positive in every year of the parliament, and by more than four percentage points of GDP in aggregate. This was a very procyclical stance. Indeed, it was more expansive than that taken by any other major economy bar the US. It even went beyond the degree of standard fiscal largesse instituted later in the wake of the GFC.

Looking in more detail at the fiscal metrics of the time, total government outlays jumped from 37.25% of GDP to 41.75%, with net government investment spending rebounding from its post-war lows to around 2% of GDP. By 2007, health spending accounted for around 17% of total managed government outlays. However, the 8.5% of GDP target was never reached under New Labour, with the peak being 7.5%.

Total government revenues, meanwhile, increased from 37.5% of GDP to 38.25% of GDP. The net result of this was that the overall budget swung into significant deficit, with the red ink running to some 3.5% of GDP for the years 2003, 2004 and 2005. Having begun the period with one of the OECD economies' relatively scarce budget surpluses, the UK ended it with a shortfall that was well above average. Against this background, the net government debt ratio rebounded to around 31.5% of GDP, but this was still low by the standards of the other advanced economies. Moreover, with average borrowing costs much more modest than they had been in previous decades, the government's net interest burden fell under 2% of GDP: well below the equivalent figures in the 1970s, 1980s and 1990s.

A DALLIANCE WITH THE EURO

Away from the minutiae of monetary and fiscal stabilization, the foremost macroeconomic policy issue of the second New Labour term was that of membership of the euro.

Labour's relationship with the EEC and then the EU had blown hot and cold over the decades: at different times, official policy had ranged from cautious enthusiasm through indifference to outright disdain. Furthermore, as with the Conservatives, attitudes towards Europe had tended to be far from consistent across the party. For some, the EU was a capitalist conspiracy; for others, it was the future.

Blair and Brown were both Europhiles at heart, and they had no objection in principle to UK membership of the single currency. There was no great ideological rift between the two on Europe, as there was between John Major and members of his cabinet. That said, there were differences of opinion between the two men about the urgency of the euro issue and the nature of the process that might lead to accession to the single currency.

Blair was keener than any UK prime minister since Edward Heath to put the country at the heart of Europe, not least in regard to its institutional evolution and reform. To him, euro membership would expand UK power and influence across the continent and beyond. This meant that his mind was more open than most to flexibility where Britain's sovereignty was concerned.

Brown was more cautious, and because of his position as chancellor he was more focused on the economic detail of euro entry. He was strongly influenced in his views by Ed Balls, his chief advisor, and he was keen to minimize the risk of a repetition of the ERM debacle. Brown had been a strong advocate of ERM membership in 1992, when he was shadow chancellor, and he had been badly burned when sterling was so unceremoniously ejected. As for the Treasury, the humiliation of Black Wednesday cut deep. It was not something it wanted to see repeated. It was therefore quite happy to concur with the chancellor's wariness on the issue.

It is also noteworthy that as Blair and Brown's personal relationship deteriorated, the latter became more proprietorial over policy towards the euro. He saw a more circumspect line as a means to exert his own influence and authority within cabinet and the party – perhaps even a way of making life difficult for a prime minister that he was by then desperate to replace and that he thought should step aside in his favour.

In the lead-up to the 1997 general election, in no small part to avoid roiling Rupert Murdoch and the Eurosceptic UK tabloid press, Blair and Brown had committed New Labour to holding a referendum on euro membership: a strategy first floated in 1991 by the recently defenestrated Margaret Thatcher. Brown and Balls also sketched out a series of five economic tests that would have to be passed to determine whether the UK was ready to join the euro, which despite the trials and tribulations of the ERM in the early 1990s was to be launched on 1 January 1999. On coming into power, Brown and Balls asked the Treasury to assess the five tests. The new government, meanwhile, reiterated its manifesto line that the UK would not be among the first wave of members. Brown subsequently added that euro membership was unlikely to happen 'in this parliament', although Blair was less dogmatic on this point.

Towards the end of October 1997, Brown more formally detailed the tests in a statement to parliament in an effort to provide greater clarity and coherence in its policy towards EMU. Provided the single currency proved a success – and there were many influential people both in the UK and in the putative euro area itself who were sceptical about this – a decision for the UK to join would be determined on the basis of

- whether business cycles and economic structures were compatible, so that the UK and others could live comfortably with euro interest rates on a permanent basis;
- whether there would be sufficiently flexibility to deal with problems were they to emerge;
- whether joining EMU would improve conditions for firms making long-term decisions to invest in Britain;
- what impact entry into EMU would have on the competitive position of the UK's financial services industry, particularly the City's wholesale markets; and
- whether joining EMU would, in general, promote higher growth, stability and a lasting increase in jobs.

The tests were in effect supplementary conditions to the Maastricht Treaty criteria for prospective euro members of interest rate convergence; specified limits on budget deficits, public debt and inflation; and two years of exchange rate stability within the confines of the ERM. They made sense, but they were also unavoidably opaque, and judging whether they had been met, or might soon be met, would involve considerable judgement, extending far beyond economics and into politics. Some would always claim that the tests were designed not to be met; others that they could always be met if the government wanted them to be.

With hindsight, it might also have been wise to add a sixth test that looked at the issue from the opposite angle: would remaining outside the euro leave the UK on the margins of the EU, reduce its policy influence, and strengthen the position of those who wanted to withdraw from the entire entity, in the process inflicting severe damage on the economy? But such concerns were, at the time, second order. Almost thirty years on from EEC accession, EU membership was generally viewed as part of the UK's institutional architecture.

What was extraordinary, especially in the wake of the ERM debacle and given the strength of the pound at that time, was that no mention was made of what might be an appropriate level for sterling in advance of entry.

It was the first test that was judged to be the most critical, as it essentially amounted to whether or not the UK – which had traditionally had a very different economic structure to prospective members of the single currency and had been more prone to boom and bust – could cope with a one-size-fits-all monetary policy handed down by the European Central Bank (ECB).

The Treasury's preliminary judgement in the autumn of 1997 was that the UK economy was not sufficiently converged with that of the rest of the EU and nor were the two economies sufficiently flexible to justify a recommendation of membership. However, these divergences were likely to diminish over time because of the impact of the single market, because of the increased premium being put on greater economic stability in the UK, and because of the likely evolution of structural reform.[21] The chancellor therefore pledged to return to the tests early in the next parliament and to publish a revised assessment at that time. With Blair keen to force the pace somewhat, in due course this came to mean by June 2003. The hiatus, meanwhile, would allow New Labour to prove that it could run the economy competently, without outside influence or support.

This did not stop speculation intermittently mounting in the press about UK entry, especially with Blair and Brown dropping regular hints about their own evolving (and often-inconsistent) preferences on the matter. However, what was also evident during this period was that popular support for euro membership was never strong.

The Treasury's second assessment of the case for euro entry was led by Ed Balls and initially, on the official side, Gus O'Donnell, who understandably favoured a cautious approach to the whole idea of euro membership given his role as John Major's press secretary at the time of Black Wednesday. Once O'Donnell had been elevated to Permanent Secretary in 2002, David Ramsden took over, leading a vast cohort of economists in a huge analytical enterprise. O'Donnell, however, continued to oversee the process.

The second assessment, which was undertaken in conditions of extraordinary secrecy, was essentially complete by Christmas of 2002, but Brown saw fit only to drip feed its contents to the prime minister, and its final conclusions – presented to all intents and purposes as a fait accompli – were not delivered to Number 10 until the following April. The cabinet was brought into the discussion only weeks later, and then cursorily.

When it was published in its entirety in early June, the assessment ran to around 250 pages and was backed up by no fewer than eighteen supporting documents on subjects such as the monetary policy transmission mechanism, the cost of capital, labour market flexibility, and the euro area's monetary and fiscal frameworks. In addition, and in contrast to the provisional 1997 appraisal, the Treasury also looked at the exchange rate.

It was a remarkably thorough and detailed body of work. Indeed, it was at the time the most extensive economic policy review that had ever been conducted in the UK, and one that other countries that took the decision to join the euro only to subsequently suffer chronic macro instability during and after the GFC would have been wise to replicate.[22] At the very least, the Treasury's paper on 'Modelling shocks and adjustment mechanisms in EMU' should have been required reading for the single currency's more peripheral members.[23]

The Treasury's overall conclusion was that the case for joining the euro in principle remained strong. The UK could look forward to various important microeconomic benefits: closer trading links, more intense competition, a lower cost of capital, more transparent pricing, and lower transactions costs, for example. What is more, there had been important progress on convergence since 1997.

However, there were still significant structural differences between the two economies, not least when it came to the housing market. Equally, while the UK's flexibility had improved, the Treasury could not be confident that it was yet flexible enough to deal with potential shocks. The same was true of other participants in the single currency. Euro membership was judged likely to increase investment, but only if convergence and flexibility were sufficient. Finally, growth, stability and employment stood to increase as a result of euro membership, but again only if convergence and flexibility proved adequate. The only one of the five tests that was judged to have been clearly met was that the City would benefit from euro membership.

The assessment encompassed serious misgivings about the pace and breadth of euro area structural reform, and about the existing institutional framework of euro area macro policy, including the way the ECB went about its business. It also warned that if UK interest rates were to converge rapidly with those of their euro area counterparts, whose rates were much lower, it would require a sharp – and potentially politically damaging – tightening of fiscal policy to forestall a destabilizing boom. It further concluded that 'the right rate' of entry for sterling was around €1.37, or between 5% and 10% below where it had latterly been trading.

The overriding conclusion, therefore, was that the economics of euro membership were not yet right. Convergence was incomplete, and entry without adequate convergence would risk instability and enduring damage to the UK economy. The question was one of how this conclusion should be 'spun'. Should the glass be presented as half full or half empty? Would a referendum effectively remain on the agenda, or would it be kicked into the long grass?

The presentation of the Treasury's assessment left much to be desired. In fact, it was something of a public relations disaster. Brown was prickly and suspicious throughout. There were endless, fraught arguments between the prime minister and his chancellor about the relative importance of different elements of substance in the assessment, about the breadth of the messaging involved, about the timing of its release, and even about who should deliver the announcement of the verdict (in the end Brown did so). These disagreements inevitably leaked out to the press, caused confusion in the markets and among the public, and led to a further worsening of the troubled relationship between the two men – a deterioration from which the friendship never recovered. The Treasury's assessment of the five tests was, along with the Iraq War, to cast a pall over the remainder of New Labour's time in office.

The essential issue was that Brown and his closest advisors fell very much into the 'half empty' camp, and he did not want his authority on such a matter of paramount importance to the country's future undermined. The prime minister and many of those around him were disappointed by the assessment's conclusions, as was the Foreign Office. Many people were deeply disappointed. At the very least they would have preferred to have accentuated the more positive aspects of the Treasury's work and left the door to a referendum on entry ajar. But their efforts to massage the drafting significantly made scant progress.

Brown threatened to resign if his judgement was overridden. Blair questioned whether Brown should ever succeed him, and considered calling his bluff, or even sacking him. In the end, both retreated from their respective 'nuclear options'. Blair was acutely aware of the damage that a bitter Brown backed by a significant coterie of supporters – a putative 'king over the water' – could do to him from the back benches. Brown eschewed a course of action that could have ended his chances of realizing his lifetime's ambition: that of becoming prime minister.

Equally, however, beyond the divisions over the economic judgements and the political spin that should be attached to them, winning a referendum on euro entry at this time – a period when the Iraq War was already going awry and UK public opinion about the government, and in particular its prime minister, was increasingly sharply divided – would have been difficult. It would have taken a monumental political effort and required the party's two figureheads to be working in close harmony. And losing a euro referendum would have been disastrous for Labour's prospects at the next general election.

The fact was that in June 2003 the stars were not aligned for sterling's entry into the single currency. To have forced the issue would have been folly. The government therefore ruled out UK membership of the euro for the duration of the parliament. To maintain the fiction that Britain was still serious about joining thereafter, a series of studies were commissioned about how to accelerate economic convergence, including one on the housing market, where a preponderance of floating-rate mortgages and high home ownership made the UK disproportionately sensitive to policy rate changes. However, after New

Labour was re-elected for a second time in May 2005, with a sharply reduced majority of sixty-six, debate on a European Constitution and the subsequent Treaty of Lisbon tended to supersede any further substantive discussions on euro membership.

In his first press conference after succeeding Tony Blair as prime minister in June 2007, Brown ruled out membership for the foreseeable future, adding that the decision not to join in 2003 had been right for Britain and for Europe. The GFC was to add weight to this judgement. Indeed, it is possible that had the UK been in the euro during the crisis and its aftermath, it would have led to a repeat of the events of September 1992, and even to the single currency's disintegration.

OPENING THE DOOR TO BREXIT

Before we turn away from the subject of Europe and the euro, we should look at another decision that was made around this time that was to have huge consequences for UK politics and the country's economy a decade or so later. In 2004 the EU expanded eastwards, with ten new countries joining, including Poland. Existing members were given the option of applying temporary restrictions on immigration from the new members, but the Blair government was a keen advocate of the principle of free movement and therefore chose not to do so. It was encouraged in this by a Treasury and a business sector that saw significant economic benefits in an influx of highly skilled and highly motivated foreign workers. The Home Office initially estimated that something in the region of 50,000 migrants would arrive in the UK from the accession countries. The eventual total was in excess of a million.

The impact of eastern European immigration on economic growth was clearly positive in the following years, but the new arrivals put pressure on already-hard-pressed public services in some of the regions in which they congregated, and the perception took hold that the UK was an open house for migrants. Their presence, and indeed their success, was subsequently scurrilously used by politicians from the UK Independence Party and from the right wing of the Conservative Party to claim, incorrectly, that indigenous workers were losing jobs and income and were having their access to healthcare and other welfare benefits curtailed as a result of the flow of migrants.

WHAT LAY BENEATH

In the two years or so between the 2005 general election and the GFC, the UK economy continued to perform well – outwardly, at least. Real GDP growth ran at an annual rate of between 2.5% and 3%. Unemployment edged back above 5% of the workforce but remained relatively low, and with the Bank of England guiding policy rates upwards to a peak of 5.75% in July 2007, CPI inflation remained close to the amended 2% target despite creeping higher in the context of sharply higher oil prices.

The problem was that the imbalances noted earlier were continuing to build. Asset markets, and in particular the housing market, remained ebullient. The burden of private sector debt spiralled ever higher. The household saving rate trended ever lower, dipping below 5% of disposable income. Banking sector assets (predominantly loans) accounted for around 450% of GDP by 2007: they had doubled on this basis over the previous decade. Growth was increasingly driven by domestic consumption. The external deficit had widened further, swelling the nation's external liabilities and suggesting that sterling was overvalued and headed for a fall.

FROM PRUDENCE TO PROFLIGACY?

In the meantime, the fiscal stance remained excessively accommodative. Overall public sector outlays continued to account for some 41.5% of GDP, with net investment spending accounting for between 1.5% and 2% of GDP, as against less than a half a percentage point of GDP around the turn of the decade. But the Treasury's forecasts for growth, and therefore revenues and borrowing, tended to be too optimistic. Gordon Brown's repeated claims to have conquered boom and bust were increasingly factored into official views of the future.

Although the UK was characterized by a widening positive output gap, the cyclically adjusted budget deficit averaged more than 4% of GDP between 2003 and 2007 and the burden of public sector net debt continued to increase. Nor could much of this be blamed on Britain's involvement in the conflicts in Iraq and Afghanistan. The total cost of these wars to 2010 is estimated at £20.3 billion, or the equivalent of around 1% of GDP in that year.

On these metrics, Britain was an underperforming outlier by the standards of the other OECD economies, yet Brown was reluctant to admit that anything was wrong – he had long displayed a rather constipated approach to apologizing – or that he might be taking liberties with his own fiscal rules. Ultimately, however, to ensure that the economy kept within the rules' guidelines across the one and only complete cycle that the Treasury had arbitrarily judged had occurred under New Labour before the GFC, the government was forced to revise its estimate of the cycle's onset to 1997 from 1999 and to raise taxes and moderate some spending programmes in 2005 and 2006. Moreover, with the current budget balance in deficit, meeting the rules in the next cycle was going to be difficult, no matter what macroeconomic circumstances the country was confronted by.

The UK's procyclical fiscal laxity in the mid 2000s was to prove unwise and inopportune, and it fuelled demand in an economy with less spare capacity than the government claimed. However, the problems should not be unduly exaggerated – the absolute level of public debt (32.7% of GDP) and the burden of public debt interest payments (1.7% of GDP) were still historically and relatively low in 2007 – and nor should the government's approach be seen as a primary cause of the subsequent GFC. The crisis denuded the government's hard-won reputation for fiscal probity nonetheless, and left it open to political attack as well as reducing the degree of fiscal firepower subsequently available to fight the most catastrophic economic downturn seen since the Great Depression.

SUPPLY-SIDE REFORM

In his later years as prime minister, Tony Blair was desperate to prove that his leadership was about more than providing military and diplomatic backup for the Bush administration's wars in Iraq and Afghanistan. Besides never quite letting the idea of euro membership go, he focused his attention on public sector reform, not least where the NHS and education were concerned, in an effort to encourage levels of efficiency commensurate with the significant additional resources that had been ploughed into them. Blair was this as a means to shore up New Labour's legacy, but Gordon Brown was increasingly pursuing a more traditional social democratic line. Brown was always less convinced than Blair that Labour could only win by being exclusively 'new'.

The reality, however, was that little was achieved in this area. True, the prime minister's newly established 'delivery unit', set up to hold policies and policymakers to greater account, enjoyed some successes. But there was an opacity and incoherence in Blair's determination to achieve greater choice and higher public sector efficiency via bigger roles for the private sector, competition and local accountability. Markets can be ill-suited to taxpayer-funded public services delivered free of charge, such as healthcare, as the consumer is not sovereign. Use of healthcare resources is unpredictable and unplannable. If scarce resources are increasingly channeled towards efficient hospitals, the inefficient will just become more and more hopeless.

Nor were Blair's plans helped by his restless reshuffling of cabinet positions, by the often muddled lines of authority, or by his limited interest in the mechanics of the civil service. There was more to reform than just issuing orders to be obeyed.

Notwithstanding the difficulties in its calculation, public sector productivity essentially flatlined in the 2000s. Furthermore, Blair's desire for reform often served only to intensify Brown's opposition to change and his antipathy towards him. The more assertive Blair became, the more difficult and duplicitous was his chancellor. Blair's authority, once paramount, had increasingly drained away.

The shortcomings of public sector reform and productivity pose the question of whether there was a broader malaise in the supply side of the UK economy during the years of Blair's premiership. In fact, the record shows that, thanks to vibrancy in the market sector, underlying UK economic performance remained reasonably impressive in overall terms during the period 1997–2007. GDP per head grew some 20% over this period, equating to around 2% a year. This was a faster rate than in France, Germany, Italy, Japan and the US. The expansion of GDP per hour worked was second only to that seen in the US.

At the same time, factors such as the relatively low taxes on labour, the moderate levels and duration of unemployment benefit, the fall in union density and the high levels of temporary working meant that the labour market stayed highly flexible and that the interaction between wage inflation and price inflation was limited and largely benign. Earnings typically increased at a faster pace than prices, but not disturbingly so, while industrial disputes became rarer. The improvement in UK employment figures between 1997 and 2007 actually exceeded that seen in the US. This was despite the sharp increase in net immigration to more than 200,000 a year after the EU was expanded. The natural rate of unemployment had declined. The old Phillips curve had shifted inwards and flattened.

The gentle reversal of decades of long relative decline continued, even if absolute UK productivity levels still remained some way below those of the US, Germany and France. Neither does the UK's improved productivity performance seem to have been merely the result of unsustainable bubbles in finance, property, oil or public spending. The contribution made by the finance sector to the 2.8% annual average productivity growth in the economy's market sector was only 0.4 percentage points. Distribution and market services were larger contributors.

Analysis of other indicators of business performance – including foreign direct investment flows,[24] use of information and communications technology, innovation, entrepreneurship and skills – supports the notion that the gains in productivity were real, although this is not to deny that some important inadequacies endured, not least low levels of investment, especially in research and development and in vocational training and skills. Notwithstanding Gordon Brown's attraction to workfare, outlays on active labour market policies remained low relative to most of the UK's European competitors as a percentage of GDP.

The economy's supply-side performance was undoubtedly encouraged by the delayed effects of previous structural policy initiatives, including the Conservative labour market reforms of the 1980s and 1990s and membership of the European single market. The competitive forces unleashed by globalization also provided an encouraging backdrop, as indeed did the eschewing of renationalization.[25]

Competition policy is one of the most important elements of structural policy. Competition raises product awareness, keeps prices down, boosts real incomes, encourages differentiation, stimulates the more efficient use of resources and increases consumer satisfaction. There is also, for the most part, a strong positive correlation between competition and productivity, and this is especially true for firms that are either far from or close to the technological frontier.

The competition regime was strengthened through the 1998 Competition Act and the 2002 Enterprise Act. These led to the evolution of the Office of Fair Trading and enhanced the powers of the Competition Commission. Indeed, the competition framework Brown established was probably one of the most liberal in the industrial world.

Unlike under previous Labour administrations, and in particular those of the mid-to-late 1970s, there was a sense that the government had a rational framework for supply-side policy – one that was focused on market imperfections and failures rather than on becoming an (often ad hoc) adjunct to social policy that impeded the reallocation of resources from low-productivity sectors and firms to higher-productivity ones.

New Labour also sunk additional resources into university education, resulting in an increase in the proportion of the workforce with a degree: from under a quarter in 1997 to over a third by 2010. Moreover, overall public spending on education rose persistently, both in real terms and as a percentage of GDP, under Blair.

Finally, it can be argued that it was during the Blair administrations that climate change was first taken seriously by a British government.[26] The prime minister was certainly interested in the subject and his chancellor came to follow his example (although this may have to some extent reflected a desire on the part of the latter to seize the initiative on the matter when personal relations between the two New Labour heavy hitters were at a low ebb).

The Stern Review on the Economics of Climate Change, released in October 2006, was commissioned by Gordon Brown when Stern was the head of the Government Economic Service.[27] The thorough and well-researched document was positively received internationally, and it had a significant impact on global opinion and on the thrust of government policy, even if the Treasury was resistant to adopt the associated recommendations on taxation. In due course, Stern's work underpinned the Climate Change Act of 2008, which set out emission targets for UK compliance. These were the first legally binding climate change mitigation targets set by any country.

Overall, beyond presiding over various public service and PFI inefficiencies, allowing the shares of both government spending and tax revenues in economic activity to rise too rapidly in the 2000s, and complicating the tax system, New Labour's supply-side interventions are hard to characterize as especially malign. They seem to have done nothing significant to undermine the economy's aggregate productivity performance after 1997, and they may have served to enhance it in some respects. That said, certain long-standing shortcomings of the UK economy – such as the poor quality of much of the management class and the relatively wide regional disparities in industrial efficiency – were largely left unaddressed, and some of the gaps in the structural reforms of the previous Conservative administrations were never closed.

There was, however, one area of supply-side policy that was storing up trouble for the future: financial regulation and supervision, unhappily shared as it was across three separate public sector institutions. New Labour was only too happy to go along with the faith of previous governments in self-correcting markets and in the risk management skills and benign influence of senior managements, and with a generally 'light touch' approach. This was to prove disastrous. The financial sector became grotesquely bloated. Between 2000 and 2007, financial leverage exploded from a reasonably consistent forty-year average of some twenty times capital to fifty times capital. As a result, the UK was to prove especially vulnerable to malign global forces.

INEQUALITIES

As noted in chapter 2, for all its economic and political traumas, UK society was as 'equal' in the 1970s as it had ever been. The picture changed dramatically in the 1980s during the Thatcher years, as the welfare state was scaled back; unemployment was allowed, if not encouraged, to escalate, and was then left persistently high; various regressive tax reforms were implemented; and those at the top of the income distribution, and especially those at the very top, enjoyed rapidly rising real earnings and significant increases in the value of their asset holdings. This all went hand in hand with deindustrialization, widening regional income disparities and a sharp escalation of poverty and deprivation.

The pace of change in the distribution of income and wealth slowed sharply during John Major's premiership, but the trend was still, if anything, towards greater inequalities. Under Blair, various indicators – including the Gini coefficient, the 90/10 ratio and the share of income going to the richest 1% of the population – all suggest that overall income inequality broadly stabilized. Regional income disparities also remained much the same as they were in 1997.

Breaking the data down into sub-periods demonstrates that there was little change in the income distribution in Blair's first term, a significant drop in inequality in his second term, and then a rebound in inequality during his third.

In aggregate, therefore, Britain remained a relatively unequal society by the standards of the EU and the OECD as a whole. However, this is not to deny that there were important shifts in the relative positions of certain groups in society. For example, asset price gains helped many of the old to become richer. Meanwhile, the young were increasingly being priced out of the housing market.

What is also clear is that the rate of growth of median real earnings began to slow in the 2000s. Indeed, median real incomes stagnated between 2003 and 2008, in a period during which real GDP grew by more than 10%. The economy had relatively full employment and a flexible labour market, but many of the jobs that were being created were lower-paying jobs. Around a fifth of UK workers earned less than two-thirds of the median wage compared with around one in ten across the rest of Europe, and it was the sectors where the trade unions were least in evidence where the low paid were congregated. Meanwhile, the relative stagnation for those in the middle of the income distribution was increasingly compensated for by the accumulation of debt – a process that was inevitably finite.

The period-to-period trajectory of poverty under Blair was similar to that of income inequality: after an initial period of little change, significant falls in poverty in the period 2001–5 were partially unwound thereafter. In overall terms, therefore, relative poverty was somewhat lower at the end of the Blair governments' period of office than it was at the beginning. This was especially so for families with children and for pensioners, the two groups that benefitted most from Gordon Brown's tax credits and benefit reforms, as well as from the increases in health and education spending that characterized the onset of the new millennium.

Inequalities of various sorts, together with perceptions of unfairness, represent further important forms of economic imbalance or disequilibria that can encourage significant social disquiet and political turmoil over time, and that can become unsustainable. New Labour's failure to significantly unwind the sharp increase in inequalities seen during the 1980s, not least among the party's traditional supporters in the poorer regions of the country, was to come back to haunt both it and the nation as a whole over the next decade and a half. It could and should have done more.

A NICE DECADE

By the standards of some previous post-war epochs and of the tumultuous decade and a half that followed, the years 1997 to 2007 look like a time of relative tranquillity and progress. New Labour avoided any major economic catastrophes and presided over ten years of sustained and reasonably robust expansion, over a further period of modest productivity catch-up, and over a time of low inflation and borrowing costs. Furthermore, the public services were significantly improved, with NHS funding for once reasonably adequate.

This record can in part be traced to a number of important institutional changes in the way that economic policy was conducted, of which the granting of operational independence to the Bank of England to pursue relative price stability was the most obvious and, at least in a narrow sense, the most successful.

The new framework for fiscal policy proved less effective, though, as time wore on. In the absence of robust independent oversight, the government assumed that trend-like economic growth could be relied upon to continue indefinitely, while it increasingly took other liberties with the way its fiscal rules were applied. The fundamental Keynesian nostrum that governments should save in the good times to afford themselves the scope to dispense largesse in the bad times was progressively downplayed, if not ignored. That said, Gordon Brown and New Labour were hardly alone in their inability to envisage a major crisis in world finance. Officialdom worldwide was essentially caught off guard by the GFC.

New Labour's successes were also grounded in the benign economic inheritance it enjoyed, courtesy of the previous Conservative administration and of a number of benevolent international trends. In sharp contrast to the situation in 1964, 1970, 1974, 1979 or 1992, the economy was already performing well, and it exhibited few evident stresses or strains in mid 1997. Blair and Brown were also wise enough to embrace rather than discard much of the 1980s Thatcherite supply-side policy settlement that had endured into the following decade. At the same time, globalization, together with the ICT revolution, led to the increasing integration into the international economy of a number of rapidly growing low-cost producers, with China being the most conspicuous example.

New Labour dodged a bullet, furthermore, by eschewing euro entry in its second term. A decision to have joined the single currency in 2003 would at the very least have invited considerably more macroeconomic and political volatility in the following years. And at most it could have led to early defeat at the polls, or even to a repeat of 1976 or 1992.

Beneath this veneer of success and stability, however, problems were brewing in the form of the growing antipathy between the government's two dominant figures and with the development of various financial imbalances and unsustainable processes within the economy that received insufficient attention from policymakers.

Even though Blair and Brown temporarily called a truce to fight the 2005 general election, sharp divisions between the occupants of Numbers 10 and 11 Downing Street inevitably became inconsistent with optimal policymaking. It could sometimes seem as if there were two entirely separate governments.

Meanwhile, the external account became prone to significant deficit; private sector debt burdens swelled alarmingly; and asset prices, and in particular house prices, became increasingly divorced from underlying economic fundamentals. These problems reflected in part a flawed framework for financial regulation and supervision, and a laissez-faire attitude towards finance that was grounded in questionable theory. The financial sector accounted for almost 9% of GDP by 2007, as against 5.7% in 2001. Risk appetite had gone far beyond the prudent. Parts of some financial entities had become laws unto themselves. It was a house of cards.

Blair's governments, like all Labour administrations before them, were pulled in several different directions. To achieve power and to maintain it they had to woo the middle classes and appease the financial markets, while simultaneously advancing social progress to keep the party's traditional base happy. This was a delicate balancing act – New Labour had to succeed with the first two goals to achieve the third – and it became harder and harder to sustain. Macro stability helped, but various enduring inequalities and the limited gains seen by those in the middle of the income distribution did not. Moreover, all governments that remain in power for an extended period tend to tire, become complacent, make mistakes and lose momentum. Blair's administrations certainly suffered this fate, not least because the Iraq War undermined faith in the prime minister's leadership.

What really killed New Labour off, however, was the GFC.

CHAPTER 9

The Global Financial Crisis and Great Recession

Success breeds disregard of failure. The absence of serious financial difficulties over a substantial period leads to a euphoric economy in which short-term financing of long-term positions becomes a normal way of life. As the previous financial crisis recedes in time, it is quite natural for central banks, government officials, bankers, and businessmen and even economists to believe that a new era has arrived.

— Hyman Minsky, 1986[1]

CARDIAC ARREST

In the second half of 2007 the global financial system entered a period of acute and escalating crisis that was to reach its apogee towards the end of 2008, following the collapse of the US investment bank Lehman Brothers. Burgeoning solvency issues for banks and other financial institutions around the world triggered what was then the most dramatic downturn of the post-war period: a recession that was not only very deep but also disturbingly obdurate, and which exerted a malign influence that endures to this day.

The essential specifics of this episode are sobering.[2]

Between 2007 and 2009, the pre-tax profits of the world's largest 1,000 banks declined from $800 billion to a low of $100 billion. The return on equity for US banks, which had long averaged around 15%, went negative for a period in 2009. Bank and investment bank equity prices fell by an average of 60–80% before recovering, significantly underperforming overall equity indices, while bank credit default swap spreads leapt from around 20 basis points to peak around 450 basis points.[3] Total global bank assets as a percentage of GDP stopped growing, even edging down for a period. In the major economies, outstanding non-performing loans jumped from between 1% and 2% of the outstanding total to between 7% and 8%. Lending standards became eye-wateringly tight and credit growth collapsed, turning negative in many advanced economies. Gross capital flows to emerging markets fell by almost two-thirds from their pre-crisis highs, with cross-border loans turning sharply negative.

In the broader financial markets, the major stock indices typically fell from peak to trough by something in the region of 50%. Measures of market volatility surged to unprecedented levels. The funding markets seized up. Corporate bond spreads blew out. Corporate bond issuance, and in particular asset-backed security issuance, slumped. In the desperate search for safe havens, long-term government bond yields sank to unprecedented lows. Real estate markets plummeted – the fall in US real house prices approached a third.

The macroeconomic landscape was similarly devastated. Global real GDP declined marginally in 2009 – the first drop since 1945. World trade volumes suffered a 17% retrenchment. Peak-to-trough falls in output in the major economies amounted to anything between 4.5% (US) and 8.5% (Italy). The equivalent figure for the UK was some 6.5%. Investment spending, and in particular residential construction investment spending, bore the brunt of the downturn. Gross fixed capital formation fell by an average of around 14%, with the UK registering the largest fall in the G-7 at 18%. Unemployment surged, reaching double digits as a proportion of the workforce in many economies, and within these totals the long-term jobless came to account for a significantly increased proportion.

Inflation cratered (albeit after a lag) as commodity prices slumped, transmitting the crisis to the developing world in the process. Corporate pricing power evaporated and wages stagnated. Annual CPI measures of price pressure turned negative for a period in many countries, and inflation expectations dropped alarmingly.

Policy rates gravitated towards the zero bound. Budget deficits swelled towards the equivalent of around 10% of GDP, as cyclical developments caused tax revenues to slump and welfare-related outlays to surge, while there was widespread resort to activist fiscal policies to support financial sectors and economies more generally. This in turn led to a sharp increase in public sector debt burdens, with the average advanced economy figure swelling to more than 100% of GDP in gross terms. The recession also marked the onset of a further slowdown in productivity and potential output growth, particularly in the UK.

The grave crisis that engulfed the world between 2007 and 2009 – and which cast a shadow over the next decade – had its origins beyond these shores for the most part, not least in the US and its financial sector. Fundamentally, however, it was a huge market failure, and a story of how two basic human motivators – fear and greed – conspired in an environment of permissive macroeconomic policies and a lax regulatory framework to break both trust and confidence, ushering in a catastrophic financial and economic meltdown that for a period threatened nothing less than a complete collapse of the capitalist system.[4]

It is not easy to get to grips with the principal mechanisms involved, because the crisis was truly international and systemic. It had multiple overlapping and often-complex causes that mutated and malignly interacted with one another, both within and across borders. The crisis was intrinsically non-linear. It is therefore almost certainly pointless to look for a single trigger or tipping point. When a system is teetering on the verge of collapse, almost anything can push it over the edge. And besides, a tipping point is a place or a moment, not a cause.

MACRO EXCESS

For a decade or more leading up to 2007, the major advanced economies had had – or certainly their policymakers had perceived themselves as having – difficulty in maintaining aggregate demand at an adequate level. Growth rates had generally trended lower, with weak private investment an important contributing factor. Central banks were tending to undershoot their mandated inflation targets. Consistent with the writings of Keynes, Kalecki and Marx, globalization played a role in this. As China, India and other relatively low-wage emerging economies became more integrated into the system of world trade, there ensued more intense competition, an excess supply of workers and a related shift in factor shares in favour of profits and against labour. Inequality remained high and continued to increase.

While the Asian economies were well placed to export their way out of this problem, the world's largest economic entities did not have that option. Hence, in the US, partly for these reasons but also on philosophical and domestic political grounds, fiscal policy became unambiguously expansionary in an effort to support domestic spending. The Bush administration cut taxes in 2001 and then did so again in 2003, at the same time as electing to fight a major war. This amounted to some four percentage points of GDP of fiscal largesse over four years. Other countries, particularly those in the euro area, were more circumspect, but both the UK and Japan ploughed a similar expansionary fiscal policy furrow for at least part of the immediate pre-crisis period.

Policy interest rates trended progressively lower, and central banks if anything erred on the side of accommodation during periods of policy normalization. A simple 'Taylor rule' calculation, whereby the requisite policy rate is dictated by estimates of excess capacity and the deviation of actual inflation from target, suggests that the official interest rates of the OECD economies as a whole were around 180 basis points 'too low' in aggregate in 2003, and 270 basis points too low in 2004. By this measure, it was only in 2007 that they returned to their appropriate level.[5]

This widespread monetary accommodation was transmitted to other countries via fixed, quasi-fixed or artificially depressed exchange rates, thereby amplifying the whole effect. This was particularly the case in the emerging economies.

And all the while macroeconomic imbalances were accumulating, particularly importantly in the US. The broadly defined US budget deficit amounted to some 5% of GDP from 2002 to 2008. This compares to an average of just 0.5% in the five previous years, and an average for the euro area over the same period of just over 2% of GDP. As we have seen, the UK's budget position coincided more closely with that of the US than with those of European countries.

US house prices almost doubled between 2000 and 2006. This exceeded the rise in the 'Roaring 20s'. At the peak of the boom, US housing investment accounted for some 6.75% of GDP, far above its long-term trend of between 3% and 5%. The rise in property prices helped to push household net worth from 400% of GDP to 490% of GDP, encouraging personal consumption to surge. Meanwhile, the ratio of household indebtedness to disposable income, which had been rising gently since World War II, took off, surging by forty percentage points in just seven years.

As a consequence of the strength of domestic spending, from 2001 the US economy started absorbing considerably more resources than it produced, running a current account deficit that averaged a little over 5% of GDP. It would not be correct, however, to pretend that the course of the US economy was unwelcome to others: had the US authorities not sustained the growth of domestic demand, economic growth everywhere else in the world would have been weaker. The Europeans and others were happy to piggyback on the US's growing excesses and disequilibria.

Without doubt, these circumstances were sufficiently novel at the time for it to be hard to know for certain how they would ultimately play out. Nevertheless, there were some important pointers.

First, there was what might be termed the *reductio ad absurdum*. No entity, be it an individual, a household, a company, a government or a country, can indefinitely consume more than it produces. There comes a point, even for the world's largest economy, where lenders start to become circumspect about extending further credit.

Second, there is the trusted rule of thumb known as the Qvigstad rule, which posits that trouble lies ahead for an advanced economy if any of its key macroeconomic indicators – the public sector deficit (as a percentage of GDP), the current account deficit (as a percentage of GDP), or the inflation rate – exceeds a value of 4%.[6] On that basis, the US data had long been signalling trouble: every year since 2002 in respect of its current account deficit; every year since 2003 in respect of its public sector deficit; and in 2008 in respect of its inflation rate, which peaked above 5%. A number of other major economies, including that of the UK, also breached at least one of the Qvigstad rule ceilings.

However one looks at it, the global macroeconomic configuration – and particularly that in the US – was unsustainable. And as the American economist Herbert Stein famously observed: 'Things that can't go on for ever, don't.'[7] The only questions were when the inevitable correction would come about, and how.

FREE-FOR-ALL

The pervasive light-touch regulation of the pre-crisis period had its roots in two theoretical propositions.

- The first was that well-designed monetary policy is all that is needed to encourage financial stability. This meant monetary policy based on the new classical–new Keynesian synthesis, focused predominantly on low inflation and delivered by an independent central bank.
- The second was that, on average, financial markets price risks correctly. This was a conclusion drawn from the EMH, which implied quite simply that bubbles and crises could not occur.

In the aftermath of the GFC, the FSA was to produce a remarkably candid description of where these two propositions left the thinking of the UK authorities on the eve of the crash. I have summarized their position below, and I believe it represents a reasonably accurate portrayal of the attitude of policymakers across the major economies at the time.

- Financial market prices provide an indication of rationally evaluated economic value.
- Securitization, based on the development of new liquid markets, has enhanced the allocation of resources and the stability of the financial sector.
- The riskiness of financial assets can be determined by mathematical means, so as to elicit dependable quantitative metrics of trading risk.
- Market discipline is an effective mechanism to moderate excessive risk taking.
- Financial innovation is generally constructive because market competition should ensure that innovations that do not provide value-added do not survive.

And the following assumptions follow from the above description.

- Markets will generally prove self-correcting, with market discipline a more effective instrument than government regulation and oversight.
- The primary responsibility for the management of risk should lay with the senior management and boards of individual firms, as they are better placed to assess threats to particular business models than regulators and because they can be relied upon to make appropriate decisions for their institution about the balance of risk and return.
- Satisfactory customer protection is likely to result not from product regulation or direct intervention in markets but from ensuring that those markets are as free from interference and as transparent as possible.[8]

With hindsight, these appear to be very misguided assumptions.

It is now appropriate to consider the ways in which the unsustainable underlying macro forces interacted with one another in this remarkably permissive context to bring about the inescapable adjustment.

THE ROAD TO CRISIS

In November 1999 a fundamental change that had long been observable in US financial framework conditions was finally recognized and formalized by the abolition of the Glass–Steagall Act. This departure from the past saw Alan Greenspan, who was Federal Reserve chairman at the time, playing an important role. The Glass–Steagall Act had both founded the Federal Deposit Insurance Company (FDIC) and separated commercial and investment banking. The latter measure was taken in an effort to eliminate conflicts of interest that arise – as they did in the 1930s – when the granting of credit-lending and the use of credit-investing were undertaken by a single entity. In the wake of Glass–Steagall's abolition, such conflicts multiplied once again.

Equally important, however, were the six principal ways in which behaviour unfolded. I will summarize these below.

First, savers, seeking yield, were relatively relaxed about moving into assets that had historically been judged risky, in part because inflation was quiescent by the standards of recent decades. Indeed, at the beginning of the new millennium, many – including senior policymakers at the Federal Reserve, such as Ben Bernanke, who was strongly influenced by the persistently sub-target level of inflation – considered deflation to be the greater threat.

Second, banks and investment banks borrowed extensively on the wholesale money markets, lending the proceeds to households through mortgages and other loans, fuelling the property market and pushing up prices.

Third, mortgage mis-selling became rife, particularly in the US. Salesmen were frequently paid per sale while bearing no responsibility for the consequences. They therefore lent to people who had little hope of servicing their loans over the longer term, often eschewing any downpayment, offering low initial 'teaser' mortgage rates and providing negative amortization loans, whereby the difference between a low mortgage rate and the market rate was added to the loan principal.

Fourth, investment banks, responding to the search for yield, developed increasingly complex, highly geared investment vehicles, such as asset-backed securities (ABSs)[9], mortgage-backed securities (MBSs)[10], collateralized debt obligations (CDOs)[11] and credit default swaps (CDSs). Many of these securities were fashioned around mortgage loans, a significant portion of which were 'sub-prime', or poor quality, in nature, but which were sliced, (geographically) diced and combined with lower-risk loans in a such a way that their inherent risk could be concealed from view.

Fifth, sub-prime mortgages accounted for 23.5% of the overall US mortgage market by 2006, up from less than 10% in the late 1990s, and 70% of all new mortgages fell into this category. Of these, more than two-thirds were so-called 2/28 ARMs: thirty-year home loans with an initial two-year fixed interest rate, after which the rate floated, based on an index rate plus a margin. It could be argued that these were hardly mortgages at all, but rather leveraged bets on the direction of house prices.

And finally, banks created off-balance-sheet special purpose vehicles (SPVs), which acted like mini-banks but operated beyond the bounds of bank regulation. They issued short-term debt to investors (mainly in the form of asset-backed commercial paper (ABCP)[12]), and they used the cash raised to buy longer-term assets from their parent companies. Many of the assets purchased were drawn from the alphabet soup of new financial vehicles, some of which would be divided up and mixed and matched into ever-more-complex securities. This was an approach widely adopted by Lehman Brothers.

The overall numbers involved were huge. In August 2007 SPVs linked to the large US financial institutions had assets of more than $300 billion. Legally, these shell companies were independent entities, but in practical terms they were attached to their parents, providing them with guaranteed credit lines that could be drawn down if needed.

This 'shadow banking system' was not confined to SPVs either. It went much further, extending to hedge funds, private equity firms and other highly leveraged and largely unregulated financial entities. Indeed, the latter provided the core of the demand side of the trades in the investment banks' increasingly exotic financial product development, and further contributed to an explosion of leverage.[13] It is estimated that the global shadow banks held assets of some $60 trillion in 2007 – more than 25% of the total financial system.[14]

The net result was to disperse the risks embedded in the new financial products around the world. However, despite the assumptions made by the FSA and others, there was little understanding of the true extent of these risks in the event of a crisis, or indeed where the risks were concentrated. Nor was there much understanding of the practicalities of unwinding highly leveraged portfolios of such products at a time when a large number of investors were seeking to do the same thing. Beneath the surface, the potential for radical uncertainty to take hold was pervasive.

Meanwhile, although official interest rates remained low by the standards of previous decades, monetary policy had for some years been on a tightening trend. In 2007 this tightening appeared to reach a critical mass: not only did real estate prices begin to roll over but a broad spectrum of asset values turned. Confidence and trust suddenly collapsed, and leverage, which until that moment had seemed like everyone's friend, turned into a savage enemy.

WHY WAS ALL THIS NOT FORESEEN – AND STOPPED?

There has been much debate as to why this situation was allowed to develop, but it seems clear that much of the explanation lies in the misguided precepts of the regulatory regime. The regulators did a poor job. They relied too heavily on the assumption that companies were 'doing the right thing' while having too few ways to check whether they actually were. They failed to achieve a basic alignment of risk and reward, or of financial regulation with financial activity.

Financial crises tend to occur when innovation outpaces the ability of regulators to understand what is going on. A policymaking community brought up on, and wedded to, the basic tenets of the REH and the EMH appears to have been both complacent and ignorant. For example, like much of the economics and financial market cognoscenti, the Federal Reserve chairmen Alan Greenspan and Ben Bernanke were both in denial in the early-to-mid 2000s about the degree of excess in the US housing market and about the potential for an economy-wide housing collapse.

At the same time, because they often work in silos, the regulators failed to grasp the interconnectedness of different areas of the financial system. This meant that when a bubble inflated, it was hard to know the full extent of it until it had burst. This was particularly the case if you believed that bubbles were exceptionally rare, or indeed that they could not exist.

Many participants in the excesses of the 2000s were strongly incentivized to keep the good times going. One-sided incentive structures at financial institutions encouraged traders to make unwarrantedly risky bets. If they paid off, they were paid handsomely, but if they failed, it was someone else's money that was lost and they were allowed to move on. But this cannot be the whole story. Traders did not function in a world without individual risk limits, even if they could be unduly generous: the ultimate responsibility therefore rests with the management of these banks (often themselves former traders), because it was them who set the guidelines.

Contrary to the authorities' assumptions, risk analysis was often poor. This had various dimensions. Within the banks and investment banks, many economists (though less prevalently in the US) repeatedly warned of the unsustainability of the global macroeconomic configuration, and particularly that in the US. Unfortunately, however, while economists in general are proficient at identifying disequilibria, they are much less adept at predicting when or how they will unwind. This meant that their advice was ignored by traders, salespeople and business heads within the financial sector. It was not seen as sufficiently practical.

At the same time, some risk managers were insufficiently concerned that the mathematical risk models they used did not adequately take underlying macroeconomic risks into account. They just blindly 'turned the handle' on their computer programs without any notion of the broader context.

For their part, many senior risk managers were reluctant to admit that they did not really understand their own bank's risk models. It is certainly the case that most management teams did not appreciate that – for contractual reasons or for reputational ones – sponsors would not be able to avoid responsibility for their supposedly off-balance-sheet products.

Risk management had become increasingly model – and statistics – based, with value-at-risk (VaR) analysis at its core, not least because that measure is consistent with the EMH and the regulators encouraged it. However, this technique is overreliant on the past to predict the future. In this particular case it had two serious limitations. First, while there were many observations around the medians of the various distributions examined, information about the extremities, which is where the catastrophic risk lies, was sparse. This was particularly true after fifteen years of exceptionally low macroeconomic volatility. In practice, the probabilities of extreme events were obtained almost wholly by assumption. Second, framework conditions evolve, and accommodating this required a structural approach, which a statistical distribution alone cannot provide. In the limit – and therefore, it was hoped, only occasionally – the model simply might not describe reality at all.

Senior corporate management proved unwilling to act. Unduly focused on their company's quarterly reports, many senior executives felt unable to 'leave money on the table'. Chuck Prince, Citigroup's chairman and chief executive, implicitly spoke for the majority in July 2007 when he said: 'When the music stops, in terms of liquidity, things will be complicated. But as long as the music is playing, you've got to get up and dance. We're still dancing.'[15]

Boards of directors proved too weak, or too ill informed, to challenge apparently successful CEOs in financial companies. Management teams increasingly seemed to be running companies for themselves, and shareholders proved unwilling, or unable, to rein in their senior executives.

'Grade inflation' by the credit rating agencies (CRAs) implied, for example, that a mortgage vehicle rated as 'triple A' (the highest rating that the CRAs could offer) carried the same risk as similarly graded major advanced-economy government bonds. The principal reason for this remarkable state of affairs was that the agencies were paid by the issuers of the securities (the banks) rather than by the investors. At the same time, CDOs and other derivatives were so complex that investors became overly reliant on the CRAs.

Financial sector capital ratios proved to be inadequate, given the leverage that had been permitted to accumulate. When asset values collapsed, not only did the shareholders lose all, but the investment banks were revealed to have reached systemic importance. The total amount that the financial sector had written off by 2009 – well over $1 trillion – was more than 100 times its collective VaR assessment of eighteen months previously.[16]

The procyclical impact of mark-to-market valuation techniques exacerbated the capital inadequacy of banks. When crashing 'fire sale' values are used by auditors to value a bank's assets, they induce fire sales to spread, thereby making matters worse.

A deficient understanding of corporate self-interest led regulators – from the chairman of the Federal Reserve down – to believe that management teams would always have their company's survival as their primary objective, and would therefore avoid actions that might unduly jeopardize that survival.[17] However, this faith underestimated three important forces: management's own personal short-term goals, the unawareness of many CEOs of the scale of the risks of macroeconomic origin to which they were exposed, and the degree to which competitive pressures obliged each to do broadly what all the others were doing.

The relevant multilateral organizations also failed to press the point. The BIS, especially via the views of William White, the former head of its monetary and economics department, was one of the few institutions that did sound a loud warning, but it was largely ignored. The IMF, the OECD and the ECB also made cautionary noises about macro and financial developments, but their warnings were neither loud enough nor clear enough, and in the policy world as a whole, much as in the investment banks, few really wanted to hear.

Politics inevitably intervened. There are few if any votes to terminate bull markets in asset prices.

And so it was that the crisis erupted.

THE IMMEDIATE POLICY RESPONSE

The role of government in the major economies was typically in the region of some 40% of GDP in 2007. Hence, the automatic fiscal stabilizers played a key role supporting aggregate demand. Nevertheless, it rapidly became evident that a major discretionary policy response was essential, and in sharp contrast to the inertia that characterized the early years of the Great Depression, that response was delivered. Over time, and all around the world, it extended to numerous packages of measures consisting of most, if not all, of the following.

- The provision of central bank liquidity support to any important financial market that experienced dysfunction or seized up altogether, e.g. the commercial paper market and interbank lending.
- Coordinated and dramatic official interest rate reductions in all of the major economies. Gradualism is no use in a major financial crisis. A large shock requires a large policy counter shock. It is important not to fall too far behind the curve, and to push real borrowing costs into negative territory to establish a floor under confidence. If it transpires that the policy response is excessive, it can always be wound back. Policy rates fell rapidly towards zero in the US, the UK and Japan. The process was slower in the euro area, in that there were rate hikes in 2008 and 2011. Both of these represented major policy errors – errors that were perhaps even on a par with the Federal Reserve's decision to raise the US discount rate to maintain the US dollar's fixed link to gold at the height of the Great Depression.
- The employment of central bank bond purchase programmes and forward interest rate guidance to reduce long-term interest rates, moderate credit spreads and increase the supply of money: so called quantitative easing and credit easing. In late 2008 and early 2009, US credit spreads were at levels last seen in the early 1930s, and they threatened to encourage an economic collapse of similar proportions to the Great Depression. They had to be brought back down closer to earth.
- Discretionary fiscal stimulus to supplement the operation of the automatic stabilizers. This combined fast-acting transfers to the income-constrained (or VAT cuts) with accelerated public investment outlays. With interest rates at rock bottom, with business and consumer confidence at a low ebb and with considerable excess capacity, there was little danger of 'crowding out' private sector activity for an extended period.

- Guarantees on all bank deposits, at least for individuals and often for all depositors for a significant period.
- Efforts by the authorities to prevent major banks from failing by providing liquidity and recapitalization.
- The removal of compromised assets from the balance sheets of private financial institutions by government-sponsored and government-financed mechanisms.
- The provision of government or central bank loans, loan guarantees and large-scale equity injections directly to troubled, systemically important corporations.
- The easing of the repayment terms on existing mortgage holders in order to reduce the flood of defaults and foreclosures that would otherwise have occured.

However, even when all of this was done, the most that could be hoped for was that the policy response would ameliorate the downturn and prevent recession from going as deep, and lasting as long, as it would have had it been left unaddressed. History provides no end of examples to prove that recessions associated with serious crises in financial sectors are the most painful and enduring, on occasion lasting more than a decade. Furthermore, many of the fundamental macroeconomic conditions that gave rise to the situation still needed to be addressed.

There was one encouraging feature though, and that was that policymakers proved determined to avoid the traps of protectionism, bilateralism, unilateral debt default and crass competitive devaluation that swept the globe in the 1930s, and which further deepened and prolonged the Great Depression.

THE LONGER-TERM POLICY RESPONSE

It was clear after the crisis that beyond dealing with the immediate consequences, other fundamental and long-lasting reforms were warranted to reduce the threat of the story being repeated. In the event, some of the required policy responses were enacted, but others were not, and still have not been. And anyway we know that, even if they exhibit similarities, future crises will of course inevitably differ in important respects from those of the past. There is also the fact that many regulators retain an underlying belief that 'efficient markets' are largely able to look after themselves, while in many jurisdictions financial regulation is spread across too many entities. The US provides the most obvious example of this. The UK, by contrast, has moved to the opposite end of the spectrum. Financial regulation was once again overwhelmingly concentrated at the Bank of England after the crisis – something that can of course lead to 'groupthink'.

In outline, the longer-term policy requirements included the following.

- The need for the regulatory authorities, or some macroprudential body, to report on the potential financial sector implications of macroeconomic imbalances.
- The establishment of ex ante conditions whereby it is appropriate to take over a distressed bank. Ideally, a failing bank should be taken over while its net worth is still positive, so that it can continue as a going concern while management and shareholders are changed.
- The mandating of higher capital adequacy ratios, at least for any bank that operates with its deposits guaranteed. These should also be extended to systemically important non-bank intermediaries.
- The institution of procyclical liquidity policies.
- Changes in the way that the CRAs function, such that their failures of the pre-GFC years cannot be repeated.
- The discouragement of off-balance-sheet activities.
- Where macroeconomic policy is concerned, greater attention should be paid to imbalances, such as are indicated by how credit is evolving relative to GDP, by the share of residential construction in GDP, by total financial assets relative to GDP, by sharp increases in the current account deficits, and so on. It might also make sense to direct an element of policy at any major macroeconomic variable that departs significantly from any historical relationship.
- Accept that asset bubbles exist and agree a method of identifying them.
- Aim for better symmetry between monetary and fiscal policy and for less dependence on monetary instruments for macro-stabilization.
- Reanimate structural reform policies to foster competition and innovation, improve education and training, boost research and development outlays, and thereby enhance productivity and flexibility in the face of shocks.

HOW MATTERS STAND FIFTEEN YEARS ON

Naturally, the two basic drivers of financial crises – greed and fear – endure. And they will be with us forever. And, as we shall see, it would be difficult not to conclude that numerous other features of the global macroeconomic and financial landscape that prevailed in the run-up to 2007 – and which, in principle, policy could have dealt with – have either been inadequately addressed, left unattended or returned. As ever, time breeds complacency.

Politics has also intervened. Populism has come to exert a stronger influence over the way that economies and financial systems are run, and in the process this has bred nativism and a search for scapegoats. The net result is that international cooperation to address these issues has been insufficient. Moreover, in the US at least, some policy levers that were important circuit-breakers during the crisis may no longer be available in future. For example, the Fed can no longer lend as widely under the 'exigent circumstances' criteria of Section 13.3 of the Federal Reserve Act.

Overall, systemic financial crises remain hard-wired into the capitalist system. Hyman Minsky's fundamental point that time – and, more importantly, stability – breeds complacency remains apposite. Another major trauma will come along before too long. Perhaps the only certainty is that it will be different to the last. In chapter 11 it will be demonstrated that, to the extent that policy lessons were learned from the traumas of 2007–9 and that changes were made, they were largely designed to fight the last war.

CHAPTER 10

Poisoned Chalice

Everyone is a Keynesian in a foxhole.

— Robert Lucas, October 2008[1]

FLAWED CANDIDATE

On 27 June 2007, after thirteen exhausting and frustrating years waiting to follow in Tony Blair's footsteps, Gordon Brown became prime minister. In many obvious respects he was well qualified for the job. He had a first-rate intellect, he was widely read and he had dominated domestic policymaking for a decade. He had also had a full year to prepare for the role following Blair's announcement that he would stand down. He should therefore have had a clear idea of what he wanted to do, and how he wanted to do it.

In fact, though, Brown seems to have entered Number 10 Downing Street with only the sketchiest of plans. Beyond a continued attachment to delivering macro-stability and a desire to be different to his predecessor, and be seen to be so, it is unclear what his vision was.

There had long been a sense that Brown considered himself to be more socialist, more 'serious', more about substance and less about presentation than his predecessor. At the same time, he was used to working in a bipolar, rather than unipolar, regime, and as Tony Blair and others at the core of government had concluded, there was much in his character that suggested he would prove ill-suited to the job.[2] Being prime minister is a multidimensional role. It requires strategic thinking and an ability to prioritize; a willingness to consult, delegate and compromise; and especially, in an age of twenty-four-hour news coverage, a deft touch with the media.

Brown was wanting in all of these latter respects. He could be seduced by his own propaganda. He was inflexible, distrustful, prone to rages and something of a control freak. And he also struggled to multitask. These had not been insurmountable problems when he had had only one department to manage, but it could be a recipe for disaster when his policy outlook was so broad and when unexpected events were bound to intervene. And on this score, Brown was to prove one of the most unlucky prime ministers of the modern era. It could be argued that the GFC was, at the time, the biggest test of leadership for a British prime minister since World War II.

Between the 2005 general election and Brown becoming prime minister he had lost his two most trusted advisors, Ed Balls and Ed Milliband, to their own parliamentary careers. Additionally, Brown agonized over who should step into his shoes as chancellor. The obvious candidate was his old sidekick Balls. He had made himself unpopular with the Blairites in the party, however, and Brown anyway baulked at having such an ambitious and intellectually authoritative former colleague in charge of the government's purse strings, and thereby as arguably the second most important member of the cabinet.

In the end, Balls was appointed Secretary of State for Children, Schools and Families, and Brown instead turned to the understated lawyer Alistair Darling. Darling had previously held a number of lesser economic and financial portfolios and he was another one of Brown's acolytes, but he was an altogether less intimate, less strident and less partisan politician than Balls. There was more than a suggestion with this appointment that the prime minister intended to continue to exert a strong overarching influence on economic policy. Indeed, this was to prove an understatement. Brown's relationship with his chancellor was enduringly tense, and occasionally toxic. Ironically, given his fury when another cabinet minister strayed onto his terrain when he was chancellor, Brown constantly second-guessed Darling's forecasts and policy choices over the next three years.

For his part, Darling was to run a very different Treasury to his predecessor. He was more open and collegiate. The atmosphere in the department lightened. Despite the remarkable challenges he faced, and the on-occasion crass efforts of the prime minister to undermine him, he rarely appeared ruffled and he dealt courteously with his officials.

OUT OF THE BLUE AND INTO THE RED

There was little expectation in government in 2007 of any abrupt change in the UK's economic fortunes. After fifty-eight consecutive quarters of economic growth, Brown's final budget as chancellor, brought down in late March of that year, included a considerable self-congratulatory element, at the core of which was the conviction that his policy architecture and prescriptions had put an end to the UK economy's long-standing cycle of boom and bust.

The budget forecasts suggested that economic growth would slow from a slightly above-trend rate that year to a trend rate of expansion of 2.75%

a year over the course of the period to 2011–12. Inflation, meanwhile, was anticipated to fall back to the 2% target and then stay there. On the basis of these benign projections, Brown felt that he could maintain an accommodative fiscal stance. He signalled two-percentage-point cuts in both the basic rate of income tax and corporation tax to be implemented in 2008,[3] while also promising to continue with significant real increases in education and skills spending and to further raise the share of net public investment spending in GDP. Nevertheless, he still hoped to bear down gradually on the headline budget deficit and to meet his fiscal rules.

Over the course of Brown's decade as chancellor, the Treasury had twice revised its estimate of the UK's trend growth rate upwards by a quarter point. These revisions increased his projected fiscal space, as future revenue growth would be commensurately higher, but they represented another clear example of policymakers mistaking extended cyclical buoyancy with underlying structural improvement. Although hardly unique among the economics profession, Brown's March 2007 outlook was to prove a hopelessly complacent view of the future. The three-year period to the general election of May 2010 was anything but stable. Not only did it see one of the most traumatic cyclical busts of the modern era, but it also exerted an enduring degenerative effect on the UK's productive potential. Trend growth would slow significantly.

The UK was overwhelmed by the GFC. It was particularly exposed because of its large financial sector, its high household indebtedness and its strong cross-border linkages. Notwithstanding what proved over time to be a forceful and wide-ranging policy response, activity contracted sharply as numerous adverse feedback loops cascaded through the economy, causing both the supply of and the demand for credit to spiral downwards.

Between October 2007 and March 2009, the broader equity market was to fall by more than 40% before staging a (hesitant) recovery, with individual bank stocks declining by anything between 40% and 95% over this period. House prices, meanwhile, tumbled by more than 20%, and commercial property prices fell by double that amount. Long-term government bond yields went from more than 5% in mid 2007 to less than 4% in early 2009, before establishing a series of historical lows over subsequent years, culminating in a decline to below 0.50% in 2020. Index-linked bond yields became persistently negative.

The economy slowed sharply towards the end of 2007, although the average expansion rate for the year of 2.6% was reasonable enough. Real GDP then began to fall precipitously in 2008, with the pace of decline accelerating through the year. The contraction continued into the first half of 2009, stretching to six successive quarters, before a modest pick-up in activity took hold. The peak-to-trough decline in real GDP was 6.3%, with personal consumption dropping by a similar amount, and gross fixed capital formation slumping by almost a quarter. It took five years for real GDP to recover fully, and real incomes did not increase consistently until 2015. In the meantime, the unemployment rate began a long rise from its Q4 2007 low of 5.2% of the workforce to a high of 8.5% in October 2011. Long-term unemployment increased from just above 1% to around 2.75%.

CPI inflation was initially boosted by international commodity price trends (and particularly by oil prices that for some time appeared to defy gravity) and by the effect of a sharp 25% depreciation of sterling in effective terms as the UK's risk premium soared. However, having peaked above 5% in mid 2008, inflation slumped well below target, to around 1%, just a year later, before hikes in indirect taxes and international factors shocked it higher again for a period. Wage growth decelerated sharply from a peak of around 4.5% a year in 2007 to just 1% in late 2009. A sharp squeeze on real incomes therefore extended well into the recovery.

Turning to the UK's twin deficits, the chronic weakness of domestic activity and the positive influence on competitiveness of the pound's fall brought the current account shortfall to heel. The external imbalance declined from some 3.5% of GDP in 2008 to under 2% of GDP in 2011. Moreover, with most of Britain's large portfolio of external assets denominated in foreign currencies, the income balance improved; additionally, the UK's net international investment position strengthened significantly due to valuation effects.

On the other hand, the budget deficit widened sharply, reaching a peak of around 10.5% of GDP in 2009 and only dropping below 5% of GDP six years later. The net debt burden followed a similarly explosive trajectory, more than doubling from 32.5% of GDP in 2007 to 70.5% of GDP in 2011, and then continuing to rise thereafter, finally peaking at 79.75% in 2015. New Labour's much-vaunted, but increasingly massaged, fiscal rules were overwhelmed by the crisis and were suspended.

Furthermore, Britain's public finance metrics were to deteriorate more rapidly, and to a greater extent, than those of most of its major competitors. Government revenues were especially sensitive in the UK to asset prices and financial activity. Indeed, around 25% of UK taxes were derived from the financial sector. The synchronized downturn of the economic and asset price cycles therefore led to a rapid fall in income tax and corporation tax, VAT and asset-price-related revenues, while current spending (which had already been growing rapidly for a number of years) continued to surge ahead. In 2008 and 2009 the government also applied discretionary fiscal stimulus equivalent to some two percentage points of GDP, although its effect on the deficit and the debt level was minor compared with the impact of the automatic stabilizers and the loss of asset-price-related revenues.

NORTHERN SHOCK

The GFC progressed through several phases, with the first hints of the coming turmoil manifesting in August 2007. Tighter monetary policy had encouraged the US property market to roll over, and the sub-prime sector in particular was under duress. Banks and the broader investment community around the world began to recognize that they had significant, but indeterminate, exposures to such assets. This sparked a swathe of write-downs as well as a sudden loss of confidence and trust between financial counterparties. There developed an increasing reluctance for institutions to lend to each other. Activity in the money and credit markets, much of which was collateralized by MBSs, began to freeze up. The off-balance-sheet entities that made up a significant part of the shadow banking system found themselves under particular strain. Bank stocks swooned.

The ECB was the first central bank to react. It felt it necessary to make successive large injections of liquidity into the money markets, to the tune of €156 billion in total, after France's biggest bank, BNP, revealed that it had significant US sub-prime mortgage exposure, through three of its investment funds, that it was struggling to value accurately. The Federal Reserve, itself concerned by the July collapse of two hedge funds backed by US investment bank Bear Stearns, and by a growing dearth of liquidity in US securitization markets, then rapidly followed the ECB's example.

The Bank of England was much slower to respond. This was despite the fact that its markets division, led by future deputy governor Paul Tucker, had started to identify pockets of dysfunction in the wholesale money markets from early July, and that a number of UK banks were, as a result, quick to request emergency liquidity assistance.[4] These included the Newcastle-based Northern Rock.

A former building society, Northern Rock had little direct exposure to US sub-prime. However, it had latterly been on something of a tear, experiencing massive growth in both assets and market share as it built a reputation as Britain's most aggressive mortgage lender. By 2007 it was the country's seventh largest bank and a FTSE 100 company to boot. Any difficulties it might encounter therefore stood to have systemic implications. Northern Rock's problem was that, rather than customer deposits, it was 70% dependent on short-term borrowing from the wholesale money markets to finance its long-term loans. When credit conditions tightened, it was subjected to a damaging funding squeeze.

The Treasury and the FSA were both sympathetic to the liquidity requests of the distressed banks, including that from Northern Rock. However, Mervyn King, perhaps reflecting his roots as an academic economist, seemed to be consumed by concerns about 'moral hazard', and he was determined that those who had taken excessive risks should be taught a lesson rather than bailed out.[5] The Bank remained willing only to provide emergency liquidity at a penalty rate and in exchange for limited forms of safe collateral.

Unlike his predecessor Eddie George, who had assiduously built up an extensive network of contacts and confidential conduits of information during his tenure, King had kept his distance from City institutions and personalities. As a result, he seemed at times to lack intuition for the markets. Despite continuing requests for more generous support, at King's behest the Bank remained unflinching in its approach throughout August. Nor did Darling at the Treasury have the authority to force an alternative approach.

Early September saw a screeching about-turn, however. The Bank belatedly found that it had no alternative but to provide the increasingly desperate Northern Rock with more generous backing. And then, with rumours of an urgent need for a full-scale rescue operation circulating, a run developed on the bank – something that, remarkably, had not happened in the UK since 1866. In these extraordinary circumstances King was forced to sanction large-scale cash injections to the system as a whole and to widen the range of acceptable collateral to include mortgages. Darling, for his part, had to announce a blanket government guarantee for all of the Northern Rock's depositors to ease the panic.

The events of August and September 2007 revealed that the tripartite structure of financial sector oversight instituted by New Labour in 1997 was unfit for purpose. The system had long been on autopilot, reflecting in part an underlying belief (consistent with the theoretical conventional wisdom described in chapter 7) that the market knew best and was a source of stability rather than instability.

Neither Gordon Brown nor Tony Blair had given financial stability much thought over the previous decade. The Bank's macroeconomic model of the time, like those of most central banks, reflected many of the elegant perfections of new classical theory, and it was largely devoid of any reference to banks or to the broader financial sector and its role in credit creation. In this model, economic actors were rational automatons. There were no financial frictions and no space for defaults. The secular rise in private indebtedness and leverage in the banking system, which were crucial elements of most previous financial crises, were for the most part overlooked.

At the same time, the Bank's financial stability arm had been allowed to wither away. Northern Rock never appeared on any Bank of England watchlist, nor did the Bank's Agent for the North East (effectively the central bank's eyes and ears) ever publicly express any anxiety about Northern Rock's underlying health. The FSA, meanwhile, had become unduly focused on consumer finance matters, and the Treasury rarely looked beyond its fiscal policy rules and the delivery of tax credits. Precious few officials from any of the three entities responsible for financial stability had any experience of a crisis, and there had been little interaction between those in leadership positions.

The extent of the threat to overall stability was underappreciated; the initial response was maladroit. It was unclear what each entity's precise role was or who had the final say on policy, while the still-callow chancellor hesitated to override the stubborn and overbearing Mervyn King. Overall, the British reaction to the onset of the crisis did not inspire confidence. It damaged the reputation of the authorities and, in particular, that of King, whose reappointment for a second five-year term as Bank governor was cast into doubt. He kept his job in the end, but largely because there was no obvious replacement and because of the assumption in the markets and beyond that Bank governors serve two terms. Replacing King could potentially have generated additional turbulence during what was already a chaotic time. As we shall see, however, the governor's relationship with Darling and Brown was to remain fraught, especially towards the end of the parliament.

FROM BAD TO WORSE

Northern Rock was just the beginning. Banks around the world began to report the sub-prime losses on their books. The UK housing market followed the US's example and rolled over, triggering balance sheet distress across the private sector; business and consumer confidence ebbed away; lending activity slowed; and the economy began to slide into recession. Before long, the new prime minister – who had eschewed an opportunity to call a general election and seek his own personal mandate that autumn – would have to come to terms with the fact that his much-heralded age of macro-stability had evaporated and also that his time in office was likely to be truncated.[6]

Northern Rock was nationalized in February 2008 after a number of expressions of interest in taking the bank over came to nothing and it was concluded that it could not be salvaged. By the time the government took possession, Northern Rock's liabilities to the Bank of England had reached some £26 billion.

The following month witnessed a much bigger shock. Bear Stearns, which was the fifth largest bank in the US and one renowned for its heavy involvement in the securitization markets, had to be rescued at a fire sale price by J.P. Morgan. Moreover, the rescue happened only after the New York Federal Reserve had first agreed to take some $30 billion of Bear's toxic sub-prime assets on to its own balance sheet and after the Federal Reserve had extended $13 billion to Bear via Morgan under Section 13.3 of the Federal Reserve

Act. This allowed it to lend to any entity under 'unusual and exigent circumstances', but it was an authority that had not been used since the 1930s.

Bear was the first big domino to fall in the GFC, and it suggested that other well-known global financial entities were likely to find themselves similarly compromised. The atmosphere in the City of London was grim, and the Bank of England's MPC found itself on the horns of a dilemma. The financial sector's woes and the burgeoning weakness of both asset prices and the economy pointed to a significantly easier monetary stance. But, with food prices soaring and the cost of crude oil heading towards a record $147 a barrel, headline CPI inflation had moved far above target and was rising rapidly towards 5%, a figure not seen since 1992. The recently reappointed governor was therefore tasked with writing a series of explanatory open letters to the chancellor detailing why this was happening and what he proposed to do about it.

However much the commodity markets were defying fundamental forces, and however forward thinking the Bank wanted to be, this was not an environment in which it could comfortably cut official interest rates aggressively. In the end, it had to content itself with two quarter-point adjustments – one in February, one in April – necessarily supported by some convoluted explanatory language. As late as August, one hawkish MPC member was still voting for a rate *hike*.

Reflecting the more challenging global environment and the liberties taken with the public finances over previous years, the 2008 budget was a low-key, neutral affair. Nevertheless, it was constructed on a series of what now seem to have been risibly optimistic economic forecasts, on the basis of which the government's fiscal rules would continue to be met. Rather than a brief dip in the growth rate below trend followed by recovery, as the Treasury suggested, the UK economy was approaching an abyss. The fiscal position was about to go to hell in a handcart.

This period did, however, see the launch of one joint Treasury and Bank of England initiative that was to provide crucial support to the financial sector in the months and years ahead. In April 2008 the Special Liquidity Scheme was established. In return for a 'haircut',* and without full disclosure, commercial banks were allowed to temporarily swap higher-quality (but illiquid) mortgage-backed (and other) debt securities for UK Treasury Bills

---

* A 'haircut' is the difference between the current market value of an asset and the value ascribed to that asset for the purposes of calculating regulatory capital or loan collateral. The amount of the haircut reflects the perceived risk of the asset falling in value in an immediate cash sale or liquidation.

(a near-cash equivalent), and in the process start to address their rapidly deteriorating liquidity situation.

Underwritten by the government, the Treasury Bills were lent to the Bank by the Debt Management Office. The Bank initially assumed that take-up for the Special Liquidity Scheme would be in the region of £50 billion, but in the event it was utilized by thirty-two banks and building societies over the following nine months alone, providing £185 billion of funding in exchange for £287 billion of illiquid assets.

As the spring of 2008 turned into summer, the ramifications of the collapse of the US housing and other bubbles were continuing to metastasize. The US economy was now in recession. As had been feared, numerous other large US banks and investment banks were plagued by similar balance sheet frailties to Bear Stearns. US stock prices, and especially those of financial corporations, continued to trend downwards, while credit spreads widened inexorably. Confidence and trust were in short supply. The wholesale money markets were dependent on central bank life support.

Adding to the sense of impending doom was a sharp deterioration in the finances of the Federal National Mortgage Association, which was known as Fannie Mae, and the Federal Home Loan Mortgage Corporation, known as Freddie Mac. These two government-sponsored entities were the anchors of the US mortgage system. They guaranteed more than $5 trillion of mortgage debt, and by the second quarter of 2008 they were effectively the last major source of mortgage funding.

Trillions of dollars of Fannie and Freddie's securities were dispersed around the global financial system, not least in the investment portfolios of central banks and sovereign wealth funds, which regarded them to all intents and purposes as being guaranteed by the US government. Yet rising delinquencies were hurting Fannie and Freddie's insurance divisions, which guaranteed millions of prime mortgages, and the collapse of the sub-prime market inflicted huge losses on their investment arms, which had accumulated more than a trillion dollars of mortgages and mortgage securities. Their share prices were collapsing, and the international investment community was losing faith in them. They were effectively insolvent.

To avoid a significant increase in the cost of home loans, which was the last thing the economy needed, the US government had no choice but to intervene to save Fannie Mae and Freddie Mac. They were effectively nationalized in early September, new management teams were appointed, and the US Treasury injected $110 billion into each to avoid looming defaults on their debt and mortgage-backed securities.

This action arrested the run on the two government-sponsored entities themselves, but the broader run on the US financial system only accelerated, with the investment bank Lehman Brothers becoming an increasing focus of attention.

CATACLYSM

Gordon Brown's popularity was in headlong retreat by the autumn of 2008, and he was careering from one disaster to another. He was finding the job of being prime minister much more challenging than he had imagined, and the weaknesses in his political make-up, and in his character in general, were being exposed. There were even rumours of a coup against him in the cabinet. This was hardly the most reassuring position from which to address the GFC as it entered its gravest phase.

Lehman Brothers was a New York-based investment bank that had a significant presence beyond the US, including in the UK, where it employed some 5,000 people in London's Canary Wharf financial district. In April 2004 Brown had himself formally opened the bank's new offices at 25 Bank Street, in the process eulogizing about the technical excellence of a financial services industry that at the time was perceived to be at the forefront of Britain's international competitiveness.[7]

Lehman was also in many ways the personal fiefdom of Dick Fuld, its stubborn and belligerent CEO.[8] Under his single-minded guidance, the bank had been one of the first Wall Street firms to move into mortgage origination, and it subsequently migrated away from being a mere brokerage house to increasingly specialize in real estate investment, leveraged lending and private equity finance, predominantly funding itself through the short-term repo market using MBSs as collateral.[9] This was a high-risk, capital-intensive model. By 2008 the firm had become absurdly over-leveraged, at thirty-one times an asset base of just over $500 billion. The value of its loan collateral was collapsing, it was struggling to roll over its liabilities, and the huge bets it had made on the real estate market were sour and illiquid. Its financial situation therefore became increasingly unsustainable. Desperate, the firm's management resorted to creative and unethical accounting and balance sheet manipulation, but to negligible effect. Lehman's losses mounted, and with the firm's stock price plunging, the expectation was that it was about to go the same way as Bear Stearns.

As Lehman stumbled towards extinction in the summer of 2008, the US authorities struggled to find a 'white knight' to ride to its rescue, either from within the US financial fraternity or from beyond it. There were expressions of interest, but Lehman was judged to be too compromised and too hazardous, while Fuld's truculence and obduracy had left him with few favours that he could call in. Both Bank of America and the Korean Development Bank pulled back from takeover deals at the death, the former deciding to instead rescue Merrill Lynch, another US household name that was on the verge of collapse but with a slightly less daunting balance sheet.

At the same time, bailing out another investment bank had become politically unappealing both to the notionally free-market Republican Bush administration and to a Federal Reserve that had already repeatedly stretched the boundaries of its legal authority to intervene in support of the financial sector. US Treasury Secretary Hank Poulson made a final desperate attempt to persuade Alistair Darling to facilitate a takeover of Lehman by UK clearer Barclays, but the chancellor and the FSA took the view that Lehman was too big a risk for an economy whose banking sector was four times larger as a percentage of GDP than that of the US.[10] Hence, on 15 September Lehman was allowed to fail, creating the biggest bankruptcy in history.

Neither Darling and the UK Treasury nor King and the Bank of England expected Lehman to be permitted to go bust in this manner, and there was a keen sense in the UK and elsewhere that letting it happen was a grave mistake on the part of the US authorities. Lehman's demise had not been discounted, and it precipitated a series of extraordinary financial and policy convulsions that rapidly reverberated around the world.

Lehman was hard-wired into the global financial system via some $440 billion of trades of one form or another. It had more than 100,000 creditors. It was also the prime broker and the major source of financing for around a hundred hedge funds. Its sudden departure from the scene undercut numerous counterparties at a stroke and sparked new levels of fear and panic. Stock markets crashed and gyrated wildly, with financials once again particularly badly hit. Even Goldman Sachs and Morgan Stanley – which were the elite of the US investment banking community and which, like Lehman, had extensive operations in the UK and Europe – came under threat. To reassure the markets, the Fed subsequently saw fit to allow them both to become bank holding companies and thereby benefit from the protection of government deposit insurance on condition that they immediately raise significant private capital. This they duly did: from Warren Buffet and Mitsubishi Bank, respectively.

Meanwhile, the wholesale money markets, which were already severely impaired, required another huge injection of central bank liquidity, collateralized with whatever was available, to function at all. US money market mutual funds suffered mass withdrawals. Borrowing costs for banks and companies exploded higher. The dollar – the world's safe haven currency – became super precious, such that the Fed had to establish extensive swap lines with more than a dozen other central banks, including the Bank of England, to ease the associated funding pressures. In the process, the Fed effectively became the lender of last resort not just for the US but for the world.[11]

BACK FROM THE BRINK

Such was the mayhem at this time that just a day after allowing Lehman Brothers to fail, the US authorities were forced to abandon their red line on more financial lifeboats. On 16 September the Fed provided an $85 billion credit line to rescue AIG, the huge US insurance company. AIG provided insurance cover of various categories to some 76 million people, including 180,000 businesses that employed two-thirds of the US workforce. It also held around $2.7 trillion of derivatives contracts, mainly in the form of CDSs, insuring troubled sub-prime mortgage bonds. If it had gone under, any number of banks and non-banks would have lost their disaster insurance just as they needed it most. Had this been allowed to happen so soon after Lehman's demise, the effect would have been catastrophic and it would have rapidly pushed the US into a deep depression, akin to that of the early 1930s. With no possibility of a solution coming from the private sector, Poulson at the Treasury and Bernanke at the Fed had no choice but to move to save AIG. The US central bank's huge loan was made in exchange for an 80% stake, again via recourse to the all-purpose safety-net of Section 13.3 of the Federal Reserve Act.

To stop money haemorrhaging out of money market investment funds, many of which had held significant quantities of Lehman's short-term debt, the US Treasury was forced into yet another extraordinary policy improvisation a few days later. It offered a guarantee to any fund that was willing to pay an insurance fee, with the cover backed by $50 billion taken from the Exchange Stabilization Fund. The latter had been established in 1934 to manage the dollar's value in the wake of the collapse of the Gold Standard. It was the only source of funds immediately available.

The shock waves from the Lehman bankruptcy, the near failure of AIG and the loss of confidence in US money market funds were immediately felt in the UK. The banking sector had borrowings of around £750 billion that had to be regularly refinanced, and at a stroke this became much harder. LIBOR–OIS spreads – a widely used measure of credit risk in the banking system – surged, eventually peaking at more than 350 basis points, while financial stock prices slumped further.[12] It became clear that several UK banks – most notably Royal Bank of Scotland (RBS), HBOS and Bradford & Bingley – had no viable future as then configured. The situation had become a systemic solvency crisis rather than a liquidity crisis.[13] And as the Japanese and Scandinavian banking crises of the 1990s had demonstrated, relying on the private sector or markets for a solution is pointless in such circumstances. In order to steal a march on the problem, policymakers needed to rapidly acknowledge its scale, provide the banks with new capital, and excise a considerable proportion of the associated bad debts. Any residual concerns about moral hazard had to be cast aside.[14]

It was also clear, however, that whatever the UK or other nations did in this regard would be insufficient to stem the tide of the crisis in the absence of similar action in the world's largest economy, the US. The situation was complicated, though, by the inconvenient fact that a presidential election campaign was in full swing. In this febrile atmosphere, many on the right were happy to demonstrate their commitment to free market economics and their antipathy towards big government through their apparent willingness to embrace the hands-off, 'liquidationist' strategy that had marked US policy-making at the onset of the Great Depression. In sharp contrast, many on the left were incensed by the previous failings in oversight from the Fed and the Treasury and by the malfeasance that was being unearthed within the financial sector. They wanted both retribution and a meaningful rebalancing of government priorities from Wall Street to Main Street.

Seeking to tread the narrowest and most delicate of paths within this economic and political firestorm, US policymakers settled on a plan to apply $700 billion of public funds to the financial sector (equivalent to nearly 5% of GDP). The initial assumption was that in order to avoid anything that smacked of the nationalization that was such anathema to Republicans, and indeed to most US citizens, the bulk of the money would be used to purchase and remove toxic assets from financial sector balance sheets. However, the hastily cobbled together so-called Troubled Asset Relief Programme (TARP) in reality provided the US Treasury with almost unlimited scope to use the funds as it saw fit. In legal terms, it gave it carte blanche.

To the astonishment of most observers around the world, when the admittedly extraordinarily thin and opaque TARP Bill was hurriedly presented to Congress on 29 September, it was promptly rejected by 228 votes to 205. Too many saw the bill as amounting to a request to US taxpayers to provide a huge blank cheque for a less than fully thought through scheme. And they had a point, even if this was not a good time to be too pernickety: some form of publicly funded bailout plan, however vague, was better than no plan at all.

The initial rejection of the TARP Bill sparked yet another even-more-gut-wrenching round of market mayhem. The S&P 500 index closed down some 9% that day (its biggest loss on record), with financial stocks down more than 10%. Other global markets plunged in their wake. Policymakers everywhere were staring into the void.

Thankfully, however, the nosedive in stock prices together with the news that two more large US financial entities – Washington Mutual and Wachovia – were in terminal trouble concentrated minds on the bigger picture. Resubmitted with amendments that split the bailout funding into three separate

tranches and balanced support for the banks with tax breaks for middle earners and support for homeowners, the TARP Bill was passed into law with
reasonable, if hardly wholesale, bipartisan support on 3 October.[15]

It was Britain, however, that came to effectively define the nature of the
global effort to rescue the banks. As the US Treasury, the Federal Reserve and
Congress grappled with the TARP, and as global markets convulsed, Brown,
Darling and King concluded that there was no alternative but to put in place
a bold and decisive bank recapitalization plan. Events were moving so rapidly,
especially where RBS (one of the world's biggest banks) and HBOS (Britain's
largest mortgage lender) were concerned, that inaction or undue delay threatened further bank runs, and possibly the implosion of the entire UK financial
system. That is to say: no functioning ATMs; no possibility of cashing cheques;
no acceptance of credit cards; no wages paid; indeed, no financial transfers of
any kind. This outcome – tantamount to societal breakdown – would have
been far beyond anything experienced during the Great Depression. And if it
had happened in the UK it would have proved contagious and happened elsewhere too. It had to be avoided at all costs. A firebreak had to be put in place.

In the meantime, something called emergency liquidity assistance (ELA)
was hastily concocted in order to keep RBS and HBOS afloat and to avert
further bank runs. This was a secret Bank of England facility (underwritten
by a partial Treasury indemnity) that allowed RBS and HBOS in particular
to access tens of billions of pounds in emergency financial assistance in return
for collateral (much of it highly questionable) and substantial fees. At its peak
on 17 October, RBS would draw £36.6 billion from this facility, while HBOS
drew £25.4 billion on 13 November.[16] The loans were repaid, however, and
the banks' collateral was returned in December and January, respectively.
Whatever outrage and alarm the secrecy and the size of the facility would
subsequently elicit, it did its job.

The more enduring strategy that emerged to save the banks owed much
to the extraordinary diligence of Treasury, Bank and FSA officials, with Tom
Scholar, who ran the Treasury's International and Finance Directorate, playing a vital role. Beyond officialdom, however, Shriti Vadera (the Minister for
the Cabinet Office, a former investment banker and a Brown confidant), the
tough and uncompromising Paul Myners (the newly appointed Financial Services Secretary, or 'City Minister'), and a number of seasoned financial market
experts untainted by the crisis – all of whom were co-opted into government
– were also key actors at this critical juncture. The latter proved particularly
invaluable given the lack of micro-financial expertise or experience of many
Treasury and Bank officials.

Overriding the manifestly absurd and reprehensible lingering reluctance of
UK bank chairs and chief executives to admit to the extent of their problems,

Darling presented a £500 billion rescue package (equivalent to some 26% of GDP) as the markets opened on 8 October. The package included three key elements.[17]

- A £200 billion (10.4% of GDP) extension of the Bank of England's Special Liquidity Scheme, which allowed banks to exchange illiquid assets for government debt.[18]
- A requirement for the UK's eight major banks to draw up recapitalization plans. They could raise the additional resources privately or they could draw on a Bank Recapitalisation Fund that would provide an initial £25 billion (1.3% of GDP) of support, with a further £25 billion to be made available if required. The size of any government stake would be negotiated with the individual bank as soon as possible. In return, each recipient would have to restrict executive pay and dividends to existing shareholders and agree to maintain the supply of credit. It would in effect amount to partial nationalization.
- Loan guarantees of some £250 billion (13% of GDP) to temporarily underwrite new debt issued by participating banks.

On the same day, the world's major central banks announced the most comprehensive coordinated official interest rate cut in history. While only the day before, fearing that the UK banking system could experience significant outflows to Irish banks following the announcement of a blanket guarantee on savings there on 30 September, the UK government had increased its bank deposit guarantee to £50,000, or £100,000 for joint accounts.[19] The pace at which policymakers were having to respond to the crisis was relentless, their ingenuity extraordinary.

The extent to which banks participated in the recapitalization programme varied according to the financial strain they were under, and with the markets still beset by panic – and the government in no mood to haggle – the precise terms and conditions were negotiated in less than a week, finally emerging on the morning of Monday 12 October.[20] The main recipients of government recapitalization funds were the effectively insolvent RBS, which took £20 billion, and the recently merged HBOS and Lloyds TSB, which together accepted £17 billion. This left the government as a majority (70%) shareholder in RBS and with an approximately 40% holding in HBOS Lloyds. By contrast, HSBC UK drew on £750 million of capital from its parent company, while Barclays sought to raise its own capital from private investors.

As the finer detail of the bank rescue plan was being settled, both Darling and Brown were abroad. Darling was attending a meeting of G-7 finance ministers in Washington, during which the exhausted Hank Poulson admitted to the UK chancellor that there was in reality no alternative to using TARP funds for the recapitalization of US banks. Seeking to create markets for hundreds of billions of dollars of toxic assets at a time of unprecedented market illiquidity and volatility, as had initially been mooted, was impractical (to say the least). The public funds had to be directly injected into the banks, and in due course the US government would opt to sink up to $250 billion into bank equity. The meeting's communiqué echoed this putative change of course, strongly suggesting that mass bank recapitalization was the way forward for counties hit hard by the crisis. For his part, Brown was in France as the guest of a meeting of euro area leaders. They too broadly hitched their wagon to UK-style bank recapitalization. Bailouts similar in nature to that of the UK were launched within days in the the US, France, Germany, Italy, Spain, Switzerland and many other countries, from Australia to South Korea.

The global pivot towards bank recapitalization was an important turning point, although there would be little evidence to confirm this for many months to come. Both the supply of credit and the demand for it remained very weak. The banks that were receiving UK government loans had to pay an annual interest rate of 12% until 2013 and then 7% annually plus three-month LIBOR thereafter. Such a high premium provided a strong incentive both to preserve capital and not to advance any remotely risky loans. The government's insistence that banks receiving public funds should maintain the supply of credit was wishful thinking.

The fact that Britain, with Gordon Brown as its figurehead, had led the way in recognizing the underlying nature of the problem and pushing the only viable solution encouraged a brief revival of the prime minister's tarnished reputation, granting his ailing premiership a stay of execution. The irony was that this short-lived resurrection came when he effectively returned to being chancellor, of not just the UK but the world.

BREAKING THE RULES

In October 2008 Darling formally admitted that there was no hope that the government's fiscal rules could be met and that they had therefore been abandoned. They had been rendered irrelevant by the fast-moving crisis. To have attempted to continue to meet them would have exacerbated an already-devastating recession.

Meanwhile, with borrowing costs falling rapidly, and with the emergence of huge and enduring excess capacity,[21] it was difficult to argue that a reasonable dose of Keynesian fiscal expansion would crowd out private sector activity or trigger inflation. Over the first half of the year, the UK economy had contracted by around 1.5%, and it was clear that the GDP figures for the third and fourth quarters were going to reveal much steeper declines – indeed, what was expected was a recession the likes of which had not been seen since before World War II. This was the view of the IMF and the G-20 too, both of which called for global budgetary expansion equivalent to 2% of GDP around this time.

On Monday 24 November Darling delivered an emergency budget that included a major discretionary fiscal stimulus, albeit following considerable debate within the Treasury, and between the Treasury and Number 10, about its size and content. Brown, supported by his erstwhile trusted advisor Ed Balls, wanted a massive response and a strong bias towards the prime minister's favoured policy mechanism of tax credits. With the budget deficit already soaring towards a double-digit proportion of GDP and likely to continue on its upward trajectory, however, the Treasury and Darling were more circumspect, favouring a simpler strategy that could have a more immediate effect and that was, when the time came, easier to reverse.

What emerged was a compromise. VAT was cut from 17.5% to 15% (the maximum cut permitted under EU rules) for thirteen months, giving consumers an immediate temporary boost to their real incomes and an incentive to spend quickly, while personal income tax allowances were increased, public infrastructure plans were accelerated,[22] and new incentives for trading in less environmentally friendly vehicles were announced. As a partial compensation, employee and employer national insurance contributions were increased by half a percentage point and the top rate of income tax, which had stood at 40% since 1988, was raised to 45%. November's expansionary package totalled some £20 billion (1.2% of GDP), while the overall impulse to real activity in 2009 from fiscal policy approximately matched the 2% of GDP recommendation of the IMF. Meanwhile, both public spending's share in GDP and net government debt approached 50% of GDP.

However, while it was important not to subject fiscal policy to an unnecessary straitjacket in such extraordinary times, there remained a requirement to demonstrate that the government was aware of the need for longer-term budgetary discipline and that it had a credible plan for its re-establishment if market confidence was to be maintained. What this commitment to longer-term fiscal probity should consist of at such an extraordinary time was by no means obvious, however, and the matter was to prove a recurring bone of contention between Darling and Brown during New Labour's remaining time in power. Through a series of specific targets, Darling wanted to make it absolutely clear that the government was committed to reducing borrowing and the debt burden once the crisis was past. Brown, on the other hand, was much more focused on the policy here and now and on retaining the maximum possible room for manoeuvre until the storm was past. It was as if he was driven almost exclusively by Keynes's famous admonishment to economists fixated on the far future that 'in the long run we are all dead'.

In the end, in place of the golden rule and the sustainable investment rule, Darling announced a 'temporary operating rule'. This stated that the government would set policies to improve the cyclically adjusted current budget each year once the economy had emerged from the downturn. It would therefore eventually reach balance, and public sector debt would fall as a proportion of GDP once the global shocks had worked their way through the system. In the circumstances, it was a reasonable stance to take.

GOING UNCONVENTIONAL

With CPI inflation collapsing from the middle of 2008, and with wage inflation also extremely low, the Bank of England no longer had any need to drag its feet on monetary policy relaxation and therefore sought to play catch up. By the end of 2008 official interest rates had been slashed to 2%. This was their lowest level since the early 1950s, and was the level that had prevailed through most of the 1930s. Bank officials also began thinking about more unconventional strategies, and in particular about some form of quantitative easing (QE).

QE really came onto the agenda early in 2009, as economic activity continued to slump, unemployment surged and bank lending and monetary growth fell dramatically. It became clear that, despite the efforts of the previous October, more needed to be done to save the financial sector. UK bank shares had come under renewed pressure following the announcement of huge losses by two of the surviving large US financial institutions, and RBS remained a particular problem. Its total liabilities were almost £2 trillion. To put that in context, the UK's GDP at the time was around £1.5 trillion.

A further frantic round of deliberations ensued between Treasury, Bank and FSA officials, with many of the external advisors that had played a prominent role in policy formulation a few months earlier also involved. Full nationalization of the most-damaged entities was discussed, but it was rejected because of uncertainties about the quality of the bank liabilities that would at a stroke be transferred onto the government's balance sheet. Despite initial Bank of England scepticism, it was instead decided to allow the banks to offload the toxic assets on their balance sheets to a safe haven, via an asset protection scheme (APS). This was a mechanism under the aegis of the Treasury that would provide banks with insurance against loan defaults. The banks would pay the government a flat fee and in return they would be insured against 90% of their possible losses.

Aimed in particular at RBS and Lloyds, the APS was announced by Darling on Monday 19 January 2009, together with new capital injections that were estimated to run to at least £50 billion, or some 2.5% of GDP. It was another extraordinary initiative. The APS meant that the government and the British taxpayer were in effect assuming £5 trillion of risk (the combined balance sheet of the banking system), leaving them potentially responsible for many billions of pounds of losses.

The APS was to remain in place until October 2012, although by that stage it was a backstop for RBS alone. Despite considerable initial scepticism in the media, the APS contributed to the maintenance of financial stability and prevented the huge economic and social cost of the failure of a major UK bank. However, there was only partial success when it came to one of the scheme's subsidiary goals: encouraging bank lending.

The following month, a new special resolution scheme for dealing with failed banks was also legislated, while in due course financial supervision became more systematic and the banks were forced to embrace better disclosure. The associated Banking Act gave the Bank of England a statutory financial stability objective, and it also established a Financial Stability Committee to work alongside the MPC.

By early March, Bank Rate had been cut to a historic low of just 0.5% – a level that was then considered by the central bank to be the practical minimum, and which contrasted with an average of around 4.75% since the Bank was established in 1694.[23] Despite this aggressive move, it was decided by the MPC that additional stimulus was necessary to move inflation back up to target. This would be provided by a £200 billion programme of large-scale asset purchases (LSAPs), mainly from non-bank financial institutions (such as pension funds and insurance companies) in secondary markets and financed by the creation of additional central bank reserves.[24] In this sense, the Bank was following an example set by the Federal Reserve the previous November and by the Bank of Japan as early as March 2001.[25]

By the end of January 2010 the Bank's balance sheet as a proportion of GDP was three times its level before the onset of the crisis in the summer of 2007, and it was larger than it had been at any point in the last 200 years. The Bank's purchases of gilts represented almost 30% of the market's 'free float' (the amount of non-official holdings), and they were equivalent to some 14% of GDP.

The theoretical case for QE was derived from variations on the theme of the so-called liquidity trap first described by Keynes in his *General Theory* in the mid 1930s but subsequently developed by various other economists, not least Nobel laureates Sir John Hicks and Paul Krugman.[26] The idea of a liquidity trap is, in essence, that circumstances could prevail in which a zero, or near-zero, short-term interest rate was insufficiently low to encourage longer-term commercial lending rates to fall to a level consistent with the stabilization of demand and output, and therefore prices. However, by acquiring government stock, and a quantity of targeted corporate debt, a central bank could moderate risk premia, further reduce long-term interest rates and induce investors to rebalance their portfolios.[27] This would generate positive wealth effects, facilitate new issuance of securities and swell the money supply. A further effect would be to lower the government's debt service costs, although this was not an explicit goal. The round of QE announced in March 2009 was to be the first in a series of such programmes employed over subsequent years to sustain growth and moderate the risk of a slide into deflation.

QE was undoubtedly controversial. Central bank purchases of public sector debt and deliberate efforts to accelerate the expansion of the money supply had historically been associated with 'fiscal dominance', and with traumatic losses of price stability and sometimes bouts of hyperinflation.[28] In the modern era, such practices tended to be confined to dictatorships and failed states. The government was assiduous, however, about abiding by a number of important institutional guard rails to ensure that such pitfalls were avoided.

The Bank retained its operational independence and the MPC employed the same personnel and procedures to reach and explain policy decisions. The 2% inflation target remained the focal point of monetary policy. The Bank was committed to complete transparency around the programme. To protect the integrity of its balance sheet, it would conduct its LSAPs via the special Asset Purchase Facility (APF) that had been set up a couple of months earlier as a means to reliquefy dormant credit markets. The APF was a separate legal entity from the Bank. It would only make purchases in the secondary market, and not directly from the Debt Management Office. Any losses the APF made would be indemnified by the Treasury, and the latter would receive any profits the scheme made. Finally, the Bank did not require approval from the Treasury to curtail the programme.

For the reasons outlined in chapter 1 about the difficulties of economists conducting scientific experiments because of the near impossibility of avoiding contamination by other factors, estimating the effects of QE is complex and subject to numerous caveats. Moreover, those effects seem to change over time, depending on the exact circumstances in which the policy is employed (although this is also the case with official interest rate adjustments).

In particular, QE's impact seems to have been greater when it was first applied: it had a 'novelty effect'. Estimates by IMF staff, the BIS and the Bank of England itself suggest that the first round of QE reduced bond yields by between 50 and 100 basis points. The Bank has further estimated that it acted to raise real GDP by between 1.5% and 2%: an impact equivalent to a policy rate cut of 150–300 basis points.[29]

The reasons behind QE being most potent during its first iteration and the fact that it was destined to become less so subsequently are bound up with the mechanisms involved in its application, of which there are generally considered to be three.[30] First, there is a 'bank lending channel'. This puts stress on the importance of banks' liquid assets, and on the potential constraints that a lack of reserves can impose on their willingness to lend. Second, there is the 'portfolio balance channel'. This puts stress on the positive impact on asset prices of the central bank's purchases, and on the potential for holders of assets whose prices have risen, and whose yields have fallen, to sell them in exchange for other (riskier) assets, such as corporate bonds or equities, or to benefit from higher collateral values when seeking to borrow. Third, there is the 'signalling effect', which suggests that what is really of importance with QE is what it implies about the thrust of future policy, and in particular the prospective path of future official interest rates.

The first two of these channels are likely to be most potent when markets are most dysfunctional – when many asset classes are illiquid and the demand for central bank liquidity is highest. This point would clearly have come around the depths of the crisis. The potency of the third effect depended on how the central bank communicated its intentions. In the first phase of QE, great emphasis was put on it being an additional string to the central bank's bow, as it sought to ease monetary conditions for an extended period. It was designed not only to lower the term premium – the additional yield demanded by long-maturity bond investors beyond their expectations of future short-term rates – but also to bring future short-term interest rate expectations down closer to the zero bound. After this had successfully been done once, it would become progressively harder to do again.

BROWN'S BIG MOMENT

On 1 January 2009 the UK took over the chair of the G-20 intergovernmental forum. Although the G-20's membership accounted for some 80% of global GDP, before the crisis erupted it had been of modest importance; its activities were largely confined to technical macroeconomic or financial matters, and to the production of dry (and largely unread) communiqués.[31] However, with the global economy in the throes of the most severe synchronized downturn of the modern era, with his own popularity low both with the public and within his own political party, and with markets still skittish and depressed, Brown was instrumental in encouraging world leaders to elevate the G-20 above the more familiar G-8 in importance. Inspired by Brown, the G-20 became a conduit for a more coordinated effort to bolster falling global demand, to provide support to the emerging economies, and to rebuild business and consumer confidence.

The group's November 2008 meeting in Washington, chaired by President George W. Bush, had confirmed the membership's common desire to overcome the slump and to reform global finance, and it had also committed it to a more forceful and coordinated macro and regulatory policy response and to the avoidance of protectionism. It was also at this event that the IMF's managing director Dominique Strauss-Khan first called for a global, 2%-of-GDP fiscal stimulus to support aggregate demand.

Brown, however, saw the group's next meeting, scheduled for London in early April, as an opportunity to raise this shared commitment to another level, and in particular to underpin it with further explicit and quantified pledges.

The British government's planning for the April 2009 meeting was meticulous. Brown invited the leaders of every member country, visiting many of them in person ahead of time during a preparatory world tour. The initial reaction to his efforts was often sceptical and unfocused. The Europeans were less than convinced, publicly at least, by Brown's openly Keynesian rhetoric, and they were more interested in action to cleanse tax havens and reform the shadow banks. The Chinese and the Russians seemed content to plough their own particular furrows. And nor did Mervyn King help Brown's cause when, in late March, he warned the House of Commons Treasury Select Committee that the UK's fiscal situation was increasingly unsustainable and that more budgetary stimulus would be an error. However, the prime minister was nothing if not determined. He kept up the pressure for a meaningful outcome, not least on Barack Obama, who was about to attend his first major overseas event as US president and with whom Brown was keen to establish a strong relationship.

At a dinner on the eve of the meeting, Brown sought to concentrate the minds of attendees on a positive outcome by contrasting the lasting achievements of the Bretton Woods Conference of 1944 with the abject failure of the London Economic Conference of 1933.[32] After a tense thirty-six hours or so, Brown, by knocking heads together and massaging various outsized egos, and with Obama providing important support, succeeded in hatching an agreement. In addition to a reiteration of the case for coordinated monetary and fiscal stimulus and against the perils of protectionism, it was established that the IMF would receive $500 billion in additional resources to lend to member states experiencing financial difficulty; a further $250 billion was pledged to support trade finance; the developing nations would receive $250 billion to supplement their foreign exchange reserves via a new issue of SDRs; and $100 billion would be made available for the multilateral development banks. Meanwhile, a new Financial Stability Board would be established as a coordinating body for national regulators, and it would be tasked with the job of devising an improved global regulatory environment.

The London G-20 meeting did not deliver additional conventional Keynesian stimulus, but it drew on the lessons of previous modern-era financial crises and delivered potent policy firepower of an alternative, but no less important, variety. Even allowing for the inevitable fudges and obfuscations that underlay the resulting commitments, it represented an impressive collective effort.

In some ways, the two days of the London G-20 meeting were the zenith of Brown's premiership, and they undoubtedly provided a fillip to market sentiment. Global stock markets bottomed out and began to recover, and the second quarter of 2009 was to mark the nadir of the economic cycle.

Brown's success rang hollow at home, however. The technical details of G-20 agreement meant little to an average voter struggling with the damaging fallout of the recession. Furthermore, with the public sector deficit at a peacetime record, the 2009 budget saw Darling disregard the hectoring of his next door neighbour and eschew a further round of fiscal expansion: instead he announced a second increase in the top rate of income tax (to 50% in 2010). And history suggests Darling was right to be cautious. The UK had by this stage used up the bulk of its fiscal policy leeway.

ENDGAME

The final year of Gordon Brown's time in office had a certain tragic quality to it. He was by this time physically and mentally spent. His previous pledges of budgetary prudence and an end to boom and bust looked faintly ridiculous. He did not have enough financial room for manoeuvre to provide the electorate with much that was new or exciting. A House of Commons expenses scandal, and revelations regarding the malicious briefings of one of his closest confidants, hit his personal popularity and that of the party hard. There were significant cabinet resignations and repeated calls for him to step down. Antipathy towards the banks and the policies that had nourished their excesses and malfeasance festered. Recovery was painfully slow, only really gathering any sort of momentum in Q2 2010 (the quarter in which the general election that saw his defenestration was held).

Nevertheless, Brown continued to push desperately for more budgetary largesse while seeking to frame the contemporary political debate as 'New Labour investment versus Tory cuts'. The Conservative Party had, after all, been critical of Labour's fiscal activism throughout the crisis, including when it played a vital role in the global policy effort to address the downturn. In order to force the fiscal policy pace, Brown even tried to replace Darling with Ed Balls at one stage, as he thought the latter would be more amenable to his expansionary bias. But he found that he no longer had the authority to engineer such a pivotal change in personnel without Darling resigning from the government – something that was unconscionable given the prime minister's political frailty. That said, it must clearly have been discomforting for Darling to know that his boss wanted him gone.

The communiqué released after the September 2009 G-20 meeting in Pittsburgh stated that fiscal policy support to economies should not be withdrawn with undue haste, but by this stage the international debate was moving on, and the tide was turning against expansionists such as Brown. As the panic and chaos of late 2008 and early 2009 subsided and output began to rebound around the world, the markets' focus increasingly turned to the unprecedented scale of budget shortfalls, and in particular to the egregious fiscal laxity of peripheral euro area countries such as Greece.

There was no post-crisis spike in UK bond yields, but with the UK deficit at record levels, Darling and many of his officials – including, importantly, Permanent Secretary Nicholas MacPherson – were fearful that further Keynesian initiatives might spark a loss of investor confidence.[33] The internal Treasury debate increasingly became about how fast the budget should be brought back into balance and in what manner. In the background, meanwhile, Mervyn King seemed only too happy to break the convention that the governor of the central bank should not publicly comment on the government's fiscal policy.[34] He too was troubled by the deficit and sympathetic to the need for a forceful programme of medium-term budgetary restraint along the lines being sketched out by the Conservative opposition.[35]

Brown seems to have bowed to the inevitable towards the end of 2009 and accepted that his quest for a more expansionary fiscal stance would be fruitless. In February 2010 Darling was able, to his considerable relief, to announce a new Fiscal Responsibility Act. This committed the government to a series of year-on-year reductions in the budget deficit, such that borrowing as a percentage of GDP would be reduced by more than 50% by the end of financial year 2013–14 and such that the public sector debt burden began to fall in financial year 2015–16.

That said, the pace of fiscal consolidation embodied in New Labour's plans remained relatively pedestrian. The 4% of GDP consolidated budget deficit anticipated in March 2010 for fiscal year 2014–15 would still have been larger than that in all but two short periods of pre-GFC UK post-war history. Moreover, that projection relied on a series of optimistic growth forecasts. It was also unduly dependent on tax increases (including a banker's bonus levy) and public investment cuts rather than focusing on reducing current outlays.[36]

If any further stimulus were needed, the implication was that it should be provided by monetary policy, even though official interest rates were close to zero. In Britain, as elsewhere, the return of explicit fiscal Keynesianism was a brief affair, lasting not much more than a year.

By this stage Brown must have sorely regretted the fiscal incontinence, on his watch, during the 2001–5 period. Those years saw a positive budgetary impulse of more than 4.5 percentage points of GDP. Notwithstanding the huge support provided to the financial sector during the GFC (between 2007 and 2009), the fiscal stance was only eased by about 3.5 percentage points.

Overall, the GFC and its painful immediate aftermath were an ignominious denouement for New Labour. Its dominance of UK politics had been built on the presentation and positioning abilities of Tony Blair; on a sense that it was a force for change and modernization; on an extended period of solid economic growth and overall macro-stability; on belated but significant investment in education, health and other public services; and on a divided and incompetent opposition that consistently failed to deliver a clear message. By 2010, each of these pillars had been severely damaged, if not demolished. Brown, meanwhile, was yesterday's man. His shortcomings as a leader had been brutally exposed, his authority was shot, his personal ratings were lower than his party's, and the electorate's trust in him was exhausted.

When the May 2010 general election came, it was no surprise that New Labour lost the sixty-six-seat majority won by Blair in 2005. The polls had been pointing in that direction for some time. However, despite a significant swing to the Conservatives in terms of votes and seats, they still fell twenty short of an overall majority. In this sense, New Labour exceeded the expectations of many, including a sizeable proportion of its own supporters. The nation was therefore confronted with only the second hung parliament of the post-war era. The election outcome also provided something of a warning: there was evidence in it that the electorate was breaking away from familiar voting patterns.

Both Labour and the Tories subsequently sought out the support of the Liberal Democrats – who had secured fifty-seven seats under the leadership of Nick Clegg – in an effort to form a workable administration.[*] In the end, after five days of intense negotiations it was David Cameron's Conservatives who prevailed. This was despite Brown resigning as leader of the Labour Party in an effort to forge a deal, and despite the Liberal Democrats having long been seen as politically and emotionally more sympathetic to New Labour than to the Conservatives. Indeed, during the Blair years the party was often further to the left than the government on many key issues.

Brown stood down as prime minister on 11 May, bringing down the curtain on thirteen years of Labour government. The Conservative–Lib Dem government that followed was the first coalition ever to result directly from a UK election. Aged forty-four, Cameron was the youngest holder of the office of prime minister for more than 200 years.

---

[*] Labour would also have required the support of other smaller parties to establish a majority.

HISTORY RESTORED

The origins of the traumatic events of 2007–10 can, to a significant extent, be traced back to the financial deregulation and ascendency of free market economics that marked the 1980s, not just in the UK but more widely. That said, subsequent administrations, and not least the governments of Tony Blair and Gordon Brown, were happy to embrace much of the policy consensus of that time. Naturally, there were different biases and tweaks here and there as the electorate was pandered to and certain lessons were learned, but the conventional policy wisdom in the later 1990s and early 2000s had much more in common with the Thatcher era than with that of the 1970s.

Even though prices were relatively stable and growth continued, private sector debt was allowed to accumulate to unheard-of levels, asset prices became detached from underlying fundamentals, and the financial sector was largely left to its own devices and permitted to expand and mutate in an increasingly hazardous manner. While outwardly performing reasonably well, the economy became inherently fragile and unstable. In hindsight, it was only a matter of time before disaster struck.

When it arrived, the GFC revealed a catalogue of errors, misapprehension and complacency. At a stroke, various fundamental economic principles that had been taken for granted were revealed to be flawed, or even entirely invalid. To address the disaster, large-scale policy responses had to be made on the hoof; old, forgotten options were resurrected; and new, untried and untested, initiatives were applied. It was a case of learning, and relearning, by doing.

The recession that followed was both deep and lengthy, as private financial and non-financial balance sheets necessarily adjusted and various unsustainable trends reversed. Indeed, for a period, the damage to financial sectors and the associated precipitous downturn threatened to shred the very fabric of society. In such circumstances it would have been difficult for any governing party to survive. Too much wealth was lost. Too many lives were damaged. Too many apparent certainties were upended. Too much malfeasance was unearthed. But this was especially the case for a government that was exhibiting the fatigue that comes with an extended period in power, and one led by a prime minister who was ill-suited to the role.

That said, after an initial hiatus the UK response to the crisis became impressively forceful and wide ranging, and it helped to turn the economic tide both at home and, by setting a positive example, further afield. Moreover, for all his failings Gordon Brown played a vital role in all this.

Banking sector liquidity was shored up. Significant public capital was injected into the most compromised entities. Troubled assets were ring-fenced. In total, the gross resources committed to financial sector support, including the increase in contingent liabilities, ran to more than 60% of GDP, although the net cost to the taxpayer was ultimately to prove much smaller.

There was also a recognition that there was a requirement for the UK's financial sector oversight to be strengthened. In due course, this would mean both a new institutional architecture and the development of macroprudential instruments to mitigate the amplitude of the credit cycle and negative feedback loops between finance and real activity.

Meanwhile, monetary policy was relaxed to an unprecedented extent (and in an increasingly unconventional manner) and significant temporary discretionary fiscal stimulus was applied around the bottom of the cycle. Both of these measures went some way towards stabilizing the perilous situation.

The financial crisis and the subsequent recession were bound to cast a long shadow, however. The GFC dealt a severe blow to the supply side of the economy. There was a sharp decline in the rate of capital accumulation, as investment plummeted, and restructuring rendered some of the capital stock obsolescent. Productivity was further depressed by lower spending on research and development and by a reduction in the finance available for riskier projects. Younger companies, which often improve their efficiency at the fastest rate, had few financing alternatives to the bank loans that were in increasingly short supply. The small and medium-sized corporate sector more broadly tended to be most reliant on property collateral for loans, meaning that lower property prices tightened their collateral constraints. The flows of capital and labour between companies through which technology and ideas are diffused tended to slow down. What is more, labour participation declined, and there was a drop in net migration flows.

The IMF has suggested that the loss to potential output that resulted from the crisis amounted to between four and five percentage points of GDP. They also estimate that the UK's medium-term growth rate was reduced by 0.5–0.75 percentage points as a result of these considerations. Other assessments were more negative still.

The GFC was to mark the beginning of an extended period of muted, historically depressed, productivity growth and stagnant living standards, even in the face of what seemed to be remarkable technological progress.

As far as inequality is concerned, it is well documented that it tends to move cyclically, rising in recessions and falling back in expansions because unemployment tends to be more cyclical for the lower paid. It is therefore no surprise that measures of inequality such as the Gini coefficient and the 90/10 income ratio edged upwards during the GFC and then began to fall back as recovery took hold. However, the high trend in UK income inequality observable since the early 1990s was undisturbed.

The problem came to be that, despite UK society not becoming significantly more unequal during the GFC, the severe cyclical downturn and reduced growth potential meant that real income growth slowed further. The aspirations that had been shaped over previous decades for more rapid improvements in living standards were thereby becoming increasingly frustrated. And if the overall cake had shrunk, and was unlikely to expand very rapidly in future, the only way for an individual to improve his or her lot significantly was at the expense of someone else.

These sorry facts together with the manifest failure of neoliberalism and the concept of self-regulating markets were seen by many commentators to be fertile ground for a shift in the political centre of gravity to the left. Those who were themselves on the left certainly hoped so, and they expected that even if Labour lost power in 2010 it would be only a temporary blip. But this did not turn out to be the case. Instead, the GFC and its aftermath were to presage political fragmentation, institutional decay and the rise of populism – just as had been the case after the Great Depression. During both periods, deep recession and its consequences weakened class consciousness and strengthened native solidarity. And on both occasions, entropy and perceived alienation served to benefit the right rather than the left, and the radical right more than the conservative right. The politics of ideas was to be overtaken by the politics of identity – and successful politicians seized on this.

CHAPTER 11

Theory and Policy in the Wake of the GFC

The deployment of austerity as economic policy has been as effective in bringing us peace, prosperity, and crucially, a sustained reduction of debt, as the Mongol Golden Horde was in furthering the development of Olympic dressage.

— Mark Blyth, 2012[1]

PHILOSOPHICAL INERTIA

The enormous ructions of the GFC shattered the complacency of the years of the Great Moderation. Over a three-year period, the world changed – and not for the better.

The crisis reached existential proportions in the US, the UK and much of the developed world. Market and broader macroeconomic events occurred that had hitherto been thought to be nigh-on impossible by much of the economics profession. Not only was the GFC an indictment of the way that Wall Street, the City of London and other financial centres functioned, it also represented a catastrophic failure of economic analysis and policy, and of economists' imagination. The presumption that economies were largely self-stabilizing and that they were immune to catastrophic breakdown was revealed to be hopelessly optimistic; the hands-off approach to finance and the belief that the resilience of individual financial institutions was a necessary and sufficient condition for ensuring the stability of the system as a whole were reckless; and the onus placed on monetary tools to the exclusion of other policy levers was proven to be dangerously narrow.

Extrapolative expectations and positive feedback loops first proliferated and then unwound mercilessly. Non-linearities burgeoned. Temporary disturbances had enduring effects. Unorthodox – and sometimes long-ignored, if not almost forgotten – policy responses were then resorted to in desperation during the depths of the crisis, and they proved decisive in turning around a situation that for a time seemed utterly hopeless.

It might have been expected, therefore, that such a dramatic shock to the global financial and economic systems would encourage profound changes in macroeconomic theory and its application to policy, and that the previously dominant new classical–new Keynesian conventional wisdom would be superseded by very different thinking and action – even if that new thinking offered a less-alluring vision than that of a perfect, frictionless, market system. This is, after all, what happened following the Great Depression – although admittedly it took a decade or so to come to fruition. Generally speaking, however, this was not the case after 2009. Notwithstanding the efforts of a small group of largely US-based economists to resurrect a particularly extravagant form of unreconstructed Keynesianism (so-called modern monetary theory, or MMT), there was no radical transformation of beliefs or approach – no revolution in thought or action.

This is not to deny that some new life was breathed into the subject of economics. There were, for example, greater efforts to incorporate elements of sociology, anthropology, psychology and history, in order to better understand how individuals, companies, markets and whole economies function and how economic rationality could be undermined. Larger data sets were assembled so that researchers could dig deeper into labour and financial market dynamics. More resources were dedicated to the development of controlled experiments in order to assess the impact of policy interventions in advance. And some British universities – such as the University of Manchester, the University of Cambridge and University College London – went out of their way to change the way that they approached the subject.

In general, however, the teaching of macroeconomics continued much as before, with only a few tweaks here and there in acknowledgement of recent events. Existing models were enriched to include a more realistic representation of the role of the financial sector, but the treatment of labour and product markets – the very core of economies – remained largely unaltered.

So much time and intellectual capital had been sunk into pre-crisis models, and they had been embraced with such confidence by so many, that there was a reluctance to question their underpinnings, let alone write them off and start again. Hence, by and large, the emphasis remained on economic rationality, consistent micro foundations and a fixation on the mathematical elegance of what unencumbered free markets could achieve for overall welfare if only they were allowed to exist. Much of the profession continued to romanticize beauty over truth.

Government intervention was still often viewed as being more of a problem than a solution. Rules continued to be favoured over discretion. Monetary instruments continued to dominate stabilization policy and to be applied by independent central banks that were formally targeting inflation, albeit in increasingly unconventional ways. Fiscal activism was frowned upon, reserved only for the most exceptional of circumstances. It was solely in the area of financial regulation that rapid change emerged. Macroprudential policy was developed to prevent the sort of build-up of asset market excess and financial imbalances that preceded the crisis.

MACROPRUDENTIAL REDUX

The years following the GFC witnessed a recognition that taking the EMH too literally, and assuming that stocks and other financial assets were always perfectly priced and never in a state of excess of one form or another, was unwise. Furthermore, the associated application of the so-called Greenspan doctrine, which suggested that asset bubbles could not be recognized in real time and could only be properly addressed after the event, was acknowledged to be potentially flawed. Rather, experience suggested not only that some asset bubbles and episodes of financial immoderation were blindingly obvious from a relatively early stage – think Japan's land prices in the late 1980s, the US tech sector in the late 1990s, or various housing booms in the UK and elsewhere in the 2000s – but that the asymmetries in macro policymaking implicit in the Greenspan doctrine could actually be a catalyst for such events.

In short, narrow inflation targeting had been found wanting. Even if central banks and governments could deliver relative price stability and consistently high rates of employment, there was a danger that they would nurture unsustainable macroeconomic disequilibria, or even financial excess, and that resource misallocation on a grand scale would result. What is more, when such tendencies unwound they had a propensity to do so with disastrous consequences, not just for the financial sector but for the economy as a whole. And these consequences could cast a long shadow over future economic performance.

At the same time, however, it was recognized – consistent with the writings of Robertson and Keynes in the interwar years – that focusing conventional monetary policy on financial stability alone was itself likely to lead only to unacceptable macroeconomic instability.[2] Monetary policy operates with significant, but unreliable, lags, and its ultimate effects are uncertain and spread far beyond the financial sector. A small official interest rate premium put in place to encourage financial stability can lead to the worst of both worlds: uncomfortably low inflation and continued asset price excess. Taking aggressive official interest rate action to counteract an asset boom could easily encourage the opposite: it can plunge the real economy into deep recession and encourage outright deflation, especially where indebtedness is high.

Conventional monetary policy was too blunt a tool to be routinely used to address the cyclical risks to financial stability.

There was therefore a desire to identify a series of separate regulations and controls that could be tightened up as asset market and other financial extravagances become manifest, thereby supplementing 'standard' monetary and fiscal policy to avoid the development of destabilizing Minsky-like financial sequences. There was a need to develop a countercyclical policy for the financial cycle. This was particularly the case in an environment of historically low interest rates, where investors might be encouraged to take excessive risks in order to generate higher returns.

It was recognized that in such a strategy of 'leaning against the financial wind', particular attention should be paid to credit growth, which has a habit of accelerating procyclically as bank balance sheets become the beneficiaries of strengthening output and still-low rates, in the process fuelling asset prices, and particularly real estate prices. Housing markets have long acted as a primary conduit for the transmission of monetary conditions to the broader economy.

By focusing on credit growth, it was hoped that official interest rates would rarely have to be higher than would be consistent with existing inflation targets; that the credibility of those targets would better preserved; and that the sort of damage to the economy that might accrue from, say, any related exchange rate strength could be avoided.

The macroprudential tools touted ranged from dynamic or countercyclical capital and liquidity buffers, to limits on loan-to-value and loan-to-income ratios, to adjustable margin requirements. Variations on some of these themes were subsequently applied in a number of economies – with the UK often being at the leading edge of policy evolution – to buttress the minimum standards for microprudential (or institution-by-institution) regulation set by the 2010 Basel III international accord. That said, the overall pattern of deployment remained patchy.[3]

None of these tools were entirely new: they were a throwback to an earlier age. For much of the period from the end of World War II until the early 1980s, rather than managing credit entirely through the manipulation of its price (i.e. through interest rates), the preference across the major economies was for direct controls on it and on other aspects of banks' activities. This was an era of caps on deposit rates; of the rationing of consumer instalment loans; of ceilings on loan maturities; of minimum downpayments for mortgages; of constraints on overall bank lending; and of the active management of bank reserve requirements, often within the broader context of trade and capital controls. Hence, as we saw earlier, British consumers, investors and economists regularly had to struggle with the minutiae of UK hire-purchase controls (effectively loan-to-value ratios) and with 'the corset': a system of 'supplementary special deposits' designed to limit bank advances.

On a basic level, these less-than-subtle intrusions into the process of financial intermediation were a success. The years from the late 1940s to the mid 1970s were devoid of the sort of chronic financial crisis that peppered the pre-war period and that resurfaced in 2007.

On the other hand, though, the ability of the authorities to prevent exaggerated business cycles waned and higher inflation became embedded. At the same time, the financial sector became more adept at circumventing the controls, and the authorities therefore faced a continual battle to minimize regulatory arbitrage and leakages into the non-bank financial sector. The system of controls became more complex, while the associated costs increasingly outweighed the benefits.

As a consequence, the early iterations of macroprudential policy morphed into outright financial repression and the creation of captive markets that governments could exploit. Innovation and competition within the financial sector were stymied. Consumer choice was rationed. The efficient allocation of resources was impeded, and success in addressing one form of financial excess merely encouraged another. Unsurprisingly, this provoked a reaction, and there followed a renaissance of faith in free market forces in finance during the late 1970s and into the 1980s.

Perhaps the overriding message of the past seventy-five years, then, is that neither ultralight regulation nor the overbearing regulations of the Keynesian period stood the test of time. Instead, what was required was a middle way: one that took account of the fact that while macroprudential initiatives could be a useful addition to the existing policy armoury in the right circumstances, they were unlikely in themselves to be sufficient.

There is no escaping the fact that macroprudential controls are distortionary. They are also arbitrary, and they are politically charged through distributional effects that fall heavily on particular groups. Moreover, their effects are not yet well understood, and they are therefore hard to calibrate with the business cycle. They are ultimately likely to be evaded by a financial sector that is adept at circumventing regulations; and however they are framed, they may prove ill-suited to the next crisis: no two crises are exactly alike. Finally, they may encounter tensions with microprudential policy in a downturn. For example, macroprudential policy may be aimed at encouraging financial institutions to take on more risk and to lend, while micro regulation may be more concerned about preventing bank failures.

All that said, the negatives associated with macroprudential policy can be attenuated if the risks it seeks to address are clearly identified and if unduly complex regulatory structures are avoided. It must also operate within a sound institutional framework under the guidance of a single, technically proficient, transparent authority, and it needs to be backed by a strong lender of last resort, such as has been the case with the Bank of England and its Financial Policy Committee, established in 2013.

Most importantly of all, prudential policies can only be a complement to an appropriate overall macro policy setting, not a substitute for one. They are not an enduring alternative to the pursuit of sound fiscal and monetary policy. If aggregate demand significantly exceeds aggregate supply because of lax macro policy, no amount of macroprudential intervention is likely to neutralize the effects. And in a globalized world, this means that macro and macroprudential policies have to be coordinated internationally: a role that has fallen on the shoulders of the Financial Stability Board, established in 2012, which comes under the auspices of the G-20.

Macroprudential policy must not be allowed to become the modern-day equivalent of incomes policy: a dam that can at best temporarily stem a flood of excess demand and that, if subjected to pressure for too long, is ultimately breached.

ENDURING FINANCIAL FAULT LINES

The early record of the renaissance of macroprudential policy shows that the global financial system continued to exhibit structural and cyclical vulnerabilities – some old, some new – after the application of the new measures.

The so-called shadow banks remained an issue. Risks continued to migrate from banks to non-banks, where many entities were still dependent on short-term funding, were highly leveraged, were often weighed down by derivative exposures and were subject to a lighter burden of supervisory and regulatory standards. The shadow banks have also established a larger geographical footprint than was the case during the GFC, with rapid growth observable in China and in the financial centres of Europe. In 2019 the shadow banking system's assets were around $100 trillion, up from $92 trillion in 2015 and $60 trillion in 2007.[4] These assets have grown faster than GDP in many jurisdictions, and especially in the emerging markets.

Many riskier assets – and higher-yielding bonds and emerging-market debt in particular – remained prone to high volatility and damaging liquidity shortages.

The spread of low-fee, passive, exchange-traded funds proliferated, their total assets swelling from less than $1 trillion in 2007 to more than $6 trillion in 2019.[5] These funds can have a propensity to distort price discovery, to encourage procyclical (or 'momentum') investing and to undermine the role of fundamental stock research, and they are also susceptible to liquidity mismatches between the underlying securities and the funds themselves.

Financial intermediaries have shrunk, while end users have become bigger and more complex. This has been associated with liquidity shortages in important markets.

Much of the banking sector has yet to put the crisis behind it. Cross-border bank lending fell away sharply after 2007 and struggled to return to its previous highs thereafter. Returns on equity have also remained depressed relative to the pre-2007 period, even allowing for the effects of a larger equity base. This was particularly the case in Europe.

Interest rates that were, until the recent war in Ukraine, historically low left insurance and pension companies under duress, as they struggled to match their assets with their liabilities.

The application of macroprudential tools, while representing an important additional string to the policymakers' bow in the post-crisis era, was never a cure-all for financial instability. Furthermore, applying those rules remains inconsistent and a work in progress. Indeed, a degree of reform fatigue had set in by 2017, and in some jurisdictions (not least the US) there was a political backlash against the reforms. And, of course, the dramatic economic effects of the Covid-19 pandemic added another layer of complexity to the process of financial oversight and reform after 2020.

There is one particular potential conduit of macroprudential policy that has not yet been actively applied but that could prove to be a useful addition to the policymaker's arsenal: the central bank balance sheet. As we have seen, LSAPs were employed aggressively, and with considerable success, during the crisis to bear down on long-term interest rates, to address issues of market illiquidity (and excess risk premia), and to thereby provide additional monetary stimulus. Furthermore, this continued to be the case well into the recovery in the UK and beyond.

There has so far been a reluctance, however, to manipulate asset markets symmetrically, using specific asset sales to moderate areas of market excess and undue risk taking.[6] This may merely reflect the absence to date of financial exuberance to compare with the run-up to the GFC. However, if asset sales are ultimately used more frequently, central banks will have to operate with permanently large balance sheets that have significant weightings to riskier assets such as MBSs, corporate bonds or equities. This would mean that they were confronted by a greater threat of incurring intermittent losses on these holdings, which would require us to question how, and to what extent, they should be indemnified against such losses by government.

Importantly, however, the symmetrical use of the balance sheet would allow central banks to pursue two objectives – price stability and financial stability – with two tools – official interest rates and the structure of their balance sheet. They would thereby meet the so-called Tinbergen rule, which specifies that policymakers trying to hit multiple economic targets need to have control over at least one policy tool for each policy, as the achievement of certain economic goals precludes the achievement of others.[7]

FISCAL MYOPIA

Despite the positive countercyclical role played by discretionary fiscal policy around the depths of the GFC, and the view expressed by the IMF, the G-20 and others that the stimulus applied in 2008 and 2009 should not be withdrawn precipitously, there was a rapid reversion to fiscal conservatism. From mid 2010 the focus switched to the longer-term issue of public sector debt sustainability. This hasty about-turn emanated in the main from continental Europe: the economics of Keynes had never achieved the influence there that it enjoyed in the Anglosphere, and there was a burgeoning sovereign debt crisis that threatened to destroy the euro. There were also some strident anti-Keynesian voices in the US on the Republican right, and they came to exert an increasingly austere influence on US fiscal policy after the Democratic Party's defeat in the 2010 midterm elections (even if that approach was rapidly jettisoned after the election of Donald Trump in 2016).

Notwithstanding the constraints on monetary activism around the zero interest rate bound, for their part UK policymakers proved reluctant to buck the conservative fiscal policy trend. Indeed, they seemed only too happy to run with the pack. This reflected a number of theoretical considerations – considerations that were controversial and that, in due course, proved erroneous.

SHIFTING MULTIPLIERS

Estimates of the multiplier effects of the fiscal stimulus that was resorted to as the GFC deepened were low at the outset. At the end of 2008, with output falling sharply across the major economies, the IMF put the average multiplier at just 0.3–0.8. This suggested that while fiscal expansion would contribute little to the stabilization of output, fiscal contraction, when it was subsequently employed, would do little harm. The notion that it would not be very costly to reduce budget deficits was reinforced by further estimates published in March 2009 that indicated that the negative multiplier for tax increases was between 0.3 and 0.5, and that for spending cuts the multiplier was as low as 0.3. The paucity of the effects of fiscal policy was in keeping with a world of near-rational expectations.

By 2013, however, the IMF had completely changed its tune, admitting in a review of evidence from twenty-six countries that it had significantly underestimated the decline in domestic demand and the rise in unemployment associated with fiscal consolidation. Consistent with standard Keynesian theory, the IMF acknowledged that fiscal multipliers were much larger in an environment of zero (or near-zero) interest rates. Indeed, they could substantially exceed 1, especially for government investment.[8]

But by this stage it was too late. The damage to the recovery in the UK and elsewhere from premature fiscal adjustment had already been done. The trajectory of the cyclical upswing was typically shallow and disappointing relative to most official forecasts.[9]

(OXY)MORONIC NOTIONS

A second encouragement for the early reversal of the fiscal expansion of 2008 and 2009 was provided by the contradiction in terms known as the 'expansionary fiscal contraction'. This phenomenon can be traced to the Bocconi School in Italy, and to the analysis of previous episodes of fiscal restraint undertaken by Alberto Alesina and various colleagues. Their claim, built around strong assumptions of rational expectations, was that a credible programme of budgetary consolidation – and especially one that is heavily weighted towards cuts in current spending rather than tax hikes or lower public investment – would actually have a net positive impact on aggregate demand. Such a strategy would encourage lower longer-term interest rates and exchange rate depreciation, and it would rebuild private sector confidence and the willingness to spend in anticipation of a lower future tax burden.[10] In other words, Keynes had got it all the wrong way round.

These ideas were popular among hard-pressed European policymakers during the euro area sovereign debt crisis, but they also garnered support within the UK Treasury.

The problem was that the analysis subsequently attracted heavy criticism from the OECD and the IMF, among others, for factual omissions and 'data mining'. Alesina was therefore forced to water down his conclusions dramatically. The truth was that, apart from under very specific circumstances, fiscal contractions do indeed 'contract'. Moreover, policies such as those advocated by Alesina and his colleagues can be especially damaging if they are applied when output is already falling, while economic performance is generally better when fiscal stimulus is not withdrawn too soon.[11] Again, however, by the time Alesina *et al.* had been forced to row back, the damage was done.

A third inspiration for fiscal conservatives emerged from the magisterial work of Carmen Reinhart and Kenneth Rogoff on the history of financial crises. Their research suggested that sovereign debt crises followed banking crises some 80% of the time. More pertinently, they claimed that when the public debt burden exceeded a figure of around 90% of GDP, growth tended to decelerate.[12]

But this too proved bogus. Reinhart and Rogoff's analysis was found to be based in part on a spreadsheet error. With the application of more robust statistical techniques, the 90% 'growth cliff' disappeared. All that remained was a modest negative correlation between public debt burdens and growth, with more than a suggestion that the causation typically went from growth to debt rather than in the other direction.

UNDEREXPLOITED AUTOMATICITY

Against this backdrop, and despite the controversies associated with unconventional monetary initiatives, little was done to enhance the role that fiscal policy could play in stabilization policy.

The most timely, predictable and effective fiscal response to moderate shocks is delivered by the 'automatic stabilizers': variations in taxes, subsidies and transfers that occur mechanically in response to changes in output and employment. To stabilize aggregate demand satisfactorily, the automatic stabilizers need to be substantial and to function well. And if they are allowed to operate symmetrically over the cycle, they should prove broadly fiscally neutral.

The amount of support that automatic fiscal stabilization offers depends on the make-up of a country's tax and benefits systems, its income level, its openness to trade, the size of its government sector, and the nature of the shock with which it is confronted – in particular, how much unemployment that shock generates. The UK's automatic stabilizers are estimated to have offset roughly 40% of the effects of the GFC. This is more than in the two previous downturns, and significantly more than was the case in the US, but somewhat less than in some other EU countries.

Today's stabilizers have typically grown out of social programmes rather than being explicitly designed as tools to stabilize aggregate demand. They could usefully be improved in terms of both timeliness and effectiveness by reorientating them to some degree. This could be achieved by the cyclical variation of investment tax deductions, property taxes, VAT, transfers to local governments and the substitution of estimated current-year-based income tax collection for previous-year-based income tax collection. This would require the establishment of pre-specified 'triggers' for when these initiatives kick in.

As useful and effective as automatic stabilizers are, though, there is a limit to their efficacy. If a shock is particularly large, or if it is sector specific, or if it leads to a protracted shortfall in aggregate demand, then the automatic stabilizers are likely to prove inadequate. Discretionary fiscal policy may then have to play a greater role, as it did during the GFC.

DISCRETIONARY OVERSIGHTS

Whatever half-truths and misrepresentations are espoused by the fiscal conservatives, it is true that discretionary fiscal initiatives face major challenges. The first challenge is that they risk unsettling bond market investors if they are deemed inappropriate or excessive. The second is that they are difficult to calibrate to the business cycle with any precision, in that large tax reductions and expenditure increases involve significant lags in terms of information, decision-making and implementation. And the third major challenge is that they are open to malign political influence, and 'fiscal dominance'.[13]

The first of these three anxieties is most likely to be allayed by joining in with an internationally coordinated relaxation of fiscal policy. It could also be dispelled somewhat by emphasizing the asset side of the public sector balance sheet more. In the past, short-termism has too often dominated: public investment projects have been slashed and assets have been sold off, thereby harming the prospects of future generations (who of course cannot vote). To the extent that future borrowing is directed to the financing of investment, public sector net worth will be promoted.

Public infrastructure investment spending, and the public sector capital stock, underpin growth potential. Infrastructure rich in pathbreaking technology tends to be especially potent over the long term. There is also a greater need for projects that address climate change in the years ahead. It makes sense, therefore, to keep the share of net public investment in GDP over the course of the business cycle at a level consistent with the maintenance of – if not an increase in – the economy's growth potential, and therefore consistent with the future tax take.

The OECD has suggested that advanced economies invest a sum equivalent to some 3.5% of GDP a year into infrastructure (public plus private) to avoid detrimental implications for living standards, quality of life and competitiveness. The UK fell consistently short of this target in the 2010s.

The second issue – that of timing – may be rendered irrelevant if, such as often occurs in the wake of a financial crisis, the recession is deep and the recovery slow. It can also be remedied to some extent by the government having available a pre-vetted, 'shovel-ready', buffer stock of investment projects to be activated or sped up at short notice – projects that are part of the government's publicly stated infrastructure plans. These need not be grandiose. The multiplier effects of investment spending that addresses even minor transport bottlenecks can, when considering its supply-side effects, run into double digits.

A number of constructive institutional initiatives in this regard have been forthcoming in the UK.

One example is the £40 billion UK Guarantees Scheme (2% of GDP), which was established in 2012 to support private investment infrastructure projects by helping potential projects to access debt finance.

Another is the National Infrastructure Commission, which was set up in October 2015 to make independent recommendations to the government on infrastructure priorities. The intention was that there would be a greater focus on planning, consents, cost management, the prioritization of nationally significant projects and the attraction of private expertise and involvement. Successive National Infrastructure Assessments and delivery plans were published, setting out a pipeline of projects, the prospective roles of the public and private sectors, and the potential burden on different industries and the skilled labour force. A National Infrastructure Projects Authority was also created in 2016 to oversee the delivery of infrastructure projects. All this should over time improve the quality and scheduling of infrastructure spending, but the problem of the total amount budgeted has endured, as has a sense that the Treasury is reluctant to initiate new projects without overwhelming proof that they would address a significant market failure.

And the third major challenge faced by discretionary fiscal initiatives – that they are open to malign political influence – is again something that can be addressed by an appropriate institutional framework, and in particular by the establishment of a credible independent watchdog to generate forecasts for the public finances, to undertake relevant analysis and to police the fiscal rules. The establishment of the Office for Budgetary Responsibility (OBR) in 2010 met this requirement.

MONETARY ENDGAME

A combination of low inflation and low inflation expectations, together with a further decline in growth potential in the advanced economies, meant that the period after 2010 was characterized by historically low interest rates in both nominal and real terms. Indeed, the average global long-term real interest rate is estimated to have been near zero, if not persistently negative, by 2016, compared with a 700-year average of around 4.75% and a 200-year average of about 2.6%.[14]

The inflation shortfall reflected significant excess capacity – the OECD output gap was the equivalent of four percentage points of potential GDP in 2009 and closed only gradually thereafter – together with a related collapse in global commodity prices.

The decline in growth potential mirrored the tendency for desired savings to exceed desired investment (alluded to in chapter 9) to continue. This had its origins in a range of factors.

On the savings side, the key considerations included high levels of out-standing private debt and a desire to deleverage; the ageing of the population, which encouraged a higher overall rate of asset accumulation to pay for retire-ment; inequality; excessively high profits in certain sectors; and self-insurance by emerging-market governments in the form of currency undervaluation and foreign exchange reserve accumulation.

On the investment side, the most important issues extended to GDP becom-ing less resource intensive in the context of ICT innovation and the rise of the services sector; a fall in the relative price of capital goods; slower labour force growth; elevated uncertainty; and an increase in financial sector regulation.

A major implication of the excess of ex ante savings over ex ante invest-ment was that nominal policy rates gravitated towards the zero bound, not just in the UK but everywhere, and the fear was that they might stay there for an extended period. The liquidity trap described in the previous chapter would therefore remain a semi-permanent feature of the economic landscape. The zero-interest-rate bound would therefore continue to bind policymakers. There would be limited scope for those policymakers to use policy rates to manage demand.

This meant that central banks – which, in an environment of near-universal fiscal restraint, had to shoulder the overwhelming burden of macro-stabilization policy – were forced to resort to the use of increasingly unfamil-iar and unconventional tools to exert a meaningful influence on aggregate demand and thereby meet mandated inflation targets. They also often had to do this in the shadow of a crisis, and when the effects of these departures were both highly uncertain and inconsistent from period to period.

The Bank of England repeatedly resorted to rounds of QE after 2010, or to the use of LSAPs to influence longer-term interest rates.[15] In the process, the central bank's balance sheet exploded in size, ultimately approaching the equivalent of 50% of GDP – some two and half times its previous peaks dur-ing the Jacobite rebellions in the middle of the eighteenth century, during the Napoleonic Wars and during World War II. It also made efforts to define its forward interest rate guidance more formally, providing greater detail about its reaction function; to reduce uncertainty about the dovishness of the mon-etary policy outlook; and to underwrite targeted commercial bank lending schemes (so called funding for lending).

At different times, however, the Bank considered further innovations that had been tried in other countries. These included a negative policy rate; the reorientation of LSAPs more towards private, even foreign, assets; a formal target for longer-term yields; new goals designed to depress real interest rates, such as a temporary commitment to overshoot the 2% inflation target, an increase in the target to, say, 4%, a price level objective, or a nominal GDP growth or level target; the taxation of money in an effort to effectively 'remove' the zero bound, and to accelerate spending; and even the direct financing of the budget deficit by the Bank – something long considered by conventional economists to be the ultimate macro policy taboo.

NEW WINE IN OLD BOTTLES

Direct monetary finance – or a central bank purchasing government debt in the primary market as opposed to the secondary one, as is the case with QE – is a major plank of MMT. The essential elements of MMT can be summarized as follows.

- A government that creates its own money generally need not, and will not, default on debt denominated in its own currency.
- A government deficit is necessarily mirrored by an equivalent private sector surplus.
- Monetary policy is less effective than fiscal policy during a slump.
- A government can buy goods and services without the need to collect taxes or issue debt.
- Interest costs can be constrained through money creation.
- Government spending and money creation need only be limited to the extent that employment becomes 'over-full', thereby encouraging inflation.
- Should inflation arise, it can readily be controlled by higher taxation and bond issuance to remove excess liquidity.

The core inference and contention of MMT is, therefore, that the budget deficit and public sector indebtedness should be allowed to adjust to the level necessary to secure full employment.

Despite the use of 'modern' in its name, MMT has its roots firmly in the past. Indeed, it looks very much like the 'functional finance' (FF) gospel preached by Abba Lerner in the early 1940s.[16]

Lerner was a Russian-born British economist who worked alongside both Hayek at the London School of Economics and Keynes at Cambridge before teaching at a number of top US universities. Something of a maverick, albeit a brilliant one, Lerner's macroeconomic philosophy can be distilled down into the notion that, so strong is the economic, social and moral case for achieving high employment and relative price stability, policymakers should not be fussy about how they go about it. Policies should be judged on their ability to achieve these goals rather than on notions of 'soundness' or compliance with the tenets of traditional economics. What matters is maintaining an adequate flow of total expenditure, and if that means that the boundaries between monetary and fiscal policy become increasingly blurred, so be it. Lerner believed that if the direct financing of budget deficits by the central bank was the only option left for boosting aggregate demand and keeping output in line with potential, then that option should be robustly employed.

Interestingly, Keynes, while certainly prepared to be radical, was cautious about FF. By the early 1940s he was a senior Treasury official and was intimately involved in the practicalities of financing the war and planning for peace. Operating very much in the real world, he believed that policy should be measured, steady, consistent and credible. While Keynes therefore acknowledged Lerner's brilliance, and expressed sympathy for the logic of his framework of thought, he saw FF more as a pedagogic device than as a basis for a rigorous policy programme. He considered Lerner to lack practical intuition and thought that he paid insufficient heed to what Keynes described as the public's 'allergy to extremes'. Perhaps most importantly, Keynes feared FF's potentially damaging effects on debt sustainability and private sector confidence, and the risk it presented for inflation.[17]

Whatever its intellectual heritage, at a basic level MMT, like FF, is little more than an expression of a macroeconomic judgement and a political reality. High unemployment and excessive inflation are ills that are best avoided, and ones that almost all politicians want to minimize. Government policy should therefore prioritize their prevention. In the process, policymakers may, *in extremis*, need to be inventive in how they combine monetary and fiscal policy to achieve these goals.

At the same time, it is also clear that government investment has been neglected over recent years; that inequality is a burning social and political issue that urgently needs to be addressed; and that, despite historically high public debt often being portrayed as a serious constraint, the limitations on fiscal expansion are much reduced when interest rates are close to zero.

Thus, there is a lot at stake, and the policy inferences of MMT therefore need to be considered seriously. The very least that can be said is that they do not compare unfavourably with calls for fiscal and monetary rectitude that are grounded either in narrow accounting logic or myopic adherence to the quantity theory of money. Judgements on the appropriateness of a policymaking framework cannot usefully be made without regard to the state of the business cycle or to the strength of private sector animal spirits.

As always, however, the devil is in the detail, and the cheerleaders for MMT are inclined to skate over many of the technical and political complexities of their prescriptions. For example, MMT – again like FF – is based implicitly on a closed-economy model. It makes no allowance for the possibility of monetary expansion causing the exchange rate to fall rapidly. MMT overlooks the potential for monetary expansion and an extended period of low interest rates to create the conditions for domestic financial instability. MMT's disciples pay little attention to the structural component of unemployment, which is unlikely to prove responsive to stimulus of demand. In the real world, full employment is a dynamic phenomenon, and the inflation process is continual: transition to a state of inflation at full employment is not the obvious and discrete process that MMT portrays. Advocates of MMT say little about the effects on wealth distribution of a reliance on monetary finance. They overlook the fact that interest is regularly paid on the new money that is created in the form of reserves held by the commercial banks at central banks. Hence, even entirely money-financed deficits cause public sectors to incur debt. MMT ignores moral hazard. The disruption of the connection between government decisions about the size of their budget deficits and the willingness of the private sector to fund those deficits at interest rates that it deems reasonable destroys at a stroke one of the most important disciplines the market imposes on politicians. And with that discipline swept away, the door is open to irresponsible fiscal policies and to a plethora of crackpot schemes.

Finally, it is an inescapable fact that debt accumulation cannot go on indefinitely, and it is also true that public sector debt ratios are already historically high. In the limit, total liabilities cannot exceed total wealth, and as the debt burden escalates inducing people to hold that debt will require ever-higher returns. Much depends on whether the average interest rate payable on debt is higher or lower than the economy's sustainable growth rate. If it is lower, then the level of government debt is of less consequence. But if it is persistently higher, debt will snowball. Hence, at some point, a government would be obliged to run a large enough primary budget surplus to stabilize debt growth. And this could involve dramatic tax increases or public expenditure cuts, which are politically unpalatable, and sometimes impossible, to deliver.

The overwhelming conclusion is the same one that Keynes came to in the 1940s: resorting to the policy prescriptions of MMT is appropriate only in the most exceptional situations, where economies are far from full employment, deflationary pressures are strong and interest rates are at the zero bound.

In the end, however, the UK authorities eschewed all the additional radical policy options mentioned above, including resort to direct monetary finance. This in part reflected the fact that the worst fears of the Bank of England and the government failed to materialize. However, direct monetary finance generated particular concerns, as it raised the spectre of a total loss of budgetary discipline, central bank insolvency, currency collapse, runaway inflation and perhaps even total economic breakdown.

YOU WOULD NOT WANT TO START FROM HERE

The damaged condition of macroeconomic theory and the inertia that surrounded it, the (real and imagined) constraints on various policy levers, and the inclinations of the time all meant that policymakers in the UK and elsewhere were ill-equipped to deliver a strong recovery in the aftermath of the GFC.

The government's macro strategy would have to evolve as reality bit and as various priors were shown to be misguided, although on the other hand, the sluggishness of the cyclical upswing would itself narrow the options available. At the same time, the strategy's evolution was also impacted by the rise of populism, a political creed that has resulted in considerable policy error over the centuries, as well as poor economic outcomes.

Populists typically view the world through what economists term a partial, rather than general, equilibrium framework. When they identify an unacceptable anomaly, their response is usually narrow and clumsy, confusing symptom with cause. They give little thought to broader ramifications. Furthermore, inasmuch as the consequences of their suggested interventions prove inconvenient or intolerable, those consequences are likely to be addressed with further heavy-handed initiatives. The net result once this process has cascaded through the economy is an outcome far more malign than the original issue.

A VERY DIFFERENT APPROACH

Just as Blair and Brown had, in 1997, distilled the conventional theoretical wisdom of the 1990s into an economic strategy for government, so too did David Cameron and, in particular, his chancellor George Osborne in 2010. Indeed, the pair had already developed a successful political narrative built around many of the issues outlined above while the GFC raged and while Brown and his government struggled to bring it under control. In particular, they sought to blame the country's cavernous budget deficit on the supposed profligacy of New Labour in advance of the crisis.

The general election campaign of 2010 was therefore framed in exactly the manner that Gordon Brown had spent twenty years trying to avoid: Labour's recklessness versus the Conservative's frugality and economic good sense. And, of course, the divisions between the more expansive Brown and the more cautious Darling in 2009 and 2010 did nothing to help New Labour's cause.

George Osborne would subsequently claim that Reinhart and Rogoff were the economists that had influenced him the most, and despite the detail of their conclusions on the impact of high public debt on growth being successfully challenged, he would refer to their work as he sought public support for his austere policies.

Overall, Osborne was happy to tread a similar path to that of the interwar Treasury. He applied a policy mix similar to that employed in Britain under the chancellorship of Neville Chamberlain during the initial recovery from the Great Depression: a combination of severe budgetary restraint, low short-term interest rates and a competitive exchange rate. The only element missing was trade protectionism.

What Osborne was less forthcoming about, however, was the fact that the UK's post-Great Depression upswing ran out of steam in 1937, and the economy slumped back into recession. It was only reanimated by a hefty dose of fiscal expansion. The UK began to rearm in earnest in 1936, and over the period up to the outbreak of World War II the country enjoyed budgetary stimulus of some seven percentage points of GDP as a result of its efforts to re-equip the armed forces! By the time war was declared in September 1939, the UK's economy was growing rapidly.[18]

CHAPTER 12

Flawed Recovery

By insisting on cuts in government spending and higher taxes that could easily have been postponed until the recovery from recession was assured, the government delayed the recovery by two years. And with the election drawing nearer, it allowed the pace of austerity to slow, while pretending that it hadn't.

— Simon Wren-Lewis, February 2015[1]

ANOTHER DUUMVIRATE

David Cameron had become leader of the Conservative Party in 2005, just four years after entering parliament. From a wealthy upper-middle-class background, he was educated at Eton and Oxford and then joined the Conservative Research Department in 1988. He subsequently worked in an advisory capacity for both Norman Lamont (including during the ERM crisis of 1992) and John Major, but in 1994 he moved into the private sector with the media company Carlton Communications. He became the Member of Parliament for Witney in 2001.

Engaging, energetic, confident, socially liberal but Thatcherite in his approach to economics, Cameron initially saw his job as being to modernize the party after its three election defeats at the hands of Tony Blair. In this he was strongly influenced by the approach taken by New Labour in the 1990s, including the remorselessness of its media strategy. Cameron was a great admirer of Blair. Indeed, Blair was Cameron's role model as a political leader.

Just as Tony Blair and Gordon Brown had formed a commanding duo at the head of New Labour, Cameron had his own political sidekick in the form of George Osborne. Similarly socially privileged, also educated at public school and then Oxford, and again formerly a party apparatchik, Osborne too was one of the Conservatives' new MPs after the 2001 general election. In return for running Cameron's successful party leadership challenge, Osborne was appointed shadow chancellor at the age of just 34, and over the following five years he developed into Gordon Brown's most relentless critic in parliament and beyond.

In 2010 Osborne became the youngest chancellor of the exchequer since Randolph Churchill in 1886. Like Brown between 1997 and 2007, Osborne was largely left alone to do his job. And also like Brown, he relied heavily on a favoured close advisor: in this case Dr Rupert Harrison. However, despite initial reservations relating to his previous association with Brown and Darling, Osborne also came to put great faith in Nicholas MacPherson, Permanent Secretary to the Treasury.

Osborne developed a reputation for being extraordinarily tribal and politically calculating. He was also to find himself criticized for his arrogance and insensitivity, and for the overt politicization of his department's work, not least during the Scottish independence and EU referendum campaigns.

Cameron and Osborne might not have dominated the Conservative administrations of 2010–16 to quite the same extent that Blair and Brown dominated the New Labour governments of 1997–2007, but they were very much its leading lights. Furthermore, unlike their New Labour counterparts they stayed closely aligned on most policies, and their personal relationship remained intact.

ECONOMIC OVERVIEW

Britain's GFC downturn was deeper and longer than those seen in most advanced economies, and the country's recovery was to prove weaker than had been seen after the two previous recessions and, indeed, in the wake of the 1930s Great Depression. The previously bloated financial sector's share in total output fell consistently in the post-crisis period, contracting by the equivalent of more than a percentage point of GDP in total.[2] The years 2011–13 proved particularly sluggish and disappointing. Even allowing for the fact that there was some loss of productive capacity in the wake of the crisis, the output gap, at some 3.5% of potential GDP in 2009, remained significant until the end of the parliament. The UK did, however, avoid the secondary dip in real activity suffered by much of Europe in the context of the euro area sovereign risk crisis, and towards the very end of Cameron's first five years in office the economy was growing above its diminished underlying trend rate.

The stock market recovery that had begun in April 2009 continued but, echoing the performance of the real economy, it was a shallow bull market, and there were a number of setbacks before the pre-GFC high was re-attained in April 2014. The protracted slide in long-term government bond yields that had begun in 1990 continued, with the ten-year rate establishing new all-time lows and threatening to breach 1.5% in January 2015. House prices recovered contemporaneously with the broader economy, as mortgage rates were dragged down by the Bank of England's unconventional policies. House price inflation peaked at a little above 10% in October 2014 before moderating over the rest of the parliament.

With the burden of household debt historically high and with balance sheet adjustment a priority, the personal savings rate initially spiked to more than 11% of disposable income. It subsequently proved reluctant to fall until the latter part of 2012. This further constrained consumers that were already being pressured by a sustained period of negative real income growth.

Investment was much slower to pick up than it had been in previous cyclical upswings. Real business investment had slumped by some 20% during the GFC and it recovered only in the most hesitant and uneven fashion. Its share in GDP remained low in both historical and relative terms.

In some important respects, the labour market performed better than expected. The 2011 peak in the unemployment rate was, at 8.5%, much lower than in the 1980s and 1990s, and by 2016 joblessness had dropped back below 5% of the workforce despite a significant fall in public sector employment. The persistent weakness of the exchange rate appears to have been an important mitigating factor. Sterling fell by more than 25% during the crisis and remained weak through 2013, after which it staged a recovery.

There was, however, a significant degree of underemployment, in the form of an increase in part-time working for many who wanted to work full time, the acceptance of jobs for which people were overqualified, and growth in precarious 'zero-hours contracts'. The total underemployment rate is estimated to have peaked at more than 10% of the workforce towards the end of 2011: around twice its level in the pre-crisis period.

The relative resilience of the labour market weighed heavily on productivity. Indeed, the tendency of output per hour to flatline for an extended period was unprecedented and was one of the most striking and disturbing features of the recovery. While all the major economies suffered a slowdown in productivity in the wake of the GFC, the UK's experience was particularly acute. Moreover, it was broad-based, and not just related to a decline in capital deepening. Growth in GDP per capita only surpassed its pre-crisis peak in 2015, leaving the UK behind the US, Japan, Germany and Canada, albeit slightly ahead of France and well ahead of Italy.

Headline CPI inflation initially significantly exceeded the Bank of England's 2% target, peaking above 5%, as currency and commodity price shocks interacted with the impact of changes in indirect taxation. However, despite the rapid recovery in employment, wage growth remained subdued and underlying CPI inflation was therefore better behaved, remaining below 4%.

The headline rate began to come down in 2011, and by 2015 it had become uncomfortably low, averaging close to zero.

With balance sheet reconstruction leaving bank credit and broad money growth extraordinarily weak, and with inflation expectations remaining well-anchored, the Bank chose to look through the initial jump in headline inflation. It kept its policy rate at the 0.5% level established in early 2009, and its asset purchase programme remained constant at the £200 billion level reached in February 2010. However, as the inflation risks reversed there was further resort to QE in October 2011, February 2012 and July 2012, although it remained overwhelmingly focused on gilt purchases. The Bank was enduringly squeamish about buying significant amounts of riskier assets.

The broadly defined budget deficit declined from its historic high of more than 10% of GDP in 2009 to just over 4% of GDP in 2015. However, it remained well in excess of the euro area average and, for that matter, considerably higher than the average for the OECD as whole, and the pace of improvement consistently fell short of official forecasts and targets. The ratio of net government debt to GDP therefore continued to escalate, only peaking in 2016, at 81.5% of GDP – some two-and-a-half times its level when the GFC hit. On the other hand, the low and falling level of borrowing costs brought net debt interest payments back down to just 2% of GDP – or just slightly above their pre-crisis level.

Despite the sharp fall in sterling's nominal effective value during the crisis and its immediate aftermath, the external balance remained in significant deficit throughout the parliament, with the red ink rising from just under 2% of GDP in 2011 to a record of more than 5% of GDP in 2015. For the most part this reflected a sharp deterioration in the income balance and unusually low returns on UK investments abroad. However, export market share also fell, continuing the pre-GFC trend, as unit labour costs rose at a relatively fast rate.

A GOVERNMENT IN A HURRY

It can be argued that the first Cameron government began as a radical administration – particularly when one considers that it was a coalition. Its initial policy agenda was certainly more ambitious than that of the 1997 Blair government. It extended beyond a pledge to eradicate the current budget deficit and see the net debt burden falling by the end of the parliament, to financial policy reform, to sweeping changes in the NHS and welfare provision, to what was to all intents and purposes a partial privatization of the university system via a trebling of university fees, to the introduction of a Fixed-Term Parliaments Act to ensure Cameron's government served a full five years, and to a commitment to hold referenda on electoral reform and all future EU treaties.

In the end, however, the results were mixed at best. Cameron and his chancellor were in too much of a hurry, and they were overconfident – even complacent – about the challenges they would face. They underestimated the complexities, trade-offs and externalities of government decision-making, and they came to be defined – and not in a positive way – by their resort to referenda, something altogether peculiar for the UK.

FISCAL FLAM

Following the unrelenting criticism aimed at the fiscal policy choices of Gordon Brown and Alistair Darling while the Conservative Party was in opposition, the centrepiece of the new government's economic strategy was an extended programme of uncompromising budgetary consolidation. The thinking seemed to be that, as long as this was satisfactorily delivered, everything else would fall into place: sustained growth, business dynamism and flexibility, and price stability.

When introducing his post-election emergency budget in June 2010, Osborne ignored the fact that Alistair Darling had already begun the job of putting the UK's public finances on a sounder footing. Instead, he peppered his speech with melodramatic language to the effect that, because of the extravagances of the previous government, Britain was on the verge of bankruptcy. The banking crisis had supposedly evolved into a fiscal sustainability crisis. Hence, if international confidence was to be maintained, and if Britain was to avoid the fate of Greece and other European fiscal delinquents, a forceful programme of austerity was inescapable.

The chancellor outlined front-loaded budget savings that went far beyond those promulgated by his predecessor. The initial programme of spending cuts was to total more than £6 billion, and over the parliament as a whole the government planned a total retrenchment of £113 billion, or more than 6.25% of GDP. Their measures would, supposedly, bring the headline budget deficit down to just 1% of GDP in 2015–16 and reduce the net debt burden to 67.5% of GDP. The plans included a two-year pay freeze for public sector employees, a three-year freeze on child benefits, sharp reductions in central government funding of local authorities (not least for social housing and transport infrastructure), and the paring back of all departmental budgets with the exception of health and overseas aid.

At the same time, VAT was not simply returned to its pre-crisis level but hiked in January 2011 from 17.5% to 20%: a tax rise that itself alone withdrew purchasing power equivalent to one percentage point of GDP. Capital gains tax and the post-crisis levy on banks were also increased.

On the other hand, a costly, poorly targeted and politically crass pension 'triple lock' was initiated,[3] personal income tax allowances were increased, and the corporate tax rate was to fall incrementally by a percentage point each year for the next four years. More than three-quarters of the planned austerity would therefore be derived from spending cuts, from which much of the Conservative Party's core support escaped lightly.

Notwithstanding some reservations about the precise composition of the strategy, Osborne enjoyed the endorsement of most of the Treasury in all this, including its Permanent Secretary, and was also supported by a Bank of England governor who, as already noted, had undiplomatically campaigned for more aggressive fiscal restraint since late 2009. This was despite the large degree of excess capacity in the economy, the historically low level of interest rates, and the absence of any evidence that the Debt Management Office was having difficulty funding the budget deficit.

The June 2010 budget was the first delivered in conjunction with the OBR. It had long been the case that the official budget forecasts were tweaked and massaged by senior government figures. Indeed, this appeared to have been particularly the case during Gordon Brown's time in Number 11 and when he was prime minister. As a result, international bodies such as the IMF had been recommending that governments set up independent fiscal watchdogs to undertake the forecasting process and to provide broader objective analysis of the public finances.[4]

The OBR was one of the first of what has become a profusion of such institutions. Its remit was to produce detailed five-year forecasts for the economy and for public finances twice a year, to evaluate performance against targets, to assess the long-term sustainability of the public finances, to explore fiscal risks, and to scrutinize tax and welfare policy costing. Initially under the temporary directorship of Alan Budd and then under Robert Chote, the former head of the Institute for Fiscal Studies, it represented an important improvement in the fiscal policy framework, and despite some unfortunate initial errors it has stood the test of time well.

In examining the record of fiscal policy over the following years, it is difficult not to conclude that, while market indicators of fiscal sustainability remained well behaved and the public finances were returned to a more even keel, it failed on its own terms. Furthermore, it left in its wake significant collateral damage.

Osborne's austerity drive failed on its own terms in the sense that the budget deficit and the debt burden consistently exceeded the forecast levels, largely because growth was weaker than expected and because the automatic stabilizers were allowed to do their job.[5] In permitting the latter, Osborne and the Treasury were more Keynesian than they liked to admit. But as a consequence, year after year, projections for when the government's formally stated goals of a return to a current budget balance and a decline in the burden of net debt were repeatedly pushed back. The expectation that rapid fiscal consolidation could be achieved without inflicting much damage on the real economy proved hopelessly optimistic.

The OBR originally suggested that the austerity drive would reduce real GDP by only 0.4% over the following two years. It predicted growth of 2.25% in 2011, 2.75% in 2012 and just under 3% in 2013. The actual figures turned out to be 1.5%, 1.5% and just under 2%. The OBR was forced into a humbling admission that it had significantly underestimated the size of the fiscal multiplier because it had based its assessment largely on pre-crisis data, when the economy was close to full capacity and interest rates were well above the zero bound. This was a ludicrous error.

It turned out that fiscal consolidation was not expansionary, or even relatively neutral, after all. Rather, it weighed heavily on growth, as standard Keynesian theory suggested it would. Encumbered as they were by debt, by the squeeze on real incomes and by the weakness of domestic demand in Europe (also encouraged by widespread fiscal restraint), rather than being set free, private sector animal spirits remained at a low ebb well into the upswing.

The overall impulse of fiscal policy was negative in every year but one from 2010–11 to 2015–16, and in the other (2012–13) it was neutral. It was also moderated in advance of the 2015 general election, allowing the economy belatedly to pick up some steam. The cumulative deflationary effect amounted to some four percentage points of GDP, bringing the cyclically adjusted deficit down to just under 4% of GDP. This exceeded the extent of discretionary fiscal retrenchment in the euro zone over the same period and was on a par with that delivered by the first Thatcher government between 1979 and 1982.

Current spending in real terms was essentially flat throughout the parliament, but outlays on both social security and education fell, particularly on a per capita basis. The NHS might have been singled out for more generous treatment, but the efforts to reform it descended into chaos that made the Blair governments' struggles in this regard look quite impressive in hindsight. The legacy of Cameron and Osborne's reforms was one of fragmentation, additional layers of bureaucracy and diminished transparency.

Public sector employment declined by around 400,000. The real value of unemployment benefits, which was already very low by OECD standards, was further curtailed. Real outlays on child benefit dropped by 10%, while other in-work payments were also cut back. A formal benefit cap, limiting the amount of state benefits that an individual household could claim per year, was introduced in April 2013.

Turning to capital spending, public sector net investment's share in GDP ran consistently below 2% of GDP and fell as low as 1.6% of GDP in 2013–14 and 2015–16, compared with a peak during the crisis of 3% of GDP. Public spending's overall share in GDP fell from some 46% in 2009–10 to 40.75% in 2015–16, while that of revenues increased by a mere half a percentage point, from 36% to 36.5%.

Besides significantly slowing the immediate pace of recovery, fiscal austerity inflicted more enduring damage on the economy, and thereby on its tax-raising potential. As output growth consistently fell short of potential, some of those who remained out of work or were underemployed saw their skills eroded and their attachment to the workforce become more tenuous. Meanwhile, the incentive for private investment in additional capacity and the pursuit of greater efficiencies was reduced. The weakness of public investment also weighed on growth potential, as indeed did an increasingly complex – and incoherent – tax system, not least where property and pensions were concerned.

Austerity had wider consequences for society. Public spending fell short of social needs, and long-held income and wealth aspirations continued to go unmet. Such considerations weighed especially heavily on those in the bottom half of the wealth distribution, who relied most on government transfers, tax breaks and subsidies and on public transport, education and healthcare.

Outwardly, the government's line on welfare was that, consistent with Conservative doctrine, its focus was on employment incentives and on supporting hard-working members of the labour force. With this in mind, it announced a progressive increase in the National Minimum Wage (NMW) from around 50% of median hourly earnings in 2010 for those over 25 to closer to 60% by 2020, leaving it one of the highest in the advanced economies. However, the NMW actually fell in real terms between 2010 and 2016. This was in marked contrast to the experience in the Blair years, when, although initially set at a low level, it rose by around a third in real terms. Overall, increases in the NMW would offset only around 20% of the drop in household incomes associated with benefit cuts.

The fact was that support for the UK Independence Party and political dissatisfaction in general correlated strongly with regional exposure to austerity.[6] Extended fiscal restraint in due course played a significant role in encouraging Brexit, and contributed to damaging developments in the nature of political discourse in the UK more broadly.

MONETARY INNOVATION

While in opposition, Osborne had been highly critical of the Bank of England's resort to QE, characterizing it as the last resort of a desperate government. In office, however, he changed his tune, becoming a staunch supporter of the Bank's unconventional efforts to address the fallout from the financial crisis and underpin economic activity. In so doing, he was acutely aware that, to the extent that fiscal retrenchment restrained recovery, monetary policy would have to fill the gap.

Despite the wayward behaviour of headline CPI inflation over the course of the first year or so of the parliament, the Bank of England opted to keep its policy rate and the size of its balance sheet unchanged, and the thrust of monetary policy remained unambiguously accommodative. The overwhelming consensus on the MPC was that the jump in inflation was largely the result of considerations beyond its control, and that with inflation expectations and wage growth remaining in check it would come to heel, as indeed it began to do during the second half of 2011.

With growth also falling short of expectations, the pace of disinflation was such that QE was resumed in October of that year and then further extended in February and July 2012. This became known as QE2, and it expanded the holdings of the Bank's APF to £375 billion: the equivalent of approaching 25% of GDP and more than a third of the outstanding debt stock. At the end of QE2, the Bank's balance sheet had never been larger on either basis. However, the muted market reactions to the announcements of gilt purchases meant that QE2 was less effective than the Bank's first round of purchases (or QE1). As detailed earlier, QE worked best when financial markets were dysfunctional. Thereafter it suffered diminishing returns.

The shallow nature of the recovery, together with the enduring post-crisis tightness of credit conditions and the weakness of bank lending and broad monetary growth, encouraged a further innovative policy departure in July 2012. The Bank was concerned that cutting Bank Rate to below 0.5% might damage the commercial banks' still-fragile profitability, but it nevertheless wanted to boost the effects of QE. It therefore joined forces with the Treasury to initiate a Funding for Lending Scheme (FLS). This was designed to lower funding costs and boost credit supply by providing loans to banks and building societies for an extended period at below-market rates, with the specific conditions linked to a financial institution's performance in providing credit to the real economy.[7] In the spring of 2013 the scheme was extended until January 2015, with the pricing structure modified to strengthen incentives for lending to SMEs. The latter accounted for more than 50% of private sector employment and had suffered particularly badly during the post-GFC credit crunch.

This extension of the FLS coincided with the announcement of a number of tweaks to the Bank's remit ahead of the installation of Mervyn King's replacement as governor. These provided formal endorsement of the flexible manner in which inflation targeting had been operated since 2010. Moreover, in an indication of things to come, the chancellor stated that the MPC could, in the manner of the US Federal Reserve and other major central banks, offer explicit guidance about the future path of interest rates. Finally, it was specified that the governor, while still required to write an explanatory open letter to the chancellor about one-percentage-point deviations from the 2% inflation target, could wait until the publication of the minutes of the MPC meeting before doing so, in order to offer a fuller explanation than in the past.

SMOOTH OPERATOR

Mervyn King reached the end of his second term as Bank of England governor in June 2013, after a twenty-two-year career in Threadneedle Street.[8] King had his critics. He could be haughty and inflexible. He also made some serious misjudgments: he put too much trust in the efficiency of markets, he neglected to establish a strong enough network of contacts within the City, he became too monocular in his focus on monetary analysis in pursuit of the inflation target, he failed to address the pre-GFC build-up of leverage, he was too fixated on moral hazard as the crisis erupted, and he made interventions in the arena of fiscal policy in 2009 and 2010 that were inappropriate and arguably misguided.

Nonetheless, King was a fine economist. He was also a canny – and sometimes highly entertaining – communicator, and as governor he came to command widespread respect around the world among the central banking elite. And in important ways he was both the architect of the UK's inflation-targeting regime and a key player in making the Bank's independence a success (for the most part). He also demonstrated considerable imagination during the depths of the GFC, as monetary policy became increasingly unconventional. He would be a difficult act to follow.

The initial list of candidates to replace King was a long one. It included a number of internal contenders, of which Paul Tucker, the deputy governor, was the favourite – until he was caught up in the so-called LIBOR scandal at least. It also included many revered UK economists, including Adair Turner, who had run the FSA during the depths of the crisis, and Jim O'Neill, Goldman Sachs's chief economist.[9] George Osborne was keen to cast a wide net, however, and the political peacock in him leant towards the appointment of a 'name' from the world of international economics and policymaking.

In the end he settled on Mark Carney, hitherto the governor of the Bank of Canada (BOC). An Anglophile, Carney was educated at Harvard and Oxford, where he received a PhD in economics. He spent thirteen years working for Goldman Sachs, albeit never as part of the firm's feted economics department, before moving into public service first at the Canadian Department of Finance and then at the central bank. He was not the economist his predecessor was, and he could on occasion be prickly, but he was more collegiate, he projected a highly polished and open public persona, and he proved to be a capable administrator and a positive force for change where the Bank's culture and diversity were concerned.

In 2007 Carney was the youngest central bank governor in the G-20, and he had had a good crisis. He was widely praised for overseeing a strategy of aggressive monetary policy relaxation, which in April 2009 extended to forward interest rate guidance, even if the BOC stopped short of the QE employed in the US and the UK. Canada, with a relatively small and more tightly regulated financial sector, avoided the worst ravages of the GFC, and it was the first advanced economy to see both its GDP and its employment recover to pre-crisis levels. In November 2011 Carney had also been named the part-time chairman of the Basel-based Financial Stability Board, which had been set up to monitor and make recommendations about the global financial system. He was the first non-Briton to be appointed Bank of England governor since the institution was established in 1694.

Conscious of both the UK economy's lacklustre recovery and the role that tight fiscal policy had played in it over the previous three years, Carney was keen to achieve a faster 'escape velocity' from the crisis. To this end, soon after his appointment he piloted through the MPC a variation on the BOC's strategy of forward guidance. In August 2013, with some fanfare and a considerable amount of explanatory material, he announced that so long as (i) inflation remained no more than half a percentage point above target, (ii) inflation expectations were well-anchored and (iii) there was no threat to financial stability, the Bank intended to hold its policy rate and QE settings in place until the unemployment rate had fallen below 7% of the workforce.[10] The jobless rate was 7.6% at the time, or just under a percentage point down from its post-GFC peak.

Forward guidance was grounded in finance theory, and the notion that longer-term interest rates are determined by the expected path of short-rates plus a term premium influenced by a range of considerations, including uncertainty, risk aversion, market liquidity and preferred investor habitats.[11] The idea behind such 'state-contingent' guidance was to provide greater clarity about the Bank's reaction function, to reduce ambiguity about the monetary policy outlook, and to thereby encourage the entire gilt market yield curve – and related borrowing costs – to shift lower.

The decision to go down this road certainly made Carney a hostage to fortune, and it was greeted with a degree of scepticism both within the Bank and beyond. Some argued that to maximize the effect, the Bank should have backed up its words with more asset purchases, i.e. it should have put its money where its mouth was. Others doubted that complex macroeconomic circumstances could, or should, be collapsed into a small number of metrics, and they feared that in the context of the Bank's other conduits of communication, such as its regular Inflation Reports, it might encourage information overload rather than greater clarity about future policy. There was also the question of whether the specified triggers would be 'hard', and therefore lead to rapid policy adjustment, or 'soft', and therefore merely encourage policy review.

As it turned out, there was substance in the criticism. The original form of the policy was rapidly overtaken by events that did not exactly gel with the Bank's view of the future in August 2013. Bond yields edged up rather than falling. The unemployment rate dropped far more quickly than the MPC had expected, dipping below the specified 7% threshold as early as January 2014. And yet, simultaneously, the inflation rate fell back below target, and it looked set to remain there for some time. Indeed, the governor was to write a succession of explanatory letters to the chancellor about the significant undershooting of the inflation target over the next three years.

Carney and his colleagues therefore had little choice but to reframe the policy. In February 2014 the unemployment threshold was set aside and the Bank embraced much less specific guidance. It would seek to use policy to absorb the economy's spare capacity, of which much remained; and when the MPC started to raise Bank Rate, it expected to do so gradually, with the endpoint well short of the pre-crisis average.[12]

Overall, however, together with the belated impact of the FLS, forward guidance (or at least the notion that policy would remain accommodative until recovery was better established) seems to have played at least some role in encouraging a pick-up in the pace of growth around this time. Private sector uncertainty declined, business confidence improved and corporate spending and hiring decisions were accelerated in late 2013 and early 2014, although it should not be forgotten that the euro area, by far Britain's largest trading partner, also began to emerge from its second dip in the middle of 2013.

REWIRING THE FINANCIAL SECTOR

The Cameron government sought to overhaul the architecture of UK financial regulation in the wake of the failure to rein in indebtedness and other excesses in the runup to the GFC and of its shortcomings during the run on Northern Rock. This also allowed it to sustain the narrative of blaming the Blair and Brown governments for the crisis.

Within a month or so of coming to power, acting on the advice of Sir James Sassoon (a former investment banker and Treasury representative in the City under Labour), George Osborne outlined his determination to end the tripartite system of financial oversight and wind up the FSA.[13] Despite the Bank of England's missteps in the noughties, and particularly in August 2007, the quest for greater financial resilience was to be built around a re-expansion of its remit.

This would extend to the creation of a new BOE Financial Policy Com-mittee (FPC), which was tasked with providing high-level macroprudential oversight, producing a biannual Financial Stability Report, working alongside the existing MPC (there would be some overlapping membership of the two committees), promoting effective coordination across all the relevant public sector institutions, and making specific policy recommendations, including for countercyclical capital buffers.

At the same time, a Prudential Regulatory Authority (PRA), which would also be a subsidiary of the Bank, would offer micro-oversight of the individual banks, building societies, insurers and large brokers. The remainder of the FSA's old responsibilities would be taken on by another new entity, the Finan-cial Conduct Authority (FCA), which would police how financial companies interacted with customers, counterparties and competitors in various markets. The new regime formally came into force in April 2013, although the FPC operated informally from June 2011.

The regulatory reform agenda also focused on ensuring that financial insti-tutions could fail without threatening financial stability or exposing taxpayers to losses. The Special Resolution Regime hastily cobbled together by Labour in 2009 was overhauled in a series of steps, including through the December 2013 EU Bank Recovery and Resolution Directive, which was transposed into UK law.

These changes in the structure of financial regulation were broadly aligned with the global regulatory reform agenda, in which the UK played a leading role.

This period saw a steady, if unspectacular, improvement in the health of the banks. Stress tests were conducted and passed. Liquidity positions improved, with the major banks reducing their reliance on wholesale funding while also increas-ing deposits. Capital positions gradually strengthened, supported by improved asset quality. The ratio of non-performing loans had fallen to around 1.5% by the end of 2015: around a third of its post-crisis peak. At the same time, domestic lending increased at the expense of foreign lending, and credit exposure to other financial entities was reduced. Aggregate advances to the corporate sector were slow to pick up, however, and the annual growth rate did not turn positive until the end of 2015. The ratio of outstanding household and corporate credit to GDP continued to correct lower from its previously elevated level.

Profitability also recovered only slowly, weighed down as it was by lower trading and net interest income and by high legacy misconduct costs. It remained low relative to historical levels. The return on the assets of UK banks in 2015 was approximately half what it had been before the crisis, and bank stocks typically traded at about half their previous multiples. Returning RBS (in which the government retained nearly a 75% share) to profitability proved particularly tough going.

The one major challenge to the new financial stability regime came from the housing market. Housing supply remained inelastic in the face of a lack of available land to build on, tight planning laws, a long-standing and chronic shortfall of social housing construction,[14] and low levels of security in the rental market. Demand, meanwhile, was stoked by historically low mortgage rates and by the government's 2013 Help to Buy scheme, which provided cheap loans and guarantees to first-time purchasers. Annual house price inflation accelerated steadily from early 2012, with the national figure reaching low double digits by Q2 2014. This led to tougher mortgage lending requirements and an FPC-mandated restriction that no more than 15% of a lender's new mortgages should be at or above a loan-to-income ratio of 4.5. Though the latter was not binding for most lenders, it appears to have had a signalling effect that prompted them to reduce high loan-to-income mortgages. Between mid 2014 and mid 2015 house price growth decelerated somewhat, and the percentage of new mortgages with high loan-to-value or high loan-to-income ratios declined.

Overall, despite the sovereign risk crisis in the euro area and the unambiguously accommodative tenor of monetary policy, financial instability was not a principal concern in the immediate wake of the crisis. The new regime functioned relatively smoothly, although this was unsurprising given the extent of the balance sheet shrinkage that was taking place and the sluggishness of economic growth. That said, the much less regulated shadow banking sector – of hedge funds, private equity firms, crowd-funders, SPVs and so on – remained a source of concern.

SAVING THE UNION

The issue of independence for Scotland had not been a burning issue during the Blair years. The Labour Party, both historically and in its New Labour guise, had dominated Scottish politics throughout the latter decades of the twentieth century and in the early years of the twenty-first, and while in government at Westminster it had succeeded in keeping the more zealous forms of nationalism at bay through the progressive devolution of power, culminating in the establishment of a Scottish Parliament in 1999. In the background, meanwhile, the so-called Barnett formula – named after Denis Healey's number two at the Treasury, Joel Barnett, and introduced merely as an interim fix ahead of the 1979 general election – had resulted in a good deal of stability in the way in which public funds were allocated to Scotland. Indeed, Scotland enjoyed consistently higher per-capita public spending than England.

Labour's hold on power in Scotland slackened dramatically, however, during the GFC and its aftermath, and it was the Scottish National Party (SNP) that benefitted most. The SNP won an overall majority in the Scottish Parliament in 2011, and immediately pushed for the referendum on independence that had been a central element of its election manifesto. Early the next year, Cameron – whose party remained something of a pariah across much of Scotland despite Labour's collapse – bowed to SNP pressure and, in October 2012, made the decision to allow a September 2014 vote on Scotland's continued membership of the Union. The Electoral Commission subsequently determined that the most appropriate way the matter should be put to the Scottish electorate was with the question: 'Should Scotland be an independent country?'

The independence debate ranged widely, touching on issues as diverse as agricultural subsidies, the complexion of future citizenship, the role of the monarchy and the location of Britain's independent nuclear deterrent in Scottish waters. However, it was four economic issues that came to dominate matters: Scotland's future trading relationship with England; the impact of independence on Scotland's financial sector, and particularly on the large banks that had a substantial footprint across the UK; the viability of Scotland's fiscal position; and what currency Scotland might use were it to set out on its own.

Despite the Tory party's paltry parliamentary representation north of the border, Cameron and Osborne were determined that Scotland remain part of the 300-year-old Union. Their party's full name was, after all, the Conservative and *Unionist* Party. Osborne therefore decided to deploy the Treasury's considerable intellectual firepower to this end. In this he enjoyed the support of his Permanent Secretary, Nick MacPherson, himself a Scot and a passionate Unionist.

Supported by David Ramsden, who had been the official responsible for the assessment of the 'five tests' for entry to the euro back in the early 2000s, MacPherson oversaw a mass of analysis putting the economic case for the political status quo. In all, fifteen papers, running to some 1,400 pages, were produced over the two years leading up to the referendum, with eight different government departments contributing.

The primary concern in Whitehall when it came to trade was that Scotland and England were deeply interwoven, codependent economies. Any barriers to commerce between the two would therefore involve enormous inconvenience and very significant cost. The situation was further complicated by the fact that if Scotland left the UK, it would also have to leave the EU, and it was unclear how easy it would prove to rejoin. Doing so would require unanimous agreement among member states, and Spain was likely to prove a particular stumbling block given its own issues with Catalonian and Basque self-determination.

Where financial services were concerned, the Treasury view was similarly disobliging. The Scottish financial sector was important, accounting for some 7% of Scottish GDP and 8% of Scottish employment. However, the majority of the customers of its banks, insurance companies and asset managers were dispersed around the rest of the UK and beyond, and they had long been regulated by the Bank of England and by other bodies based in London. Scotland would need to establish a new financial regulatory architecture, and building trust in the associated institutions would take time.

More importantly, the GFC had demonstrated the importance to financial stability of a credible central bank with a sound balance sheet, and of a national Treasury with deep pockets, especially when large international commercial banks had to be rescued. The vast sums dispensed by the Bank of England and the Treasury in 2008 and 2009 to sustain RBS and HBOS, Scotland's two largest commercial banks, would have been far beyond a Scottish central bank or finance ministry. RBS and HBOS remained enormous relative to the Scottish economy in 2014, and it is noteworthy that their management, together with those of Lloyds (which was owned by HBOS by then), the Clydesdale Bank, TSB and Tesco Bank, all indicated that they would seek to redomicile in London in the event of a 'Yes' vote. This would have done enormous damage not just to Scottish employment but to the viability of Scottish independence full stop.

The issue of the fiscal arrangements of an independent Scotland proved to be another area of controversy. The SNP and its supporters had for decades argued that the country was entitled to a greater share of North Sea oil revenues than one determined by its share of UK GDP or by its population. In 2013 the Scottish Fiscal Commission also argued that by replicating the Norwegian oil fund overseen by its central bank, the nation's long-term fiscal position could be enhanced.[15]

The Treasury, in contrast, made great play of the fact that, on the basis of the contemporary oil price, a newly independent Scotland would be running a budget deficit of some 6.5% of GDP by 2016–17: around three times the projected level for the UK as a whole and, in all likelihood, the most substantial budgetary shortfall among the advanced economies. It stressed, furthermore, that Scotland's population was ageing more rapidly, and was unhealthier, than that of the rest of the country. This meant that prospective government outlays on pensions, health and social care were likely to exert enduring upward pressure on the nation's budget deficit and debt burden.

It was the issue of an independent Scotland's currency, however, that became the most contentious of the four major economic issues, and the most uncomfortable one for the SNP. The party had for some time been in favour of EMU, and had the UK been a member, an independent Scotland would have been able to retain the euro as its currency on exiting the UK. It would still have had to establish a monetary authority as part of the European system of central banks, but the ECB would have determined monetary policy in Scotland and also overseen its banking sector, thus addressing many of the regulatory issues outlined above. However, the Blair government's decision not to join the euro in 2003 meant that Scotland had to come up with different currency arrangements.

The Fiscal Commission sketched out four options: the continued use of the pound; the creation of a new Scottish currency linked to sterling; the creation of a new Scottish currency that was allowed to float freely; and, despite the 2003 decision, membership of the euro.[16] The SNP government came down in favour of the retention of sterling, while admitting the need for shared arrangements to ensure financial stability, and supported the creation of a Scottish Monetary Institute to work closely with the Bank of England.[17]

The problems with such an approach were twofold.

First, history suggested that a durable currency union would require the continued ceding of important spending and taxation decisions to Westminster, which was hardly what the SNP had in mind from Scottish independence. Indeed, the euro area sovereign risk crisis had amply demonstrated the pitfalls of running a currency union without a single credible fiscal backstop.

Second, it was unclear why the complex proposals set out by the SNP would find favour after independence in the rest of what had been the United Kingdom. Indeed, the reaction outside Scotland was overwhelmingly unenthusiastic. This judgement extended to both Mark Carney and George Osborne. In February 2014 the latter asserted that:

> The value of the pound lies in the entire monetary system underpinning it … It is a system that is supported by political union, banking union and automatic transfers of public spending across the United Kingdom. A vote to leave the UK is a vote to leave … those monetary arrangements … There's no reason why the rest of the UK would need to share its currency with Scotland … If Scotland walks away from the UK, it walks away from the … pound.[18]

What is more, the chancellor made the extraordinary decision to publish the advice that he had received to this effect from Nick MacPherson.[19]

This amounted to blatant politicization of the Treasury, and it ruffled a lot of feathers both in Whitehall and beyond. For its part, the SNP – which, it should be stressed, was not afraid to resort to intimidation and the dark arts itself – denounced it as a bluff and an example of 'scaremongering', or 'Operation Fear'. Yet both the chancellor and his senior civil servant were unrepentant, with MacPherson subsequently saying:

> I published that advice because I saw it as my duty. The British state's position was being impugned. Demonstrating that the political and official state were completely aligned would further strengthen the credibility of the government's position.[20]

He remained convinced that, had Scotland voted to leave the UK, a currency union would not have been forthcoming.

The challenging economics of Scottish independence, and in particular the issue of the currency, played an important role in the ultimate outcome of the referendum: a vote for Scotland to remain in the UK by a margin of 55.3% to 44.7%. Furthermore, the extraordinary efforts of the chancellor, the Treasury and the Bank of England to convince the Scottish electorate that the economic risks of going it alone were not ultimately worth the candle persuaded many swing voters to stick with the status quo.

It should not be forgotten, however, that in the last few weeks of the campaign, and with polls indicating a close outcome, Gordon Brown emerged from the shadows to reanimate the 'Better Together' campaign. In contrast to much of what had gone before, and certainly contrary to the stance taken by Osborne, the former prime minister put a positive and patriotic case for Scotland remaining in the UK, structured around a new devolution settlement that he suggested could deliver more rapid, more equitable and more sustainable change than outright independence.[21] This resonated with many voters, and it helped the government get over the line. Indeed, it is quite possible that Brown's constructive intervention – in stark contrast to Osborne's unrelenting scorn for the Scottish independence project – saved the day for the Cameron government and for the Union.

Whatever the ultimate underlying balance of reasons for the 'No' vote that prevailed in September 2014, in one important sense a rubicon had been crossed. The chancellor had achieved his desired outcome after both his highest-ranking Treasury official and the governor of the Bank of England had been permitted, indeed encouraged, to enter the political spotlight. This left him with few qualms about employing a similar strategy in the EU referendum that was to occur two years later.

In the meantime, however, and despite the referendum outcome, the SNP continued to dominate Scottish politics, and the Conservatives remained a minor party north of the border. Calls for Scottish independence refused to go away.

PRODUCTIVITY PUZZLE[22]

Whlie UK labour productivity growth had always been volatile from period to period, it had averaged a little above 2% a year over the very long term and, as we have seen, this was roughly the rate of improvement observed in the run-up to the GFC. During the downturn and its immediate aftermath, however, labour productivity growth averaged a mere 0.25% a year. In the period covered by the Cameron government, the figure was marginally better, at around 0.5% a year, but productivity gains nevertheless made only the most modest contribution to output growth after 2007. The expansion of the economy, such as it was, was overwhelmingly driven by higher employment and by an increase in the number of hours worked per employee. Output per hour at the end of 2015 was more than 15% lower than if it had continued to expand at its pre-crisis trend rate. Such a slowdown in productivity, which in many ways approximated to the sum total of aggregate frustration among the population, was unprecedented over the previous 250-odd years.

Stagnant productivity held back real wages, real GDP per head and the growth rate of productive potential. It acted as the economy's speed limit. The OECD estimated that the growth rate of productive potential averaged around 1.5% a year during the Cameron years: well below the pre-crisis and advanced-economy averages. The absolute level of UK labour productivity remained similar to the OECD average, but in 2015 it was 20–25% lower than in the US, Germany and France. Only Italy had a worse record among the G-7 economies.

The productivity slowdown affected almost every sector, not just those, such as financial services, that had suffered a significant supply shock during the GFC. The UK had a 'long tail' of low-productivity firms in every sector and every region that had failed to keep up with those operating close to the technological frontier. There were large and persistent geographical disparities, with London and the South East performing significantly better than other areas, especially relative to those with a bias towards low-tech manufacturing. These disparities in turn reflected large and persistent differences in skill levels, qualification levels, infrastructure networks and the intensity of innovative activity. Productivity tended to hold up best among exporting firms, foreign-owned firms (particularly US-owned companies) and bigger enterprises.

One possible partial explanation for Britain's seemingly dreadful absolute and relative performance is measurement issues, which are always more evident in service-dominated economies. Service sector productivity is notoriously harder to measure accurately than manufacturing productivity, and it should be noted that the Office for National Statistics bases its estimates of UK output per hour worked pretty much solely on questionnaires asking how much people work. Other nations adjust the raw data to take account of a tendency for people to underestimate how much holiday they take, and this massaging of the figures can reduce the final estimate of hours worked by as much as 20%. Applying similar tweaks to the UK data could increase measured productivity level by 10%, which would reduce the productivity shortfall with France by half and that with the US by a third. But, of course, such modifications would still leave the post-GFC *growth rate* minimal by historical standards.

Beyond the undeniable potential for statistical error, there are numerous overlapping and interrelated reasons for the UK's productivity malaise. No one explanation is sufficient, and the impact of some of those listed below continues to attract controversy among economists.

To come to terms with them it is useful to remember that labour productivity growth is determined by two considerations. First, there is the ratio of capital employed to the total number of hours worked, commonly referred to as 'capital deepening'. And second, there is total factor productivity (TFP), or the overall efficiency with which inputs are converted into output. Both of these factors appear to have played a role in the UK's predicament, but slower TFP seems to have been the dominant consideration, at least beyond the early stages of the productivity shortfall.

Many firms appear to have held on to labour, and especially skilled labour, during the crisis and in its immediate aftermath, thereby slowing capital deepening. The big shake-outs of manufacturing workers and the large spikes in productivity that were associated with the recessions of 1979–80 and 1990–91 were not seen this time around.

A reduction in the relative cost of labour in the context of the slack labour market led firms to substitute labour for capital, which further slowed capital deepening. And when labour was reallocated from areas like financial services and the oil industry, some of it found itself in less productive areas, thereby reducing TFP.

The difficulties experienced by the financial sector during the GFC raised the cost of capital and led to credit rationing, especially for new and smaller firms, which in addition saw the value of their loan collateral decline. This impaired the process of capital reallocation from less productive sectors to more productive ones, and it slowed TFP. Larger, higher-productivity firms may also have been affected by financial constraints, as they tended to be highly leveraged.

Changes in the composition of the labour force, including a rise in the participation rate of older and part-time workers, resulted in lower skill levels, which also reduced TFP.

The historically low level of borrowing costs, together with bank forbearance in the context of a high and rising proportion of non-performing loans, slowed the pace of creative destruction. Firms that would have failed in other circumstances stayed in business. Such entities were particularly common in low-tech manufacturing. This trapped capital and labour in inefficient parts of the economy, again slowing TFP.

As we have already noted, the crisis and post-crisis periods were notable for a slump in business investment and for a relatively shallow recovery thereafter. Resource utilization rates picked up only sluggishly, and in the interim companies were weighed down by uncertainty and risk aversion, some deciding to buy back their own stock rather than spend on new plant and equipment. There were particular shortfalls in transport equipment, machinery and ICT disbursements. Spending on research and development, which leads to innovation and the adoption and diffusion of new technologies, was relatively low in both the private and public sectors. Total R&D expenditure amounted to just 1.6% of GDP in 2015, against an OECD average of almost 2.5%. Of that total, the government financed 1.2 percentage points, as against an average of 1.6 percentage points in the advanced economies as a whole. Innovation and the quality of human capital were reduced. Furthermore, the investment shortfall was exacerbated by the impact of fiscal austerity on public sector infrastructure spending.

Both capital deepening and TFP suffered as a result of the weakness of investment, and it probably represented the single most important factor constraining productivity.

The slower rates of diffusion of innovation from the frontier to laggard firms and the headwinds to TFP also appear to have reflected stifled competition and greater industrial concentration. The regulation of patents and intellectual property may have played a role in this, as indeed might the growing importance of economies of scale in encouraging natural monopolies in technology-rich activities.

Finally, there is evidence of widespread management failings, especially among smaller, family-owned firms. In contrast, larger exporting and foreign-owned firms were more integrated into global supply chains and more exposed to the disciplines of global competition.

The impact of many of these productivity constraints seems to have faded over time. The banks' health gradually improved, and credit conditions eased. Labour hoarding diminished. The closer the economy came to full employment, the more efficiently labour was utilized and the greater were both the incentive to expand capacity and the demand for labour-saving technology. Business investment began to pick up more conspicuously from 2012 onwards, and a shallow and uneven upward trend in labour productivity growth followed. However, as we shall see in the next chapter, Brexit then intervened to nip this recovery in the bud.

STRUCTURAL FAULTS

The productivity slowdown pointed to shortcomings in UK supply-side policy. Indeed, it could be argued that the UK needed a second wave of structural reforms in the wake of the GFC, akin to those of the 1980s, and that the policies needed to focus on improving the performance of the long tail of underperforming firms largely situated beyond London and the South East in particular.

Besides evidence that parts of the competition regime would benefit from a revamp to stem the development of tech-related oligopolies and monopolies, the overriding priorities revealed by the post-crisis years were the need to encourage more high-quality investment and to improve the allocation of human capital.

Turning first to investment, it was clear that more public infrastructure was required, and that it also needed to be more equitably distributed. In the mid-to-late 2010s, the public sector capital stock accounted for around 45% of GDP, as against an average of around 60% in the advanced economies. According to the IMF, only when it came to ports did the UK rate higher than the OECD median. Its roads, railways and airports were all worse, with bottlenecks commonplace.[23]

The tax regime for R&D spending in the UK was broadly competitive, but there appeared to be a case for more direct government funding, especially in the least productive areas of the country, and also to encourage greater collaboration between businesses and universities. Higher education spending on R&D financed by industry was about 4% of the total, as against an OECD average of 6%.

Finally, at all levels, the fact that Britain had one of the most centralized systems of government in the OECD seemed to have become an important constraint on regional investment efficiency. Greater decentralization would facilitate policies that were better suited to local objectives.

As far as human capital was concerned, education in general was short of resources. Public spending on education fell both in real terms and as a percentage of GDP after 2010. Average levels of numeracy and literacy in the UK fell some way below the OECD average. Around a third of all spending on education (equivalent to around 2% of GDP) in the UK comes in the private sector, which is unlikely to contribute much at all to the low-skilled.

At the same time, more resources needed to be ploughed into active labour market policies (ALMPs), and especially into the training and retraining of the low-skilled and of non-specialized workers, who accounted for around a quarter of the UK workforce. UK government spending on ALMPs remained minimal – far below the OECD average and a mere fraction of the 1.5%-plus of GDP allocated to these so-called activation policies in the Nordic countries of Denmark, Sweden and Finland.

Another area in which it was clear that the UK could do better was labour mobility. There was a high implicit tax rate for second earners returning to work and childcare costs were high. Labour mobility was further constrained by the high cost of housing, which, as we have seen, was exacerbated by a lack of social housing supply, overbearing planning and construction regulations, and an emphasis on transactions rather than values in property taxation.

So, was broader tax reform warranted to enhance supply-side performance? Perhaps the first point to make in this context is that the impact of national tax burdens on productivity is ambiguous. Some highly taxed nations, such as Sweden and France, have enjoyed much better productivity records than the UK, and in any case the UK tax burden has never been particularly high relative to that of the other advanced economies, and was certainly not in the 2010–15 period.

That said, it does make sense to keep the tax system broadly internationally competitive, and there were areas in which the UK tax regime was distortionary and wasteful. These extended to property and pensions; preferential VAT rates; and other exemptions, deductions and credits. There was also a bias towards debt in the tax code as well as unequal treatment between employees, the self-employed and corporations. Additionally, inheritance tax, as configured, was a relatively inefficient means to tax wealth. Overall, however, substantial changes to the structure of the UK tax regime, while warranted for the sake of fairness and revenue-raising efficiency, were probably of largely secondary importance from the point of view of productivity.

The government recognized many of these supply-side shortcomings – at least in part. They appeared in numerous budget documents, and in July 2015, for example, the government published a report that detailed the nature of the country's productivity problem and its implications, and it sketched out, in broad terms, what might be done to address it.[24] As we shall see, however, the follow-through was insufficient. There remained a failure to adapt structural policy sufficiently broadly and with sufficient urgency bearing in mind the extent of the problem. And these inadequacies were about to be brought into much sharper relief by Brexit.

The Cameron administrations also rather soft-pedalled on climate change policy. It had become something of an afterthought during the GFC, unsurprisingly, although in November 2008, just as the market turmoil was at its height, the Brown administration did manage to pass a bill that committed the UK both to an 80% reduction in greenhouse gasses by 2050 and to a series of rolling five-year carbon budgets. Cameron himself paid a degree of lip service to the issue, but there was rarely any sense that he was strongly committed to it or, for that matter, that he was taking much of the Conservative Party with him. His substantive inertia was to prove a source of consistent frustration to his Liberal Democrat coalition partners.

Osborne, meanwhile, with his focus on fiscal austerity, was determined that such initiatives as were forthcoming in this area were implemented as inexpensively as possible. He did not want to add significantly to the tax burden or threaten the sustained supply of relatively cheap energy. Nor was he persuaded by arguments that investment in decarbonization could boost growth, in particular by addressing market failures and by promoting knowledge spillovers from new innovations – that is to say, it was argued that decarbonization might 'crowd in' investment rather than 'crowd it out'.[25]

All this meant that while the 2050 target remained in place, funding related to climate change was cut back and various related public bodies were downsized or wound up. Under Cameron and Osborne, the UK would not be setting the global climate change policy agenda. That said, it should be mentioned that the UK government did contribute constructively to COP21 in Paris at the end of 2015, a gathering which led to important progress on global emission reductions. Moreover, Mark Carney, especially towards the end of his term as Bank of England governor, was to become an important cheerleader for the stronger disclosure of climate risks by banks and insurance companies, and a keen supporter of the greening of the financial system in general. Indeed, this became something of a personal crusade for him.

A STILL UNLEVEL PLAYING FIELD

Income inequality among the total UK population remained well above the average for the advanced economies in the wake of the crisis – indeed, it was only exceeded in the US and South Korea. However, the most commonly used measures of overall income inequality, such as the Gini coefficient and the 90/10 ratio, remained relatively stable between 2010 and 2015: there was no significant increase, and neither was there any major change in either relative or absolute poverty rates, whether or not the metrics included housing costs.

But these aggregate metrics tell only part of the story. There remained huge regional income inequalities, for example, with London and the South East driving the recovery and many of the older industrial regions lagging far behind.

At the same time, there was increasing evidence of widening income and wealth differentials between generations. Millennials (those born in the 1980s and the first half of the 1990s) were the first post-war generation to have lower incomes during early adulthood than the cohort before them. Younger people, reflecting their relative decline in homeownership, were accumulating significantly less wealth than did previous generations.

Inequalities between generations can bleed into the following generation too. Elderly households were much wealthier than were their counterparts a decade or two earlier, and they were more likely to leave a large inheritance to their offspring. With the young relatively slow to accumulate wealth and with older generations wealthier than before, inheritances became increasingly important to the living standards of the young. Those with wealthy parents could expect a substantial increment to their lifetime wealth. Those without would find life more challenging.

The influence of these various forms of inequality on perceptions and attitudes was deepened by sluggish growth in disposable incomes, which in turn was exacerbated by fiscal austerity. Real incomes generally fell in the post-crisis period, with some sectors experiencing particularly dramatic declines. Labour's overall share in GDP dropped from 58% to 53% and, as already noted, this was a period of widespread underemployment and job insecurity.

Hopes and ambitions were unrealized; savings buffers were lower; vulnerabilities to income and employment shocks were greater. At the same time, life expectancy stagnated; stress, depression, obesity and drug and alcohol abuse became more pervasive; suicide was more common, and the death rate among low-income, middle-aged men increased. This must all have been a further contributing factor to lower productivity.

In reviewing all these trends, some went as far as to conclude that the five social evils identified by Sir William Beveridge almost eighty years earlier in his eponymously named report on social insurance – want, disease, ignorance, squalor and idleness – continued to stalk the land, even if their precise make-up had changed.[26]

Whether or not that was an entirely accurate depiction of the status quo in the UK, the post-crisis environment accentuated existing grievances and bred a sense of unfairness – unfairness that extended from education and training opportunities, to access to health and social care, to confinement to substandard housing. And, of course, such resentments were easy to amplify in the age of increasing social media use.

JUST WHOSE SIDE WAS THE BANK ON?

The sense of injustice extended to the activities of the Bank of England, with many commentators suggesting that the MPC's unorthodox initiatives had overwhelmingly favoured the wealthy. Some went further, suggesting that the

Bank's extraordinary interventions had taken it beyond its mandate, occupying ground normally reserved for fiscal policy and parliament.

Although essentially neutral in regard to the economy and to resource distribution over the long term, monetary policy can exert an important influence on both in the short term. Indeed, its role in macroeconomic stabilization depends on distributional effects. Movements in interest rates redistribute cash flows between savers and borrowers, and they can also influence aggregate savings and investment behaviour. Similarly, LSAPs will have rather different effects on the asset rich and the asset poor, or the heavily indebted, as well as influencing the evolution of the macro savings and investment balance.

Monetary policy must, however, be judged by its ultimate ability to stabilize the economy, and thereby its overall contribution to the welfare and prosperity of the population. Within reason, even if the economic gains from monetary interventions are unevenly spread, and some lose out, it would be nonsensical to eschew them. Rather, any such side effects should be tempered by fiscal and structural policy initiatives aimed at those who are the major casualties. Moreover, the more forceful and well targeted that any initiatives aimed at macro-stabilization and job creation are, the lighter will be the burden placed on monetary policy, with all its distributive wrinkles.

So much for the theory. Researching the distributive detail of monetary policy – and especially of unorthodox monetary policy – is difficult. There are many channels and contradictory forces to consider, some of which – such as perceptions of job security and financial anxiety – do not lend themselves well to quantification. Nevertheless, much work has been done in this area, and the Bank of England itself undertook some of the most detailed study.

Drawing on the comprehensive body of prior analysis embedded in its macro model of the UK economy, and taking in data on the UK household sector's assets and liabilities, the Bank dissected the consequences of the sharp relaxation of monetary policy between February 2008 and mid 2012. This was the period during which Bank Rate was slashed from 5.5% to 0.5% and asset purchases cumulating to £375 billion were made.[27] The results can be summarized as follows.

Absent its unorthodoxy, the Bank calculated that real GDP would have been 8% lower, the jobless rate four percentage points higher, and consumer prices 20% lower. Equity and house prices would also have been lower: by 25% and 22%, respectively, in real terms. Even allowing for wide margins of error in these estimates, the conclusion must be that the central bank's policies prevented a much deeper downturn, indeed an outright depression, and played a central role in securing recovery.

Bank of England policy had significant effects on household interest payments and receipts; wages and employment; financial, housing and pension wealth; real deposits; and debt – although the potency of these effects varied greatly depending on household wealth and income.

The average household gained in income terms by £1,500 per year, or close to £9,000 cumulatively over the studied period, from Bank policy. The average household would have been 5% worse off had the Bank not made the interventions it made, with the dominant positive impact being on jobs and wages.

The gains were reasonably evenly spread as a proportion of income, although they were slightly smaller among lower-income households and negative for the lowest income decile. Nevertheless, the UK's overall Gini coefficient was little affected. The balance of benefits was spread more unevenly on a money basis, largely because of the uneven distribution of income prior to the crisis.

The average UK household also benefitted significantly in wealth terms. The total gain amounted to some £90,000, or some 20% of net wealth, with the benefits extending to financial and housing assets and to pensions. In percentage terms, the gains were evenly spread, and the impact on overall inequality was small. However, the unequal initial distribution of wealth again meant that the absolute gains were skewed heavily towards upper income groups.

In proportionate terms, the income gains were greatest among the young, largely because of their improved employment prospects. Older cohorts lost out because of lower earnings on their savings. Wealth gains, in contrast, were evenly spread across the age spectrum in percentage terms, although the elderly benefitted most in money terms because of the positive impact on housing and pension assets.

By region, the benefits of Bank policy were evenly spread in percentage terms, and there was no significant widening of regional inequality. That said, the absolute monetary gains were heavily skewed towards London and the South East because of the unequal initial distribution.

For all its uncertainties and arbitrary elements, the Bank's monetary unorthodoxy played a key role in stabilizing the UK economy in the wake of what was then the most serious hit it had suffered since World War II. Furthermore, the impact on income and wealth was constructive and significant across the population. In the absence of the Bank's response, average living standards would have been much lower than they turned out to be.

On the other hand, while overall income inequality was little changed, the effects on the population of the various elements of the Bank's strategy differed considerably in both nature and scale. Some people benefitted through higher employment, some through lower debt repayments, others via higher wealth, and the timescales of these consequences varied considerably.

Furthermore, a distinctly unequal initial distribution of income and wealth, and the manifest variation in absolute monetary gains, rather than percentage ones, left plenty of room for subjectivity and misinterpretation to adversely colour perceptions and influence public opinion about the central bank's policies. Nor was enough done by the Bank or by successive governments to combat the development of such misperceptions.

In conclusion, the issue was not so much what the Bank did and how it did it, it was the initial distributional context within which its unorthodox policies were forced to operate.

COMING UP SHORT

The economic record of the 2010–15 coalition government is unimpressive. The pace of overall recovery was sluggish both in a historical context and relative to other economies at the time. Confidence remained low, and uncertainty and economic insecurity high. There was a huge shortfall in business investment. Productivity was chronically weak. Real incomes suffered a profound and extended squeeze. Competitiveness declined along with export market share, and the external balance registered unprecedentedly large deficits. Britain was once again one of the sick men of not just Europe but of all the advanced economies.

The degree of budgetary restraint imposed was grounded in misguided new classical theoretical precepts. In particular, insufficient weight was attached to the basic Keynesian tenets that, in pursuing more sustainable public finances, it is important to give sufficient weight to the sustenance of the denominator of the underlying calculus (nominal GDP) as well as acting on its numerator (the budget deficit), and that reductions in the latter typically feedback negatively into the former. As Keynes said in 1937, 'The boom, not the slump, is the right time for austerity.'[28] The government also neglected to adequately take into account that all of the UK's competitors were also tightening fiscal policy.

The austerity therefore proved excessive. This was particularly the case in the early years of the parliament, even if in the end the rhetoric surrounding the policy of fiscal consolidation went rather further than the substance and the government's stated fiscal goals went unmet.

Not only did fiscal restraint constrain the recovery, it also had an enduring negative effect on underlying growth potential and, via the associated cuts to welfare provision and the public services in general, it imposed unnecessary costs on society as a whole. In this context, long-standing issues of inequality festered, aspirations went unmet and dissatisfaction metastasized. The political mould began to crack.

Furthermore, the impetus of fiscal policy placed too heavy a burden on monetary policy, and in particular unconventional monetary policy, to support growth and, latterly, to prevent deflation, while leaving the Bank of England open to public criticism. That said, despite a change of leadership, the

Bank's imagination continued to prove impressively fertile in this regard, even if forward guidance was only a very qualified success and seemed to suggest that where central bank communications were concerned, less could mean more. Moreover, the longer-term consequences of the Bank's unorthodoxies, and how the Bank might eventually disengage from them, remained unclear.

At the same time, financial policy was recalibrated and the financial system was belatedly put on a sounder footing, such that credit creation was gradually reanimated.

However, structural policy fell short of what was required. The lack of investment in public infrastructure and ALMPs and the failures of competition policy and the shortcomings in the broader education system proved particularly costly. Nor was there much progress on tax reform.

Finally, the politicization of the Treasury by the chancellor during the Scottish independence referendum campaign may have helped to achieve its short-term goal of sustaining the Union, but it opened the door to further incursions into the political arena that were, as we shall see, to prove altogether less successful. What is more, the issue of Scottish independence had hardly gone away.

CHAPTER 13

The Brexit Referendum and Its Aftermath

This royal throne of kings, this scepter'd isle,
This earth of majesty, this seat of Mars,
This other Eden, demi-paradise,
This fortress built by Nature for herself,
Against infection and the hand of war,
This happy breed of men, this little world,
This precious stone set in the silver sea,
Which serves it in the office of a wall,
Or as a moat defensive to a house,
Against the envy of less happier lands;
This blessed plot, this earth, this realm, this England.

— William Shakespeare, 1597[1]

MAJORITY VERDICT

Few commentators expected the Conservatives to secure an overall majority in the general election of May 2015. The consensus was that a sluggish recovery, depressed real incomes (they had yet to return to their pre-GFC peak), the effects of fiscal austerity, the missed targets for the budget deficit and government debt, and the party's unpopularity in Scotland would prove insurmountable obstacles to an outright victory. Even within the cabinet and Number 10, another hung parliament, and therefore a continuation of the coalition arrangement with the Liberal Democrats, was seen as the most likely ultimate outcome. That David Cameron was returned to office and was able to form a single-party government with a working majority of twelve (or fifteen in practice, because of Sinn Féin's history of abstention) was a surprise on a par with John Major's unlikely triumph in 1992.

In hindsight, it appears that, helped by a slump in the price of oil and a rebound in sterling's value, there was enough of a rebound in real incomes and real activity ahead of the election to carry the Conservatives over the line. Indeed, economic growth was running at its fastest clip since the crisis, the unemployment rate was down to around 5.5% of the workforce, inflation was not an issue and asset prices were firm. The suggestion was that monetary policy had managed to offset just about enough of the austerity, and besides, the fiscal clampdown had itself been moderated when excess threatened to spill over into complete overkill. A final additional factor was that the core of the Tories' support – homeowners and pensioners – had, under Osborne's guidance, enjoyed the greatest protection from the nation's post-crisis hardships.

The Conservatives' victory was not just a matter of a well-timed mini-boom, however. Their coalition partner had lost credibility with the electorate. The perception from some was that the Liberal Democrats had contributed little to the alliance, while others thought that rather than moderating the Conservatives, as many had hoped they would, they had instead enabled them. The early sharp increase in university tuition fees proved to be a major own goal. After all, the Liberal Democrats had pledged to scrap them altogether just months before. The 2011 referendum on electoral reform – a central provision of the 2010 coalition agreement – was also a disaster for the party, as a shift from 'first past the post' to an 'alternative vote system' was rejected by 67.9% to 32.1%. These were blows from which the Lib Dems never recovered. In 2015 the party lost all but eight of the fifty-seven parliamentary seats it had won in 2010, with the Conservatives taking eighteen of them.

Labour had also lost its way. Most of the big guns of the Blair and Brown cabinets had retired from politics, and the party's new leader, Ed Milliband, who was something of a throwback to old Labour, failed to inspire the electorate or stop the Tories from dictating the economic narrative of the campaign. The public, egged on remorselessly by Britain's predominantly right-wing press, had largely swallowed the government line on the urgency of eradicating the budget deficit and bringing the burden of debt to heel, even if progress was limited, while perceptions of Labour's economic competence had regressed, since the GFC, to where they were in the early 1990s.

In Scotland, meanwhile, the continued ascendency of the SNP came at the expense of the Labour Party rather than the already largely vanquished Conservatives. Despite losing the 2014 independence referendum, the SNP took all but three Westminster seats north of the border in 2015, including forty of those won by Labour in 2010. If Labour had held on to a decent proportion of these, it would have triumphed.

Another significant political development was the rise of the UK Independence Party (UKIP), with its hardline anti-immigration stance and unabashed commitment to leaving the EU. It took some 12.6% of the vote in the election, the third highest total, and although it returned only a single MP under the retained first past the post system, it both scared the Conservative leadership and made considerable gains at Labour's expense in working class areas.

It was the advance of UKIP that had convinced the Conservatives to include in their manifesto a pledge to hold 'a straight in–out referendum on our membership of the European Union by the end of 2017'.[2] This would never have happened had the coalition endured, as the pro-EU Liberal Democrats would have vetoed it. But with an overall majority in place, Cameron had little choice but to turn these words into action.

ECONOMIC OVERVIEW

Like the political environment, the economy's performance in the mid and late 2010s was heavily influenced by the decision to hold a referendum on EU membership and then by the outcome of the vote.

The mini pre-election boom stoked by Osborne rapidly faded, as business sentiment was weighed down first by uncertainty around the outcome of the proposed Brexit vote and then by a lack of clarity about the precise nature of the exit deal that the UK would negotiate. A particular problem was the unwillingness of companies to spend on plant and equipment. Real GDP growth slowed progressively from 3% in 2014 to under 1.75% in 2018 and 2019. The latter was the slowest expansion rate among the G-7 economies, even though global growth and world trade were consistently robust. Thereafter, of course, the Covid-19 pandemic and the reaction to it plunged the economy into its deepest downturn for some 300 years.

Despite the effective elimination of the output gap and record low borrowing costs, real business investment registered no growth at all between the July 2016 referendum and the onset of the pandemic in early 2020. Because of Brexit, the overall size of the economy was at least 2.5% smaller than it would have been had the pre-referendum trend continued when Covid struck.[3] The GDP shortfall would have been greater had households not dipped into their savings to sustain private consumption.

The labour market remained resilient, however. The proportion of the workforce in employment reached record highs; underemployment declined, although it remained above pre-GFC trends; and the headline jobless rate dropped below 4%, finally bottoming out at 3.8%, a forty-two-year low, towards the end of 2019. This also helped to sustain private consumption, even as a sharp fall in sterling's value in the context of still-modest, if slightly accelerated, wage growth rekindled the long-standing squeeze on real incomes.

The pound had been trending down for the six months preceding the referendum, and it fell a further 10% in nominal effective terms in its immediate aftermath. The decline in sterling's value was centred on the countries from whom the UK imported the most, as market participants factored in the longer-term effects of changes in the UK's trading arrangements. On the other hand, sterling weakness, together with strong overseas demand, helped net exports to partially offset the softness of domestic demand, and the external deficit narrowed somewhat from its then-record level of some 5.5% of GDP in 2016. It ran at between 3.5% and 4% of GDP in 2017 and 2018, which was still above its long-run average, before falling by a further percentage point or so of GDP between 2019 and 2021.

Given the inertia in business investment, which typically accounts for some 50% of total investment, labour productivity remained chronically weak and was marked by large regional disparities. The modest pick-up seen in output per hour worked in the middle of the decade quickly faded. Productivity growth was zero by 2019, further depressing the economy's productive potential. This was especially the case as labour force growth diminished, partly due to a decline in net migration inflows from the EU. Notwithstanding some volatility around the pandemic, the level of productivity has remained little changed since.

Together with higher energy prices, the decline in the exchange rate around the time of the referendum boosted headline CPI inflation from close to zero in 2015 to back above target in 2017 and 2018, with a peak of around 3%. It faded rapidly thereafter, however, and remained below target until it began to surge higher in the spring of 2021.

In early August 2016 Bank Rate was cut by a quarter point to a new low of 0.25%, and the Bank of England restarted its QE programme with an additional £70 billion of bond purchases, taking the cumulative total to £445 billion (some 21% of GDP). Bank Rate stayed at 0.25% until late 2017, at which point it was returned to 0.5% in the context of limited remaining excess capacity. A further hike to 0.75% was made in August 2018 for the same reasons, as private sector pay growth finally began to pick up somewhat. Bank Rate was then cut to a new low of 0.1% and QE started once again as the pandemic struck. Ultimately, the Bank's balance sheet peaked at the equivalent of almost 50% of GDP.

Long-term interest rates continued their inexorable fall in the late 2010s. The ten-year gilt yield established a new low of less than 0.75% in August 2016 before stabilizing within a 1–1.5% range until the latter part of 2019, at which point a further downtrend began. It eventually bottomed out close to zero in August 2020.

UK stock prices fell sharply in advance of the Brexit vote, then rallied, before eventually settling into a volatile range. However, the UK equity market proved a consistent underperformer relative to its US and European counterparts, and it then suffered a sharp fall as the pandemic struck. Annual house price inflation peaked at just above 8% in mid 2016 before trending down towards zero in late 2019. However, the post-Covid loosening of monetary policy sparked a further rebound.

Progress in the reduction of the budget deficit – already much less rapid than originally planned – stalled in the wake of the referendum, with the broadly defined shortfall running around 2–2.75% of GDP, until the pandemic and the response to it led to a further dramatic increase in red ink. A small current surplus was finally achieved in 2018, however, and the share of public spending in GDP was for a time reduced below 40% of GDP – something last achieved by the second Blair administration. The net debt burden also peaked around this time in the low 80s as a percentage of GDP – a level last seen in the mid 1960s. The pandemic saw it surge back towards 100% of GDP.

A MAN WITH A PLAN

It was in a speech delivered in January 2013 that David Cameron had first outlined a desire to renegotiate the UK's relationship with the EU and to then hold a referendum on the new terms of membership. This was after the comfortably 'won' (from the Conservatives' perspective) electoral reform referendum but before the much more challenging Scottish independence vote. Cameron had been warned off making such a move by George Osborne and others in the party, as they feared him making himself a hostage to fortune unnecessarily, but fuelled by public concern about a seemingly inexorable rise in immigration, much of it latterly from the EU, the clamour within the Conservative Party for such a move had become hard to ignore. Parliamentary rebellions on European issues had become more common, and Cameron was fearful that if he failed to respond to them in some substantive way, there could be a rush of defections to the increasingly popular UKIP. Cameron's characteristically cavalier calculation was that a victory in such a vote would be a means to finally move on from the distraction of his party constantly 'banging on about Europe', something that was always likely to be wishful thinking.[4]

In following this path, it could be argued that he misjudged UKIP's attractions and their durability. While the party was a convenient vessel for protest votes about long-standing prejudices and gripes, especially when the electorate was experiencing tougher times than many of them had known, it was an inherently fragile political movement. Its organization and finance were chaotic. Beyond its desire to leave the EU and stop immigration, its policy platform was shallow and incoherent. And it boasted few, if any, politicians of substance or appeal beyond Nigel Farage, its charismatic and street-smart leader.

At the same time, Cameron overestimated his powers of persuasion with the electorate; with his cabinet, some of whom were long-standing Eurosceptics, if not closet Brexiteers; and with other EU leaders, from whom he would have to achieve meaningful concessions in advance of the vote. Nor was he helped in much of this by his own previous indulgence in cheap Euroscepticism. Cameron had been a weak and unconvincing advocate of UK membership in the past, and he had regularly resorted to lazy platitudes about EU regulation and its supposed overbearing influence on British life. In 2006 he had also foolishly withdrawn the Tories from the European People's Party – the network of cooperation among centre-right political parties in the European Parliament and beyond.

Just over a month after his election victory in 2015, Cameron began to outline to the European Council the reforms he sought to UK membership, the thrust of which had been outlined in the Conservatives' election manifesto. They essentially fell into two categories.

First, while underlining continued UK support for the single market, he expressed his antipathy to ever-closer union, to euro membership and associated future laws and regulation, to participation in euro area bailouts, to the further concentration of power in Brussels, and to a European army – not that any such entity seemed close to being established.

Second, he set out proposals to significantly reduce the flow of immigrants from other EU members by making it less attractive for them to come to the UK. In practical terms this amounted to an interim period during which they would be ineligible for in-work and other benefits, including social housing. Furthermore, those who failed to find a job within six months would be required to leave.

The first category of demands can hardly have come as a great surprise to his EU interlocutors. It represented in large part a formal statement of Conservative Party policy towards Europe that had de facto been in place since the time of the Major government. The real problem came with the second category. Shocking though the latter appeared to other EU members committed to the equal treatment of their citizens, it was viewed as unduly modest by the many in the UK who wanted immigration essentially brought to a halt – and preferably quickly.

The negotiations went on until February of 2016, and they were tough. In a harbinger of things to come, the EU was meticulous in its approach, and, rather than fragmenting, the bloc acted throughout as a coherent whole. In the end, though, Cameron – assisted by Tom Scholar, his most senior advisor on international affairs – secured much of what he wanted in the first category of reforms. This included, most symbolically, formal recognition that Britain would not be party to further political integration into the EU – a development that ostensibly could establish UK membership on an entirely new footing. It would certainly have provided a clearer idea of what being a member of the EU actually meant for the UK than had ever been evident before.

Unfortunately for Cameron, however, it was on the second set of proposed reforms that public, and importantly press, attention was overwhelmingly focused, and all he could secure here was a diluted version of his original pitch. Freedom of movement was a core element of the *Acquis Communautaire* of the EU, and there was a profound reluctance on the part of other members to see it undermined to any significant extent.[5]

As part of a new settlement for the UK, the EU also alluded to an ambitious future agenda of economic reform that would include the next stage of development of the single market, with a focus on bringing down the remaining barriers to trade in services, energy and digital, alongside completing major ongoing trade deals.

Eurosceptics in the Tory party and elsewhere were nevertheless unconvinced by the deal. They claimed it had gone nowhere near far enough to address their concerns about an influx of Eastern European workers and the supposed pressure this exerted on the public services. Furthermore, despite the statement discharging Britain from further obligations where political integration was concerned, the long-standing issue of UK sovereignty continued to inflame passions.

Cameron returned from Brussels with this set of accords and subsequently formally committed to persuading the electorate to vote to remain in the EU at a referendum scheduled for 23 June. Within days, six cabinet members announced that they would be supporting the campaign to leave. To Cameron's chagrin, the six included his close friend Michael Gove, who was Minister of Justice at the time. Another prominent Conservative rapidly to side with the Leave campaign was Boris Johnson, then still the mayor of London.

With these defections the vote had rapidly taken on the appearance of a Tory civil war, but conscious that he would have to try to lead a united government and party if he won the referendum, Cameron often seemed to fight it with one hand tied behind his back. He certainly lacked the unreconstructed passion and vision for Europe displayed, for example, by Edward Heath and Roy Jenkins during the 1975 referendum campaign. Indeed, it could be argued that he sometimes sounded less enthusiastic about Europe than had Margaret Thatcher, who was the newly installed Conservative party leader at the time of the 1975 vote.

Others were much less reserved. The Leave campaign was to prove an astute but unscrupulous one. Directed by Dominic Cummings, Michael Gove's former special advisor, it repeatedly made specific headline-grabbing (and often spurious) claims, while generally presenting the EU as the external source of many of the adverse influences that were making life harder for UK citizens. Its populist, anti-intellectualist approach, often grounded in rose-tinted English exceptionalist nostalgia, regularly spilled over into falsehoods, deceptions, prejudice and xenophobia, all of which were easily amplified by social media, and probably by the Russian secret service too. No caricature of Europe seemed to be too extreme.

THE RETURN OF PROJECT FEAR

Osborne realised early on that the vote was anything but a foregone conclusion. The pro-EU campaign could expect to receive lukewarm support at best from the Labour Party. Under its new crypto-Marxist leader Jeremy Corbyn, the party had shifted much further to the left, and Corbyn had been a long-standing critic of the EU. He was to prove the most reluctant of Remainers. Meanwhile, the Liberal Democrats, who were ostensibly the most pro-EU major party, were in disarray after their electoral debacle.

Osborne also felt that his position left him less constrained in his actions than Cameron, and he therefore determined to reprise the 'Project Fear' economic strategy he had employed during the Scottish independence referendum. Treasury analysis would be at the core of the arguments used by the Remain campaign.

The chancellor commissioned a thorough assessment of the long-term consequences of the UK remaining in the EU compared with various alternatives. Taking a so-called gravity approach, which estimated bilateral trade flows on the basis of the size of two economies and the geographical distance between them, the Treasury first explored EU membership being replaced by UK membership of the European Economic Area, which would mean staying in the European single market. This is the position taken by Norway, for example. Second, it examined a negotiated bilateral trade agreement, such as that which existed between the UK and Canada. And third, it assessed the option of the UK trading with the EU on the basis of World Trade Organization rules alone, which would leave the economy confronted by a wall of tariff and non-tariff barriers to trade.[6]

The Treasury's 200-page report unsurprisingly concluded that the UK's economic openness and interconnectedness would be reduced in each of the examined scenarios. Trade, investment (including inward foreign direct investment) and migration flows with the EU would all be lower, and the UK stood to be permanently poorer as a result. The overall hit to the level of GDP could, the analysis concluded, be anything between 3.4% and 9.5% over fifteen years. The losses were also presented as the annual loss in GDP per household over the same period, and on this basis they were more sobering still. Each household was set to lose £2,600 per year in the first scenario, £4,300 per year in the second and £5,200 per year in the third. There was also an effort to assess the prospective shortfall in tax receipts in each case. Here, the estimates ranged from £20 billion a year to £45 billion a year. These numbers were given context by the revelation that £36 billion was the equivalent of more than a third of the NHS budget, or the equivalent of an increase in the basic rate of income tax of some eight pence in the pound.

The Treasury's work then went on to offer a rather more questionable estimate that the reforms alluded to by the EU would boost UK GDP by some 4% over the longer term, and it asserted that many of these reforms would not happen if the UK left the EU. The ultimate economic cost to the UK would therefore be greater still, it argued.

Finally, there was reference to a range of other evaluations of the potential damage to be incurred by leaving the EU, which ranged from three percentage points of GDP over 3–5 years up to eight percentage points. A detailed assessment by the OECD – whose remit is, *inter alia*, to encourage best policy practice across its membership – that was not included in the Treasury's report put the cost at between 2.7 and 7.7 percentage points of GDP over the period to 2030.[7]

Some sense of the veracity both of the Treasury's work and of other forecasters' estimates of the potential longer-term costs of exit can be gleaned from backward-looking studies of the *positive* impact of EU membership on the UK over the previous forty-odd years. Perhaps the most authoritative research, conducted by Professor Nick Crafts of Warwick University, suggested that it had been in the region of 10% of GDP.[8] The Bank of England broadly concurred. EU membership had expanded Britain's export markets, encouraged significant inward international investment and the importation of skilled foreign workers, exposed the domestic economy to more intense competition, enhanced productivity, and provided an important supply-side policy anchor via the rules of the single market. In economic terms, it had, in short, done much of what was hoped for when Britain joined it. Casting it aside would be a painful and costly process.

That said, the Treasury's analysis was not without its critics, where both its approach and its output were concerned. But it is safe to say that remotely credible estimates of the longer-term effects of leaving the EU with an opposing sign to the government's work were rare indeed. Furthermore, those that were forthcoming tended to rely on underlying assumptions – such as the unilateral adoption by the UK of completely free trade – that stretched credulity to its limits.[9]

In May 2016, just before the actual vote, the Treasury issued a second assessment of the economy's post-Brexit prospects, this time focusing on the short term. The work was undertaken by a team led by David Ramsden, who had overseen much of the work on the 'five tests' some fifteen years earlier, and it was given a formal stamp of approval by former Bank of England deputy governor Sir Charles Bean. Its conclusions were, if anything, even more dramatic. It talked of 'an immediate and profound shock' to the economy. Even on the basis of its most optimistic scenario, leaving the EU would over two years lead to a recession, a fall in GDP of more than 3.5%, an increase in unemployment of half a million, a 12% depreciation of the pound, higher inflation and borrowing, and lower house prices. The numbers under its severe shock scenario were much worse, with the drop in GDP extending to 6% and the rise in unemployment to more than 800,000.[10]

Fearing that even this was not enough, Osborne announced in the wake of the second report's release that if there was a vote to leave the EU he would have to introduce an emergency budget to plug a shortfall in the public finances of some £30 billion. This was likely to involve higher income and inheritance taxes as well as reductions in the NHS budget, the latter assertion being a direct retort to the Leave campaign's promise that the fictitious £350 million a week they claimed would be saved by no longer contributing to the EU budget could in future be channelled into public healthcare.

What soon became clear, however, was that this second report did not reflect the same level of consensus across the Treasury and other Whitehall departments that had underpinned the initial longer-term assessment of Brexit's likely effects. It had not been widely circulated in advance, and Osborne had played a dominant role in the way that its conclusions were presented and developed into a set of austere fiscal policy implications. This gave rise to a sense that the findings had been deliberately massaged, and Osborne had therefore allowed the independence – and, thereby, the credibility – of the most powerful and important government department to be impugned. As former chancellor Nigel Lawson, by then an unabashed Brexiteer, was to put it: 'The Treasury had seemingly prostituted itself for a particular political cause.'[11]

What also became apparent, however, was that rather than scaring the undecided into voting to stay in the EU, the tone of much of the Treasury's output and the melodramatic policy implications described by the chancellor simply alienated people. For their part, die-hard Leavers dismissed it as an act of desperation on the part of a floundering Remain campaign. As a strategy, it backfired badly.

A much more powerful consideration in the way people voted was the fact that in the month of the vote, the Office for National Statistics announced that net immigration had reached 330,000 a year – problematic for Cameron, who had promised in 2010 to reduce the figure to tens of thousands. Immigration trumped economics, especially when the latter were being spun so crassly and the profession's reputation had been so seriously dented by the GFC. As Michael Gove put it in his now-infamous paean to insularity and ideological myopia: 'People ... [had] had enough of experts.'[12] In short, ignorance was bliss.

With hindsight, while the bulk of the initial Treasury assessment of Brexit continues to this day to hold water,* the second paper went awry in part because of the assumptions it was based on. In particular, it presumed that there would be a tightening of fiscal policy along the lines suggested by Osborne while oddly making no allowance for an accommodative policy response from the Bank of England.

As it turned out, the Bank did respond and there was no immediate recession or sharp rise in unemployment. The Treasury was correct, however, in its forecast of a sharp decline in sterling.

EARTHQUAKE

Despite the leadership of all the major political parties falling in behind the Remain campaign, and in spite of it having the support of the major trade unions and employers' organizations, it lost on a 51.9%:48.1% split of a turnout of more than 72% of the electorate. The latter exceeded that of recent general elections.

The general level of ignorance across the population about the EU proved extraordinarily high. At the same time, following the example of so many previous governments, Remain neglected to make a sufficiently positive case for British EU membership. Indeed, it was only when Gordon Brown again intervened towards the end of the campaign that a strong voice was heard extoling the contribution of the pan-European institutions to post-war peace and economic and social progress and detailing how they had encouraged the UK to be an outward-looking, progressive nation.[13] This time, however, the former prime minister's intervention, however erudite, proved too little and too late.

At the same time, and in common with many referenda, there was a tendency for the electorate to pose and answer its own questions rather than religiously respond to the question that had been set. And the context within which the vote took place in June 2016 was one of widespread resentment across the country about the economic travails, insecurities and frustrated aspirations of the previous eight or nine years – not least because of the fiscal austerity of the period since 2010.

---

* It appears to be a sound piece of work that identified the key issues at stake and, as far as it is possible to tell at this juncture, broadly got the prospective longer-term hit to the UK economy correct.

Neither was this the whole story. In the end, it was older voters who swung the result decisively in favour of Leave – that is to say, it was those who were best insulated against the GFC and its painful aftermath. The implication is that perceived loss of control and sovereignty, extending in particular to discomfort about globalization and high levels of immigration, together with a dislike of other latter-day cultural developments were key considerations in the way the referendum played out. It came down, in significant part, to a matter of national identity, and at the same time to a nostalgic desire to rec-reate a more stable and familiar era when Britain was a great power and could largely set its own course in the world. As the Leave campaign had intended, the EU became a scapegoat for all the forces that had taken that status away.

Any number of important facts were overlooked in this visceral response. For example, more than half of the twenty-five countries in the world in which it was easiest to do business in 2016 were EU members, and the bloc's regulatory burden was declining, in part because of UK influence in Brussels. Less than 7% of primary UK legislation and only 14% of secondary legislation was passed in order to implement EU law.[14] The UK's net contribution to the EU accounted for around just 1% of total public spending in 2018–19. The EU had no significant influence over UK government outlays on, or policies relating to, health, education, housing, pensions, welfare, infrastructure, cul-ture, defence or aid. And finally, rather than enhancing the UK's capacity for control over its own survival, the vote for Brexit threatened to reduce it. The futures of Northern Ireland, Scotland and Wales were all destabilized by it, too.

As a small island, accounting for less than 3% of global GDP, where imports and exports of goods and services together accounted for some 60% of national income and when around half of those exports went to the EU, Britain's ability to increase its control over its economic destiny was always limited. It could in theory amend the domestic regulatory architecture to ren-der it more suited to UK business needs, but UK product and labour markets were already some of the most lightly regulated in the world. There was lim-ited scope for further deregulation. The danger, therefore, was that regulatory policy morphed either into state aid that merely distorted competition and propped up inefficient companies or into reductions in worker and environ-mental protection.

Similarly, achieving greater access to alternative markets to compensate for the loss of favourable access to the market of 450 million Europeans on the UK's doorstep was easier said than done. The economic superpowers would certainly drive hard bargains, while the faster-growing emerging economies were unlikely to be very obliging either. The latter were often individually still relatively small markets, and they were frequently highly protected ones too, especially where services – which accounted for 44% of UK exports, and in which Britain's comparative advantage lay – were concerned.

Finally, the standards insisted on for trade to take place were inconsistent from country to country. The UK would still have to choose which one of the major trading blocs to align its standards with. And the most likely candidate was the geographically adjacent EU.

Contrary to the hopes and beliefs of the Leavers, Britain had, in seeking greater control and independence, chosen a solitary course – one where it was at the mercy of others, some of whom were much more powerful and inwardly focused than it was. Real sovereignty represents the capacity to act and to choose how to cooperate, rather than being bullied or coerced into commercial or political arrangements or just angrily shouting from the touchline. This means building trust and alliances and persuading others to play by the international rules designed to benefit all. Engagement with the EU had helped to amplify Britain's voice on the global stage. Brexit would muffle it, perhaps even to the point of inaudibility.

AFTERMATH

The Brexit vote was a massive shock, and in terms of being a watershed moment for the nation it was arguably more important than the Suez Crisis of 1956, the IMF crisis of 1976 and the abandonment of the Gold Standard in 1931. It left the population riven; the civil service in turn discredited and then overwhelmed; the political system at times paralysed; the domestic union subverted; and the nation's reputation for sound judgement in matters of international economic policy and diplomacy wrecked.

The immediate aftermath of the referendum was a particularly anxious and chaotic time. Although he had previously publicly insisted that he would remain in office in the event of the vote being lost, Cameron immediately resigned, his political career abruptly terminated, plunging the Conservative Party into a divisive leadership contest. This was won by Theresa May, the dutiful and determined, but insular and uninspiring, home secretary. With other candidates rapidly falling by the wayside, she became prime minister on 13 July, having had precious little time to gather her thoughts. Her default option was to operate largely as before: keeping her cards close to her chest; eschewing contact with the press, or for that matter many other MPs; and relying heavily on her two widely disliked and distrusted political advisors, Nick Timothy and Fiona Hill, for strategic guidance.

Reflecting the reality of Brexit, May rapidly sacked nine of the previous cabinet, including George Osborne, another whose political career died a sudden death. She had little choice but to shift the government to the right, and a number of prominent Brexiteers, including Boris Johnson and David Davis, were elevated to senior ministerial posts. Few of those promoted proved to be a success.

Phillip Hammond moved across from the Foreign Office to become chancellor. Like May, he was a less-than-enthusiastic, even rather idiosyncratic, Remainer, and in many ways he was the antithesis of the Machiavellian Osborne. Hitherto a fiscal conservative, if a less devout one than his predecessor, he was never close to the prime minister or to her personal advisors. Indeed, Timothy had a particular antipathy for both Hammond and the Treasury, which he saw as a hive of conventional and pro-EU thinking. In many ways, he was right. Timothy's support in July 2016 for the creation of an expanded business ministry – the Department for Business, Energy & Industrial Strategy – was a clear, if ultimately unsuccessful, attempt to clip the Treasury's wings permanently, reducing it to more of a pure finance ministry.

Over the next few years the Treasury was to find itself on occasion banished to the periphery of decision-making, in a manner that would have seemed inconceivable to Hammond's predecessors. Nevertheless, strongly supported by his senior officials, he was to prove perhaps the stoutest and most coherent cabinet opponent of a 'hard' Brexit, and a supporter of the notion that the plans for departure should reflect the narrowness of the referendum result. Despite the often-transparent hostility of May's inner circle, he came to command considerable respect as a safe pair of hands – someone whose arguments remained grounded in fact, and who fully grasped the trade-offs that Brexit involved. And he ultimately survived as long as May did.

The problem for both policymakers and businesses in July 2016 was that while Leave had won, there was limited understanding of what exiting the EU actually meant in practice. Cameron had not allowed any significant contingency planning for Brexit because he was worried that if that planning leaked out, he would be characterized as defeatist. The Leavers, meanwhile – who were as surprised as anyone that they had actually been victorious – had said remarkably little in advance about their detailed intentions, preferring instead to seek refuge in hard-to-disprove generalities or narrow, eye-catching soundbites.

Most critically, there was no agreed position on what the country's future trade arrangements should be. In particular, there was no consensus on whether the UK would leave the EU single market or customs union. It was no wonder that uncertainty ran high at this juncture.

CARNEY'S FINEST HOUR

Even if the government was all at sea, at least the Bank of England had done some preparatory work. As sterling went into an immediate post-referendum nosedive, Mark Carney appeared on television to assure the public that it had matters in hand. The banking system was liquid and well capitalized, and the Bank had overseen the construction of a number of buffers, safeguards and contingencies over previous months. There was therefore no descent into panic, and the markets continued to function smoothly. In many ways, this was Carney's most successful intervention as governor. The Bank's foresight and vigilance at this time proved invaluable.

In early August the MPC followed up Carney's words by cutting Bank Rate to a mere 0.25%, pushing it well into negative territory in real terms, and by reactivating its programme of QE. The latter included a combination of £60 billion of gilt purchases and £10 billion of corporate bond purchases (equivalent to some 3.5% of GDP). In addition, the Bank undertook a number of measures to support liquidity and lending. These included the launch of a successful Term Funding Scheme (TFS), which remained in place until the end of February 2018, and the unwinding of the half percentage point increase in the countercyclical capital buffer, which had been instituted earlier in the year.

Carney subsequently suggested that the MPC's rapid response in Q3 2016 boosted growth by between 0.5% and 1% over the following two years. Well … perhaps. Regardless, with the prospects for long-term growth reduced and with uncertainty high, confidence slumped and the sharp fall in the pound pushed inflation back up, re-intensifying the squeeze on real wages. At the same time, businesses put capital spending projects on hold, the flow of inward FDI began to ease off, and growth slowed, even if an outright contraction failed to materialize.

THE TREASURY ON THE BACK FOOT

Despite having provided additional funding for the NHS, increased personal tax allowances and made greater efforts to advance public infrastructure spending, Osborne had continued to prioritize fiscal consolidation in the two budgets he delivered in the wake of the 2015 general election. Restraint when it came to current spending, including public sector wages, had remained a primary focus. Indeed, the overall fiscal policy impulse of around −1.5% of potential output in 2016–17 was the most deflationary of his period as chancellor. It brought the headline deficit down below 3% of GDP for the first time since before the GFC, although it was still about twice the euro area average.

In March 2016, however, Osborne had signalled that a downgrade in the OBR's growth outlook, driven in part by the continued weakness in productivity, meant that the pace of fiscal adjustment would have to slow somewhat. The Brexit vote only added to the impetus for an altogether less aggressive approach to fiscal consolidation.

Hammond and May were quick to conclude that Osborne's fiscal targets were no longer realistic. The November 2016 Autumn Statement offered a recalibration of budgetary policy. The new chancellor outlined a £73 billion increase in projected government borrowing over the next four years as a result of a deterioration in the economic outlook. Rather than seeking to offset this, however, he allowed borrowing to increase, and he actually decided to add further to the deficit via an even-more-expansive attitude to public infrastructure spending and by cancelling scheduled increases in fuel duties. The persistent decline in net debt service costs, even in the face of a much higher debt burden, together with the interest collected by the Bank of England and transferred to the Treasury as a result of its QE programme provided some additional short-term room for manoeuvre.

The 'fiscal rules' were amended once again in 2017. The primary goal of fiscal policy was switched to the reduction of the structural deficit to below 2% of GDP in 2020–21 from its then level of around 2.5%, such that the net debt ratio would also begin to fall and overall fiscal balance could be achieved before the end of the following parliament. Over the next three years, the thrust of fiscal policy was essentially neutral, although under the guidance of the National Infrastructure Commission the share of public sector net investment in GDP rebounded to around 2% from its 2015 low of 1.6%.

In his 2018 budget, cheered by an unexpected tax windfall, Hammond proclaimed that the era of austerity was finally coming to an end, even if most government departments continued to be subject to keen spending limits. He introduced a series of tax breaks, extending in due course to income tax thresholds, while pledging to increase spending on the NHS by almost 3.5% a year in real terms for five years from 2019 and topping up resources for Universal Credit, the judiciously designed but hitherto-underfunded system of simplified welfare payments. Spending pressures related to the nation's ageing population were beginning to build. Hammond also announced the abolition of the PFI – the public–private mechanism for funding infrastructure projects that Gordon Brown had been so enamoured of but which proved so lacking when it came to value for money.

After May's departure from Number 10 Hammond was replaced by the free-marketeer Sajid Javid. Like his predecessor, Javid had voted unenthusiastically to Remain, and he had previously been a junior minister in the Treasury between 2012 and 2014. He would have to work with a prime minister with a very different public spending agenda and a less-than-reverential attitude towards the institutional architecture of government. Although he never publicly dissented from the austerity of the post GFC years, the populist Boris Johnson saw government outlays very much as a means to an end, and he had little interest in their tight control.

As it transpired, Javid was to be chancellor for only seven months – at the time the shortest occupancy of Number 11 Downing Street since Iain MacLeod's one-month tenure in 1970. His period in office coincided with the chaotic final months of 2019, when 'getting Brexit done' overrode all other government business. He constantly had to push back against interference from his next-door neighbour and his cohorts, not least Dominic Cummings, who had been elevated from leading the Leave campaign to becoming John-son's chief advisor. Cummings's interventions extended to suggestions that there should be a purge of senior officials and to renewed calls to develop another economics ministry as a counterbalance to a Treasury that supposedly remained staffed by orthodox thinkers and Remainers.

Javid resigned when he was informed that his special advisors would be managed from Number 10. He was replaced by his chief secretary: the Goldman Sachs alumnus Rishi Sunak. Javid never delivered a budget. The November 2019 event was cancelled because of the general election campaign. However, he did successfully steer through the installation of Andrew Bailey as Mark Carney's successor as Bank of England governor, despite the efforts of the prime minister's office to appoint a more politically malleable alterna-tive. Bailey might have been dull and uninspiring, but as a Bank lifer he was strongly committed to its independence.

Javid also proposed yet another set of fiscal rules – the eighth iteration of said rules in ten years. These amounted to the achievement of balance in the current budget within three years; the limitation of net public investment to 3% of GDP; and a threshold for debt interest costs equivalent to 6% of tax revenues, beyond which the government was obliged to reassess its borrowing plans to restrict the accumulation of debt.

The current-spending rule represented a loosening of the previous approach, while the investment ceiling was consistent with a significant increase in pub-lic sector capital spending, even if the interest cost ceiling could constrain it. It was unclear, however, why there should be a formal numerical cap on public investment at all. Logically, all public investment projects that pass the net present value test – whereby prospective returns exceed the projected discount rate – should be allowed to go ahead.

The rules were never formally evaluated by the OBR, but they seemed to be inconsistent with the expansive plans outlined in the Tories' December 2019 general election manifesto. In the end they were rendered irrelevant by the exigencies of the pandemic, but there was a sense around this time that fiscal policy was being conducted without a sufficiently credible anchor.

STRUCTURAL SHORTCOMINGS

As noted in the previous chapter, the extended weakness of productivity during the post-GFC period had become an increasingly important focus of policy debate in the middle of the 2010s. The nature of the problem was better understood by 2016 (albeit still not fully), and there was greater agreement on what was required to address it – not least the need to raise investment spending and narrow the gap between the stronger-performing regions and firms and those that were doing less well. Productivity in the latter would have to grow much faster than in the former, and for an extended period. In some UK regions, for example, productivity levels were lower than in some of the least productive areas of the entire OECD.

Brexit only increased the urgency of tackling this most fundamental of economic issues. Leaving the EU promised to weigh on productivity by reducing FDI, trade and inward migration, while many of its effects stood to fall disproportionately on the sectors and regions that already exhibited the largest productivity shortfalls relative to the UK's 'technological frontier', largely situated in London and the South East.

Britain's tradables sector would also need to boost its underlying competitiveness if it was to take advantage of the fast-growing developing markets in Asia and elsewhere – markets it would have to conquer as substitutes for Europe. A soft pound alone could not do the job. Except in a few brief periods, it had never done so before, and complex global value chains, in which there was a high import content, had in any case reduced the responsiveness of exports to the exchange rate.

Against this backdrop, there were some new and important initiatives by the May government in areas of supply-side policy.

The institutional oversight of public infrastructure was improved. With the National Infrastructure Commission playing an important advisory role, it was better planned and in receipt of much needed additional resources, for energy and transport in particular. This extended to a greater emphasis on raising public investment in the regions to address specific bottlenecks, facilitate external trade and encourage industrial agglomeration, and to embrace the positive efficiency spillovers all this might bring about. In the middle of the decade almost a third of all public sector infrastructure investment was on projects in London. London enjoyed by far the highest per capita spending flows. This had to change.

A National Productivity Investment Fund was also established in the autumn of 2016 to provide finance for small transport, digital, housing and R&D projects in those areas of the country most in need of a productivity uplift.

The vocational training regime was simplified, and efforts were made to increase the number of apprenticeships through the mechanism of a 0.5% levy imposed on large businesses' payrolls.[15]

Some government arrangements were decentralized in an effort to improve accountability and to better align decision-making with local needs. The Northern Powerhouse Strategy and the Midlands Engine Strategy, established by George Osborne to coordinate new development programmes for some of Britain's older industrial regions, received further encouragement.

Greater efforts were made to encourage cooperation between businesses and higher education in order to raise R&D spending and spur industrial innovation.

And finally, a new Industrial Strategy was set out in January 2017. It sought to provide additional context and coherence to the above-mentioned initiatives.[16] It identified 'five foundations' – ideas, people, infrastructure, business environment and places – and 'four grand challenges': artificial intelligence and data, the ageing society, clean growth and the future of mobility. In order to oversee the strategy and provide independent guidance, an Industrial Strategy Council was established in 2018, meeting for the first time in November of that year. This was the first such body the UK had had since the National Economic Development Office, which had operated from 1962 until it was abolished by the Major government in 1992.

Despite these various initiatives, however, many significant gaps and shortcomings remained – and, of course, the gestation periods of such policies are typically long, often stretching to a decade or more.

The precise role of climate change policy in all this was initially unclear. Phillip Hammond's attitude to the matter at first largely mirrored George Osborne's cautious, cost-conscious example, even though it was clearer than ever by 2016 that failing to act to control the rise in average global temperatures would generate extraordinary levels of disruption. It was only from the end of Hammond's term as chancellor, and with the arrival of Rishi Sunak in Number 11 Downing Street, that the substance of climate change policy altered significantly. The shift seems to have reflected Boris Johnson's belated conversion from climate emergency denial, the fact that the COP26 climate change conference would be held in Glasgow in November 2021, and an effort to apply an element of substance to the government's post-Brexit slogan of 'Global Britain'.

In June 2019 Britain embraced a legally binding target to achieve net zero carbon emissions by 2050, and an interim report on the economic consequences of said target was published by the Treasury in December 2020. The report accepted that there was no choice between the maintenance of economic growth and preventing serious climate change: rather, acceptable economic performance was conditional on global heating being arrested. The Treasury also significantly reduced official estimates of the associated costs, even if there was still an apparent reluctance to embrace the notion that decarbonization, if appropriately undertaken, could substantially boost growth for an extended period.

It is also notable that, in their regular assessments of UK supply-side policy, the IMF and the OECD, while applauding the actions mentioned above, continued to identify many all-too-familiar inadequacies and recommend many all-too-familiar responses. The implication was that the UK government's approach to the supply side of the economy was too timid. There remained a case for more and better-distributed public infrastructure; for more funding for ALMPs to promote upskilling and the reallocation of labour from non-tradable to tradable sectors; for more spending on R&D, especially in depressed regions; for more improvements in education and vocational training; for a more neutral tax system; for efforts to address excessive industrial concentration in certain key sectors; for the encouragement of more housing supply, especially social housing, through fewer planning restrictions and the more efficient use of publicly owned land; and for more governmental decentralization.[17]

At the same time, insufficient emphasis was placed on the black hole that was public sector productivity. While admittedly hard to measure, the level of public sector productivity was estimated to be just 3.7% higher in 2019 than it had been when Tony Blair became prime minister in 1997, which amounts to an average annual rate of increase of less than 0.25%.

Furthermore, policymakers seemed to put too much store both in the light-touch regulation of UK labour and product markets and in tax cuts for the corporate sector. As has been noted, the UK had been a modestly regulated economy in these respects for a generation by the mid 2010s. Corporation tax, meanwhile, was cut from 30% in 2007 to 20% in 2020 – well below the G-7 and OECD averages – and yet it appeared to have had little discernible impact on the pace of business investment spending or on overall economic performance.

As for the Industrial Strategy, Britain was a laggard in this area of policy relative to all other major economies. The period since the GFC had seen a flowering of interest in industrial strategy around the world, with important initiatives taken in countries as diverse as China, Germany, France and Japan. Furthermore, the May government's approach was insufficiently focused on the detailed structure of the UK corporate sector: that is, the preponderant role of services as opposed to manufacturing, the importance of fast-growing companies as opposed to SMEs, the relatively high failure rate of UK companies, and the relative lack of success of medium-sized enterprises. Nor did the Industrial Strategy become a central plank of economic policy, embedded at the heart of government with its own staff and funding. For all the hopes of Nick Timothy and others to establish alternative centres of economic policy to challenge the Treasury's dominance, the Industrial Strategy Council proved a rather tame and solely advisory body. It had few resources, and it was prevented from commenting on tax policy or making public policy recommendations to government.

In 2021 the Industrial Strategy was 'transitioned' into a 'Plan for Growth', thereby continuing the pattern of UK industrial policy being characterized by frequent policy changes and reversals and being driven by different political cycles – all while multiple, uncoordinated public bodies, departments and levels of government have been responsible for delivery.

Overall, UK supply-side policy still left much to be desired.

GETTING BREXIT DONE

The process of turning the decision to leave the EU into a practical reality proved tortuous in the extreme. From an economic damage-limitation point of view, as Philip Hammond and the Treasury made clear when they were given the opportunity to do so, it made sense to sustain as close a trading relationship with Europe as possible. However, the increasingly ascendant, ideologically driven Brexiteer majority within the Conservative Party and the cabinet progressively adopted an altogether different approach. Their focus was on what they considered to be a more comprehensive return of sovereignty, and fuller control over the nation's borders, money and trade, and they were willing to pay a high economic price to achieve that goal. Hopes of a soft Brexit – or, for that matter, a reconsideration of the entire decision to leave the EU – rapidly faded. It became a matter of how hard a variant of Brexit would ensue.

In the meantime, within a week of the referendum the EU-27 had established a number of fundamental negotiating principles, including the indivisibility of the bloc's 'four underlying freedoms': the free movement of goods, services, capital and people. Rather than the EU being weak or divided, vulnerable to UK pressure, fearful about the future or anxious to reach an early deal on whatever terms it could, from the outset it exhibited considerable discipline, unity and consistency of purpose.

With her political honeymoon period in full swing, Theresa May played to the (jingoistic media) gallery. She rapidly sloughed off any residual attachment to the Remain campaign and happily adopted confrontational rhetoric. 'Brexit means Brexit,' she proclaimed, to the delight of the Leavers in her party. Hardly Churchillian oratory, but the message was that there would be no halfway house. No backtracking.

A Department for Exiting the European Union was established, headed by the languid and one-dimensional – but always on-message – David Davis. He was to lead the negotiations with Brussels from a powerbase separate from the ideologically suspect Treasury and Foreign Office. May then delivered a speech at the October 2016 Conservative Party Conference that took a very hard line. She ruled out a European Economic Area-type trade arrangement, which would have left the UK in the single market and the customs union and under the jurisdiction of the European Court of Justice, and she proposed to trigger Article 50 of the Lisbon Treaty, setting in motion a two-year count-down to departure, by the end of the following March. In all this she was strongly influenced by Timothy and Hill and also mindful of the importance of immigration and the widespread desire for an end to the free movement of labour implicit in the Brexit vote. Indeed, it could be argued that May prior-itized ending free movement above all other associated objectives. She then followed this up by suggesting in another speech that the UK would change its economic model and become a low-tax 'Singapore of the West' off the coast of Europe if negotiations did not go its way. This threat was made despite the fact that Singapore was a tiny, near-one-party, city state, and that it was about as dissimilar an economy to the UK as it was possible to imagine.

This approach to Brexit was misguided and reckless. It unnecessarily narrowed Britain's negotiating options, repeated the long-standing tendency to overstate its bargaining power, and glossed over the inevitable painful economic and political trade-offs with which May's party and the elector-ate would be faced (including the vexed issue of Northern Ireland's border with the Republic of Ireland). At a stroke, May truncated the time available for three things: the establishment of a clear vision of exactly what the UK wanted to achieve (rather than what it did not want to be party to); the nec-essary negotiations on a huge range of trade, financial, legal and institutional arrangements; and, of course, the preparations on the part of the civil service and business that would be necessary to minimize disruption to the economy. Hammond, who was not consulted on any of this, was aghast.

May had repeatedly ruled out an early general election since becoming prime minister, but once Article 50 had been triggered she performed a remarkable volte-face on the advice of Timothy and Hill. In April 2017 she sought and secured the two-thirds House of Commons supermajority required to overturn the Fixed-Term Parliaments Act of 2011. She would go to the country after all – three years ahead of schedule – in an effort to strengthen her hand in the Brexit negotiations and afford her government greater room for domestic policy manoeuvre.

May's strategy backfired spectacularly, in the process revealing how capri-cious and divided the nation was. She also laid bare her questionable political judgement and the limited faith that her insular and robotic style of leader-ship was capable of inspiring. Despite facing a Labour Party that, under the leadership of Jeremy Corbyn, offered an unreconstructed socialist cocktail of high state spending and nationalization, the Conservatives lost their overall majority and became dependent on the politically blinkered Northern Irish Democratic Unionist Party to rule. Part of the explanation for the Tories' poor performance was no doubt the re-intensification of the squeeze on real incomes, but it also reflected a dreadful campaign waged by a maladroit prime minister who was frequently reduced to the staccato repetition of platitudinous stock phrases.

History suggested that May's minority government would struggle. The four such administrations seen during the twentieth century were all short-lived, and three of them had to battle major economic crises. May's was no exception to this rule.[18] With her position severely weakened, she had no choice but to sack her two key advisors, but this did nothing to alter the fact that both May and the country were now confronted by a period of precarious political purgatory. Her thankless task was to thread the needle of negotiating a reasonable EU withdrawal deal that she could get through parliament while the English nationalists on the right wing of her party pressed with almost Maoist fervour for an ever-tougher approach. Meanwhile, it did not help that the the Democratic Unionists retained an effective power of veto over proposed trade arrangements in Ireland. The only recent political epochs that come close to matching the recurring nightmare of the second half of May's rule were Callaghan's in the late 1970s and Brown's in the wake of the GFC.

What followed was more hollow posturing, followed by various compromises, fudges, the odd false dawn and some humiliating retreats. In mid 2018 May did, however, eventually succeed in negotiating a withdrawal agreement and a political declaration setting out a framework for future relations with the EU.

May's withdrawal agreement encompassed four key elements. First, it established a transition period that would last until the end of 2020, during which existing arrangements would remain. Moreover, it could be extended by mutual consent for up to two years, provided a decision was made by 1 July 2020. The hope was that both a comprehensive free trade agreement (FTA) and numerous other issues relating to future UK–EU cooperation could somehow be settled during the transition period. Second, the withdrawal agreement included a financial 'divorce settlement' (then estimated at £35–39 billion) that would cover the UK's outstanding obligations to the EU and vice versa (including during the transition period). Third, the withdrawal agreement sought to clarify the future rights of expatriate EU and UK citizens working in either jurisdiction. And finally, the withdrawal agreement included 'backstop' trading arrangements between Northern Ireland and the Irish Republic in the event that the talks on an FTA failed.

The backstop was designed to protect the Good Friday Agreement (which underpins Northern Ireland's peace process) by keeping an open frontier on the island of Ireland. As a result, the whole of the UK would remain in what amounted to a temporary customs union with the EU, at least until July 2020.

Tariff arrangements would remain unchanged, and Northern Ireland would also stay aligned with some EU rules, including aspects of the single market. Although a joint UK–EU committee and an arbitration panel would try to resolve any disputes, the European Court of Justice would also retain an oversight role in Northern Ireland, and to some extent in the rest of the UK as well. Nor could the UK unilaterally abandon the backstop until the risk of a hard border had evaporated.

The political declaration ran to a mere twenty-six pages, but *inter alia* it sought to establish in general terms how the UK and the EU would trade with each other once the UK had left the bloc. The document was not legally binding, but it defended the core principles that were dear to each side: the integrity of the single market and the customs union for the EU, and sovereignty for the UK. It also stated explicitly that future ties should be as close as possible.

When it was presented to the cabinet, however, the deal infuriated the Brexiteers and sparked the resignation of several ministers, including Johnson and Davis. The backstop provisions were seen as being particularly problematic. The Brexiteers' fear was that UK independence would be seriously compromised if customs union membership was indefinite, not least in the sense that it could prevent the UK from applying trade deals made with other countries. May's government had suffered the first of a series of damaging defections, and her ability to force her deal through had thereby become much harder.

In the meantime, government and Bank of England economists produced rough assessments of the effects of the agreement in November 2018 that suggested that May's deal would undoubtedly be better for the economy than crashing out of the EU without any agreement at all. They also concluded that Britain would ultimately be far better off staying in.[19]

The Bank concluded that a no-deal Brexit, and the blizzard of tariff and non-tariff barriers to trade and movement that went with it (not least across the service sector), could unleash a recession worse than that which had followed the GFC, with GDP potentially falling by around 10%.[20]

Government economists suggested that an outcome similar to the exit deal struck with the EU – one involving some new trade frictions at the border and sharp restrictions on immigration – would leave UK GDP some 4% lower than it would have otherwise been over fifteen years. On average, each member of the population would be some £1,100 worse off a year.

The Bank's assessment of May's deal was more circumspect, concluding that much depended on just how close to the EU the UK economy ultimately remained, but it warned that the 'harder' the eventual Brexit settlement, the greater the damage to the economy.

Just as with the Treasury analysis presented by George Osborne in 2016, the reaction in Brexiteer circles to these evaluations was as scathing and dismissive as it was delusional and self-deceptive. But the real problem with May's deal was that it satisfied no one: not the hard-line Brexiteers; not the pro-Remain Tory moderates; and not the newly empowered Democratic Unionists, who were against anything that set Northern Ireland apart from the rest of the UK. Even the opposition Labour Party rejected the political declaration on the grounds that it was too vague.

Unsurprisingly, therefore, May failed to get her exit agreement through parliament – despite having three attempts at doing so. Indeed, it was defeated by huge margins on each occasion. Brexit demanded a prime minister of vision, imagination, cunning and epic powers of persuasion. She possessed none of those attributes.

In the end May had little choice but to resign in July 2019, leaving the floor to Boris Johnson, the shambolic Old Etonian showman with an ethical deficit. Never a politician with an eye for detail, a long attention span or a close relationship with the truth, Johnson's strategy was to put the population out of its misery as soon as possible. He would talk tough, resort to deceit, sophistry and evasion, and do whatever was necessary to get Britain out, preferably with some sort of withdrawal deal, however tawdry, but without one if absolutely necessary. Thereafter, he would declare victory and move on. Meanwhile, UKIP, resurrected by Nigel Farage as the Brexit Party, cheered from the sidelines.

Facing bitterly divided and weak opponents, Johnson's high-risk strategy worked, at least in a narrow sense, even if he had to play fast and loose with the law and with parliamentary procedure in the process and, humiliatingly, ask the EU for a temporary extension of the UK's EU membership. The substance of the withdrawal deal Johnson negotiated with the EU was little different to that proposed by May, apart from his willingness to place Northern Ireland in a different position from the rest of the UK and a few tweaks to the political declaration designed to keep the more outspoken Brexiteers happy.

The whole of the UK would leave the EU customs union, thereby allowing the UK to strike trade deals with other countries in the future. Legally, there would be a customs border between Northern Ireland (which would stay in the UK) and the Republic of Ireland (which would stay in the EU), but in practice there would be no checks along that border. The necessary inspections would instead occur on what was effectively a customs border between Great Britain and the island of Ireland. The backstop was therefore, in essence, replaced by a 'full stop', whereby Northern Ireland would remain aligned to the EU from the end of the transition for at least four years from December 2020.

The revised political declaration restated that both sides would work towards an FTA. However, the references to a 'level playing field' – the degree to which the UK would agree to stick closely to EU regulations in the future

– were removed from the legally binding withdrawal agreement and put in the non-binding political declaration. Both sides would merely aim to retain the same high standards on state aid, competition, employment and social rights, the environment, climate change and 'relevant tax matters'.

As such, Johnson's deal did not really 'get Brexit done' at all. Brexit was always going to be an extended process rather than a single event. *Inter alia*, there was still a requirement to strike the FTA with the EU. And that meant there was still the risk of 'no deal' – or, as Johnson disingenuously put it, 'Australian-style trading arrangements'. Australia had no trade deal with the EU.

Nevertheless, when Johnson sought the backing of the British people for his deal in another snap election in December 2019, the public, exhausted by the previous three and a half years of political agony and scared off by Corbyn's ever-more-extravagant public spending pledges, gave Johnson the largest Tory majority since 1987. The most extraordinary aspect of Johnson's landslide victory was the way that so many Labour seats in the economically vulnerable old industrial heartlands of the Midlands and the North turned blue. It was the elderly – pro-Brexit – vote that was largely behind this trend, and it made Johnson the most powerful prime minister in the modern era.

With a comfortable majority, Johnson was easily able to push his narrowly framed exit deal though parliament. The UK would leave the EU at the end of January 2020, although it would remain in the single market and the customs union during an eleven-month transition period that saw the onset of the Covid pandemic.

In the end, after more complex and bitter negotiations, an FTA was forthcoming at the eleventh hour, on Christmas Eve 2020. Under the agreement, tariff- and quota-free trade between the UK and the EU would continue. But this too was a strikingly thin set of arrangements, and it said little or nothing about the service sector. There would be a swathe of new customs checks and formalities, technical regulatory barriers, complex rule-of-origin procedures and a mass of balls-aching documentation, all of which kicked in at the start of 2021. The contrast with the ease of trading within the single market would be stark.

COUNTING THE COST

In his 2019–20 new year address, the ever-bloviating Johnson proclaimed that the 2020s would see a repeat of the 'Roaring 20s' of the previous century. The irony was that this was a complete misrepresentation of that period in UK economic history. The Roaring 20s boom was a US phenomenon. In the UK, the 1920s was a dark valley of swingeing public expenditure cuts and a deep recession followed by a shallow recovery. It was a time of a chronically overvalued exchange rate, of price and wage deflation, of high unemployment, of exaggerated regional inequalities, and of unprecedented industrial unrest. The year 2020, meanwhile, was to see Britain's deepest recession on record.

As I write, the economic narrative of the last three years has undoubtedly been heavily influenced by an extraordinary epidemiological event and its aftermath, and by the onset of the first major war on continental European soil since 1945. It is hard to the point of impossibility to accurately abstract from these considerations. Nevertheless, there can be little doubt that Brexit – and, more specifically, the particular nature of the UK's exit deal – has played an important role in the economy's woeful performance, and that it stands to continue to do so.

Cumulative growth in real GDP per capita over the period 2015–22 was less than 5%, a figure far below the G-7 average and less than half that achieved by the US and the EU. The overall size of the economy has yet to return to its pre-pandemic peak, leaving the UK very much in the slow recovery lane, while the OBR, the Bank of England and the IMF all believe that a relapse into recession beckons, especially in the wake of the extraordinary recent fiscal policy debacle and subsequent U-turn perpetrated by Johnson's successor Liz Truss and her chancellor Kwasi Kwarteng.

International trade brings with it a plethora of positive influences, including enhanced competition, greater choice, the encouragement of economies of scale and specialization, and the diffusion of new technologies and business practices. However, it is not just that the UK's reliance on trade with the EU has declined since the exit from the single market and the customs union, it is that the UK economy has become much less trade dependent more generally. Trade with non-EU countries has declined as well, and the UK has missed out on much of the post-pandemic recovery in global commerce. According to the OBR, the trade intensity of GDP has fallen by almost 15% since 2019, which is more or less as it originally predicted. Smaller companies have struggled particularly badly, with their trading relationships with the EU dropping by about a third in the face of mounting red tape. For many of these firms it has no longer been worth the effort trying to sell overseas.[21] It is also worth noting that lower trade intensity tends to be associated with higher levels of inequality.

At the time of writing, the UK has signed continuity trade deals with more than sixty nations since the decision to exit the EU, and it has also agreed a selection of new trading arrangements. However, none of the new FTAs negotiated with countries outside the EU stand to have a significant effect on total trade or economic growth. For example, the much-vaunted agreement with Australia that was signed in December 2021 is estimated by the government to raise both UK exports and imports by some 0.4% of GDP over the next fifteen years, but the impact on the level of GDP is put at a trivial 0.1% – effectively a rounding error.[22]

Business investment and productivity have continued to flatline. Each exhibited considerable period-to-period volatility during and after the pandemic, but despite both the progressive decline in the standard rate of corporation tax and £25 billion of super deduction capital allowances over recent years,[23] real business investment remains some 6% below its level around the time of the Brexit referendum, and around 22.5% below its extrapolated pre-referendum trend.

The overall level of productivity has risen by less than 2% since 2019, and it is a mere 7% higher than it was when the GFC began in mid 2007. This is a far worse performance than that seen in other advanced countries, and the UK's productivity shortfall has widened again commensurately. The OBR continues to assume that the new trading relationship between the UK and the EU will reduce long-run productivity by 4% relative to remaining in the EU, and that around two-fifths of the 4% impact (i.e. 1.6 percentage points) had already occurred by the time the EU–UK Trade and Cooperation Agreement came into force as a result of uncertainty weighing on investment and capital deepening.

FDI is generally seen as a particularly fruitful source of technological advancement and best industrial practice, and until the Brexit vote the UK was one of the largest recipients of such inflows, with about 40% coming from other EU countries. The single market and the UK's flexible labour market made it an attractive destination for multinational companies. However, FDI has slumped since the Brexit referendum, from all major source markets and especially where supply chains are concerned. The year 2016 witnessed a record for FDI due to a few high-value mergers and acquisitions, but the number of inward FDI deals fell by more than 9% in 2017–18 and by another 16% in 2018–19. The number registered a small increase in 2019–20 but then fell again, by 17%, in 2020–21. The value of net FDI flows into the UK was £20 billion in 2021: the fifth successive year of decline since 2016.

During the pandemic Boris Johnson talked of building on the success of the UK's coronavirus vaccine programme (success that, it should be stressed, owed nothing to Britain's departure from the EU regulatory framework), such that Britain would transform itself into a global science superpower. But R&D investment has fallen by around a fifth since 2014; the UK share of global investment in R&D projects in health and life sciences has dropped from 4.2% in 2014 to 3.4% in 2019; and the UK ranks eleventh in the OECD universe for total R&D spending.[24]

So far, the government's new, tighter, post-Brexit migration regime has cut the net inward flow of workers to the UK from the EU from more than

180,000 a year to closer to 60,000, although there has been a compensatory increase in immigration from other areas. The evidence is that prior to Brexit, and contrary to the common view that immigration reduced the pay and job chances of those born in the UK, migration into the UK from the EU had a positive impact on overall employment, productivity and GDP. Many of the arrivals were highly skilled, and a significant proportion were overqualified for the jobs they took on. Furthermore, European migrants paid more in taxes than they received in benefits and contributed much more financially and through work than they consumed in public services.[25]

It appears, therefore, that there are major risks for the UK economy and for the country's public finances from reducing EU migration, with potentially marked effects on those industrial sectors and regions where EU migrants have congregated. Offsetting these impacts by retraining British-born workers is likely to take time – perhaps as long as a decade – while recruiting substitutes from non-EU jurisdictions will depend both on future trade deals and on the appetite of the domestic population for such inflows, which so far remains limited.

The financial sector, presented by many Brexiteers as a part of the economy with the potential to flourish in the post-Brexit world, has done nothing of the kind. The UK is no longer considered to have the world's most competitive financial sector.[26] Indeed, its ranking has fallen away sharply over recent years, and it now lags well behind the US. The size of the sector remains well below its 2009 peak, at some 8.3% of GDP.[27] Its growth rate slowed sharply after 2016, and it actually contracted for three successive years between 2018 and 2020. Financial service exports have flatlined since 2017, as has the trade surplus in financial services. At the same time, the BIS has reported that, while the UK remains the most important hub for currency and interest rate derivatives trading, its share of both markets has declined over recent years. London accounted for 38% of foreign exchange market turnover in early 2022, down five percentage points since 2019. Its share of over-the-counter derivatives trading fell from 51% to 46% over the same period.[28] Meanwhile, the market capitalization of the Paris stock exchange has caught up with that of London's.

And then there is the impact on young Britains entering the labour market. Since a UK passport is now of less use in the single market than a Bulgarian or Latvian document, it is harder for UK citizens to get taken on, trained or promoted by transnational firms, which generally treat the EU as a single commercial and human resources space. Over time this will limit the skillset of UK nationals.

A further important handicap of Brexit is a loss of policymaking insight. All EU policy areas – energy, consumer protection, research priorities, updated regulation for data or the tech sector, new qualifications, anti-dumping and so on – have EU working groups that allow the relevant officials in member states to exchange the intelligence, ideas and practical solutions that are being used within their countries. Moreover, there has been evidence that the European Commission has deliberately avoided informal policy discussions with UK officials because of the lack of trust that now exists.

Brexit also appears to have exacerbated the UK's recent inflation problem. The decision to leave the EU, together with the related advance of populist politics, has undermined trust in the government's ability to run a disciplined economic strategy; has added to selling pressure on the pound; and, as a result, has loosened the mooring of inflation expectations. At the same time, the reduction in the level and elasticity of labour supply in the context of the exclusion of European migrant workers has encouraged a growing mismatch between available workers and jobs while enhancing the bargaining power of domestic labour.

Finally, despite Johnson's public commitment to 'levelling up' those regions of Britain that had fallen behind, and the publication of a long-awaited White Paper on the issue, there was no evidence by the time he was chased from office in disgrace in the summer of 2022 that any progress had been made or that inequality had been lessened in any sense since the Brexit referendum.[29]

Brexit is already proving to be a devastating supply shock for the UK economy, and it is likely to continue to be one regardless of the fantasies spun by the Brexiteers. Moreover, Brexit has been interacting malignly with two other supply shocks: one related to the Covid pandemic and another with its origins in the war between Russia and Ukraine. In his desperation to 'get Brexit done', Johnson was reputed to have stated that he was happy to 'fuck business'. One way or another, he seems to have had his wish granted.[30]

The UK policy response to these circumstances has been inadequate on many levels. This was especially the case in late 2022 when Johnson's right-wing populist successor, Liz Truss, and her chancellor, Kwasi Kwarteng, effectively took leave of their senses when they sought to push through a range of iniquitous, unfunded and inflationary tax cuts at a time of acute market unease. But perhaps this should not come as a surprise. British economic policy has hardly covered itself in glory over the past half century. To have expected it to have responded to recent events in an optimal manner was always likely to prove wishful thinking.

Against this background, it is little wonder that at the time of writing the polls indicate a growing sense across the population that Brexit was a dreadful mistake.

CHAPTER 14

Decline and Fall

Nostalgia is a product of dissatisfaction and rage. It's a settling of grievances between the present and the past.

— Don DeLillo, 1985[1]

A RAKE'S PROGRESS

I appreciate that my portrayal of the British economy's performance over the course of the past fifty-odd years does not make for comforting reading. It is not an uplifting tale. Indeed, for much of the time it is a depressing catalogue of misapprehensions, missteps, underachievement, wasted opportunities, crises and humiliations. The British state rarely seemed to be able to exert the requisite degree of control over its own destiny, and it regularly found itself staring into the abyss. Many all-too-familiar problems arose time and again without ever being satisfactorily addressed. The gap between aspiration and reality, and between the past and the present, only widened.

The twenty-five years or so following World War II had seen consistent – albeit unspectacular and hardly trouble-free – economic improvement. The performance of the UK economy from the early 1970s onwards, however, was generally less impressive, and the period was punctuated by a series of more challenging setbacks and conundrums. This began with the stagflation that followed the first oil price shock and the bust that followed the 'Barber boom' and it ended with Brexit, the damaging economic fallout from which was exacerbated by the worst global pandemic in a century and by the eruption of a major war on the European continent.

Some of the problems the UK encountered reflected the unavoidable consequences of global events that were beyond the control of a medium-sized open economy and its policymaking community. But others had origins that were more firmly rooted in domestic considerations, and in particular policy errors on various levels. Even when the causes of these sporadic trials and tribulations were predominantly external, policy shortcomings had a habit of making things worse than they would otherwise have been. Meanwhile, the deliberate manipulation of the rate of growth of the economy and of the tax burden for political purposes, especially around general elections, remained a perennial source of instability, even in the face of institutional departures that were designed to constrain it.

Reflecting an ageing population structure and slower technological progress, among other considerations, the trend rate of growth slowed over the course of the period under scrutiny, as indeed it did across all the advanced economies. The steadily increasing prosperity of the 1950s and 1960s became an increasingly distant memory, ultimately to be replaced by an environment more akin to secular stagnation. The average annual rate of growth in UK productive potential progressively retreated to levels not seen consistently since the early nineteenth century and the initial stages of the Industrial Revolution. That is to say, perhaps as low as 1% per annum.

Perhaps more pertinently, the UK's slowdown proved somewhat greater than the advanced economy average, compounding the fact that the initial starting point had also been sub-par. The pace of expansion in the UK rarely impressed for extended periods, and when it did it typically succumbed to major imbalances and proved unsustainable, necessitating a bout of fundamental policy adjustment. The cycle of boom and bust was never broken. Productivity and business investment were perennial sources of disappointment and frustration. There was an enduring lack of innovative dynamism across vast swathes of the economy, not least in the SME sector. The quality of both management and labour was repeatedly found wanting.

The UK was a relatively equal society in the 1970s, with an extensive welfare state, albeit a costly and often inefficient one. However, the latter part of that decade saw both the onset of what was to prove a lasting, if erratic and uneven, effort to contain social security outlays and a dramatic increase in income and other inequalities that has never subsequently been unwound to any significant extent. These various inequalities, together with lingering pockets of poverty, some of it abject by advanced-economy standards, increased perceptions of unfairness and insecurity, frustrated people's ambitions and, over time, bred social and political fragmentation, polarization and general disquiet – a cocktail that ultimately found a voice in populism.

The housing market experienced a succession of booms and busts that correlated with the business cycle, but the trend in real house prices remained a distinctly positive one and was an important contributor to the catalogue of inequalities observable after the 1970s. Homeowners have emerged from the last fifty years relatively unscathed.

The stock market also traced a familiar pattern of bull and bear phases, but average annual stock returns in the UK fell short of those of most of the nation's rivals. Long-term government bond yields followed the global trend downwards from the early 1980s, but until the granting of operational independence to the Bank of England in 1997 they were, for the most part, higher and more volatile than in the other major economies.

Inflation, particularly wage inflation, was initially deeply embedded into the structure of an economy characterized by a powerful and often-militant trade union movement, and by employers that were weak in a collective sense. It proved hard to tame, but labour and product market reform along with the decline of a number of hitherto-dominant industries helped to bring it to heel. It was ultimately only beaten into submission, though, by the sky-high real interest rates and the deep recession that followed sterling's ill-timed and ill-conceived entry into the ERM in October 1990. Thereafter, inflation targeting and formal Bank of England operational independence, together with the powerful disinflationary impetus of globalization and new technologies, kept it at bay.

Indeed, the opposite problem increasingly reared its head. From the late 1990s until the malign interaction of the three destabilizing supply shocks in the early 2020s, it became more difficult to sustain the rate of change in prices at the Bank of England's mandated target without progressively lower official interest rates and the regular employment of monetary policy unorthodoxies – most notably repeated doses of QE.

That said, in an environment of largely free international capital movements, to a significant degree the Bank was merely reacting to the broader forces acting on interest rates of ex ante global savings and investment flows. The MPC's ability to drive interest rates away from the borrowing costs dictated by these overarching influences was limited.

The government's consolidated budget was rarely in surplus, and when it was it never stayed there for long. Britain's default position was to run a significant deficit, which peaked at more than 10% of GDP in the wake of the GFC and at an even higher level during the Covid pandemic. The share of national income taken up by government spending oscillated between the high 30s and high 40s in percentage terms. It ended the 2010s around the same 40%-or-thereabouts level observable in the early 1970s.

The burden of government debt, meanwhile, ebbed and flowed. It at first declined, in large part because of persistently high inflation and because of the repression of investor choice that resulted from government regulation and an increasingly antiquated and uncompetitive financial sector. Notwithstanding intermittent budgetary emergencies, there then followed a period of reasonable stability in the 1980s and 1990s, before a further leg down in the early years of the twenty-first century (aided by the longest episode of continuous growth during the period under observation) and by historically low borrowing costs. However, in the wake of the GFC and its policy exigencies, it again rose sharply. Despite an extended bout of fiscal austerity after 2010, the burden of government debt was significantly higher at the end of this period than it was at the beginning, and it was well in excess of the EU average.

This rapid accumulation of government liabilities was allowed to happen despite the fact that the future pressures on the public finances from demographic change in areas such as pensions, health and social care had become much greater, and in spite of the fact that there was a growing need to prepare the ground to combat such challenges, along with the existential threat of climate change.

Because of the long-standing shortfall in public investment, the end of the period under study saw the fabric of the UK's economic and social infrastructure stretched dangerously thin. After the extended austerity of the 2010s, transport links and power generation resources were increasingly overloaded. Furthermore, many public services entered the pandemic struggling to cope with the demands on them, with extended waiting lists, reduced access, staff shortages, missed targets for reform, and other stark indicators of diminished standards.

The NHS was under particular duress. The National Audit Office concluded in 2020 that vast swathes of its estate failed to meet the demands of a modern health service, and that the whole had come to represent considerably less than the sum of its parts. Not only was it inefficiently managed, poorly incentivized, and lacking in both modern equipment and adequately trained employees, but some 14% of its physical bricks and mortar predated its establishment in 1948, while outstanding maintenance requirements continued to balloon, threatening catastrophic failure. Needless to say, the situation has only deteriorated over the past few years.

Competitiveness proved to be an enduring concern, as indeed was an external balance prone to often-egregious deficit. As Bank of England governor Mark Carney succinctly put it, Britain remained reliant throughout on 'the kindness of strangers' to finance its recurring current account shortfall.[2] Nor was such generosity always easily forthcoming. Domestic policy regularly had to be reorientated to garner the necessary international confidence.

Britain's once proud and dominant manufacturing sector, meanwhile, was permitted, and at times even encouraged, to wither away. Many of its traditional heartlands were thereby consigned to economic and social decay and to deprivation. Britain's share of global output and trade continued the retreat that had been in evidence since the late nineteenth century. Rather than being invested for the future, much of the bonanza of North Sea oil was squandered on tax cuts for the wealthy for ideological reasons and political expediency, fuelling an unsustainable consumer boom in the 1980s. Sterling lost its residual reserve currency status after the IMF crisis of 1976. The importance of UK financial assets to global investment funds diminished. The nation's political influence and diplomatic clout went the same way.

The economy enjoyed a modest but patchy renaissance between the mid 1980s and mid 2000s, encouraged by supply-side reforms and improvements in the institutional architecture of policy, and latterly supported in no small part by sympathetic external circumstances – including, importantly, membership of the European single market. But Britain's long-standing relative decline accelerated alarmingly once again towards the end of the period.

The GFC cast an enduring shadow over the economy's productivity and supply-side performance. Against this backdrop, average real household disposable income was no higher at the end of 2019 than it had been in the run-up to the crisis. This represents the longest, and most acute, squeeze on living standards for 300 years.

The decision to leave the EU, and the manner in which that decision was implemented, delivered a further significant shock to productive potential. The shock was subsequently exacerbated by the Covid pandemic and by the war in Ukraine, and these events are yet to fully play out. And with the rise of populism, a series of maladroit – some would say incompetent – leaders was elected, some of whom had a questionable attachment (to say the least) to the maintenance of sound institutions or even to the truth. This was only to add to the difficulties of achieving anything akin to an optimal mix of economic policies.

THE CAPRICIOUSNESS OF POLICY

Throughout the epoch under examination there was a restlessness and an impulsiveness about both UK economic policy and the debate that surrounded it. The iterations and recalibrations were countless, as indeed were the inconsistencies. This was driven partly by the nature of specific events, and in particular by how various crises had a habit of sweeping away previous convictions. And the effect was compounded by the inevitable strategic adjustments that follow transfers of power from the left to the right, and vice versa. It also reflected the evolution of economic theory, with two of the more obvious examples being the collapse of the post-war Keynesian consensus, which had for a generation after World War II become particularly hard-wired into UK political consciousness; and the exposure of the shortcomings of naive monetarism in the early 1980s.

Despite the shift away from traditional Keynesianism after the 1970s, too much emphasis continued to be placed on short-term demand management of the economy relative to efforts to enhance supply-side performance. This no doubt reflected the five-year electoral cycle and the fact that supply-side policies have a long gestation period. Reflation, even when not explicitly presented as such, will invariably deliver some improvement in growth, incomes and employment in short order, together with a degree of additional electoral popularity, even if it proves to be fleeting. But in contrast, the costs of structural reform immediately fall on often-powerful vested interests, while the benefits are more thinly spread and accrue over a timespan in excess of a single parliament. Much the same can be said of efforts to address climate change. However powerful the underlying logic for a significant reorientation of approach, there are always sound political reasons to soft-pedal in the present.

The Thatcher era was something of an exception to the rule on supply-side policy, but even then her governments' record on structural reform was inconsistent. There were numerous important gaps and oversights. Indeed, it is remarkable how constant the criticisms of UK supply-side policy have been over the past five decades. Low investment, inferior education and training, outdated and overburdened infrastructure, insufficient finance for smaller and rapidly growing companies, inadequate research and development spending, and the over-centralization of government have all been repeatedly identified as shortcomings.

Furthermore, Thatcher and her government seriously underestimated the social consequences of their reforms, which were intricately bound up with the sharp rise in inequalities in the 1980s. She and her second chancellor, Nigel Lawson, also failed to grasp how structural policy can interact with macro policy to supercharge a cyclical upswing to the extent that it runs out of control.

CAPTIVE TO THE PAST

Whatever the influence of external events, of the political pendulum or of the progress of economic theory, the large number of UK policy regimes, and their often-ephemeral nature, cannot be fully explained without reference to the economy's enduring underlying malaise. This has inspired an often-desperate search for a panacea that could arrest the nation's relative decline and return it to its supposed former glories. All economies and, for that matter, all economic policymakers are to a significant extent prisoners of their own history. But this seems to apply more to the UK than is customarily the case.

This nostalgia for the glory days of the past – notwithstanding the fact that they were increasingly distant and that they went hand in hand with colonial exploitation – became tyrannical in its influence. It infected programmes with wishful thinking, and on occasion it inspired what can only be described as panic. This bred inadequately thought through initiatives that were blindly borrowed from other structurally dissimilar economies, that flew in the face of painful experience, or that were drawn from the theoretical (and therefore divisive) extremes. Britain lost an empire, and time and again it failed to find an enduringly workable economic policy framework.

It is ironic that what is arguably the most successful UK macro policy regime of this period (albeit one that is far from perfect) – that of inflation targeting by an independent central bank – came about in the wake of sterling's ERM exit largely because it was more or less the only viable alternative left to which the government of the day could turn.

THE BLAME GAME

All this makes one wonder how responsibility for the impermanence, the contradictions and the overall shortcomings of UK economic strategy should be apportioned between politicians and civil servants at the Treasury, at the Bank of England and in other government departments.

In any democracy, the buck must stop with the politicians, and especially with those at the top of the pyramid of power. However complex and challenging the trade-offs they are confronted with, they are the ultimate directors and arbiters of policy, and they must stand accountable to the electorate for its success or failure. And the fact is that many senior British politicians during the period under review were often tone deaf to advice, unduly headstrong, ideologically myopic or fixated on the exploitation of short-term political gain to the extent that they ignored the longer-term costs of their actions.

All that said, officials cannot escape censure. Their job is to develop ideas that work and to save governments from themselves. They could have shouted louder during the period covered by this book, and they could have constructed their arguments more persuasively to deter ministers from questionable courses of action. They too were guilty of expressing opinions that suited their own preconceptions and biases. They too fell foul of groupthink. And they also, just like their political masters, sank into the trap of impulsively searching for a magic economic bullet. The unsatisfactory record of the past fifty years is there for all to see, and officialdom must assume a certain level of culpability for it. Furthermore, given that even after the granting of operational independence to the Bank of England and the ructions of Brexit, the Treasury was, and remains, the most powerful department of state, it should shoulder the lion's share of the responsibility for the UK's economic failings at the official level.

That said, however, over the course of the half century or so under scrutiny, the UK civil service produced some extraordinarily dedicated and talented individuals. People who frequently managed to knock the rougher edges off proposed policies and prevented yet more egregious errors. Furthermore, on occasion – not least during and in the aftermath of certain crises – the civil service exhibited remarkable fertility of imagination and performed nothing short of miracles. Its accomplishments during the GFC and in the aftermath of Brexit, for example, were extraordinary, as indeed they were in many respects during the Covid pandemic, which fell largely beyond the remit of this book.

A RUNNING SORE

Europe stands out as a destabilizing theme throughout the period under review, but especially from the time of Britain's entry into the ERM. Thereafter, the subject left the Conservative Party increasingly riven and became a ticking time bomb, not just for the Tories but for the economy and the country as a whole. No Conservative leader succeeded in bringing the issue under control. Major's premiership was consumed by it, and, in seeking to reach an enduring settlement on the matter, Cameron, May and Johnson seemed to opt for the wrong option at almost every turn and in so doing they ended up presiding over perhaps the greatest post-war policy error of all: Brexit. This catastrophic episode, and the manner in which it was handled, was to all intents and purposes tantamount to a collective loss of sanity.

The progressive triumph of Euroscepticism is clearly another topic where the present was consistently coloured by the past – or, more accurately, by what might be described as rose-tinted hindsight.

The history of Britain's relations with its European neighbours in the twentieth century was indelibly coloured by the experience of two world wars. This experience fostered an undercurrent of arrogance and superiority, while at the same time encouraging a quite different attitude towards European integration than was seen within its continental neighbours. In the UK, from the outset, the association with Europe was somewhat reluctant and was viewed as overwhelmingly commercial and transactional, rather than being considered as more salvational and constitutional, as was the case elsewhere.

At the same time, decades after the UK's accession to the EEC, and then the EU, there remained a hankering across much of society for the distant days when the country had no need to seek collective European security, either economic or political, and was free from the interventions in its affairs of politicians and bureaucrats from beyond the country's shores. There was therefore always a risk that, sparked by a particular set of challenging circumstances, an emotional spasm grounded in these prejudices would result in a schism. This is what happened in the 2010s.

As the economy foundered during the GFC and after it, a plethora of iniquities and disparities festered, hopes and ambitions increasingly went unmet, cultural divisions within society percolated to the surface and widened, and there was an inevitable search for a scapegoat to shoulder the blame. Moreover, such sentiments became bound up with elements of free market ideology and populism. This proved a lethal cocktail. Economic populism exhibits all the shortcomings that it attributes to orthodox thinking: it is narrow and inflexible, and unable to adapt as facts change; and it is blind to the trade-offs and unforeseen consequences of policy action. Hence, as the Brexit debate heated up, the knowledge and experience of experts was scorned, and even the most objective analysis of the economic pros and cons of EU membership was dismissed as propaganda. The glaring logical inconsistency between Britain's domestically perceived exceptionalism and its widely touted victimhood at the hands of its nearest neighbours was overlooked. In the meantime, the positive case for Europe was never sufficiently powerfully articulated.

The net result was an extraordinary aberration: one of the more remarkable acts of economic and political self-harm by any country in the modern era. The hardline realization of Brexit amounted in effect to a medium-sized economy with enduring productivity and competitiveness problems, onerous levels of debt across both the private and public sectors, and a highly suspect policy reputation turning inwards and waging an extended trade war against itself. Elsewhere in Europe, the UK's experience has proved to be one of the best advertisements for EU membership.

THE PASSABLE, THE BAD AND THE UGLY

The economic track record of individual governments over the course of the past fifty years varies enormously, and each government was often inconsistent even during their period in office, with a tendency for policy to be most impressive in the wake of crises before subsequently going off the rails. In this sense, there was a Mynskian tendency for stability to breed instability, or for good policy to inevitably descend into bad.

Some prime ministers exerted a more profound influence on economic strategy than others. Heath, Thatcher, Major (at least initially) and Brown immediately spring to mind as leaders who, for extended periods, dominated economic decision-making. Others were more content to leave things to their chancellor for the most part, and to perhaps intervene only to pursue a particular, favoured policy or to deal with a crisis. Wilson, Callaghan, Blair, Cameron, May and Johnson seem to fall more into this latter category.

There are inevitably elements of hindsight and subjectivity when one seeks to rank the performances of various political administrations. Gordon Brown's stewardship of the economy around the depths of the GFC was in many respects admirable, even if it proved to be a lost cause politically. But perhaps the best extended records of economic management, or at least the best economic outcomes, came under the Major government in the wake of the ERM crisis and during Tony Blair's decade in office, and especially during his first two terms. There was a sense during the period from the mid 1990s to the mid 2000s that Britain was on the right track, even if this was in significant part down to sympathetic external circumstances. The record of the three Thatcher administrations, although often held up by her disciples as transformative, was in fact more mixed, in terms of both its immediate achievements and its longer-term legacy.

Heath: Tragedy and Farce

The Heath administration's record was in overall terms disastrous, and it cast a long and unfortunate inflationary shadow over the economy for the next two decades. Heath was panicked by rising unemployment into an extraordinary juxtaposition of hopelessly inconsistent and unsustainable policies. While it must be noted that his government was confronted by unfamiliar and difficult external circumstances, especially in 1973, Heath and his chancellor fundamentally misunderstood how the economy worked. They were beset by Keynesian wishful thinking and by overreach that went beyond anything that Keynes himself is likely to have endorsed.

His administration ultimately descended into a combination of monetary and fiscal debauchery and industrial relations purgatory. Heath's only saving grace was to deliver UK entry into the EEC – an achievement that in due course provided considerable, if underreported, economic benefits, albeit with political consequences that became increasingly toxic for his own party.

Wilson and Callaghan: The End of an Era

The Wilson/Callaghan Labour administrations were confronted with the thankless task of cleaning up the mess handed down to them by Heath. Their parliamentary weakness, the difficult international environment, the militancy of a strong trade union movement, the ideological divisions within the Labour Party, and the continued failure to grasp the inappropriateness of many aspects of Keynesian policymaking made this impossible. In particular, there remained undue emphasis on the fiscal fine-tuning of aggregate demand at the expense of adequate monetary control, together with unsustainable efforts to control wages and prices directly. Such attention that was paid to the underperforming supply side of the economy was dominated by regional and social interventions that in some respects made things worse.

The IMF crisis of 1976 proved to be an enduring humiliation that marked an inflection point in the nation's post-war economic and political history. Despite the serendipitous arrival of North Sea oil, Britain could no longer claim to be a major power, and economic policymaking could not go on as before. The 1978–79 Winter of Discontent simply served to underline all this further.

That said, one cannot but wonder how different history might have been had Callaghan listened to the advice of many around him and gone to the country and won an election in late 1978. Could a weaker, reconstructed form of 1970s corporatism possibly have endured? Would a radical change in direction merely have been delayed? Might Margaret Thatcher have ended up being a political footnote akin to the failed Tory party leaders of the late 1990s and early 2000s?

Thatcher: A Discordant False Dawn

Margaret Thatcher's decade in power initially saw a very different approach to economic policymaking – one that was grounded in the monetarist–new classical counter-revolution in economic theory and that reflected the searing experiences of 1970s stagflation and industrial unrest. The case for major changes in strategy at the time was undoubtedly strong, but Thatcher and her governments repeatedly fell into the trap of believing that there were simple solutions for complex problems. They also underestimated the painful trade-offs involved in their initiatives. There were therefore repeated retreats from ideological purity, and over time there was reversion to a more pragmatic approach that necessarily embodied elements of previous regimes, even if the rhetoric remained more dogmatically free market in tone.

In the end, she and her colleagues were undone by their hubris, and the all-too-familiar failing of losing control of the business cycle. The long-standing sequence of stop and go continued, as indeed did the manipulation of the economy around general elections. Nor were things helped by Thatcher's keenness to always bring official interest rates down to help homeowners.

Thatcher's most solid accomplishments were therefore less in the realm of macro policy – which was repeatedly inconsistent, confusing and flawed – and more on the supply side of the economy. But even there, the helpful role of EEC membership should not be underestimated. Nor should the unprecedented increase in various inequalities over which she presided be forgotten, the poisonous effects of which continue to ramify to this day – and let us not ignore the excesses that her commitment to financial deregulation were ultimately to unleash either.

Major: Accidental Success

John Major's period as prime minister will forever be associated with sterling's chastening ejection from the ERM in 1992, which was another important milestone on the road to relative decline, not least in the manner in which it encouraged the UK's march away from Europe. That said, Major's government did finally manage to flush inflation out of the system, even if it came at the cost of eye-wateringly tight monetary policy and another catastrophic downturn.

Moreover, the years after the ERM debacle witnessed an extended cyclical upswing and a period of relative economic calm. This owed much to the delayed effects of Thatcher's supply-side agenda; a benign international environment, which included both the development of the European single market and the rise of globalization; a successful inflation-targeting regime, established by Norman Lamont after September 1992; and the willingness of his second chancellor, Kenneth Clarke, to eschew, in large part, the crass manipulation of the business cycle.

Unfortunately for Major and the Tories, four years of sound economic management was not enough to make up for the earlier disasters, for the widening divisions over Europe and for the myriad other political failings.

Blair: Stability Has Many Elements

Tony Blair and his all-powerful chancellor, Gordon Brown, were also the lucky beneficiaries of the continued effects of Thatcher's supply-side reforms, while the second Major administration's failed efforts to turn sound economics into political success provided a Labour government with a rare constructive inheritance. Furthermore, like their immediate predecessor, they too profited from the benevolent influence of various international developments.

Brown initially went out of his way to apply the latest theoretical thinking and to slough off the reputational baggage of the Labour Party's past failures as he looked to develop policy credibility in the eyes of the markets. Not only did he buttress inflation targeting with the widely applauded granting of operational independence to the Bank of England, but he also instituted a set of coherent rules within which fiscal policy could sustainably operate.

Both the government and the country dodged a bullet when Brown vetoed euro entry in 2002, but over time, and in an all-too-familiar pattern, the chancellor got carried away with his own propaganda as the good times rolled. Cyclical strength was confused with structural improvement; the fiscal rules were massaged; there was too much fine-tuning of tax policy; and various destabilizing imbalances were allowed to burgeon, particularly in the lightly regulated financial sector.

By the time Blair finally handed on the prime ministerial baton to Brown in 2007, the economy was in mounting disequilibrium and was acutely vulnerable to shocks. And, unfortunately, it was about to be struck by one of the biggest shocks of the post-war period: the GFC.

Brown: A Flawed Saviour Discarded

Gordon Brown's premiership was dominated by the GFC. After a maladroit beginning, Brown and his chancellor, Alistair Darling, ably supported by the Bank of England, did a laudable job, often having to improvise in ferociously difficult circumstances. In a number of ways – including bank recapitalization, international policy coordination, fiscal expansion and unconventional monetary policy – the UK helped to set the strategic agenda, playing an important role in reversing a pernicious global negative feedback loop and, in due course, encouraging recovery. Without the interventions instituted by Brown and his government, things would have probably been a good deal worse – not just at home, but more broadly too.

In the end, however, the huge collateral damage done to the economy by the crisis, together with Brown's broader prime ministerial shortcomings, meant that New Labour's previous achievements counted for little in the electorate's eyes. Its extended period in office drew to a close in 2010.

The crisis left behind a painful legacy of inflated public sector debt, uncomfortably low inflation and moribund productivity, all of which exerted a profound influence on the policy debate over the next decade.

Cameron: Reaping the Whirlwind of Austerity

Like Tony Blair, David Cameron largely left the running of the economy to his chancellor – George Osborne in this case. Indeed, on the one occasion that he overruled Osborne on a major policy issue – the Brexit referendum – it ended in unmitigated disaster both personally and for the nation as a whole. Cameron is likely to always be remembered for that one fateful decision above all else.

For his part, Osborne allowed ideology, and in particular anti-Keynesianism, to unduly colour his macro strategy, with the result that the post-GFC policy mix lacked balance, with undue onus being placed on unconventional monetary policy for stabilization. His unnecessarily aggressive fiscal squeeze slowed the recovery, weighed on private investment and growth potential, further entrenched various inequalities, and encouraged resentments that found their voice in the Brexit vote. He also presided over a tactless politicization of the Treasury that was to weaken its influence for the next five years.

On the other hand, under Osborne's watch the OBR was established as a much-needed independent fiscal policy watchdog, infrastructure planning improved (even if spending remained inadequate), and financial regulation was tightened up, with macroprudential policy acquiring a coherent form for the first time.

May: Wrong Place, Wrong Time, Wrong Path

Theresa May's period in office was consumed by the fallout from the electorate's determination to extricate the UK from the EU, in the process rejecting forty-odd years of constructive competition and economic integration. If ever a Conservative leader was handed a poison chalice upon taking the reins, May was the recipient of it – but she also proved to be astonishingly ill-equipped to cope with the situation, repeatedly making poor choices and ultimately being forced out of office by the right wing of her own party.

Her chancellor, Phillip Hammond, established fiscal policy on a less austere footing than his predecessor, but with the Treasury under a post-referendum cloud he could do little to influence the drift towards a hard form of Brexit, with all its immediate disruptions and longer-term damage to the economy.

Johnson: Populism Prevails – with the Customary Results

With the elevation of Boris Johnson to Number 10 Downing Street, the overwhelming policy priority became exiting the EU at almost any cost. This was duly delivered, and a subsequent general election was comfortably won, but the ultimate withdrawal deal was a wretched one. The harm done to the UK economy and to the country's wider reputation continues to metastasize, not least as the Brexit supply shock has been amplified by the structural changes wrought by the Covid pandemic and by the subsequent war in Ukraine.

Beyond the issue of Brexit, economic policy took on a distinctly populist tone, with all the customary blather, short-sightedness and deficiencies that go with such an approach. The long-standing relative decline in the UK economy that had been held in abeyance from the mid 1980s until the GFC therefore accelerated once again, and in the minds of many commentators was viewed as terminal.

THE MORALS OF THE STORY

There are many lessons to be drawn from this sobering historical narrative, but perhaps the ten most pertinent can be summarized as follows.[*]

Uncertainty Is Different to Risk

Just as Keynes described in chapter 12 of *The General Theory*, unquantifiable uncertainty – as opposed to measurable risk – is a fact of life. And

---

[*] It is worth mentioning that I believe that most, or perhaps all, of my ten lessons would apply to any economy, not just to that of the UK.

beyond a certain point, uncertainty can dominate all other considerations in decision-making. By clouding the future, and damping animal spirits, it can constrain spending and profoundly undermine aggregate demand.

As a consequence, economies do not necessarily rapidly self-regulate, smoothly returning to equilibrium if disturbed by some shock or other. Instead they can become divorced from any notion of full resource utilization for a protracted period. It is therefore imperative that policymakers seek to nurture confidence rather than neuter it. Political and economic stability are far more important to investment than any short-term programme of tax cuts.

Stability Has a Tendency to Encourage Instability

Unfortunately, however, to the extent that they can be realized, periods of macroeconomic and financial tranquillity tend to embody the seeds of their own destruction, in that they encourage complacency and risk taking, both in the private sector (especially in finance) and among the policymaking community.

What is more, the downturns that follow large financial crises are typically the most intractable and those that cast the longest shadow over productive potential.

There is an Overwhelmingly Compelling Case for Macroeconomic Policy Activism

The business cycle, such as it is, should not be left to its own devices. Doing so can, *in extremis*, prove disastrous for social and political instability. While the fine-tuning of aggregate demand should be largely eschewed, the progress of total expenditure should be actively managed and sustained in a transparent, consistent and accountable manner, within appropriate institutional guardrails.

While it is undoubtedly a powerful impetus for innovation and enterprise, the danger inherent in putting too much store in the free play of market forces and 'creative destruction' is that it delivers a low ratio of creation to destruction.

It Is Important for Economic Policies to Be Balanced

Monetary policy is not the answer to every question. It is no cure-all, even when it is pursued by a group of the most competent, politically independent technocrats operating within the most appropriate of institutional frameworks. It is not always as potent as policymakers would wish it to be. It generates costs as well as benefits, and it can become overloaded. It works less well around the zero interest rate bound, when it enters less conventional territory, when there is major private sector balance sheet adjustment, and when uncertainty about the future is elevated.

Policy activism should therefore extend to fiscal, macroprudential and broader regulatory departures. Moreover, the various levers of policy, and in particular fiscal and macroprudential tools, should be aimed in part at macro imbalances, such as debt accumulation and asset prices. Even if they build slowly, they are wont to unwind in a sudden and disorderly fashion.

Fiscal Policy Requires Independent Oversight and Should Start with the Automatic Stabilizers

It is important that the condition of the public finances is transparently and objectively assessed by an independent entity to constrain political manipulation and so that longer-term pressures that accrue from considerations such as demographic trends are considered.

The automatic stabilizers should play a central role in the management of normal, relatively mild business cycles, and where they are not already sizeable and designed to act on aggregate demand in short order they should be expanded and made timelier and more efficient.

Discretionary fiscal stimulus is more suited to deep and extended downturns such as those that follow large financial shocks, although better preparations could be made to improve the timeliness and suitability of such interventions for combating less egregious downturns. Discretionary fiscal interventions also work better when they are internationally coordinated and around the zero interest rate bound, where the financial constraints on their employment significantly abate.

Beware Concerted Fiscal Consolidation

Just as discretionary fiscal stimulus is enhanced by international coordination, the effects of fiscal restraint are magnified when others are pursuing the same strategy or, for that matter, when the private sector is aggressively deleveraging.

'Expansionary fiscal contractions', meanwhile, are rare beasts. They occur only in very specific circumstances, and in particular when confidence has been lost in the public finances and debt service costs have exploded higher.

Fiscal Austerity Has Its Limits

Sovereign debt crises are usually the result of private sector credit booms turning to bust. Beyond one or two countries, the GFC had relatively little to do with public sector profligacy per se, even if historically high government debt burdens complicated the fiscal policy response to it.

More than anything else, reducing the burden of public debt significantly requires sustained economic growth, and a consistently positive, if moderate, inflation rate. High public debt levels are unlikely to be addressed by fiscal austerity alone. Indeed, the danger is that excessive fiscal restraint feeds back negatively on growth and inflation, rendering the public debt position more intractable.

The Pursuit of Structural Reform
Should Be an Open-Ended Process

Demand management is not enough. It can only achieve so much, however well it is designed and executed. To maximize economic performance and welfare over the longer term it is necessary to pursue structural policies that encourage the flow of resources from declining and less productive activities into growing and more productive activities, and which leave an economy and its population better equipped to absorb shocks. That is to say, initiatives that increase the nation's capacity to adapt to change. Never has this been more important than in the context of global warming.

This means that we should look to adopt strategies that foster competition in product and labour markets; improve education and training; encourage research and development; expand infrastructure networks, especially beyond London and the South East; promote trade; and inspire inward FDI.

While seeking to restrain the size of the public sector and lowering the overall tax burden might play a positive role in all this, it is far from clear that either measure is, in and of itself, a panacea. Furthermore, it is doubtful that either will prove possible at a time when then the population is ageing, when climate change needs to be addressed, when inequality is such a burning issue, and when the social services are so substandard. It is much more likely that upward pressure on public spending and on the overall level of taxation will prove irresitible for political and other reasons. The challenge for future governments will be to ensure that it is not excessive and that it happens in a coherent and efficient manner.

In the meantime, arguably more could be achieved in terms of the structural enhancement of the UK economy by simply rejoining the EU customs union and single market, if not the EU itself, than could be gained from any round of tax cuts or shrinkage of the government sector.

Fight the Current Battle and Prepare for the Next

Too often, policymakers continue to fight the last battle long after it has been won or lost, and when some new challenge is emerging. And the next crisis is usually different to the last.

It is therefore important that minds are kept open, that dogma and ideology are restrained, and that the universe of advice available to policymakers is a broad one.

Policy Change Has to Be Sustained

Major shifts in underlying economic performance over short periods are rare. Influences come and go, but economies are typically largely prisoners of long-term considerations such as demography and the pace of technological progress, and often of their own history, institutions, culture and politics. And this means that various kinds of inequality must be kept within limits. There has to be a reasonable sense across the population that economic policy is fair.

To exert an enduring, transformational impact, policy changes must be substantive, coordinated and persistent in nature. But they also have to be socially acceptable.

*

Can we expect UK policymakers to follow this template in future? Judging from the way events have played out during the time I have been writing this book, that is certainly very much open to question. The Truss/Kwarteng episode of ideologically driven and wholly unsustainable initiatives represented a truly scary interlude for those of us who believe in evidence-based policy. It amounted to nothing short of the economics of the madhouse. It is to be hoped that it was an aberration and that lessons have been learned. Yet, given the divisions in UK society and politics there remains a risk that economic policy again mutates away from the principles laid out above rather than gravitates towards them. Rather than pedestrian competence, we are therefore saddled with more populism, short-termism and incompetence.

The suggestion is, therefore, that Britain's relative decline is only likely to continue. It is just a matter of how far and how fast it progresses, and of how soon Britain drops out of the top league of economies – following in the unfortunate footsteps of Argentina. Indeed, such is the current conjuncture that it would be an accomplishment to merely arrest the pace of decline. To repeat the limited revitalization achieved in the later 1990s and early 2000s would be a major success.

That said, things can and do change, of course. The unexpected can and does happen. Perhaps the reacceleration of decline will convince the nation of the need to look forwards, not back, in due course, and will prove a catalyst for a sustained and fundamental shift towards the sort of broad and mutually reinforcing range of policy initiatives required. Perhaps the international environment, which looks so challenging at present, will be transformed for the better. Maybe that will encourage the process of positive change. Perhaps technology will ride to the rescue. Indeed, it is easy to argue that it must if the existential threat of global warming and climate change is to be successfully confronted. Perhaps the advent of a coalition government will usher in proportional representation and yield a more consensus-orientated approach and greater policy consistency.

Micawberism, however, is hardly a proven strategy.

Main Sources and Further Reading

The underlying narrative of this book was developed in particular from the following sources.

Barrell, R., Kirby, S., Metz, R., and Weale, M. 2005. The Labour government's economic record and economic prospects. *National Institute Economic Review*, No. 192 (April).

Benn, T. 1989. *Against the Tide: Diaries 1973–76*. Hutchinson, London.

Bernanke, B., *et al.* 2019. *Firefighting: The Financial Crisis and Its Lessons*. Profile, London.

Blyth, M. 2013. *Austerity: The History of a Dangerous Idea*. Oxford University Press.

Blyth, M., and Lonergan, E. 2020. *Angrynomics*. Agenda, Newcastle.

Brown, G. 2017. *My Life. Our Times*. Bodley Head, London.

Cairncross. F. (ed). 1981. *Changing Perceptions of Economic Policy: Essays in Honour of the Seventieth Birthday of Sir Alec Cairncross*. Methuen, London.

Callaghan, J. 1987. *Time and Chance*. Collins, London.

Cameron, D. 2019. *For the Record*. Harper Collins, London.

Campbell. A. 1994–2010. *The Alastair Campbell Diaries*, various volumes. Hutchinson, London.

Cassidy, J. 2009. *How Markets Fail: The Logic of Economic Calamities*. Allen Lane, London.

Chote, R., *et al.* 2010. The public finances: 1997 to 2010. Election Briefing Note No. 6 (IFS BN93), Institute for Fiscal Studies.

Clarke, K. 2016. *Kind of Blue: A Political Memoir*. MacMillan, London.

Clarke. P. 2009. *Keynes: The Twentieth Century's Most Influential Economist*. Bloomsbury, London.

Conaghan, D. 2012. *The Bank: Inside the Bank of England*. Biteback, London.

Darling, A. 2012. *Back from the Brink: 1,000 Days at Number 11*. Atlantic, London.

Davies, H. 2022. *The Chancellors: Steering the British Economy in Crisis Times*. Polity, London.

Dell, E. 1996. *The Chancellors: A History of the Chancellors of the Exchequer, 1945–90*. Harper Collins, London.

Dow, J. C. R. 1998. *Major Recessions*. Oxford University Press.

Healey, D. 1989. *The Time of My Life*. Michael Joseph, London.

Henessey, P. 2000. *The Prime Minister: The Office and Its Holders Since 1945*. Allen Lane, London.

HM Treasury. 2002. *Reforming Britain's Economic and Financial Policy. Towards Greater Economic Stability*. Palgrave, London.

HM Treasury and Bank of England. 1993. ERM project: the UK's membership of the ERM (21 December).

Jones, R. 1987. *Wages and Employment Policy 1936–85*. Allen and Unwin, London.

Jones, R. 2014. *The Itinerant Economist: Memoirs of a Dismal Scientist*. London Publishing Partnership.

Kay, J., and King, M. 2022. *Radical Uncertainty: Decision Making for an Unknowable Future*. Bridge Street Press, London.

Keegan, W. 1984. *Mrs. Thatcher's Experiment*. Allen Lane, London.

Keegan, W. 1989. *Mr. Lawson's Gamble*. Hodder and Stoughton, London.

Keegan, W. 2012. *The Prudence of Gordon Brown*. Wiley, Chichester.

Keegan, W. 2014. *Mr. Osborne's Economic Experiment: Austerity 1945–51 and 2010–*. Searching Finance, London.

Keegan, W. 2019. *Nine Crises*. Biteback, London.

Keynes, J. M. (various years). *The Collected Writings of John Maynard Keynes*. MacMillan, London.

Lamont, N. 1999. *In Office*. Little Brown, London.

Lawson, N. 1992. *The View from No. 11: Memoirs of a Tory Radical*. Bantam, London.

Major, J. 1999. *The Autobiography*. Harper Collins, London.

Mankiw, N. 1996. *Macroeconomics*. Worth, New York.

NIESR. 2019. Beyond Brexit: a programme for UK reform. NIESR review, No. 250 (November).

Peden, G. C. 1985. *British Economic and Social Policy: Lloyd George to Margaret Thatcher*. Philip Allan, London.

Rawnsley, A. 2010. *The End of the Party: The Rise and Fall of New Labour*. Viking, London.

Richards, S. 2019. *The Prime Ministers*. Atlantic, London.

Rogers, I. 2019. *Nine Lessons in Brexit*. Short Books, London.

Skidelsky, R. 2004. *John Maynard Keynes 1883–1946. Economist. Philosopher. Statesman*. Pan, London.

Skidelsky, R. 2009. *Keynes: The Return of the Master*. Allen Lane, London.

Skidelsky, R. 2018. *Money and Government: A Challenge to Mainstream Economics*. Allen Lane, London.

Slater. M. 2018. *The National Debt: A Short History*. Hurst, London.

Smith, D. 2015. *Something Will Turn Up*. Profile, London.

Smithers. A. 2022. *The Economics of the Stock Market*. Oxford University Press.

Stephens, P. 1996. *Politics and the Pound: The Conservatives' Struggle with Sterling*. MacMillan, London.

Stephens, P. 2021. *Britain Alone: The Path from Suez to Brexit*. Faber and Faber, London.

Thatcher, M. 1993. *The Downing Street Years*. Harper Collins, London.

Thomas-Symonds, N. 2022. *Harold Wilson: The Winner*. Weidenfeld and Nicolson, London.

Tooze, A. 2018. *Crashed: How a Decade of Financial Crises Changed the World*. Allen Lane, London.

Tugendhat, C. 2022. *The Worm in the Apple: A History of the Conservative Party and Europe from Churchill to Cameron*. Haus, London.

Turner, P. 2011. Fiscal dominance and the long-term interest rate. Financial Markets Group Special Papers SP 199 (May).

Weldon, D. 2021. *Two Hundred Years of Muddling Through*. Little Brown, London.

*

I also made extensive use of various commentaries I authored and co-authored while at Llewellyn Consulting between 2013 and 2020, the OECD's annual Economic Surveys and the IMF's regular Article IV consultation reports on the UK, together with the Bank of England's Inflation Reports and Monetary Reports and the extensive documentation that is issued with every UK budget.

For statistics, my most commonly mined sources were the Bank of England's exhaustive 'A Millennium of Macroeconomic Data' database (www.bankofengland.co.uk/statistics/research-datasets), the Office for Budget Responsibility's 'Public Finance Database' (https://obr.uk/data/) and the databases of the OECD (https://data.oecd.org/) and the IMF (www.imf.org/en/Data).

Where necessary, more explicit references are provided in the notes on the following pages.

Notes

PREFACE

1 This work was published as R. Jones. 1987. *The Wages Problem in Employment Policy 1936–85*. Allen and Unwin, London.
2 During this period I contributed, *inter alia*, to A. Cairncross. 1985. *Years of Recovery: British Economic Policy 1945–51*. Methuen, London. E. Plowden. 1989. *An Industrialist in the Treasury: The Post-War Years*. Andre Deutsch, London.

CHAPTER 1

1 J. M. Keynes. 1972. A memoir of Alfred Marshall. *The Collected Writings of John Maynard Keynes* (ed. D. Moggridge), Vol. X. MacMillan, London. (The *Collected Writings* will henceforth be referred to as simply JMK.)
2 The prize was won by David Card, Joshua Angrist and Guido Imbens for their leading role in developing the 'design-based' approach to economics to answer questions for society.

CHAPTER 2

1 A. Cairncross. 1998. *Living with the Century*. Inyx, Fife.
2 A. Smith. 1776. *An Inquiry into the Nature and Causes of the Wealth of Nations*. Penguin Classics, London.
3 Robbins was subsequently to recant, and become a committed Keynesian, albeit a conservative one. See L. Robbins. 1971. *Autobiography of an Economist*. MacMillan, London.
4 H. Hoover. 1951. *The Memoirs of Herbert Hoover: The Great Depression, 1929–41*. MacMillan, New York.
5 A classic summary of the 1920s 'Treasury view' is to be found in 'Memoranda on certain proposals relating to unemployment, presented by the Minister of Labour to parliament', May 1929. HMSO, London.
6 Only thirteen democracies remained in 1940.
7 JMK. 1971a. *The Economic Consequences of the Peace*, Vol. II. JMK. 1981a. *Activities 1922–29*, Vol. XVIII. JMK. 1981b. *The Return to Gold and Industrial Policy*, Vol. XIX.
8 JMK. 1971b. *A Tract on Monetary Reform*, Vol. IV. JMK. 1971c. *A Treatise on Money*, Vol. V. JMK. 1971d. *A Treatise on Money*, Vol. VI.

9   JMK. 1981c. *Activities 1929–31: Rethinking Employment and Unemployment Policies*, Vol. XX. R. F. Kahn. 1931. The relation of home investment to unemployment. *Economic Journal* 41(162), 173–198. JMK. 1973a. *The General Theory and After*, Vols VIII and IX.

10 J. M. Keynes. 1936. *The General Theory of Employment, Interest, and Money*. MacMillan, London. Also published as JMK. 1973b. *The General Theory of Employment, Interest, and Money*, Vol. VII.

11 A. Badger. 1989. *The New Deal: The Depression Years, 1933–1940*. MacMillan, London.

12 A. Tooze. 2007. *The Wages of Destruction: The Making and Breaking of the Nazi Economy*. Penguin, London.

13 R. Jones. 2014a. *Takahashi's Ghost*. Llewellyn Consulting Comment (6 March). See also Bank of Japan. 1996. *Annual Review*. Bank of Japan, Tokyo.

14 The first UK national accounts were developed by James Meade and Richard Stone in Whitehall in the early 1940s. Both men were disciples of Keynes and subsequently became Nobel laureates. They were in significant part inspired by Keynes's work on war finance, initially outlined in his pamphlet 'How to pay for the war'. In this, his intention was to present a strategy to avoid a repetition of the inflation that plagued Britain in World War I. He described the concepts of 'inflationary' and 'deflationary gaps', essentially episodes of excess and inadequate aggregate demand, which could be acted on, and indeed closed, by government action on public spending and taxation, including compulsory saving. JMK. 1978. *Activities 1939–45: Internal War Finance*, Vol. XXII.

15 HMG. 1944. *Employment Policy*. Cmd. 6527. HMSO, London.

16 Defined here as the share of non-employment income in total domestic income.

17 In nominal trade-weighted terms, sterling lost 37% of its value from its June 1972 'float' until November 1976. In real terms, the decline was some 23%.

18 Until the aftermath of the GFC, there were only three months in which the annual rate of CPI inflation was negative in the UK. These were in 1959 (June) and 1960 (January and March).

19 Jones (1987).

20 JMK. 1980. *Activities 1940–1946: Shaping the Post-War World: Employment and Commodities*, Vol. XXVII, p. 381. A more detailed perusal of Keynes's writings on the post-war world suggest that he thought an unemployment rate of around 5% a more reasonable goal.

21 A. W. Phillips. 1958. The relationship between unemployment and the rate of change of money wages in the United Kingdom, 1861–1957. *Economica* 25(100), 283–299.

22 Jones (1987).

23 'The Radcliffe Report', published in 1959, offers the most widely cited exposition of this approach to monetary policy. It attracted considerable criticism for having understated the importance of monetary instruments, and over time became a very controversial document. See HMG. 1959. *Report of the Committee on the Working of the Monetary System*. Cmd. 827. HMSO, London.

24 R. C. O. Matthews. 1968. Why has Britain had full employment since the war? *Economic Journal* 78(311), 555–569.

25 J. C. R. Dow. 1998. *Major Recessions: Britain and the World, 1920–95.* Oxford University Press.

26 P. Stephens. 2021. *Britain Alone: The Path from Suez to Brexit.* Faber and Faber, London.

27 The Conservative government of the early 1960s targeted growth of 4% a year. In 1965 the Labour government's 'National Plan' committed it to a 25% increase in output over six years.

28 Labour's chief economic advisor in the 1960s, Nicholas Kaldor, was an exception to this rule. One of the most thoughtful and innovative Keynesian economists, he recognized that economies of scale encouraged output in manufacturing to rise faster than employment, raising productivity as markets expanded, and thus encouraging a virtuous circle of rising efficiency and increased exports. He therefore sought to encourage the flow of resources from services into manufacturing via a selective payroll tax.

29 Cairncross (1985).

30 Defined as the sum of the current account and long-term capital account balances.

31 R. Roberts. 2017. *When Britain Went Bust: The 1976 IMF Crisis.* OMFIF, London.

32 Because of the threat posed by the sterling balances to the pound, there was a belief that they should be 'funded', which meant coming to an agreement with holders to exchange them for medium- or long-maturity bonds, which would reduce the risk that sterling was summarily dumped. However, such a solution meant deciding that sterling's role as a reserve currency was over, which was a matter of national prestige and of broader political significance. It was only in the wake of the 1976 IMF crisis that the issue of the sterling balances was addressed and sterling reserve currency status effectively ended.

33 See E. Conway. 2014. *The Summit: The Biggest Battle of the Second World War – Fought behind Closed Doors.* Little Brown, London. See also JMK. 1980a. *Activities 1940–44: Shaping the Post-War World: The Clearing Union*, Vol. XXV. JMK. 1980b. *Activities 1941–46: Shaping the Post-War World: Bretton Woods*, Vol. XXVI.

CHAPTER 3

1 NIESR. 1974. *National Institute Economic Review*, Vol. 67, No. 1 (February).

2 D. Kynaston. 2001. *The City of London. Volume IV: A Club No More.* Chatto and Windus, London.

3 Competition and Credit Control grew out of a Bank of England consultative document published in May 1971, and it was also detailed in the Bank of England's *Quarterly Bulletin* of Q2 1971. The policy was implemented in the final quarter of the year.

4   The property price bust also made it necessary for the Bank of England to launch a lifeboat for a number of specialist real estate lenders that it believed threatened broader financial stability.

5   It was the fifth time Heath had declared a State of Emergency in just over three years. Prior to June 1970 it had happened only twice before in post-war Britain: during the national rail strike of 1955 and during the seamen's strike of 1966.

6   One senior advisor to Wilson has written of him 'preparing to lose' in the run-up to the election. B. Donoughue. 2005. *Downing Street Diary: With Harold Wilson in No. 10.* Jonathan Cape, London.

7   D. Healey. 1989. *The Time of My Life.* Michael Joseph, London.

8   Perhaps the best candidate to be chancellor in 1974 was Roy Jenkins, who had been successful in restoring the economy to equilibrium in the wake of the late 1967 devaluation, but Jenkins was unacceptable to the left wing of the Labour Party.

9   In January 1974 an IMF Committee of Twenty statement called on countries to eschew strategies that would aggravate the problems of others, and to instead pursue 'policies that would sustain appropriate levels of economic activity and employment.' See M. Garritsen de Vries. 1985. *The International Monetary Fund,1972–78: Co-operation on Trial.* IMF, Washington.

10 The vote was 67.2% in favour of the renegotiation and 32.8% against. Every social class, every age group and all regions of the country apart from Shetland and the western isles of Scotland voted 'Yes'. The contrast with the detail of the 2016 Brexit vote is stark.

11 UK North Sea oil output amounted to 0.5% of GDP in 1976, 3.3% of GDP in 1979 and 5.9% of GDP in 1982.

12 It has been claimed in the official history of MI5 that Jones, a former member of the Communist Party of Great Britain, had frequently passed information about Labour Party business on to the Soviet Union. See C. Andrew. 2010. *The Defence of the Realm: The Authorised History of MI5.* Penguin, London.

13 J. Callaghan. 1987. *Time and Chance.* Collins, London.

14 Callaghan subsequently claimed that this portion of his speech, drafted in large part by Peter Jay (his son-in-law and the economics editor of *The Times*), should be seen in the context of the moment. He needed to appease the markets, encourage potential financial assistance and impress upon his own party how parlous Britain's position was. He never fully abandoned an essentially Keynesian view of the world, even if a rather cynical one. See Callaghan (1987).

15 The two best short summaries of the 1976 crisis are to be found in Roberts (2017) and in K. Burk and A. Cairncross. 1992. *Goodbye Great Britain.* Yale University Press, London. The most thorough study is D. Wass. 2008. *Decline to Fall: The Making of British Macroeconomic Policy and the 1976 IMF Crisis.* Oxford University Press.

16 Healey also considered the use of selective import controls, but as much as a negotiating tactic as anything else. They were never the centrepiece of his strategy.

17 In late November 1976 Benn circulated to his colleagues the cabinet minutes from July 1931. A narrow majority of the Labour cabinet followed the prime minister, Ramsay MacDonald, in supporting a cut in unemployment benefits in order to obtain a loan from American bankers. But others could not go along with the cuts. The government fell, but MacDonald stayed on as prime minister in a coalition government dominated by Conservatives. Labour was decimated at a subsequent general election.

18 In fact, the previous Labour chancellor, Roy Jenkins, had at the IMF's bidding adopted a target for DCE following the 1967 devaluation.

19 With the progressive imposition of cash limits on public spending, government departments became so frightened by them that they underspent, sometimes dramatically so.

20 The original members of the ERM were Germany, France, Italy, Holland, Belgium, Luxembourg and Ireland. They would later be joined by Spain in 1989, the UK in 1990 and Portugal in 1992.

21 The ERM was based on the concept of fixed currency exchange rate margins, but with exchange rates variable within those margins. It was therefore a semi-pegged system. Before the introduction of the euro, exchange rates were based on the European Currency Unit (ECU), the European unit of account, the value of which was determined as a weighted average of the participating currencies. A grid (known as the Parity Grid) of bilateral rates was calculated on the basis of these central rates expressed in ECUs, and currency fluctuations had to be contained within a margin of 2.25% on either side of the bilateral rates (with the Italian lira and Spanish peseta allowed to fluctuate by ±6%). Market intervention and loan arrangements were expected to protect the participating currencies from excessive fluctuations, but there were numerous realignments, especially in the system's early years.

22 There are only two direct references to a budget deficit in *The General Theory*. Keynes's *Collected Writings* run to twenty-nine volumes. Budget deficits take up five lines of the index, or one-tenth of one column out of 746.

23 JMK. 1980. *Activities 1940–46: Shaping the Post-War World. Employment*, Vol. XXVII.

24 The theory was originally formulated by Polish mathematician Nicolaus Copernicus in 1517, and was subsequently restated by philosophers John Locke, David Hume and Jean Bodin.

25 R. Skidelsky. 2000. *John Maynard Keynes. Vol. III. Fighting for Britain*, p. 53. MacMillan, London.

26 The original 1944 White Paper on Employment Policy was couched in terms of sustaining a high level of total nominal expenditure. See HMG (1944).

CHAPTER 4

1 K. Joseph. 1976. *Monetarism Is Not Enough.* Centre for Policy Studies, London (October).

2   M. Friedman. 1957. *A Theory of Consumption Function*. Princeton University
    Press.

3   M. Friedman and A. Schwartz. 1963. *A Monetary History of the United States,
    1867–1960*. Princeton University Press.

4   M. Friedman. 1970. *The Counter-Revolution in Monetary Theory*. Wincott
    Memorial Lecture, Institute of Economic Affairs, Occasional Paper 33.

5   M. Friedman. 1975. *Unemployment versus Inflation? An Evaluation of the Phillips
    Curve*. Institute of Economic Affairs, Occasional Paper 44.

6   M. Friedman. 1977. *Inflation and Unemployment: The New Dimension of Politics*.
    Institute of Economic Affairs, Occasional Paper 51.

7   L. Walras. 1877 [1954]. *Elements of Pure Economics*. Irwin, Homewood, IL.

8   J. Muth. 1961. *Rational Expectations and the Theory of Price Movements*.
    Econometrica 29, 315–335.

9   See, for example, R. Lucas. 1995. *Monetary Neutrality*. Nobel Memorial Prize in
    Economic Sciences 1995 prize lecture, 7 December. R. Lucas. 1981. *Studies in
    Business-Cycle Theory*. MIT Press, Cambridge, MA.

10 G. Stadler. 1994. Real business cycles. *Journal of Economic Literature*
    32(December), 1750–1783.

11 E. F. Fama. 1991. Efficient capital markets: II. *Journal of Finance* 46(5), 1575–
    1617. See also E. F. Fama. 1965. Random walks in stock market prices. *Financial
    Analysts Journal* 21(5), 56–60.

12 JMK. 1983. *On Friedrich Hayek's Prices and Production*, Vol. XII, p. 252.

13 N. G. Mankiw. 2008. New Keynesian economics. In *The Concise Encyclopaedia
    of Economics. Library of Economics and Liberty*.

14 F. Hayek. 1944. *The Road to Serfdom*. Routledge, London.

15 Budd, it should be said, had previously served at the Treasury under the
    Barber regime. In due course he was also to question the morality of the initial
    Thatcherite revolution, suggesting that in the eyes of some members of the
    Conservative Party it amounted to class war. In particular, he mused whether
    their willingness to accept subsequent high levels of unemployment was what
    Marxists would term an effort to create a 'reserve army of the unemployed' to
    break the trade unions and boost corporate profits. See D. Trilling. 2010. A
    nightmare experience. *New Statesman*, 8 March.

CHAPTER 5

1   A. J. Woodman (ed.). 2019. *Tacitus. Agricola*. Cambridge University Press.

2   The government produced a Green Paper on 'Monetary Control' in March 1980
    that recommended focusing on restricting the monetary base rather than broad
    money, and thereby copying the approach to monetary restraint applied in the
    US by the Federal Reserve at this time. However, this proposal was never acted
    upon, not least because such techniques had the potential to generate extreme
    volatility in interest rates. HMG. 1980. *Monetary Control*. Cmd. 7858. HMSO,
    London.

3   Milton Friedman himself doubted the veracity of this assertion. He told the
     Treasury Select Committee: 'The key role assigned to targets for the PSBR
     … seems to me unwise. There is no necessary relation between the PSBR and
     monetary growth.' Quoted in C. Johnson. 1991. *The Economy under Mrs.
     Thatcher, 1979–90.* Penguin, Harmondsworth.
4   C. Goodhart. 1975. Problems of monetary management: the UK experience. In
     Papers in Monetary Economics, Vol. 1. Reserve Bank of Australia, Sydney.
5   The story behind the letter is described by one of its initiators in R. Nield. 2014.
     The 1981 statement by 364 economists. In *Expansionary Fiscal Contraction:
     The Thatcher Government's 1981 Budget in Perspective* (ed. D. Needham and
     A. Hotson). (See https://bit.ly/41zc3Z4.)
6   Quoted in W. Keegan. 1984. *Mrs. Thatcher's Economic Experiment.* Allen Lane,
     London.
7   The most famous occasion on which she did so was at the October 1980
     Conservative Party Conference, when she uttered the now famous words: 'You
     turn if you want to. The lady's not for turning.'
8   G. M. Dillon. 1989. *The Falklands, Politics, and War.* St Martin's Press, London.
9   Victory in the Falklands War may have increased the Conservative vote by some
     25% in the 1983 election according to S. Price and D. Sanders. 1994. Economic
     competence, rational expectations, and government popularity in post-war
     Britain. *Manchester School* 62(3), 296–312.
10   See, for example, Y. Funabashi. 1988. *Managing the Dollar: From the Plaza to the
     Louvre.* Peterson Institute, Washington.
11   ERM membership had been discussed by Thatcher and Howe as early as the
     autumn of 1981 but had received little support.
12   After five years of painful negotiations, Thatcher achieved a 66% rebate on
     the UK's EEC Budget contribution. In many Tory circles, this was greeted in
     triumphalist fashion almost on a par with the victory in the Falklands War.
13   This became known as 'The Lawson Doctrine'. See N. Lawson. 1992. *The View
     From Number Eleven: Memoirs of a Tory Radical.* Bantam Press, London.
14   European Commission. 1989. *Economic and Monetary Union in the European
     Community.* Brussels (April).
15   N. Lawson. 1984. *The British Experiment.* Mais Lecture (June). Available at
     margaretthatcher.org.
16   Lawson (1992).
17   European Commission. 1985. *Completing the Internal Market.* COM (85) 310
     (June).
18   Lord Cockfield's reward for his hard work was to be sacked by Thatcher.
     See R. Denham. 2007. Lord Cockfield. *The Guardian*, 11 January (www.
     theguardian.com/news/2007/jan/11/guardianobituaries.obituaries).
19   D. Parker. 2012. *The Official History of Privatisation, Vol. II: Popular Capitalism,
     1987–97.* Routledge, London.
20   See H. Phelps Brown. 1981. Labour market policy. In *Changing Perceptions of
     Economic Policy* (ed. F. Cairncross). Methuen, London.

21 P. Krugman. 1990. *The Age of Diminished Expectations: US Economic Policy in the 1990s.* MIT Press, Cambridge, MA.
22 N. Crafts and G. Toniolo. 1995. *Economic Growth in Europe.* Cambridge University Press.

CHAPTER 6

1   N. Lamont. 1992. *Chancellor's Statement.* HM Treasury (16 September).
2   The contrast with the legacies bequeathed to Labour in 1964 and 1974 is stark.
3   W. Martin. 1991. *Shades of '25.* UBS Phillips and Drew Economic Research (November).
4   Bank of England. 1991. *Quarterly Bulletin,* Vol. 31, No. 1 (February).
5   Germany's CPI inflation rate of 4% in 1992 was twice the Bundesbank's unofficial target and exceeded the G-7 average by a percentage point. Nothing like the latter had been witnessed since the war. Hitherto, even when German inflation picked up, it tended to remain relatively low.
6   The transformation of the EEC into the EU went beyond semantics. The EU would become an entity in international law, and those living within it would become citizens of it as well as their own countries. This received little attention in the UK at the time.
7   Outside government, calls for an alternative economic strategy were growing in vehemence, and extended to both monetarist and Keynesian economists. One particularly noteworthy critic was Alan Walters. In an echo of the 364 economists who protested against the 1981 budget, he, along with five other monetarist economists, wrote to *The Times* (published on 14 July 1992) to warn that sterling's membership of the ERM risked turning recession into depression.
8   Bank of England. 1992. *Quarterly Bulletin.* August.
9   National Savings and Investment (NS&I) is a state-owned savings bank. Its aim is to attract funds from individual UK savers for the purpose of funding the government's deficit. NS&I attracts savers through offering savings products with tax-free elements, and a 100% guarantee from HM Treasury on all deposits.
10 By 1992 the ERM had a series of divergence indicators, to gauge the relative extent of each currency's deviation from its central parity. Any movement of a currency beyond 75% of its maximum allowed divergence was a trigger for remedial action in the form of intervention and/or a change in monetary policy.
11 Ken Clarke, speaking on *The Major Years*, Part 2. BBC 1, 18 October 1999.
12 HM Treasury and Bank of England. 1993. *The Cost of Intervention.* 23 August.
13 Keynes had actually advocated what we would now call an inflation targeting regime in his *Tract on Monetary Reform* of 1923. In the context of price instability in the international economy after World War I, he recommended a policy of exchange rate flexibility, appreciating the currency in response to international inflation and depreciating it when there are international deflationary forces, so that internal prices remained more or less stable. The

Swedish Riksbank instituted the first explicit policy of targeting of the price level between 1931 and 1937.

14 A target range of 0–4% was retained for M0, and a monitoring range of 4–8%, subsequently amended to 3–9%, for M4.

15 The group was initially made up of Gavyn Davies, Patrick Minford, Wynne Godley, David Currie, Andrew Brittan, Andrew Sentance and Tim Congdon, and their meetings were chaired by Chief Economic Advisor Alan Budd. This was a motley crew. Minford (new classical monetarist) and Godley (unreconstructed Keynesian), for example, were about as far apart on how the economy functioned and how policy should be framed as it was possible to be.

16 In the summer of 1993 German reunification resurfaced as an existential faultline for the ERM. The Bundesbank remained troubled by domestic inflation and continued to soft-pedal on monetary easing. Official rates were permitted to decline only slowly. The Irish punt succumbed to speculative pressure in February, and the peseta and escudo did the same in May, before attention turned to the French franc. The Bundesbank initially provided the franc with the sort of assistance that it had denied to sterling the year before, but it remained reluctant to tailor German monetary policy entirely to external considerations. The ERM was in the end only saved from obliteration by the widening of the parity bands to 15%.

17 The first phrase was popularized in 2004 by then Federal Reserve governor Ben Bernanke, the second in 2007 by Bank of England governor Mervyn King.

CHAPTER 7

1 R. Lucas. 2003. Macroeconomic priorities. *American Economic Review* 93(1), 1–14.

2 See, for example, J. Buchanan. 1987. *The Constitution of Economic Policy*. Nobel Prize lecture, republished in *American Economic Review* 77(3), 243–250.

3 D. North. 1991. Institutions. *Journal of Economic Perspectives* 5(11), 97–112.

4 R. Lucas. 1980. The death of Keynesian economics. *Issues and Ideas* (Winter), 1–20.

5 Labour Party. 1997. *New Labour, Because Britain Deserves Better*. London (www.labour-party.org.uk/manifestos/1997/1997-labour-manifesto.shtml).

CHAPTER 8

1 From a speech in the House of Commons. Quoted in D. Smith. 2016. *Something Will Turn Up: Britain's Economy. Past, Present, and Future*. Profile, London.

2 B. Bernanke. 2004. *The Great Moderation*. Speech to the Eastern Economic Association, 20 February. Federal Reserve. Although these forces resulted in growing inequality domestically in most countries, they also lifted millions out of poverty for the first time in their histories.

3   Beyond the prime minister, only two other cabinet ministers were advised in
     advance of it happening: John Prescott, the deputy prime minister, and Robin
     Cook, the foreign secretary. The full cabinet had not even met for the first time
     when it was announced.
4   Bank of England independence was also one of the conditions set out by the EU
     for membership of the European single currency.
5   Tom Scholar's father, Sir Michael Scholar, had played a similar role in the work
     done on central bank independence in the late 1980s.
6   Budd was to become one of the first members of the Bank of England's MPC,
     however.
7   This was in contrast to the Federal Reserve and the ECB, which themselves
     defined what they meant by price stability. There was concern at the Treasury
     that, if left to its own devices, the Bank might prove overzealous in its pursuit of
     stable prices.
8   In due course the MPC was to number among its members many of the great
     and the good of the economics fraternity not just in the UK but more broadly.
     These included Willem Buiter, Charles Goodhart, Charles Bean, Tim Besley,
     Martin Weale, Sushil Wadhwani, Kate Barker, David Blanchflower, Kristin
     Forbes and Catherine Mann.
9   Over time, the number of speeches given by MPC members has multiplied,
     leading to criticisms that they have created an excessive degree of noise around
     policy.
10   As we shall see, this was not always to be the case when it came to the Bank
     governor commenting on fiscal policy.
11   Interview with former MPC member David Blanchflower.
12   J. K. Galbraith. 1958. *The Affluent Society*. Houghton Mifflin, New York.
13   The institution of fiscal rules had been growing in popularity and was to
     continue to do so. According to the IMF, between 1985 and 2015 they had been
     extended to over ninety countries. IMF. 2015. *Fiscal Rules Database*. See https://
     www.imf.org/external/datamapper/FiscalRules.
14   This was a phrase employed during Brown's budget speech of 17 May 1998.
15   K. Clarke. 2016. *Kind of Blue: A Political Memoir*. Pan, London.
16   This was a figure quoted by former cabinet secretary Richard Wilson in an
     interview. H. Davies. 2022. *The Chancellors: Steering the British Economy in
     Crisis Times*. Polity, London.
17   The system became triennial in 2007.
18   The decision to converge with euro area practice was a sop to those in New
     Labour who continued to hope for euro membership after the Treasury's
     negative assessment of the case for entry in 2002.
19   D. H. Robertson. 1928/1966. *Theories of Banking Policy*. Lecture at the LSE,
     13 February 1928. Reprinted in *Essays in Money and Interest*. 1966. Collins,
     London.
20   Quoted in *The Guardian*, 19 June 2007.
21   HM Treasury. 1997. *UK Membership of the Single Currency: An Assessment of the
     Five Economic Tests*. October.

22 HM Treasury. 2003. *UK Membership of the Single Currency: An Assessment of the Five Economic Tests.* Cmd. 5776. June.

23 P. Westaway. 2003. *Modelling Shocks and Adjustment Mechanisms in EMU.* HM Treasury, London.

24 Foreign-owned firms tend to display higher productivity than their domestic competitors.

25 Railway infrastructure and maintenance were brought back under public control in 2001 and 2004, respectively, but this was largely because the privatization structure bequeathed to New Labour by the Conservatives proved unworkable.

26 Global warming is an existential problem. The estimates of the likely probabilities and potential damage from climate change are so large that they are difficult to grasp. In its 'likely' climate sensitivity analysis, the Intergovernmental Panel on Climate Change estimates the median temperature increase at different levels of atmospheric concentration of carbon dioxide equivalents. It concludes that, even if governments keep their current promises, atmospheric greenhouse gas concentration will reach 700ppm, resulting in a 10% chance of the increase in global temperature exceeding 6 degrees centigrade. This would be catastrophic. Either mankind will manage the transition to net zero emissions by transitioning the economy or nature will do it for us by depopulating and deindustrializing the planet.

27 N. Stern. 2007. *The Economics of Climate Change: The Stern Review.* Cambridge University Press.

CHAPTER 9

1 H. Minsky. 1986. *Stabilising an Unstable Economy.* McGraw Hill, New York.

2 The statistics outlined in the following paragraphs are drawn from various editions of the IMF's *World Economic Outlook*, the BIS's *Annual Report* and the OECD's *Economic Outlook*, and also from A. Haldane. 2010. The contribution of the financial sector: miracle or mirage? Bank of England, 14 July.

3 CDSs are akin to insurance policies. The buyer pays a regular fee to the seller, who will pay out in the event of a default on a loan. They allowed risky assets to be removed from bank balance sheets, thereby freeing up capital for alternative uses. The buyer of a CDS does not necessarily have a corresponding loan on its books. CDSs can therefore be a vehicle for pure speculation on a default.

4 The rest of this chapter is drawn from a presentation at Birkbeck College, University of London, by the author and Dr John Llewellyn for the Society of Professional Economists in February 2019.

5 The Taylor rule was developed by Stanford economist John Taylor. See J. Taylor. 1993. Discretion vs. policy rules in practice. Stanford University (http://web.stanford.edu/~johntayl/Papers/Discretion.PDF).

6 J. Qvigstad, J. Llewellyn, N. Husom Vonen and B. Dharmasena. 2012. The 'rule of four'. *Business Economist* 3(1), 31–44.

7 Quoted by Paul Krugman in the *International Herald Tribune*, 5 November 2003. Others remember Stein slightly differently, but the point remains the

same. See, for example, Greenspan on Stein at www.nabe.com/am2000/grnspnvid.htm.

8   A. Turner. 2009. *The Turner Review: A Regulatory Response to the Global Banking Crisis*. FSA, London.

9   ABSs are securities backed by a pool of illiquid assets such as car loans, student loans, credit card debt, mortgages and so on. They are all associated with a cash flow.

10   MBSs are a form of ABS secured by a pool of mortgages. The pooling of mortgages was designed to decrease the default risk of an entire portfolio. Hence, they were given a low risk weighting and allowed to be used as collateral. This relied on the assumption that defaults on mortgages were not highly correlated with one another.

11   CDOs can be backed by any form of debt – mortgages, corporate bonds, even other ABSs – and are split into tranches of varying risk and maturity, each offering a different return, so as to give investors greater choice.

12   ABCP was seen as low risk because it was backed by the assets held by the SPV.

13   Leverage can be defined as a bank or financial institution's ratio of debt to equity.

14   BIS data.

15   *Financial Times*, 10 July 2007 (http://blogs.ft.comgapperblog/2007/11/wall-streetsbrhtml/). Cited by John Gapper.

16   J. Nugée. 2009. *Failure and Reconstruction: The Financial Sector in 2008 and 2009. A Personal View of the Financial Crisis for EFFAS-EBC*. (See https://bit.ly/41C09hj.)

17   Alan Greenspan's influence should not be underestimated. He could not believe that firms would not stamp out malfeasance, as such action was in their own interest. However, in October 2008 he admitted to Congress that he had 'made a mistake presuming that self-interest ... of banks and others [was] such that they were best capable of protecting their own shareholders and their equity in the firm'. (See https://oversight.house.gov/sites/democrats.oversight.house.gov/files/migrated/20081023100438.pdf.)

CHAPTER 10

1   As quoted in J. Fox. 2008. Bob Lucas on the comeback of Keynesianism. *Time Magazine*, 28 October.

2   See, for example, the various volumes of Alastair Campbell's diaries covering his time as a close advisor to Tony Blair.

3   The cut in the basic rate of income tax went hand in hand with the abolition of the lower 10% band and cuts in tax credits. When it became clear that this would make up to 5 million people worse off, the government had to hastily rush out a compensation package to avoid a defeat in the House of Commons.

4   Tucker was the Bank's executive director for markets and was on the Monetary Policy Committee. He had something of a fraught relationship with the governor.

5   Moral hazard is a situation where an economic actor has an incentive to increase
     its exposure to risk because it does not bear the full costs of that risk.

6   Brown considered calling an election in the third quarter of 2007, and there was
     huge press speculation to that effect at the time. Just as Callaghan had done in
     1978, though, he backtracked after internal polling suggested that New Labour
     was unlikely to increase its existing modest majority and could even lose seats.
     The events surrounding Northern Rock did nothing to help his cause.

7   The author was present at this event. The hubris among Lehman management
     that day was palpable.

8   In 2006 Fuld was paid $40.5 million, including a cash bonus of $6.25 million,
     $10.9 million in restricted stock and $10.1 million in options. At the end of
     the year, Fuld owned 10.52 million shares in Lehman and 3.3 million options.
     His overall stake in the firm was $930 million. For more insights into Fuld's
     character, see R. Jones. 2014b. *The Itinerant Economist: Memoirs of a Dismal
     Scientist*. London Publishing Partnership.

9   A repurchase agreement (repo) is a short-term secured loan: one party sells
     securities to another and agrees to repurchase those securities later at a higher
     price. The securities serve as collateral. The difference between the securities'
     initial price and their repurchase price is the interest paid on the loan, known as
     the repo rate.

10   Barclays did end up taking over Lehman's US business post the latter's
     bankruptcy, and it was able to do so at a much reduced price. Lehman's
     European operations were taken on by the Japanese brokerage house Nomura.

11   The amount of central bank liquidity swaps peaked at more than $600 billion
     around the turn of the year.

12   LIBOR, or the London inter-bank offered rate, is the average interest rate that
     banks charge each other for short-term, unsecured loans. It reflects in part
     the credit risk of the banking sector. The OIS, or overnight indexed swap,
     meanwhile, represents a country's central bank rate over a certain period.
     Because the parties in a basic interest rate swap exchange not principal but
     the difference of the two interest streams, credit risk is not a major factor in
     determining the OIS rate. The LIBOR–OIS spread represents the difference
     between an interest rate with some credit risk built in and one that is virtually
     free of such hazards. When the gap widens, it is indicative of a financial sector
     that is under duress.

13   A bank, or any business, is solvent when the value of its total assets covers its
     total liabilities. Defaults on a bank's loans will erode the value of its assets
     relative to its liabilities. Liquidity, on the other hand, is the ability to meet
     short-term obligations. A bank, for example, has to have access to enough cash
     to pay its depositors and other creditors on demand. If a bank's assets exceed its
     liabilities but it is unable to borrow enough cash or sell enough assets in time to
     meet its payment obligations, then it is illiquid but solvent.

14   Just as the Japanese authorities dithered, covered things up and sought relief
     in forbearance, the Scandinavians took quick and effective action, and could
     subsequently move on from their financial crisis much faster. Japan's banking

crisis was still causing major problems for its economy more than a decade on from its eruption.

15 The Emergency Economic Stabilization Act of 2008.

16 The ELA's existence was not acknowledged in the Bank's 2009 Annual Report and was only finally publicly disclosed a year after its inception.

17 In reality, the plan amounted to £400 billion, as the SLS was already in place up to a total of £100 billion.

18 Use of the SLS was to continue to run at around £180 billion throughout 2009, before gradually tapering off in 2010 and then falling more sharply thereafter.

19 The three main Irish banks, with combined balance sheets equivalent to 700% of Ireland's GDP, were all on the brink of collapse. The Irish authorities failed to give any other government – or, for that matter, the ECB – advance notice of its intention.

20 What was also extraordinary at this time was that the entire country of Iceland was going bankrupt, as its massively overextended banking sector imploded. In response to the Icelanders' refusal to pay back the billions of pounds of British depositors' money, the government had to resort to anti-terrorist powers to freeze Iceland's UK assets. To say that governments were having to fight on a number of fronts is an understatement.

21 The output gap is estimated to have peaked at more than four and a half percentage points of potential GDP in 2009.

22 A more ambitious programme of public investment was eschewed, in part because there were not considered to be sufficient 'shovel-ready' projects available. Given the manifest shortcomings of UK infrastructure that continue to this day, this is a remarkable indictment of public policymaking.

23 The fear was that with official rates below 0.5%, the money markets would stop functioning. This proved to be unduly pessimistic. In subsequent years Bank Rate was reduced to 0.25%, and ultimately to a mere 0.1%.

24 Banks acted merely as intermediaries in the transactions.

25 The Fed announced its first round of QE on 25 November 2008. It began buying $500 billion in MBSs and $100 billion in other debt in an effort to bring down credit spreads and to support the housing market that the sub-prime mortgage crisis had devastated.

26 As early as 1930 Keynes had made the point that in responding to a slump it was important that action was taken to ensure that long-term interest rates fell in sympathy with short-term rates. See JMK (1930) and JMK (1936). See also J. R. Hicks. 1937. Mr Keynes and the classics: a suggested interpretation. *Econometrica* 5(2), 147–159. P. Krugman. 1998. It's baaack: Japan's slump and the return of the liquidity trap. Brookings Papers on Economic Activity, No. 2.

27 The notion that a central bank should confine its policy instruments to the short-term rate always depended on there being smooth and unconstrained arbitrage across different assets (and therefore a high degree of substitution between short-term bills and longer-term bonds) and on banks not facing capital or liquidity constraints. Such assumptions are only realistic during periods of economic and financial tranquillity.

28 'Fiscal dominance' occurs when a government runs persistently large budget deficits, leading to a rapidly rising debt burden, and forces the central bank to prioritize keeping the government out of bankruptcy as opposed to goals such as price stability and sustained output and employment growth.

29 IMF. 2012. United Kingdom. *Staff Report for the 2012 Article IV Consultation.* IMF, Washington (July).

30 See, for example, M. Joyce, M. Tong and R. Woods. 2011. The United Kingdom's quantitative easing policy: design, operation, and impact. *Bank of England Quarterly Bulletin*, Q3.

31 The G-20's members are Argentina, Australia, Brazil, Canada, China, France, Germany, India, Indonesia, Italy, South Korea, Japan, Mexico, Russia, Saudi Arabia, South Africa, Turkey, the United Kingdom, the United States and the European Union.

32 The Bretton Woods Conference was a gathering of delegates from all forty-four Allied nations held at the Mount Washington Hotel, situated in Bretton Woods, New Hampshire, in July 1944. The aim was to regulate the international monetary and financial order following World War II. It established the International Bank for Reconstruction and Development (IBRD, later the World Bank) and the International Monetary Fund (IMF), as well as a system of 'fixed but adjustable' exchange rates. The so-called Bretton Woods system of international commercial and financial relations provided much of the institutional architecture for twenty-five years of unprecedented global economic prosperity. The London Economic Conference of June and July 1933 was a meeting of the representatives of sixty-six nations. Its purpose was to reach agreement on measures to fight the Great Depression, revive international trade and stabilize currency exchange rates. It was fatally undermined by Nazi posturing, divisions between the UK and France, and President Roosevelt's denunciation of the notion of currency stabilization. It proved symbolic of a decade of masochistic economic nationalism.

33 There is some suggestion that Brown also tried to have MacPherson moved from his Treasury post.

34 In March 2009 King told the Treasury Select Committee that he was sceptical about further fiscal expansion. Fifteen months later the Bank's May 2010 Inflation Report explicitly called for significant fiscal restraint.

35 King met shadow chancellor George Osborne on several occasions around this time and appears to have leaked sensitive material to him.

36 There is historical evidence that fiscal consolidations that rely more on cutting current spending than on reducing investment or raising taxes tend to be more enduring.

CHAPTER II

1 M. Blyth. 2012. *Austerity: The History of a Dangerous Idea.* Oxford University Press.

2 D. H. Robertson (1928/1966). JMK (1936).

3   Basel III reforms focused on four key areas of individual banks' operations: capital, leverage, liquidity and resolution.

4   Corporate Finance Institute data (https://corporatefinanceinstitute.com/resources/knowledge/finance/shadow-banking-system).

5   ETFGI data (https://etfgi.com).

6   See P. Turner. 2021. The new monetary policy revolution: advice and dissent. NIESR Occasional Paper LX.

7   The Tinbergen rule is named after Jan Tinbergen, the Dutch Nobel laureate. See J. Tinbergen. 1952. *On the Theory of Economic Policy: Contributions to Economic Analysis*. North Holland. Amsterdam.

8   O. Blanchard and D. Leigh. 2013. Growth forecast errors and fiscal multipliers. IMF Working Paper 13.1.

9   By 2015 the UK's Office for Budgetary Responsibility (OBR) had reverted to a more cautious set of assumptions. It estimated a multiplier of 1 for government investment; 0.6 for current spending; 0.35 for VAT; and 0.3 for income tax and national insurance contributions. OBR. 2015. Economic and fiscal outlook (July).

10   A. Alesina and S. Ardanga. 2009. Large changes in fiscal policy: taxes versus spending. NBER Working Paper 15434 (October). See also A. Alesina. 2010. Fiscal adjustments and the recession. Project Syndicate (vox.eu.org).

11   J. Guajardo, D. Leigh and A. Pescatori. 2011. Expansionary austerity: new international evidence. IMF Working Paper 11/158 (July). (See www.imf.org/external/pubs/ft/wp/2011/wp11158.pdf.)

12   C. Reinhart and K. Rogoff. 2009. *This Time is Different: Eight Centuries of Financial Folly*. Princeton University Press.

13   Fiscal dominance can be defined as the government forcing the central bank to prioritize the financing of the budget deficit to the exclusion of considerations of price stability.

14   P. Schmelzing. 2017. Global real interest rates since 1311: renaissance roots and rapid reversals. The Bank of England's 'Bank Underground' blog (6 November) (https://bankunderground.co.uk/2017/11/06/guest-post-global-real-interest-rates-since-1311-renaissance-roots-and-rapid-reversals).

15   QE is also subject to a lower bound, past which further asset purchases will do little to bring down longer-term interest rates. The fear was that this constraint would also increasingly bite.

16   A. P. Lerner. 1943. Functional finance and the federal debt. *Social Research* 10(1), 38–51. See also R. Jones and J. Llewellyn. 2014. Towards 'functional finance'. Llewellyn Consulting Comment (13 November).

17   For a full description of the sometimes-heated debate between Keynes and Lerner in the 1940s, see T. Aspromourgos. 2014. Keynes, Lerner, and the question of public debt. *History of Political Economy* 46, 3.

18   R. Middleton. 2010. British monetary and fiscal policy in the 1930s. *Oxford Review of Economic Policy* 26(3), 414–441.

CHAPTER 12

1   S. Wren-Lewis. 2015. The austerity con. *London Review of Books* 37(4) (https://lrb.co.uk/the-paper/v37/n04/simon-wren-lewis/the-austerity-con).

2   By 2015 it accounted for less than 8%. G. Hutton. 2022. Financial services: contribution to the UK economy. House of Commons Library (September).

3   To guarantee that the state pension would not fall in real terms, it would rise each year by the greatest of average earnings growth, CPI inflation or 2.5%. This was aimed at the ageing Conservative Party electoral base, and it was inconsistent with international best practice, which had gravitated towards indexation to the CPI.

4   Alistair Darling had wanted to set up a similar body, but was overruled by Gordon Brown, who feared that it would reflect badly on him.

5   In this sense, Tory policy diverged in a positive sense from that of the National Government of the early 1930s. By cutting unemployment benefits sharply, the latter reduced the strength of what were in any case feeble automatic stabilizers.

6   T. Fetzer. 2018. Did austerity cause Brexit? Centre for Competitive Advantage in the Global Economy Working Paper 381 (July).

7   The FLS was a collateral swap programme for banks that increased their net lending. The banks placed lower-quality collateral with the Bank with the usual haircuts and margins in exchange for higher-quality gilts that could then be used to raise wholesale funds at close to the policy rate.

8   This is a little more than half of Eddie George's forty-one-year career at the Bank.

9   The LIBOR scandal related to the manipulation by commercial banks of the London inter-bank offered rate, a key benchmark for international loans and bond issues, in order to enhance profits.

10   Bank of England. 2013. Monetary policy trade-offs and forward guidance (August).

11   The term premium is the excess return an investor demands for holding a longer-term bond, rather than a series of shorter-term bonds.

12   The year 2014 also saw Carney ask former Federal Reserve governor Kevin Warsh to conduct a review of the Bank's operations. Reporting in December of that year, Warsh produced a robust endorsement of central bank transparency. To bring it in line with international best practice, the Bank adopted three of Warsh's recommendations: the simultaneous publication of the MPC's policy decisions, its minutes, and, in relevant months, the Bank's Inflation Report; a reduction in the number of MPC meetings from twelve to eight per year; and the publication of MPC transcripts after an eight-year period. (See www.bankofengland.co.uk/news/2014/december/boe-announces-measures-to-bolster-transparency-and-accountability.)

13   Before coming into office, Osborne had commissioned Sassoon to report on the financial regulation regime. His conclusions were critical of the Tripartite

System, including the Bank. He made forty recommendations that provided the blueprint for Tory policy.

14 Social housing construction had until the mid 1970s rarely fallen below 100,000 a year, and in some it years had exceeded 200,000 a year. Subsequently, it typically ran between 20,000 and 30,000 a year, and for a period during the Blair years it even fell below the bottom of this range.

15 Scottish Government. 2013a. Macroeconomic framework. Fiscal Commission Working Group, First Report (February).

16 Scottish Government (2013a).

17 Scottish Government. 2013b. Scotland's future: your guide to an independent Scotland (November).

18 Chancellor of the Exchequer. 2014. Speech on the prospect of a currency union between an independent Scotland and the rest of the UK (13 February).

19 N. MacPherson. 2014. Scotland and a currency union. Memo to the chancellor of the exchequer (11 February). (See https://assets.publishing.service.gov. uk/government/uploads/system/uploads/attachment_data/file/279460/ Sir_Nicholas_Macpherson_-_Scotland_and_a_currency_union.pdf.)

20 Interview with Lord MacPherson, detailed in Davies (2022).

21 In due course, Scotland was to benefit from the devolution of significant tax-raising powers.

22 This section draws heavily on the annual OECD Economic Surveys and the IMF's Article IV Staff Reports on the UK.

23 IMF. 2018. Article IV 2017 Staff Report on the UK (February).

24 HM Treasury. 2015. Fixing the foundations: creating a more prosperous nation. Cmd. 9098 (July).

25 D. Zenghelis. 2019. Securing decarbonisation and growth. *National Institute Economic Review*, No. 250 (November).

26 D. Blanchflower. 2019. *Not Working: Where Have All the Good Jobs Gone?* Princeton University Press. HMG. 1942. Social insurance and allied services. Cmd. 6404.

27 P. Bunn, A. Pugh and C. Yeates. 2018. The distributional impact of monetary easing in the UK between 2008 and 2014. Bank of England Staff Working Paper No. 720. See also A. Haldane. 2018. How monetary policy affects your GDP. Bank of England (April).

28 J. M. Keynes. 1937. How to avoid a slump. *The Times*, 3 January. (Reprinted in JMK. 1982. *Activities 1931–39*, Vol. XXI.)

CHAPTER 13

1 W. Shakespeare. 1597. *Richard II,* Act II, Scene I.

2 The Conservative Party. 2015. Strong leadership. A clear economic plan. A secure future. Election Manifesto (May).

3 B. Nabaro and C. Shulz. 2019. Recent trends in the UK economy. IFS Green Budget (October).

4   Cameron had used this phrase when addressing the 2006 Conservative Party Conference.
5   The *Acquis* is the accumulated legislation, legal acts and court decisions that constitute the body of European Union law.
6   HM Treasury. 2016a. The long-term impact of EU membership and the alternatives. Cmd. 9250 (April).
7   OECD. 2016. *The Economic Consequences of Brexit: A Taxing Decision.* OECD, Paris.
8   N. Crafts. 2016. The impact of EU membership on UK economic performance. *Political Quarterly*, 18 May.
9   T. Sampson, S. Dhingra, G. Ottaviano and J. Van Reenen. 2016. Economists for Brexit: a critique. Centre for Economic Performance.
10   HM Treasury. 2016b. The immediate impact of leaving the EU. Cmd. 9292 (May).
11   Quoted in *The Guardian*, 23 May 2016. The Bank of England's central forecast at the time was for the economy to keep growing after the Brexit vote. However, the bank's governor, Mark Carney, added that in the event of a vote to leave, there could be a technical recession: output could contract for two consecutive quarters.
12   Quoted in the *Financial Times*, 3 June 2016.
13   One of Brown's interventions, made in a video filmed at the ruins of Coventry cathedral, is available at https://blogs.lse.ac.uk/brexit/2016/06/07/gordon-browns-viral-video-britain-as-a-leader-not-a-leaver/.
14   According to the Centre for European Studies. Quoted in M. Wolf. 2016. Myths and fantasies in the case for Brexit. *Financial Times*, 27 April.
15   The employers could spend the money set aside on any approved apprenticeship scheme or transfer up to a quarter of their levy pot to enable non-levy payers to fund workplace programmes. Any money unspent after two years was returned to the Treasury. It was revealed in 2022 that employers had surrendered more than £3.3 billion in unspent cash to the Treasury since 2019, and that there had been a huge drop in the number of apprenticeship starts. The programme had failed.
16   BEIS. 2018. Industrial strategy: building a Britain fit for the future (November).
17   The regular (usually annual) OECD surveys and IMF Article IV reports provide an invaluable source of information and analysis of the progress of the UK economy and policy.
18   None of the four minority governments of the twentieth century lasted more than eighteen months. The Labour minority administrations of 1929–31, 1974 and 1978–9 were all associated with, if not destroyed by, economic crises.
19   HM Government. 2018. EU exit. Long-term economic analysis. Cmd. 9742 (November).
20   Bank of England. 2018. EU withdrawal scenarios and monetary and financial stability. A response to the House of Commons Treasury Committee (November).

21   OBR. 2021. Economic and fiscal outlook (October).

22   D. Webb. 2022. UK–Australia free trade agreement. House of Commons Library, 6 September.

23   From 1 April 2021 until 31 March 2023 companies investing in qualifying new plant and machinery assets could claim a 130% super-deduction capital allowance on qualifying plant and machinery and a 50% first-year allowance for qualifying special rate assets. The super-deduction would allow companies to cut their tax bill by up to 25p for every £1 they invested.

24   S. Nanda, C. Thomas and G. Dibb. 2022. Science or stagnation. Next steps for life sciences policy in England. IPPR (October).

25   Migration Advisory Committee. 2018. EEA workers in the UK labour market. Final Report (September).

26   Z/Yen. 2022. The global financial centres index (31 March).

27   Hutton (2022).

28   BIS. 2022. Triennial central bank survey of foreign exchange and over-the-counter (OTC) derivatives markets in 2022 (www.bis.org/statistics/rpfx22.htm).

29   HM Government. 2022. Levelling up. CP 604 (February).

30   There are several instances when Johnson, either as foreign secretary or as prime minister, was quoted as using this phrase. See, for example, Robert Shrimsley's article in the *Financial Times* on 25 June 2018: 'Boris Johnson's Brexit explosion ruins Tory business credentials' (www.ft.com/content/8075e68c-7857-11e8-8e67-1e1a0846c475).

CHAPTER 14

1   D. DeLillo. 1985. *White Noise*. Viking Press, New York.

2   This was a term employed by Carney during an appearance in front of the Treasury Select Committee in January 2016.

Index